LANGUAGE WITHOUT SOIL

Language Without Soil

ADORNO AND LATE PHILOSOPHICAL MODERNITY

Edited by

GERHARD RICHTER

FORDHAM UNIVERSITY PRESS
New York 2010

Copyright © 2010 Fordham University Press

All rights reserved. No part of this publication may be reproduced, stored in a retrieval system, or transmitted in any form or by any means—electronic, mechanical, photocopy, recording, or any other—except for brief quotations in printed reviews, without the prior permission of the publisher.

Fordham University Press has no responsibility for the persistence or accuracy of URLs for external or third-party Internet websites referred to in this publication and does not guarantee that any content on such websites is, or will remain, accurate or appropriate.

Library of Congress Cataloging-in-Publication Data

Andrew W. Mellon Foundation Interdisciplinary Workshop on Adorno (University of Wisconsin–Madison)
 Language without soil : Adorno and late philosophical modernity / edited by Gerhard Richter.—1st ed.
       p. cm.
 Early versions of some of the contributions were initially presented as lectures and seminars in a year-long Andrew W. Mellon Foundation Interdisciplinary Workshop on Adorno, Humanities Center at the University of Wisconsin-Madison.
 Includes bibliographical references and index.
   ISBN 978-0-8232-3126-3 (cloth)
   ISBN 978-0-8232-3127-0 (pbk.)
 1. Adorno, Theodor W., 1903–1969—Congresses.
   I. Richter, Gerhard, 1967–   II. Title.
       B3199.A34A66   2010
       193—dc22
       2009020854

12 11 10   5 4 3 2 1
First edition

CONTENTS

	Acknowledgments	vii
	Introduction GERHARD RICHTER	1
1.	Without Soil: A Figure in Adorno's Thought ALEXANDER GARCÍA DÜTTMANN	10
2.	Taking on the Stigma of Inauthenticity: Adorno's Critique of Genuineness MARTIN JAY	17
3.	Suffering Injustice: Misrecognition as Moral Injury in Critical Theory J. M. BERNSTEIN	30
4.	Idiosyncrasies: Of Anti-Semitism JAN PLUG	52
5.	Adorno's Lesson Plans? The Ethics of (Re)Education in "The Meaning of 'Working through the Past'" JAIMEY FISHER	76
6.	Adorno—Nature—Hegel THERESA M. KELLEY	99
7.	The Idiom of Crisis: On the Historical Immanence of Language in Adorno NEIL LARSEN	117
8.	Aesthetic Theory and Nonpropositional Truth Content in Adorno GERHARD RICHTER	131
9.	The Homeland of Language: A Note on Truth and Knowledge in Adorno MIRKO WISCHKE	147
10.	Of Stones and Glass Houses: *Minima Moralia* as Critique of Transparency ERIC JAROSINSKI	157

11. The Polemic of the Late Work: Adorno's Hölderlin ... 172
    ROBERT SAVAGE
12. Twelve Anacoluthic Theses on Adorno's "Parataxis: On Hölderlin's Late Poetry" ... 195
    DAVID FARRELL KRELL
13. The Ephemeral and the Absolute: Provisional Notes to Adorno's *Aesthetic Theory* ... 206
    PETER UWE HOHENDAHL

    Appendix: Who's Afraid of the Ivory Tower? A Conversation with Theodor W. Adorno ... 227
    TRANSLATED, EDITED, AND WITH AN INTRODUCTION BY GERHARD RICHTER

    Notes ... 239
    List of Contributors ... 293
    Index ... 297

ACKNOWLEDGMENTS

Early versions of six of the thirteen contributions collected here were initially presented as lectures and seminars in the context of a year-long Andrew W. Mellon Foundation Interdisciplinary Workshop on Adorno that I co-directed with Theresa Kelley through the Humanities Center at the University of Wisconsin–Madison. The workshop attracted a sizable and lively group of faculty and graduate students from a variety of disciplines. At the University of California, Davis, Karen Embry reliably and thoughtfully assisted in the preparation of the final manuscript, and Geoffrey Wildanger prepared the index. The editorial staff at Fordham University Press ably saw the manuscript through to book form. Earlier versions of some of the chapters have appeared as follows: Theodor W. Adorno, "Who's Afraid of the Ivory Tower? A Conversation with Theodor W. Adorno," translated, edited, and with an introduction by Gerhard Richter, *Monatshefte* 94: 1 (Spring 2002): 10–23 (© 2002 by the Board of Regents of the University of Wisconsin System; reproduced courtesy of The University of Wisconsin Press and Suhrkamp Verlag, Frankfurt am Main, Germany); J. M. Bernstein, "Suffering Injustice: Misrecognition as Moral Injury in Critical Theory," *International Journal of Philosophical Studies* 13:3: 303–24 (http://www.informaworld.com; used by permission of the Taylor & Francis Group); Alexander García Düttmann, "Ohne Erde: Eine Denkfigur Adornos," *Moderne begreifen: Zur Paradoxie eines sozio-ästhetischen Deutungsmusters*, eds. Christine Magerski, Christiane Weller, and Robert Savage (Wiesbaden: VS-Verlag, 2007), 255–62 (used by permission of GWV Fachverlage GmbH); Martin Jay, "Taking on the Stigma of Inauthenticity: Adorno's Critique of Genuineness," *New German Critique*, vol. 97 (Winter 2006): 15–30 (Copyright 2006 New German Critique, Inc. All rights reserved. Used by permission of the publisher, Duke University Press); Jan Plug, "Idiosyncrasies: Of Anti-Semitism," *Monatshefte* 94: 1 (Spring 2002): 43–66 (© 2002 by the Board of Regents of the University of Wisconsin System; reproduced by the permission of The University of Wisconsin Press); Gerhard Richter, "Aesthetic Theory and Nonpropositional Truth

Content in Adorno," *New German Critique*, vol. 97 (Winter 2006): 119–35 (copyright 2006 New German Critique, Inc.; reprinted by permission of the publisher, Duke University Press); portions of Robert Savage's contribution were originally published in his *Hölderlin after the Catastrophe: Heidegger—Adorno—Brecht* (Rochester, NY: Camden House, 2008 (copyright © Robert Savage, used by permission of Camden House/Boydell & Brewer Inc.).

Language Without Soil

INTRODUCTION

Gerhard Richter

In the history of art, late works are the catastrophes.

ADORNO, "Beethoven's Late Style"

The renaissance that has developed on both sides of the Atlantic around the work of philosopher, sociologist, political thinker, musician, musicologist, and cultural theorist Theodor W. Adorno (1903–1969) has outpaced interest in other members of the Frankfurt School of Critical Theory in recent years.[1] Indeed, his multifaceted work has exerted a profound impact on far-ranging discourses and critical practices in late modernity. Adorno's analyses of the fate of art following its alleged end, of ethical imperatives "after Auschwitz," of the negative dialectic of myth and freedom from superstition, of the relentless manipulation of mass consciousness by the unequal siblings of fascism and the culture industry, and of the narrowly conceived concept of reason that has given rise to an unprecedented exploitation of nature and needless human suffering, all speak to central concerns of our time. For Adorno, every uncompromisingly critical act is performed in the name of an other-directedness, the commitment to an Other that, by extension, also is a commitment to a reconceived future. The liberatory hope in Adorno's philosophical thought, if any is to be found, resides in the ways in which language, forever at odds with its own intentions and strivings, gestures toward a futurity that does not yet possess a name, toward a form of community that has yet to be imagined, and toward that most difficult of all tasks, a learning to "live together" for which no ethicopolitical model exists. This nameless futurity, bound as it is to the belatedness of the past, calls upon us as though it belonged to the stunning and perplexing protocols of Adorno's dreams—in turn paranoid and political, optimistic and perverse—recorded upon awakening, which now have been made available to us.[2] The dreaming of which Adorno dreams has little to do with wishful thinking or political escapism. Rather, it embodies a deliberate affront to those forms of thinking that have given up on the hope embedded in a dream, a moment of contrary-to-factness that has not been exhausted once and for all. The sentences that Adorno devotes to his friend Walter Benjamin apply equally well to his own project: "In the paradox of the impossible possibility, mysticism and enlightenment are joined for the last time in him. He overcame the dream without betraying it and making himself an accomplice in that on which the philosophers have always agreed: that it shall not be."[3]

The felt contemporaneity of Adorno's thought to the concerns of our late modernity nevertheless unfolds in a certain noncontemporaneity of thinking. In 1967, two years before his death, Adorno formulates the complexity of this noncontemporaneity in the opening to his philosophical magnum opus, the *Negative Dialectics*: "Philosophy, which once seemed passé, remains alive because the moment of its realization was missed."[4] For Adorno, the missed opportunity of thinking—and especially the realization or actualization of that thinking—is to be both mourned and welcomed. While the condition of having-missed suggests a failure in and of thinking as a form of praxis, it also names, for him, the condition of possibility for any future act of thinking that still may be to come and that refuses to exhaust itself in the stale programs of the received agendas associated with this or that theoretical "orientation" or predictable political marching plan. If there is a late modernity that still can be grasped in conceptual terms—even in the wake, perhaps, of Jean-François Lyotard's well-known diagnosis of the end of all master narratives in what some call postmodernity—it, too, will have to engage its own lateness, its delay and deferral, its perpetual disruption of any adequately temporal construct of thought. This is also why, for Adorno, lateness and belatedness—in a manner contiguous with, but not identical to, Freud's insistence on the psyche's delayed action—cannot be thought in isolation from the far-reaching constellation of critical concerns that occupy him in so many heterogeneous registers. Adorno's concerns with lateness emerge as early as his 1937 essay on the complexity and madness of considering "Beethoven's Late Style."[5]

Adorno's late modernity—the modernity that always will have arrived too late and the modernity that will come into its own only later—cannot *not* be mediated by language, understood in the broadest sense of textuality and representation. Whatever late modernity will have meant in any particular instance, Adorno reminds us time and again that the time of that modernity, even its most recent past, exists only in and as representation, never as an immediately accessible object of knowledge. As he writes in his Bar Harbor notebook: "That the violence of the facts has become such a horror, that any theory, even the true kind, looks like a ridicule of that horror—this is burned as a sign into the very organ of theory, language."⁶ Any examination of our own lateness, of the myriad forms of violence that we have not been able to avoid, means to confront that lateness in the very language through which it is mediated for us. To engage this "textual" nature of lateness also means to come to terms with the uprootedness of its language, the ways in which it is not stably anchored in the native soil of self-present speech or fully transparent thought. For Adorno, the task of critical thinking is to imagine a mode of being-in-the-world that occurs in and through a language that has liberated itself from the spell of an alleged historical and political inevitability, what in his 1959 radio address "Words from Abroad" he tellingly calls a "language without soil [*Sprache ohne Erde*]."⁷

Answering German critics who had complained to him about what they felt was an excessive use of *Fremdwörter*, "foreign words" or words of foreign derivation, Adorno insists on the utopian potential associated with an "exogamy" of language that works to deconstruct the mere repetition of sameness and the imposition of what always already is known.⁸ This exogamy of language cannot but be other-directed, attuned to that which will not remain identical, even in the most fossilized automatisms of spoken and received language. For the young Adorno, he recalls, the exogamy of language even offered "tiny cells of resistance to the nationalism of World War I."⁹ What attracts the philosopher is the idea that words of foreign derivation, in their allegorical enactment of an engagement with the other, even with the other that speaks within and as the voice of the self, gives rise to a non-naïve utopian impulse tied to a language without soil, a language that is irreducible to its historical overdetermination even while it is inflected by it, a language that refuses the nationalism, narcissism, and anti-utopianism in which existence is reduced to a mere communicative functionality. Instead, Adorno suggests, language without soil acts as a kind of repository for some long-forgotten dream. "Hopeless like death-heads," he writes, "do the words of foreign derivation wait to be reawakened in a better order."¹⁰ We could say that Adorno, in this essay as in all of his works, refuses to concretize the specific content of this "better order" because to specify it would be to betray it, to empty it in advance, and thus to return it to a soil that does not nourish but imprisons it within the confines of a narrowly conceived notion of reason. In the Adornean sphere of aesthetics, the work of writers such as Marcel Proust and Samuel Beckett and of musicians such as Ludwig van Beethoven and Arnold Schönberg may come closest to embodying what precisely cannot be embodied: a language without soil.

To formulate, in the hyperprecise and yet treacherous language without soil, some of the concerns that preoccupy him—the question of ethics, the role of nature and the animal, the inexhaustible possibilities lodged in aesthetics—Adorno turns time and again to the politics of the work of art. For him, it is the work of art that in late modernity is the primary mediator of any such concerns. Here he includes not only musical compositions—sonic forms such as the radically experimental music of Schönberg and Alban Berg preoccupied him throughout his life—but also literary and poetic modes such as the condensed, epigrammatic form of short prose called the *Denkbild*, or "thought-image," that linked Adorno's work to a modern trajectory extending from Friedrich Nietzsche and Charles Baudelaire to Stefan George, Karl Kraus, Robert Musil, and Bertolt Brecht, as well as to the literary styles of friends such as Benjamin, Ernst Bloch, and Siegfried Kracauer.[11] For Adorno, the essay form also embodies the possibility of aesthetically mediated experiences of freedom, as does the practice of paratactical—rather than hypotactical—writing in poets such as the eighteenth-century German lyricist Friedrich Hölderlin.

Precisely what kind of a thinking would the politically charged work of art demand? In order to become properly political, any thinking of the work of art must enter into a relation to what is—whether affirmative or critical—in a singular way that shows itself responsible to the specific kind of relation vis-à-vis which is staged by the internal movement of the work itself. But regardless of whether the thinking of—that is, about and by—the politically charged work of art strives to solidify or to transform what is, the marching plan of its thinking is bestowed upon it from elsewhere, that is, from a so-called political reality, the empirically given force field of relations alleged to antedate the creative act and the conceptual impetus that such an act engenders. In the force field of these concerns, there can be no truly "political" work of art that is straightforwardly political or that has a manifest political content. On the contrary, the work of art is most political when it at first appears to have little to do with politics. As Adorno writes in his essay "Commitment," an engagement with Jean-Paul Sartre's political claims on behalf of literature, ours "is not the time for political works of art; rather, politics has migrated into the autonomous work of art, and it has penetrated most deeply into works that present themselves as politically dead."[12] What the truly political artwork would give us to think is also always a radical reconsideration of what the concepts "political" and "artwork" signify, for it is only in the perpetual reevaluation of its own aesthetic claims and of "the political" as such that the aesthetic object works to sustain the openness of nonreified relations that perpetuate the experience of freedom.

It is as though Adorno's own relationship to writing echoed that of Franz Kafka, in whom he and Benjamin shared a sustained interest, and to whom Adorno devoted a lengthy essay. As Kafka famously writes in a letter from 1904: "I think one ought to read nothing but books that bite and sting. If the book we are reading does not wake us up with the blow of a fist against the skull, then why are we reading that book? So that it will make us happy? . . . No, we need books that affect us like a misfortune, that cause us a lot of pain, like the death of someone whom we loved better than ourselves, as if we were cast out in the forests, cut off from all human beings, like a suicide; a book must be the ax for the frozen sea in us."[13] The force of this bite and sting, the blow of this ax—especially when they have taken shape in the materiality of an artwork that transcends any mere thematic interest or ideological assumption—are the only modes of artistic and philosophical engagement that Adorno can tolerate. This is especially true after the catastrophes of the twentieth century but also in light of the entire history of reason, including the alleged disenchantment and latter revival of superstition and unfreedom. The political in Kafka's work is inextricably bound up with a compositional style that refuses to yield to the temptations of unified sense. For Adorno, therefore, the insight that each sentence in Kafka "says 'interpret me,' and none will permit it" is a metacommentary on the way in which his language "will shoot towards" the reader "like a locomotive in a three-dimensional film."[14] If there is anything political in the work of art, it is mediated by a sustained philosophical and aesthetic confrontation with this onrushing locomotive and with language's stubborn refusal to hold still.

Adorno's finely chiseled, contrapuntal sentences work to perform a ceaseless gesture of thoughtful vigilance, a vigilance understood not in the sense of moralizing or ethical normativity but of a rigorous attention to thinking and of a mindful commemoration of catastrophe and displacement. While all of his sentences mark, in one way or another, sites of commemoration, they also remain without a proper place, soil-less traces of an absence. If Adorno imagines a radical language without soil, we should think of it in terms of the simultaneity with which aesthetic markers work to commemorate an absence even through a seemingly overdetermined presence. From that perspective Adorno would have approved of the project *Stolpersteine* (Stumbling Stones) by contemporary artist Gunter Demnig.[15] Since the mid-1990s, the Cologne-based artist has placed thousands of small, brass-fitted concrete squares on select streets in major German and European cities. These squares, each ten square centimeters in size, display the names of victims of the Holocaust and, where available, the year of birth, date of deportation, and date of murder in a Nazi concentration camp. The small squares are embedded in the sidewalk in front of the building in which the deportee—Jew, homosexual, Jehovah's Witness, political dissident, or victim of Nazi euthanasia—once lived. These buildings, or those that now stand in their place, are in each case the last known voluntary residence of the victims. Unsuspecting passers-by, caught unawares, will "stumble" upon them by chance, while others will not notice them at all or will choose to ignore them. Although sunken into the pavement, these *Stolpersteine* have a certain transient quality, not only because they are, on a regular basis, secretly removed by members of neo-Nazi groups or by residents of the buildings or neighbors who object to the local reminders of these brutal atrocities, but also because the small size and relative inconspicuousness of the *Stolpersteine* render them almost invisible. This aspect of the memorial recreates the experience of becoming aware of a horrific deed in the course of one's everyday life. Like Adorno's language without soil, these mnemonic *Stolpersteine* are silent markers without permanent soil, here and almost not here at the same time, signs of an unmastered past, a history that remains out of joint.

To return time and again to the memory and provocation of the unthought and the repressed for Adorno also means to return thinking to a never-ending contemplation of its own complicity with what it criticizes. As he writes in 1963, in language that still rings true, perhaps even truer, in light of the many disturbingly regressive tendencies that have marked the beginning of our twenty-first century:

> The theorist who intervenes in practical controversies nowadays discovers on a regular basis and to his shame that whatever ideas he might contribute were expressed long ago—and usually better the first time around. Not only has the mass of writings and publications grown beyond measure: society itself, despite all its tendencies to expand, in many cases seems to be regressing to earlier stages, even in its superstructure, in law and politics. ... Even critical thought risks becoming infected by what it criticizes. Critical thought must let itself be guided by the concrete forms of consciousness it opposes and must go over once again what they have forgotten. Thought is not purely for itself: especially practical thought, so closely tied to the historical moment that in this regressive age it would become abstract and false were it to continue to evolve from its own élan regardless of the regression.[16]

To think in this manner also requires thought to think against itself, against itself precisely in the moment where it believes simply to have overcome that which it opposes by means of the deliberate movements of its critique. Only when it is vigilant with regard to its own assumed accomplishments and interventions can critical thought continue the gesture that is at the root of the Greek *krinein*: to separate, to distinguish, to decide, and to select. But in order not to foreclose this proper gesture of *krinein*, to keep it open as a mode of undecided futurity and as the promise of the impossible, it cannot be contained by any firm soil, native or otherwise. Critical thought cannot be planted firmly in the ground in the way of a tree, static in the wake of the change of history. This thinking without the permanence of soil is a thinking that is exiled, nomadic, never at home once and for all. Adorno's thought resides in the constitutive antagonism of language itself.

His "negative dialectic," when thought in tandem with the aesthetic resistance posited by Adorno's understanding of the artistic act, marks a radical departure from the thinking of this or that relation, and even from the notion of "relation" itself, on which the conventional conjunction of aesthetics and politics so adamantly relies. We could say, then, that the wager of Adorno's aesthetic theory is that a truly political work of art, rather than entering into a specific relation to what is, will inaugurate a moment of reflection that shifts the relation predicated upon the conjunction of presentation and commentary to a different kind of relation, the relation of thinking *to itself*. Only here, in the conceptual creation of a thinking that turns against itself, can new forms of solidarity and ethico-political responsibility be articulated. As Adorno writes in *Negative Dialectics*, if "negative dialectics seeks the self-reflection of thinking, the tangible implication is that if thinking is to be true—today, in any case—it must also think against itself. If thinking fails to measure itself by the extremeness that eludes the concept, it is from the outset like the accompanying music with which the SS liked to drown out the screams of its victims."[17] The nonself-identity of thought, staged with radical singularity in the truly political work of art, is the faint promise of a concept that comes after the concept, but that "late" concept, the after-concept, is, as it were, without soil.

The essays collected in this volume, each in their own way, address the epistemo-ethical possibilities and limitations in late modernity of a mode of critical thinking that emerges from Adorno's principle of a "language without soil," broadly conceived. In his opening meditation, Alexander García Düttmann interrogates the figure "without soil" in relation to pivotal concerns in Adorno's thought. The essays that follow take up these concerns in such realms as ethics, aesthetics, history, nature, and politics.

Martin Jay explicates Adorno's dialectical engagement with inauthenticity and genuineness, two of the central tropes of his mature philosophy; the next three contributions each speak to a particular form of ethical demand. While J. M. Bernstein considers the problem of misrecognition as a source of moral injury in Adorno and in the project of Critical Theory, Jan Plug revisits the question of anti-Semitism as it emerges especially in the *Dialectic of Enlightenment,* and Jaimey Fisher refutes the long-standing prejudice that Adorno offered no concrete suggestions capable of bridging theory and praxis by scrutinizing the philosopher's contributions to German educational reforms following World War II.

Adorno's innovative understanding of nature and the historical constitutes the core of the two contributions that follow. Here, Theresa M. Kelley illuminates our understanding of nature in Adorno by excavating the manifold relations between Adorno's and Hegel's concepts of nature, while Neil Larsen casts into sharp relief Adorno's concept of history as a form of historical immanence of language. The subsequent essays are devoted specifically to problems of aesthetic theory and the philosophy of language. Gerhard Richter offers a close reading of a passage from the literary and philosophical work *Minima Moralia* that enacts Adorno's radical concept of nonpropositional truth content in philosophical aesthetics after Auschwitz. Then Mirko Wischke and Eric Jarosinski turn to related problems as they arise in *Minima Moralia,* respectively addressing the question of truth and knowledge as a function of the accessibility of language and the question of transparency in relation to the formulation of these problems. The next two essays perform case studies of Adornean aesthetics, each focusing on the philosopher's groundbreaking 1964 reading of Hölderlin. Returning to the question of lateness, Robert Savage engages the problem of the late work—both in Hölderlin and as a general problem of aesthetic theory—while David Farrell Krell offers an innovative "thetic" approach to Adorno's essay by revisiting the much-discussed concept of parataxis that Adorno first developed in his confrontation with Hölderlin's poetry and with Heidegger's ontological interpretation of it. In the concluding essay, Peter Uwe Hohendahl proposes an alternative interpretation of Adorno's unfinished *Aesthetic Theory* in which he reconsiders some of the philosopher's central aesthetic concepts, such as aesthetic autonomy, from the perspective of those moments when Adorno's writing appears to destabilize the work of art and, by extension, the philosophical claims that his theories generally are held to make on behalf of the aesthetic. Finally, the Appendix, an edited and annotated translation of Adorno's seminal 1969 interview with the German *Spiegel* magazine concerning the relationship of Critical Theory to political activism, not only situates Adorno's conversation within the epistemo-political context of its time, but also illustrates Adorno's abiding commitment to an unknowable futurity in which an ethico-political hope lodged in the unsublatable dialectical interplay between thought and action might someday emerge.

Taken together, the contributions to this volume conspire to yield a refractory and unorthodox Adorno, a suggestive and, at times, infuriating thinker of the first order, whose work continues to serve—recalling a figure from *Minima Moralia*—both as a splinter in the eye and as a magnifying glass. This volume attempts to show itself responsible to the ways in which Adorno's intellectual gestures sponsor politically conscious modes of theoretical speculation in a late modernity that may still have a future *because* its language and aspirations are without soil.

CHAPTER I

Without Soil: A Figure in Adorno's Thought
Alexander García Düttmann

For David Roberts

What is the target of the critique practiced by Adorno? Adorno's critique is targeted at what exists. But not because what exists is not as it should be, because it must be changed and instituted in some other way. In that case, critique would fall between what exists and what does not yet exist. It would be critique of what exists in the name of what does not yet exist. A critique that targets what exists sets its sights on what exists *as such*; and therefore also on attempts to hold fast to what exists, to insist on it, to repeat and to prolong the existence of what exists in a gesture that, in holding fast to it, holds it fast. Nothing that exists, nothing that insists on a thing's existence, can be exempted from critique, regardless of which existing thing is at issue, how it is historically and socially conditioned, and thus how it falls under the sway of some other existing thing.

To the same extent that what exists is inseparable from the gesture that, insisting on holding fast to it, insistently holds it fast, since this gesture first opens up a passage to it or even transforms it into an existing thing, safeguarding the existence on which it insists; to the same extent that, vice versa, the gesture of holding fast always insists on what exists; to that extent critique is called forth by what exists, by the existing thing whose continued existence proves to be the object of insistence.

"The 'yes, but' answer to the critical argument," Adorno writes in *Negative Dialectics*, "the refusal to have anything wrested away—these are already forms of obstinate insistence on existence, forms of a clutching that cannot be reconciled with the idea of rescue in which the spasm of such prolonged self-preservation would be eased. Nothing can be saved unchanged, nothing that has not passed through the portal of its death."[1] To be sure, it seems at first as if Adorno were following the usual schema here. What exists attracts critique owing to its particular constitution, and the repudiation of the "critical argument" that in turn targets such critique equates to an unreflective insistence upon what exists: a rationalization. But the idea of rescue deployed against this schema, as the "innermost impulse of man's spirit," the talk of a transformation that could not be more far-reaching and perfect because it passes through death, traversing the "portal" of death, as Adorno writes with reference to Job and the Psalter, but also to dialectics, affects the schema, forcing the reader to suspend its mode of operation. For if the relation of thought to its object and to what exists is ultimately one of rescue, a release from the "spasm" of self-preservation, if critique consequently has its measure in rescue, then it is the task of the critic to help release self-preservation from both forms of its spasmodic prolongation, that of its petrification and that of its obstinacy. Self-preservation becomes petrified with regard to what exists, the existing subject and the existing object; obstinately it insists on what exists, on itself—as subject and object. The insistence on existence "prolongs" self-preservation, which, in insisting on what exists, celebrates its first triumph over transience and, at the same time, through its defense of what exists, concedes the semblance of its triumph. The "spasm" does not set in after the event as an epiphenomenon. Without knowing it, the "yes, but" encounters itself again in what exists. The critic alone knows of this self-encounter. Were rescue to transform something that exists illegitimately in order to perpetuate something that exists legitimately, it would be robbed of its meaning, it would for its part prolong the "yes, but" and be just as much a defense as this; the "surrender" in which rescue is said first to touch upon its meaning, and that is supposed to be even that of spirit, hence the surrender of rescue itself,[2] would be nothing but a final appropriation, a final insistence on what exists. The perfect transformation that is rescue, and in whose service critique stands, thus cannot result in the institution of something that exists, in the petrification of its self-preservation and in the renewal of its obduracy. Rescue denotes the point of indifference of self-preservation and surrender.

Any claim whatsoever that is raised must be dismissed; for inasmuch as it is raised, it appeals to an existing thing and refers back to itself as something that claims existence, too. Philosophy, the medium of spirit, is not concerned with validity claims that must be redeemed, as if its task were to move from one existing thing to the next. Rather, philosophy begins by dismissing every claim, regardless of its content, its origin, or its consequences. Doing philosophy is not synonymous with recognizing the argument that proves to be the best possible and that may therefore, with the reservation of fallibility, lay claim to be valid.

If, however, philosophy returns to whatever was at stake in the claim being raised, then the claim is transformed by this return. It ceases to be a claim that must be redeemed, dismissed, or at any rate recognized. It is not simply the case that another claim takes the place of the one that was dismissed; the claim that was raised is not simply confirmed and thereby raised to the level of a justified claim. The understanding of philosophy that consists in the raising and testing of validity claims depends on what exists, on the petrification and obstinacy of self-preservation, and so forfeits precisely the element in which philosophy can first unfold: that of freedom, of a free relation to the object, which does not posit the latter from the outset as something already given or existing. This much is suggested by the fact that Adorno's idea of philosophy is that of a by-no-means fixed constellation of concepts and ("critical") arguments rather than that of a meaningful and self-contained argumentative context. His critique of speculative dialectics ultimately refers to the confusion of constellation and argumentative context, in particular to the subordination of the context, which is only ever precipitated and never subsists for itself. One cannot appeal to a context, only to an argument that has logical consistency or, if this is lacking, is no argument at all.

Freedom, the element of philosophy, proves itself as much in the conscious dismissal as in the rescuing return. The return is not that of something repressed, a claim suppressed by another claim, by the blank refusal to have anything to do with something. The fact that Adorno's thinking draws on dialectical motifs means that the conscious dismissal turns against what exists, against what is merely natural, isolated, abstract in life; the life of the spirit that has freed itself from abstraction no longer sets itself in opposition to death. It no longer takes control of death as negativity and, for that very reason, no longer succumbs to it. If one wanted to revert to Kantian terminology, one could say that philosophy is concerned with neither inclination nor respect, but with favor. It lies in the determination of what exists that it denies favor insofar as it registers an interest in what exists. In the end, it must always hold fast to itself and set itself apart from what it is not.

In his attempt to elucidate the moral-philosophical relevance of the event marked by the date September 11, Joseph Margolis argues for the abandonment of "any universalized theory of normative practice," however much it may be embedded in local contexts or in particular life-forms.³ Moral philosophy should henceforth be concerned with claims that do not deny their origin in particular "*Sitten*" [customs and practices], since they cannot shrug aside their relativity: "We begin—and we end—as partisans. But in acknowledging the diverse, even opposed voices of other societies, we begin to see how our own habitual practice and habituated judgment are effectively leavened by the confrontations of similarly generated conceptions that oppose our own [. . .]."⁴ Because claims can be raised only when a society has "its own sense of accurate and admissible description, interpretation, explanation, and appreciation," connected with a particular "reflexive [. . .] reading of its own *ethos*,"⁵ the contestation of which Margolis speaks—the provocation through different and perhaps even incompatible claims—is structurally inscribed in the raising of claims, in the moral self-understanding of a society, as what one could call the possibility of history. Where this is entirely missing, no claims are raised at all and self-understanding remains wholly abstract. A responsiveness to different, perhaps even incompatible, claims for the purpose of justifying the claims that one raises oneself demonstrates the seriousness with which one stands up for a preferred or adopted life-form.⁶ It also demonstrates, however, that claims can never be immediately raised without being dismissed, cast into doubt, confronted with questions. But is the continued existence of a claim to be secured through such a confrontation, should *Sitten* continue to exist more or less unchanged, more or less changed, between the ever-shifting borders of *minimum bonum* and *summum malum*?

The moral philosopher Raimond Gaita likewise refuses to equate morality with the outlining of "principles of conduct."⁷ But his critique of moral philosophy rests not on the assertion of a logically many-valued relativism of "second-best morality," as in the case of Margolis, but on the memory of a transcendent act of goodness or on the exception of a love, which expresses itself in considerate conduct toward another person and brings to light the singularity of individual life. Yet is not an ambiguity introduced into morality with such a memory, resulting from a contagious exposure of that which withdraws from every regulation and consists in an immediate and indubitable deed? As soon as one refers to the revelatory consequences of the experience of a transcendent goodness and love surpassing any expressible principle or justifiable demand, one turns favor into a claim: *that* is how it should be, that is how it *should* be. The infinite singularity of individual life calls for the infinity of love and goodness. The goodness that exposes and discloses itself to self-consciousness, and to which a claim may therefore appeal, becomes something existing, the continued existence of an idea or a deed to be insisted on with the impotence of the ought. The unity of the deed is thwarted. It pertains to what Adorno characterizes as "impulse," which contradicts every argumentation, every objective consideration of claims, every dispassionate recital of arguments and counterarguments. It pertains to a moral impulse to which immediate satisfaction alone can do justice and that, for this reason, is inseparable from its satisfaction. If, like Wittgenstein in his "dream experience,"[8] one has become aware of the obligation to take upon oneself what is most terrifying—it is on the basis of such an awareness that goodness and love are more than virtues and can have a revelatory effect—skepticism involuntarily creeps in. Is one even prepared to take it upon oneself?

Against the background of Margolis's and Gaita's critical and complementary approaches to moral philosophy, which converge in the extremity of intransigence, it can be seen that rescue as transformation, which, in order to ease the "spasm" of self-preservation and to withstand blindness, modifies the claim as claim, what exists and the insistence on what exists, endeavors to confront a threefold danger: that of the bad infinity of immanence; that of a contagion of transcendence and immanence; and that of the abstraction of mere transcendence.

One example of the radical critique of what exists practiced by Adorno can be found in his essay "Words from Abroad," in a passage where he refers to the idea of a "language without soil."[9] The pleasure felt by a child at the use of loanwords, which he or she drops into conversation in an exaggerated and almost capricious fashion, is said to work unconsciously toward liberating language from what exists, from "subjection to the spell of historical existence." To such "historical existence," which designates the comprehensive reification of the word into a commodity, not the nationalistically transfigured givenness of a natural language, Adorno opposes a "better order." The fact that this order would no longer be one of the earth implies, however, that "historical existence" always exerts a "spell," in the form of a linguistic nationalism or linguistic globalization. The "spell of historical existence," then, can only be that of what exists as such, the spell exerted whenever someone or something is subjected, to the same extent that what exists only knows the freedom of the partisan. Perhaps the spell of what exists or "existence," the mythic or "mythology," is even prolonged by the mutability underlined by the emphasis on history, insofar as such mutability is ambivalent. On the one hand, it is the condition of confrontation between partisans, between those who inevitably end up taking sides; on the other, every change brings about a movement that extends beyond partisan struggle. In a letter to Horkheimer from 1940, Adorno writes: "There is only as much mythology in the world as there are ties to the earth and to a particular place of abode."[10]

Would it not be a fatal misunderstanding if one were to take Adorno's admittedly infelicitous talk of a "better order" as the occasion for conceiving the liberation he has in mind as a process of generalization, of universalization or decontextualization, as a progression from the particular and arbitrary, confined and one-sided, to the true and necessary? If a utopian "language without soil" is to distinguish itself from the uniformity of reified language, then it must be a language of nuances, of "flexibility, elegance, and refinement of formulation," of "precision," one that hits the "meaning" of the matter at hand or through which the meaning of the matter is first constituted. Nuances arise and communicate their meaning, however, through considerations that bear an earthly remainder that may be neither extrinsic nor a source of embarrassment to them, since their element is a particular use of language, a language game. If one wants to understand what is meant by the curious idea of a "language without soil," one must thus investigate how Adorno speaks of the earth in different contexts, how he deploys the word.[11] The "better order" may only be one in which removal from the earth, the rejection of claims that always stand under a "spell," because they repose in an "historical existence," in something that exists and must be recognized or changed, is also a return to the earth, a rescue. The relation to the earthly remainder founded by the rescuing return is, of course, no longer one of "subjection," but a relation of freedom or a free bearing: in language games between language games, between cultures in cultures. The more precise the language, the more free and unrestrained it is. This freedom and unrestraint allows us, finally, to discern in the "language without soil" the "rushing" and "rustling" mentioned in other essays in Adorno's *Notes to Literature*.[12] Would such rushing be at all perceptible without a return to the earth? Through the rescuing return, the utmost in linguistic precision is attained as the rushing of language is set free for perception. At the border of the infinitely precise and inconspicuous, precision turns into something different.

Adorno once again speaks of the earth in a striking passage from the *Philosophy of Modern Music*, a passage that, in analogy to the current of music, suggests the interpretation of "language without soil" as rushing language. The origin and end of music in the Orphic legend and in twelve-tone works are said to communicate with each other insofar as they extend "beyond the realm of intention," beyond "meaning and subjectivity."[13] Their communication, however, makes clear what is at stake in the "expression" of *all* music: an "outpouring" [*Verströmen*] that dissolves what exists. Because it signals a return, not a simple regression or murky confluence, because it does not ecstatically consummate a "neo-heathen invocation of the earth,"[14] this "outpouring" disavows its equation with a madness, a captivity and a blindness, for which earth and soil stand as a cipher. The return to the earth transforms the latter into an earth without earth. Speculating on the origin of music, Adorno claims this origin to be "gesticulative in nature" and "closely related to the origin of tears." The gesture from which music emerges appears as that of "release":

> The tension of the face muscles relaxes; the tension which closes the face off from the surrounding world by directing the face actively at this world disappears. Music and tears open the lips and set the arrested human being free. The sentimentality of inferior music indicates in its distorted figure that which higher music, at the very border of insanity, is yet able to design in the validity of its form: reconciliation. The human being who surrenders himself [*sich verströmen läßt*] to tears and to a music which no longer resembles him in any way permits that current [*Strom*] of which he is not part and which lies behind the dam restraining the world of phenomena to flow back into itself. In weeping and in singing he enters into alienated reality. 'Tears dim my eyes: earth's child I am again'—this line from Goethe's *Faust* defines the position of music. Thus the earth claims Euridyce again. The gesture of return—not the sensation of expectancy—characterizes the expression of all music, even if it finds itself in a world worthy of death.[15]

The critique of what exists and of the insistence on what exists describes a double trajectory in Adorno. In one direction, it leads to a composure of utmost precision, in the other to an outpouring and rushing "at the very border of insanity." The idea of such critique, which is named, signified, and invoked in the formula of a "language without soil," designates the point at which the wish to keep apart composure and outpouring proves idle.

Translated from the German by Robert Savage

CHAPTER 2

Taking on the Stigma of Inauthenticity: Adorno's Critique of Genuineness

Martin Jay

To know inauthenticity is not the same as to be authentic.[1]

PAUL DE MAN

"The search for authenticity, nearly everywhere we find it in modern times," writes Marshall Berman in his book on Rousseau, *The Politics of Authenticity*, "is bound up with a radical rejection of things as they are ... the desire for authenticity has emerged in modern society as one of the most politically explosive of human impulses."[2] Even those with less radical agendas, like Sigmund Freud, have been seen as sharing the same desire. According to Lionel Trilling in his classic study *Sincerity and Authenticity*, Freud's insistence on the tragic dimension of the human condition "had the intention of sustaining the authenticity of human existence that formerly had been ratified by God."[3] Nietzsche, Trilling added, dreaded "the inauthenticity of experience, which he foresaw would be the consequence of the death of God."[4]

These testimonials to the power of authenticity as the reigning value of a society bereft of divine sanction and dissatisfied with the false comforts of modern life can be seen as symptomatic documents of the 1960s and early 1970s, at least in the American context. They can, in fact, be seen to represent the culmination of the powerful impact on American culture of Sartrean existentialism, which functioned to reinforce native inclinations, stemming from certain strains in evangelical Protestantism and the frontier experience, toward relying on individual responsibility in the face of conformist pressures from the outside.⁵ At a time when moral relativism appeared hard to overcome, authenticity also seemed to lend at least a measure of value to whatever beliefs were held with special intensity and fervor. Indeed, if recent books like Alexander Nehamas' *Virtues of Authenticity* and Geoffrey Hartman's *Scars of the Spirit: The Struggle Against Inauthenticity* are any indication, the positive glow surrounding the word "authenticity" remains strong into our own century.⁶

And yet at virtually the same time as Americans like Berman and Trilling were identifying authenticity as the highest value of their age, Theodor W. Adorno was writing an uncompromising attack on what he dubbed "the jargon of authenticity" as the latest version of "the German Ideology."⁷ This text of 1967, one of the most excoriating polemics he ever wrote, was directed largely against Heidegger, Jaspers, Buber, and other German existentialists, with an occasional nod to Sartre and a recognition that the roots of the jargon lay in the Weimar Republic rather than the postwar era.

It is particularly noteworthy that Adorno, who took so much from Freud and Nietzsche and was no less adamant than Berman's version of Rousseau in radically rejecting "things as they are," nonetheless reckoned authenticity on the side of the conformists rather than the rebels, and identified it as a particularly German rather than American ideology. What is perhaps even more striking is his having anticipated the argument of *The Jargon of Authenticity* while he was still in his American exile, in one of the most trenchant aphorisms of *Minima Moralia*, written in 1945, called "Gold Assay."⁸ In what follows I want to focus on the implications of this aphorism and argue that it was the indispensable link between Adorno's later attack on German existentialism and an earlier essay by his great friend Walter Benjamin, his celebrated "The Work of Art in the Age of Mechanical Reproduction,"⁹ which even more than the critique of Kierkegaard in Adorno's 1933 *Habilitationsschrift* provides the key arguments for his attack on authenticity.¹⁰

First, several etymological observations are in order (even as we acknowledge Adorno's own skepticism about placing too much faith in the origins of words). Authenticity (*Authentizität* in German) is derived from the Greek *autos* or "self" and *hentes* or "prepared," and implies something done by one's own hand and thus providing a reliable guarantee of quality. In German, the more common word is *Eigentlichkeit*, whose root is in *eigen*, which is the perfect participle of a verb, defunct in modern usage, for "having" or "possessing." As a result, it suggests proprietary ownership, including of the self. A third term, *Echtheit*, comes from a *niederdeutsch* term *echact*, which means following the law, an origin that alerts us to the link between *echt* and *recht*. Interestingly, the normal English equivalent, genuineness, has a very different sedimented meaning, coming as it does from the Latin *genuinus*, which means native or inborn. Although there is considerable overlap among all these terms, it has been argued by one of the most important theorists of the term that there is a genuine and false authenticity and a genuine and false inauthenticity. That theorist was Martin Heidegger, who was of course Adorno's most direct target in his critique of the jargon of authenticity.[11] What I hope to show is that Adorno himself relied on a similar distinction, albeit with very different criteria of judgment.

Now let me turn to the importance of Benjamin's "The Work of Art in the Age of Mechanical Reproduction." As has often been noted, Adorno quarreled with a number of Benjamin's arguments, especially his premature dismissal of the value of the autonomy of the artwork and his blunt advocacy of the politicization of art.[12] As late as his posthumously published *Aesthetic Theory*, Adorno would charge that the essay betrayed Benjamin's "identification with the aggressor" because it tried to reintegrate art and practical life.[13] But in one crucial respect, Adorno seems to have learned a powerful lesson from his friend's work, a lesson about the impossibility of reversing the decline of what Benjamin had called "aura" and whose alleged recovery was at the heart of ideological efforts to achieve authenticity in the present fallen world.

The issue of authenticity is addressed in Benjamin's essay fundamentally in aesthetic terms, which foreground the crucial distinction between the auratic original work and its reproduction. "The presence of the original," he writes, "is the prerequisite to the concept of authenticity.... The whole sphere of authenticity is outside technical—and of course, not only—technical reproducibility."[14] The context that gives the original artwork its special power is, however, ultimately religious: "the unique value of the 'authentic' work of art has its basis in ritual, the location of its original use value."[15] Although the cult origins of aesthetic authenticity have been effaced, their residue remains potent in the modern worship of aesthetic beauty, for "with the secularization of art, authenticity displaces the cult value of the work."[16] Whereas auratic natural objects have no comparable authenticity, art objects have an essence that "is transmissible from its beginning, ranging from its substantive duration to its testimony to the history which it has experienced."[17] Or rather they did so until the introduction of techniques of mass reproduction, such as the lithograph, photograph, and cinema, which undermine the uniqueness of the original and disrupt the smooth continuity of tradition. The result of this change, Benjamin asserted, was monumental: "the instant the criterion of authenticity ceases to be applicable to artistic production, the total function of art is reversed. Instead of being based on ritual, it begins to be based on another practice—politics."[18]

Benjamin's analysis of this epochal shift is, by now, widely known, but one dimension of it needs foregrounding and examination. In an important footnote, he argues that "at the time of its origin a medieval picture of the Madonna could not yet be said to be 'authentic.' It became 'authentic' only during the succeeding centuries and perhaps most strikingly so during the last one."[19] Valuing authenticity is itself, Benjamin claimed, a function of reproduction, not a quality of what precedes it. Thus, as Eva Geulen has recently pointed out, "authenticity is a belated effect. In the beginning was not the original, but rather the reproduction, which makes the concept of authenticity possible in the first place. Authenticity becomes 'authentic' only against the background of reproducibility. That means, however, that authenticity is compromised from the beginning, inauthentic from the start, for its origin lies not in itself, but rather in its opposite, reproduction."[20]

Adorno was skeptical about many aspects of Benjamin's argument—its wholesale disdain for the autonomous art object, its misplaced optimism about the political effects of the end of the aura, and its overemphasis on the critical implications of technology alone—but he seems to have been deeply impressed by this critique of the compromised nature of claims to authenticity.[21] By the time Adorno composed aphorism 99 in *Minima Moralia*, Benjamin's suspicions of the claims of aesthetic authenticity were enlarged to encompass more general claims about authentic human behavior as a whole.

The aphorism is entitled "gold assay" [*Goldprobe*], which invokes the practice of distinguishing rare from base metals, genuine gold from the fool's alternative. Like believers in the intrinsic value of gold, devotees of authenticity think they can isolate a standard of value before the onset of the exchange principle, which reduces everything to a fungible counter in a circulation without end. But despite his own fundamental hostility to the triumph of exchange, which was the economic equivalent of identity thinking, Adorno is at pains in *Minima Moralia* to distance himself as well from the order of valuation implied by the ontological search for an immutable standard like gold.[22] He begins the aphorism by noting that the collapse of substantive religious and ethical standards has created a vacuum that has been filled by the idea of genuineness, the imperative that everyone should be entirely what he or she really is. Not only is it evident in late bourgeois thinkers like Ibsen, Kierkegaard, and Nietzsche, but it also has found a home among the adepts of fascist philosophy, who have taken on the pathos of religious authority without any real content. Their talk of heroic "being-in-the-world" and testing oneself in dangerous "frontier situations" masks the absence of any values beyond sheer factual existence. But rather than seeing their appeal as a corruption of a more benign notion of authenticity, Adorno perceives its flaw operating at a deeper level, that of the self whose authenticity is supposedly endangered in the modern world.

"The untruth is located," he writes, "in the substratum of genuineness [*Echtheit*] itself, the individual. If it is in the *principium individuationis*, as the antipodes Hegel and Schopenhauer both recognized, that the secret of the world's course is concealed, then the conception of an ultimate and absolute substantiality of the self falls victim to an illusion that protects the established order even while its essence decays."[23] The illusion is not that the integrated individual once existed and has been destroyed or maimed in the present, nor that individuals are to be understood as eternal existential realities underlying the depredations of a world that only appears to undermine them. True self-reflection instead will show that the seemingly sovereign and self-contained individual was always a secondary effect of impulses that are more primary, which Adorno categorizes as "imitation, play, wanting to be different."[24]

Here, although he doesn't make it clear, Adorno was drawing on another of Benjamin's seminal ideas, the importance of the mimetic faculty as a source of resistance to identity thinking and the preponderance of the subject over the object.[25] Creative mimicry, the passive receptivity that avoided domination of otherness, led to a benign playfulness that could make of repetition a virtue rather than a vice.[26] The search for a pure subject prior to mimetic behavior, Adorno warned, leads to a false infinity of desire for a reality that is as elusive as the Kantian thing-in-itself. Schopenhauer was among the first to realize the impossibility of this quest when he posited the necessity of an external object as the basis for the alleged interiority of the subject, which was "nothing but an insubstantial ghost."[27] Believing otherwise, Adorno continued, was itself a function of a particular social order in which sovereign individuals were given ideological solidity. "What presents itself as an original entity, a monad, is only the result of a social division of the social process. Precisely as an absolute, the individual is a mere reflection of property relations. In him the fictitious claim is made that what is biologically one must logically precede the social whole, from which it is only isolated by force, and its contingency is held up as a standard of truth."[28]

Because the self is always imbricated in the social, any attempt, like Kierkegaard's, to retreat into naked existential interiority is complicitous with the isolation caused by society, not a protest against it. Nietzsche, despite all his insights into the workings of ideology, ultimately failed to see through the fallacy of authenticity, which betrayed his Lutheran roots and even smacked of the very anti-Semitism he decried in Wagner. In contrast, Adorno insisted, "anything that does not wish to wither should rather take on itself the stigma of the inauthentic. For it lives on the mimetic heritage. The human is indissolubly linked with imitation: a human being becomes a human being at all by imitating other human beings."[29] If there is a religious dimension of this alternative to authenticity, it comes not through speaking of the self as an absolute ontological ground, but rather as a second-order reality understood to have been made in the likeness of that supreme Other called God.

Those who celebrate genuineness, Adorno continued, also often do so for social reasons, to legitimate their priority before those who allegedly are latecomers. The precarious experience of the exile can be heard in his warning that "all ruling strata claim to be the oldest settlers, autochthonous. The whole philosophy of inwardness, with its professed contempt for the world, is the last sublimation of the brutal, barbaric lore whereby he who was here first has the greatest rights."[30] Not only is the philosophy of authentic inwardness falsely premised on some alleged founding claim in the immemorial past, but it is also a function of the very society in the present it pretends to question. "The discovery of genuineness as a last bulwark of individualistic ethics is a reflection of mass-production. Only when countless standardized commodities project, for the sake of profit, the illusion of being unique, does the idea take shape, as their antithesis yet in keeping with the same criteria, that the non-reproducible is the truly genuine."[31] Then directly echoing Benjamin's observation in the footnote to "The Work of Art in the Age of Mechanical Reproduction" cited earlier, but moving it from the register of the visual to the aural arts, Adorno added, "previously, the question of authenticity was doubtless as little asked of intellectual products as that of originality, a concept unknown in Bach's era."[32]

The fetish of the original, of the authentic, of the incommensurable is captured in the comparable fetish of gold as an alternative to mere exchange. The aphorism ends with Adorno protesting that any attempt to find such a foundation beyond social relations merely serves those relations that predominate in capitalism. "The ungenuineness of the genuine stems from its need to claim, in a society dominated by exchange, to be what it stands for yet is never able to be. The apostles of genuineness, in the service of the power that now masters circulation, dignify the demise of the latter with the dance of the money veils."[33] Gold as an absolute standard of value is thus no antidote to the empty circulation of exchange, but rather its fetishistic complement. Authenticity as an antidote to the apparent inauthenticity of the administered world is no less complicitous in what it strives to resist.

Despite the defeat of fascism, Adorno came to believe that the same constellation of ideological forces was at work in the postwar world. In his 1948 study of the *Philosophy of Modern Music*, he began his attack on "Stravinsky and Restoration" with a section called "authenticity" [*Eigentlichkeit*]. Linking it with the composer's denial of the subjective pole in music and his apotheosis of sacrifice, he argued that "the relationship to concurrent philosophical phenomenology is unmistakable. The renunciation of all psychologism—the reduction to the pure phenomenon, as the process reveals itself—opens up a realm of 'authentic' being which is beyond all doubt. In both cases, distrust of the unoriginal (at its utmost depth the suspicion of the contradiction between actual society and its ideology) results in the misleading hypostatization of the 'remains,' or what is left over after the removal of that which has allegedly been superimposed as truth."[34] In his 1956 introduction to his metacritique of Husserl's phenomenology, *Against Epistemology*, he would continue the attack by writing that "phenomenology speaks the jargon of authenticity which meanwhile ruined the whole of cultivated German language and turned it into sacred gibberish. It struck a theological note devoid of theological content or any other content except self-idolization. It feigns the incarnate presence of the first which is neither incarnate nor present. Its authority resembles that of the bureaucratic world which rests on nothing except the fact of bureaucracy itself."[35] The phrase "jargon of authenticity" then served as the title of a longer treatment of the problem originally intended for *Negative Dialectics*, but which became its own book because Adorno thought the danger was sufficiently great to warrant a separate treatment.

It begins with Adorno tracing the current jargon to the work of a group of unidentified religious revivalists in the 1920s, "anti-intellectual intellectuals,"[36] whose rediscovery of Kierkegaard had led them to seek concrete religious experience instead of abstract idealist theology. He mentions a friend who was not invited to participate in their company—perhaps Siegfried Kracauer—because his hesitation before Kierkegaard's "leap of faith" had suggested he was "not authentic enough."[37] This group, which anticipated Heidegger's appropriation of the term in *Being and Time*, was sarcastically dubbed "The Authentic Ones" by those who shared those hesitations. For Adorno, writing in the 1960s, their heirs included Karl Jaspers, Otto Friedrich Bollnow, and Ulrich Sonnemann.

Once again, Benjamin's "Work of Art in the Age of Mechanical Reproduction" provided Adorno a way to situate the cult. "The fact that the words of the jargon sound as if they said something higher than what they mean suggests the term 'aura.' It is hardly an accident," Adorno argued, "that Benjamin introduced the term at the same moment when, according to his own theory, what he understood by 'aura' became impossible to experience. As words that are sacred without sacred content, as frozen emanations, the terms of the jargon of authenticity are products of the disintegration of the aura."[38] Although now conceding that Nietzsche may have still used the word "genuineness" in a non-ideological way, Adorno contended that "in the jargon, however, it stands out in the unending mumble of the liturgy of inwardness."[39] In this liturgy lurks the ideology of subjective "mineness," "the decision in which the individual subject chooses itself as its own possession. The subject, the concept of which was once created in contrast to reification, thus becomes reified."[40] Here, significantly, Adorno seized on the root meaning of *Eigentlichkeit* rather than *Echtheit*, and as far as I can tell, never thematized the legal implications of genuineness. In any event, he argued that the choice of "mineness" failed to register the obstacles to self-possession produced by the social and political order, which is far more intrusive than the jargon assumes.

Adorno's target, it should be stressed, was as much the linguistic abuse of the terms "authenticity" and "genuineness" as what they purported to denote. "Language," he complained, "uses the term 'authentic' in a floating manner,"[41] which can give too much power to the subject doing the designating. By so doing, it undermines what he would call in *Negative Dialectics* "the object's preponderance,"[42] which is forgotten by those who embrace an undialectical nominalism. But no less problematic is the opposite mistake, which was made by the phenomenologists: seeking contact with the essential object beneath subjective mediations. "Heidegger would like to escape Husserl's dualism, as well as the whole dispute of nominalism. He remains a tributary of Husserl's, however, in the short-circuited conclusion that imputes the authentic immediacy to things, and thus turns the authentic into a special domain."⁴³ As a result, Heidegger supports the valorization of identity over non-identity, the totality over the particular, and death over life, which are the sinister earmarks of fascist thought.

To sum up, then, Adorno's multifarious charges against authenticity and the jargon that has surrounded it are as follows: it provides a hollow substitute for lost religious belief in ultimate values; it is based on a mistaken search for proprietary origins that establish rights of the earliest settlers; it rests on a dubious ideal of self-possession and integrity, which fails to credit the mimetic moment in the creation of selfhood; it entails an ontological fiction of absoluteness that falsely sees itself as the antidote to the leveling equivalence of the exchange principle; it serves as an anti-intellectual evocation of concreteness and immediacy against the alleged depredations of abstract, intellectual thought; it can be understood as a variant of the cultish notion of aura, which in fact is only itself a function of the reproductive technologies that it pretends to antedate; and finally, it paradoxically gives too much power to the subject able to designate something as authentic and to the object after that designation has been made. All attempts to derive authentic meaning from etymological priority thus share with foundational philosophy a vain search for an *Urgeschichte*, which is little more than a nostalgic fantasy of primal wholeness before the Fall.

With all of these faults, it may well seem that no viable concept of authenticity can ever be salvaged, that therefore the distinction between genuine and false authenticity made by Heidegger is not one Adorno could have embraced. As we know, however, Adorno's negative dialectics rarely rested content with a simple denunciation of a position from the vantage point of its binary opposite, which leads us to pose the following questions: Were there other usages of "genuineness" and "authenticity" that escape the gravitational pull of the current jargon? Did Adorno himself provide a less toxic use of the terms in his own writing? Were the analysis in "Gold Assay" and the comparable remarks in his other writings cited above not the last word on these numinous words? In the remainder of this essay, I want to explore a subordinate current in his work that did, in fact, gingerly give a positive answer to these questions, thus revealing a more benign usage of the term in his vocabulary.

The first thing to register is that, all the reasons listed above notwithstanding, Adorno did feel comfortable using authenticity as an honorific term at various times in his work, although, as Robert Hullot-Kentor has noted, almost always in the form of *Authentizität* rather than *Eigentlichkeit*.⁴⁴ Thus, for example, in the same essay, "Bach Defended against His

Devotees," in *Prisms*, where he criticized contemporary interpretations of Bach for assimilating his music to the philosophical search for a timeless "Order of Being," he could also contend that "authentic works unfold their truth-content, which transcends the scope of individual consciousness, in a temporal dimension through the law of their form."[45] The implication here is that artworks that register the passing of time, the inability to return to something allegedly primal and originary, can earn the positive epithet of "authentic." Thus, Adorno explicitly did not use the term in connection with the historical recovery of early instruments or original performance techniques, as was the case with the movement to restore music to its allegedly primal beginnings.[46]

The temporality of authenticity in the critical sense, that is, as transience, moreover, involved not merely an acknowledgment of the contradictory state of the present world, but also an anticipation of something better that might replace it. This is a vital dimension of what Adorno insisted was a work's truth-content. The temporality that was necessary to truth-content was therefore explicitly historical, not natural. In fact, as early as his 1930 essay "Reaction and Progress," Adorno would claim that "whatever nature may have been at the start, it is only from history that it receives the seal of genuineness [*Echtheit*]. History enters into the constellation of truth: through the dead stare of their speechless eternity the stars will strike down with confusion anyone who tries to partake of truth outside of history."[47] Accordingly, those composers who express, albeit indirectly and in mediated form, the historical realities of their day can be said to have produced authentic art.

In his own age, art might earn the accolade of true authenticity if it resisted providing instances of its false alternative, which fed the jargon Adorno so disliked. As he put it in an essay in *Eingriffe* called "Every Twenty Years," culture after Auschwitz can only avoid inauthenticity if it registers the impossibility of culture as a meaningful whole: "the authentic artists of the present are those in whose works there shudders the aftershock of the most extreme terror."[48] In *Aesthetic Theory*, he made a similar point: "Scars of damage and disruption are the modern's seal of authenticity [*Echtheitssiegel*]; by their means, art desperately negates the closed confines of the ever-same; explosion is one of its invariants."[49]

Adorno was thus, despite all of his hostility to the ideological search for an existential "gold standard," able to mobilize the rhetoric of authenticity for his own purposes. In fact, because Adorno reintroduced a notion of aesthetic authenticity in these ways, it has been possible for some of his critics to chide him for falling below the standard set by *The Jargon of Authenticity*. Thus, for example, Douglas Kellner has charged that Adorno's aesthetics are undialectical because "he operates with a binary contrast between 'authentic' art and mass culture in which the latter is primarily debased and emancipatory effects are limited to the former. This stance reproduces the German religion of high art and its inevitable elitism, and completely excludes the 'popular' from the domain of 'the authentic,' thus, regressing behind the critiques of Brecht and Benjamin—and Adorno's own critique of 'the authentic' in *The Jargon of Authenticity*."[50]

The irony of this critique from the populist Left, which is grounded in a simplistic reversal of the binary opposition it attributes to Adorno, is that it was precisely the Benjamin of "The Work of Art in the Era of Mechanical Reproduction" who inspired the attack on genuineness we have seen in *Minima Moralia* and after. And that attack, as we have noted, was indebted to an appreciation of the ways in which the mimetic quality of mechanically reproduced art undermined claims to auratic originality. That is, Adorno's praise for authenticity in art understood in a non-ideological sense is based precisely on his critique of its problematic use, which could just as easily be evident in mass culture as in high culture. Thus, in *Aesthetic Theory*, Adorno was at pains to uncouple the aura from what he thought of as the critically authentic art of his day: "Compared with authentic art, degraded, dishonored, and administered art is by no means without aura: the opposition between those antagonistic spheres must always be conceived as the mediation of the one through the other. In the contemporary situation, those works honor the auratic element that abstain from it; its destructive conservation—its mobilization for the production of effects in the interest of creating mood—has its locus in amusement. . . . Aura is gulped down along with sensual stimuli; it is the uniform sauce that the culture industry pours over the whole of its manufacture."[51] In other words, mass culture is itself the site of a resurrected auratic effect, which parallels the cult of immediacy and genuineness evident in the philosophical jargon of authenticity. A defensible—that is, critical—version of authenticity resists such phony auratic effects with their comforting illusions of wholeness and integrity, and registers instead both the shudder of alienation in the modern world and the utopian moment of mimetic relationality that Benjamin had praised in modern technologies of reproduction as well as ancient practices like astrology and graphology.

If one goes back to aphorism 99 of *Minima Moralia*, there is in fact a subtle adumbration of this position. "Indeed," Adorno writes, "not only inauthenticity that poses as veridical ought to be convicted of lying; authenticity itself becomes a lie the moment it becomes authentic, that is, in reflecting on itself, in postulating itself as genuine, in which it already oversteps the identity that it lays claim to in the same breath."[52] What I take Adorno to be saying in this compacted sentence is that the claim that something should be seen as authentic is itself a theoretical overlay, a reified conceptual subsumption, which distances specific cases of the allegedly authentic from their own particularity. Instead of maintaining their non-identical uniqueness, outside of and resistant to the exchange principle, they become mere instances of the very category of authenticity, subsumed under a general term, rather than irreducible to it. As a result, they are simply victims of another mode of commensuration, which only thinks it challenges what it dislikes in economic fungibility. Such an outcome happens in high as well as mass culture, when the aura is introduced as a way to distinguish the uniqueness of a work from the generic standard, just as the genuine individual is set apart from the herd, from Heidegger's *das Man* ("the One" or "the They"). In all these cases, the imposition of the category of auratic authenticity undermines the non-auratic alternative that Adorno sees in certain works of art in the modern era.

What are the results of tracing the concept of authenticity in Adorno's work? The ideological notion of authenticity, attacked in aphorism 99 of *Minima Moralia* and *The Jargon of Authenticity*, is based on a dangerous search for ultimate origins as legitimating fictions, a mistaken reification of the individual as a self-possessed monad, and the transfer of cultish notions of aura from the sphere of religion to art, philosophy, and everyday human existence. It evokes the myth of autochthonous rootedness to denigrate the wanderers who are condemned to permanent exile.

Against this usage are two different, more defensible notions, which are variants of non-auratic authenticity. One involves the registering of the historical disasters of modern life, the "scars of damage and disruption" that produce a shudder which is the emblem of the work's truth-content. Here authenticity means fidelity to the historical moment with all its traumatic contradictions rather than retreating to an allegedly prior state of plenitudinous wholeness before the fall into alienation. However much he may have insisted on the value of aesthetic autonomy against the reduction of art to a function of something exterior to it, Adorno never failed to praise works that indirectly expressed the depredations of modern life. Indeed, it was only the works that resist the gravitational pull of the current order and yet do not pretend to have transcended it entirely—works that, as Max Paddison has pointed out,[53] are "failures" and know themselves as such—that can gain the breathing space to express its horrors.

The second defensible use harkens back to Benjamin's celebration of the mimetic faculty, which is evident in the technologically reproduced mass culture that Adorno so often distrusted. Here authenticity paradoxically means accepting and even valorizing the necessary inauthenticity of the self, which is always dependent on the other, always in relation to the outside, always insufficiently integrated into a coherent and boundaried unit. To repeat the key sentences of aphorism 99: "Anything that does not wish to wither should rather take on itself the stigma of the inauthentic. For it lives on in the mimetic heritage." Here the derived is privileged over the putative original, an original that, as the footnote from "The Work of Art in the Age of Mechanical Reproduction" cited above shows, is itself an effect of the very reproduction it pretends to precede, a phantasmatic compensation for what is assumed to be lost. This version of mimetic relationality is not, however, a capitulation to the exchange principle, for it knows that imitation is not perfectly equivalent, that mirroring is not simple duplication of the same. It provides an alternative both to the absolute commensurability of exchange and the absolute singularity of the jargon of authenticity.

One final example will make this alternative clearer, and it ensues from the performative practice of Adorno himself. That is, if we register the extent to which Adorno's critique of genuineness in *Minima Moralia* and elsewhere was itself deeply indebted to Benjamin's defense of mechanical reproduction against the aura and his notion of the mimetic faculty, it quickly becomes apparent that many of his "own" ideas betray precisely the kind of inauthenticity that he defended against the jargon.[54] Or if one wants to rely on his critical use of the term, it shows the non-auratic authenticity of the intellectual who knows himself not to be in full possession of his own ideas. Paradoxically, in his very lack of originality, his reworking without entirely duplicating many of his friend's most arresting ideas, Adorno took upon himself the stigma he urged us all to embrace. However much we may have sought to honor him in 2003, his centenary year, it is, pace Detlev Claussen, as inauthentic follower rather than self-starting genius,[55] as creative mimic rather than wholly original thinker, as non-auratic epigone rather than charismatic lawgiver, that Adorno ironically deserves our deepest respect.[56]

CHAPTER 3

Suffering Injustice: Misrecognition as Moral Injury in Critical Theory

J. M. Bernstein

Injustice is the medium of real justice. A just world should not be defined as one that is regulated by the norm of the equal consideration of every individual's interest, nor as a world that is in accordance with Jürgen Habermas's idea that justice is now "sublimated into the concept of the impartiality of a discursively attained agreement."[1] These notions of justice, precisely, sublimate into a normative ideal the *political struggle* of the indigent subject against a dominating, sovereign Universal or, even worse, sublimate into procedures and modes for warranting the assertibility of moral and legal norms the primary world reference of justice in its biblical sense. Justice in its emphatic sense, justice as a fiery sword, is the always practical, always eventful, always political struggle for the elimination of injustice. The normative *force* of the idea of justice, its urgent claim, is parasitic upon the acknowledgment, without any mitigation, of "the undiminished persistence of suffering, fear, and threat" that remains in a world "which could be paradise here and now—[yet] can become hell itself tomorrow."[2]

It is the persistence of social suffering in a world in which it could be eliminated that for Adorno is the source of the *need* for critical reflection, for philosophy. Philosophy continues and gains its cultural place because an as-yet unbridgeable abyss separates the social potential for the relief of unnecessary human suffering and its emphatic continuance. Philosophy now is the culturally bound repository for the systematic acknowledgement and articulation of the meaning of the expanse of human suffering within technologically advanced societies that are already committed to liberal ideals of freedom and equality.[3] Philosophy is the discursive expression of the forms of wrong of needless human suffering in the midst of the continuing requirement for an acknowledgement of unpreventable suffering.

To call preventable social suffering "injustice" is hardly more than a semantic refinement. In this light, Adorno's negative dialectics could just as well be thought of as a dialectics of injustice, a thought underlined by the subtitle of *Minima Moralia: Reflections from Damaged Life*. Adorno, however, only rarely used the concept of injustice in place of suffering (damaged life, nonidentity) for two reasons. First, injustice could signify simply a regression from a known positive conception of justice, implying that our conception of justice was sound but it had failed to be applied adequately or sufficiently. For Adorno it is just this failure that is the conundrum that calls for thinking, namely, that our liberal ideals proved, and continue to prove, insufficient at the very junctures where they might matter most. And Adorno assumes that the cause for this, at least in part, is that emphatic justice has been sublimated into democratic procedures for the warranting of social norms as a means for coordinating actions among competing interests. In this respect, social norms presuppose the mutual indifference of a plurality of strangers forced to coordinate their actions with one another if they are to achieve their individual ends. Not only does this make the competitive market and its needs the model for social cooperation generally, but in so doing it quietly displaces the voice of the excluded. Saying that the excluded ought to be included, that our norms for the coordination of action ought to apply to everyone, makes evident what is nonetheless there on the surface: namely, that the goal of inclusion is only a precipitate or corollary to the idea of fair cooperative procedures. Mutual indifference is still the premise, making the relief of suffering an adjunct or ancillary to liberal justice.[4] And this might have been anticipated, since liberal justice makes justice into a means (for the coordination of action) rather than an end in itself. The priority of the right over the good—the political good become democratic procedure—by making justice into a means succumbs to the demands of instrumental rationality: now political cooperation and a just social order themselves become a means to a private end—formally the end of each citizen pursuing his or her own conception of the good life, substantially the end of capital reproduction. Liberal justice is the instrumentalization of the political. Second, the sublimation of emphatic justice by liberal justice abstracts from the material, bodily basis of moral experience. By speaking of suffering rather than injustice, Adorno placed the body at the forefront of moral experience. For him bodily suffering is the paradigm of social suffering; and bodily experiences of abhorrence, revulsion, and disgust at the suffering (bodily or otherwise) of others, together with compassion for the suffering of others, form the practical ground for ethical norms and practices. As a consequence, "what *hope* clings to, as in Mignon's song, is the transfigured body."[5]

In abjuring the language of injustice Adorno made his thought appear more politically impotent than it in fact is; that his philosophy is not politically or ethically idle no longer needs demonstrating.[6] However, making perspicuous what it means for social thought to sustain the idea that injustice is the medium of justice does still require elaboration. In my own writings I have tacitly assumed that while Adorno does not directly employ Hegel's recognitive conception of self-consciousness, nevertheless, since the master/slave dialectic is everywhere in his writings, and since the way in which the human suppression of external nature reverses to become a form of self-denial and self-repression follows the model of Hegel's notion of the causality of fate, his theory of social suffering must indirectly depend upon the recognitive model. Having already agreed that Adorno makes bodily suffering paradigmatic for social suffering, then what is needed now is an explication of how what is in effect a theory of intersubjectivity can nonetheless bind itself to bodily experience.

Recognitive theory is not new to Critical Theory. From the outset, Axel Honneth has sought to displace Habermas's communication's theoretic approach—which itself sought to sublimate recognitive demands and relations into a conception of communicative relations—with a renewed theory of recognition.[7] This sets the agenda for this essay. I will begin by reprising Honneth's recognitive critique of the communicative turn. The singular achievement of recognitive theory is to provide an account of all moral injuries, injuries that are not just misfortunes but normatively wrong, in terms of misrecognition. This thesis will be tested against Nancy Fraser's contention that inequality cannot be analyzed in recognitive terms.

Although Honneth analyzes social suffering as misrecognition, and gives a certain precedence to social suffering, his approach finally turns on providing a *formal* (and perhaps quasi-transcendental) reconstruction of the good life in recognitive terms; the price of this is to eclipse injustice and social suffering once again, and hence to again betray emphatic justice. A negative social philosophy, one bound to injustice, must give priority to history and event. Honneth's approach displaces what Adorno conceived of as the two orienting frames of Critical Theory: a contextualization of modern social forms within a fragmentary philosophy of history, and, working from the opposite pole, the provisioning of an ineliminable and primary role to event and experience. These two emphases converge for Adorno in the event of the Holocaust, and it is the injustice of it, its exemplification of injustice, that provides the moral orientation necessary for the transformation of a broken modernity: the demand that Auschwitz not happen again. In a letter to Max Horkheimer in August 1940, Adorno wonders whether what they have been wont to see from the standpoint of the proletariat has now been transferred to the Jews "in a terrifyingly concentrated form," since the Jews now represent "the opposite extreme to the concentration of power."[8] Perhaps, after Rwanda, after the killing fields of Cambodia, after ethnic cleansing in Bosnia, after the uprising of global terrorism, after the systematic torture of Iraqi civilians in Abu Ghraib, after the absence of international response to the ethnic cleansing—perhaps genocide—taking place in Sudan, and after globalization processes have made palpable and effective the subordination of political community to economic system, and the superfluousness of social masses over the globe,[9] perhaps the instance of the Holocaust no longer looks like a self-enclosed event in German history, but begins to look like a precedent, an exemplary instance in which these moments gather round it like elements of an horrific constellation; perhaps, now, unbearably, the Holocaust is coming to have for us the very sociohistorical and moral significance that Adorno attributed to it.

The Rose in the Cross of the Present: From Class to Communicative Reason to Social Movements

Following the demands of Hegelian metaphysics in which actuality precedes possibility, the Marxist critique of capitalist modernity and the emancipatory interest it promoted anchored itself in the social reality of the laboring classes. The practical import of critique derived from its being, in the first instance, an articulation of an empirical instance of injustice that could be shown to have systematic consequences for society as a whole. Despite the lapse of the proletariat as an intramundane source of transcendence, Critical Theory too was meant to be the reflective aspect of an existing historical process of emancipation. However, it is argued, the very terms of the Weberian historical sociology in which Adorno and Horkheimer attempted to explicate the dehydration of emancipatory praxis, namely, the expanding rationalization processes infecting both the intellectual and institutional practices of modern societies, effectively left no concrete social element as the bearer of intramundane transcendence; in its place arose "a barely articulated anthropology."[10] The embarrassment of being dependent upon a pre-theoretical emancipatory source incapable of being empirically demonstrated, of having, at best, only the indirect illumination provided by austere instances of high modernist art in order to chart the path from actuality to possibility and hence from potentiality to future actuality, left the praxial claims of negativist Critical Theory looking hopelessly emaciated.

This was the impasse Habermas believed himself to be inheriting: negativist critique, with its focus on an ever-escalating growth in the technological transformation of society, the continuing denationalization of economies and the consequent continuing subordination of the political system, and, finally, "the accelerated hollowing out of the human personality,"[11] unveiled a conception of the world lacking any intrinsic, systematic empirical structures and practices that, with a bit of unfettering, might unfold into freedom and happiness. Honneth pointedly limns Habermas's project for the renewal of Critical Theory through the development of a theory of communicative action as governed by three categorial gestures. The first is the shift from the Marxist paradigm of labor as world constituting to a dual-orientation in which labor and communicative action form different constitutive relations between self and other, with social progress in the emphatic sense now found in the sphere of social interaction. The second gesture is the elaboration of a pragmatics of ordinary language which depends on the demonstration that all communicative action contains a discrete set of normative presuppositions that jointly form its rationality potential. Habermas's last gesture is a developmental theory of society in which societal rationalization is shown to involve the separation, thematization, and formation of social steering media through which the normative presuppositions of communicative action become socially explicit and empirically effective.

Even at this level of generality, it is evident that Habermas's search for the rose in the cross of the present is off-base, exacerbating rather than resolving the dilemmas of negativist critique. After all, Adorno and Horkheimer never intended to deny the *ideals* of enlightened modernity: freedom, equality, universality, and hence that, even as those ideals are implicated in the reproduction of capitalist modernity—say, the ideal of a fair and equal market exchange, exchanging equal for equal—they contain an ever-suppressed moment of utopian hopefulness. Their critique was rather that, in practice, those ideals are co-implicated in the—negative—rationalization of modernity, and hence operate simultaneously as progressive and regressive forces; so, for example, Kant's Categorical Imperative pays for its real universality through its suppression of bodily affects; freedom is hence now grounded in fear and coercion—the Categorical Imperative as punishing superego and ego ideal in one. They further contended that because these ideals were either co-implicated in the rationalization of society or left as purely ideal, they either promoted the very forms of domination they meant to suppress or were empirically idle, lacking a foothold in empirical experience: in their secular form, normative ideals and principles lacked motivational authority.

Now it is evident from Habermas's first categorial gesture, the separation of communicative from instrumental reason, that he thought he could *purify* the ideals governing communicative action so that they could not logically, so to speak, be implicated in what they mean to resist, that a clean categorial separation between the progressive and regressive forces of modernity could be drawn. This is Habermas's answer to the rationalization problem, the negativist thesis that now, for all intents and practical purposes, it is instrumental reason—aka identity thinking—all the way down. But there is a systematic misprision in Habermas's response: to answer the dilemma of ideals becoming *either* co-implicated *or* merely ideal by thumping their ideality simply repeats one horn of the dilemma whilst leaving the whole in place. Worse, the false resolution is wrong in itself: arguably, purity is a religious ideal for which there logically cannot be a secular correlate; Habermas's ritual of purification is as dangerous and misguided as secular practices of purification—from the Terror to the Cultural Revolution—have always proved. The point here, the very reason purity can never be secular, and hence why, for example, a priori ideals inevitably carry with them a taint of theology, is that the meaning of ideals cannot be systematically and permanently separated from their use, from their role in mundane practice—the phrase "meaning is use" is *not* a point of departure for a theory of language, but a critical reminder of what it means to operate within a secular frame of reference, the ineliminability of empirical practices for the comprehension of meaning. Not only is a clean-hands morality impossible in practice (the meaning of our actions necessarily exceeds our intentions, so in the "guilt context of the living" no one escapes), but there are no "clean ideals" either. Idealization is the repudiation of the material and temporal conditions of meaning; once purified of their material anchor and temporal core, meanings naturally lose their foothold in empirical experience, while simultaneously belying their own intrinsic world-belonging. Finally, Habermas's communicative theory assumes that the rational *authority* of norms is derived from their formal ideality; but it must be questionable whether the process of purification, which deprives norms of motivational force, can invest them with rational authority. What is the rational authority of a norm that lacks motivational force? If the classical thesis that what makes a norm *practical* rather than theoretical is that its authority is intrinsically motivating, then the answer to the question is that it is a theoretical norm: purifying practical norms so that they lose both their complicity and motivational bearing achieves its end by effectively transforming them into theoretical ideals. Indeed, that is the way in which practical norms die: they become mere ideals, objects of contemplation or theory or reflection rather than immanent grounds for action. A central feature of the negativist critique of modernity, running from Pascal and Nietzsche, is the claim that societal rationalization has transformed practical norms into contemplative ideals, depriving them of *practical* authority, that is, the kind of authority that is intrinsically motivating.

If this is right, then at best Habermas answers a non-existent question—"What ideals are we enlightened subjects of modernity committed to that might govern our actions?"—while failing to answer the actual problem, *viz.*, what are the pre-theoretical sources within social life for which a Critical Theory of society might represent the reflective arm?[12] He answers a question about "Who?" and "Where?" with a response to a "What?" question. Habermas is not altogether unaware of this: he acknowledges that a cost of modern societal rationalization is that norms lose their anchor in the fabric of collective life, becoming ideal, and hence require a form of life to meet them "half-way" if they are to become effective in practice. Needless to say, this requirement, this hope for social collaboration, merely repeats the original problem. (Negativist critique, oppositely, thought that the first responsibility of reflection was to analyze the lapse of practical norms into contemplative ideals.)

It is a simple category mistake to attempt to replace the rationally vindicable sense of injury and injustice of the working classes with the norms of communicative action: they are intramundane sources of transcendence in utterly different ways. Honneth's more generous way of stating this thesis is to say that the processes of the communicative rationalization of the lifeworld, through which the linguistic conditions of reaching an understanding free from domination become empirically effective, develop behind the backs of the agents involved. As a consequence, neither these norms nor their violation—the colonization of the lifeworld by instrumental reason—belong immediately to the moral personality of social subjects. Social harm is not experienced as a punctual or systematic violation of the norms governing linguistic interaction; rather, Honneth avers, social agents "experience an impairment of what we can call their moral expectations . . . not as a restriction of intuitively mastered rules of language, but as a violation of identity claims acquired in socialization."[13]

Looking at sociological studies devoted to the forms of active resistance to social domination in the lower classes, it becomes evident that social protests "are not motivationally guided by positively formulated moral principles, but by the violation of intuitive notions of justice; and the normative core of such notions of justice repeatedly turns out to consist of expectations connected with respect for one's dignity, honor or integrity."[14] The concrete moral experience of suffering from injustice, Honneth contends, turns on feelings of social disrespect (*Missachtung*); and feelings of disrespect encode the feelings of recognition we feel we deserve and are being denied. If this is anything like correct it follows, and this is Honneth's central philosophical critique of Habermas, that "the normative presuppositions of all communicative action is to be found in the acquisition of social recognition."[15] This entails that all the normative work of communicative action, positive and negative, is borne by relations and structures of recognition and misrecognition.

Misrecognition and Moral Injury

> It is typical of . . . experiences of disrespect . . . that their individual consequences are always described in metaphors that refer to states of deterioration of the human body.
>
> AXEL HONNETH[16]

Let me begin spelling out the claim of recognitive theory by noting Nancy Fraser's objections to Honneth's scheme. She contends that the attempt to ground Critical Theory in a moral psychology of prepolitical suffering is inadequate because the very idea of a "single basic moral expectation underlying all social discontent," namely, "that one's personal identity be adequately recognized," is *prima facie* implausible. Are there not a diverse range of motives for social resistance "including resentment of unearned privilege, abhorrence of cruelty, aversion to arbitrary power, revulsion against gross disparities of income and wealth, antipathy to exploitation, dislike of supervision, and indignation at being marginalized or excluded"?[17] Further, does not Honneth's account unnecessarily shift the focus away from society and into the self, "implanting an excessively personalized sense of injury?"[18] And is not Honneth returning to a form of the myth of the given in searching out a wholly pretheoretical experience of injustice, as if a sense of injustice is not routinely motivated by complicated mediations that stretch across the domains of society? Were not women's experiences of daily suffering suffused with schema drawn from political feminism? Have not peasant movements been inspired by ideas drawn from liberation theology? Or workers' experiences of injustice saturated in the traditions of socialism?

In contrast to Honneth, Fraser contends that it is not a hierarchical scheme of the good life as etched by three fundamental forms of recognition (love, rights, and solidarity), but *parity of participation* that should be the guiding notion for a Critical Theory of society. The core idea here is that social arrangements should permit all adult members of a society to interact with one another as peers. There are at least two necessary conditions for parity of participation: (1) that the distribution of material resources is sufficient for each individual's independence and "voice"; and (2) that "institutionalized patterns of cultural value express equal respect for all participants and ensure equal opportunity for achieving social esteem."[19] In fine, parity of participation requires both distributive goods—condition (1)—and recognitive goods—condition (2)—and these goods cannot be reduced one to the other.

The exchange between Fraser and Honneth appears tetchy, both evidently feeling misunderstood by the other. And both are right, since each fundamentally misunderstands both the theory of the other *and* his or her own theoretical orientation. Fraser is right in opposing Honneth in that an adequate conception of injustice cannot be grounded in experiences of violations to *personal* identity *narrowly* construed; while Honneth is right in opposing Fraser in that without a conception of misrecognition she lacks an adequate account of moral injury. Fraser misunderstands her own theory of parity of participation, since she fails to see that it is *already a theory of recognition and misrecognition*, while Honneth fails to understand that recognitive theory indeed operates through projecting the minimum necessary conditions for the possibility of social participation; by emphasizing personal identity and self-realization, Honneth gives recognitive theory a more teleological cast than it can bear or than is necessary.[20]

Consider again Fraser's list of motives for social discontent: resentment of unearned privilege, abhorrence of cruelty, aversion to arbitrary power, revulsion against gross disparities of income and wealth, antipathy to exploitation, dislike of supervision, and indignation at being marginalized or excluded. What needs teasing out from this list is not the diversity of motives, but the precise nature of the moral injuries they are responding to. What one needs in each case is an explication of the *injury suffered*; if there is no suffering, then there is no injury, and hence no wrong. One may dislike supervision, but that does not mean that one does not require it in certain circumstances. And one may even have been excluded or marginalized for good reasons. If no one suffers from unearned privilege or disparities of income, then these, even if unjustified, do not morally matter; supervision and exclusion can be local phenomena, hence politically anodyne. As Fraser knows, these are not really radically diverse phenomena, since what gives them their political and moral salience is the role they play in providing and prohibiting, not parity of participation (a phrasing redolent with moral ambiguity), but the minimum necessary conditions for social participation, or stated alternatively, "to *respect* the equal autonomy and moral worth of others one must *accord* them the status of full partners in social interaction"[21]—a statement which for all the world sounds like Hegel's thesis that the freedom and independence of self-consciousness depend on the recognition of an equally independent and free self-consciousness that the first self-consciousness recognizes in turn.

What makes Fraser's critique of Honneth so untoward is that she illegitimately reduces recognitive discourse from a general accounting of the constitution of self-conscious agency into a narrow cultural theory concerned with specific forms of social identity. No one has ever supposed that inequality of income is directly or immediately equivalent to a failure of recognition; but if disparity of income is unjust and a form of injury, this is not because it violates a deontological norm that has magically descended from heaven; it is because it blocks my participation in society, and if my participation in society is blocked in this way then I have not been recognized as being of equal worth to those around me; if being "accorded" a status means anything, it means being recognized. Hence, not being accorded a status is a form of misrecognition. And if not being recognized of equal worth is a *moral* matter this can only be because it is a source of harm or injury or wounding. Unless the violation of a *norm* is simultaneously and thereby a violation of *me*, a way of actually harming me, it is not a moral norm. The provision of equality of income, or, at least, the right to sufficient resources to have the material goods necessary for social participation, are good or right because they are *forms of recognition*, forms necessary in order for me to be an independent subject in a world in which I am always dependent on those around me. Recognitive forms are those that knit together the necessary conditions for human separateness and connectedness—my independence from all others in a social setting in which I am at the same time permanently dependent on them.

Fraser can misread Honneth in the way she does because in turning Hegel's broad conception of self-consciousness into a notion of personal identity, Honneth makes it sound as if all political struggle is a form of identity politics, a matter of securing my personal identity in a diverse social world. However, since in *The Struggle for Recognition* Honneth is careful to explicate the way the development of rights occurs along a variety of axes—legal rights, political rights, welfare rights—it is safe to assume that he is, in fact, operating with a formal and broad rather than a narrow conception of personal identity. Nonetheless, since I think that Fraser's notion of social parity comes closer to Hegel's idea of recognition than Honneth's formal teleological conception of the good, I want to step back for a moment in order to elaborate a little more slowly on the presuppositions of recognitive theory.

In order to begin thinking hard about recent debates in bioethics concerning eugenics, Habermas has, surprisingly, returned to his roots in philosophical anthropology as a way of reconfiguring the fundamental ideas concerning the ethical self-understanding of the species. This is surprising because his account returns ethical self-understanding to the situation of our fragile human embodiment in the context of human sociality. His beautiful statement about this, in a language that seems as if drawn directly from an obscure text of the young Hegel, forms an almost perfect way of beginning to think about the internal relation between ethicality, recognition, and embodiment.

> I conceive of moral behavior as a constructive response to the dependencies rooted in the incompleteness of our organic makeup and in the persistent frailty (most felt in phases of childhood, illness, and old age) of our bodily existence. Normative regulation of interpersonal relations may be seen as a porous shell protecting a vulnerable body, and the person incorporated in this body, from the contingencies they are exposed to. Moral rules are fragile constructions protecting *both* the physis from bodily injuries and the person from inner and symbolic injuries. Subjectivity, being what makes the human body a soul-possessing receptacle of spirit, is itself constituted

through intersubjective relations to others. The individual self will only emerge through the course of social externalization, and can only be *stabilized* with the network of undamaged relations of mutual recognition.

This dependency on the other explains why one can be hurt by the other. The person is most exposed to, and least protected from, injuries in the very relations which she is most dependent on for the development of her identity and for the maintenance of her integrity.[22]

Any reasonably naturalistic accounting of morality must begin with the fact that unlike other animals, humans are born prematurely; it is prematurity that explicates what is meant by the idea of "the incompleteness of our organic makeup." Our organic makeup is completed, to the extent that it ever is, through socialization. Physical maturation, gaining control of our bodies in relation to the physical and social environment, occurs in tandem with socialization; hence through socialization we become the bodies we already necessarily are. Human beings not only are their bodies but, as self-conscious beings, have or possess their bodies; subjectivity is rooted in our simultaneously being the bodies we have or possess, where our having a body is "the result of the capacity of assuming an objectivating attitude toward the prior fact of being a body."[23]

Bodily integrity, the sense that my body is mine, occurs through and in tandem with the way the infant becomes a self, "the human body a soul-possessing receptacle of spirit." So, on the one hand, the human body, as body, is from the outset socially constituted in its being and integrity; while, on the other hand, the symbolically constituted subject that has this body is itself written in the language of the body: the social subject is, minimally, a body in symbolic form. The integrity of the social subject, its capacities for independence and self-direction, are, minimally and necessarily, socially mediated elaborations of embodiment, the mode in which we complete our organic makeup, become an intact, self-moving body. Personal identity, as Habermas and Honneth use that phrase, is the social inscription of bodily integrity, whilst intact bodily integrity is achieved by becoming a self-conscious agent.

On this accounting, the forms of recognition through which the fragmented, inchoate body of the infant becomes an *intact* body that is the child's own constitute bodily integrity in reflexively normative terms: the physical integrity of the body and its capacity for self-movement are simultaneously experienced as a moral whole, as what is rightfully, which is to say authoritatively and morally, "mine." And these same processes through which the body becomes one and mine are processes in which the self is formed as a social subject. Because the body's physically becoming one is simultaneously its normative constitution as mine, then what we call the moral dignity of the person, what it is that we now think of as *what demands respect, is a reimaging of the intact and integral body at the reflective level inscribing the self or subject that has a body in the image of the body it is and has.* The dignity of the person, in an older jargon someone's having a soul, is a social construction; the dignity of the person just is what comes to be through the forms of recognition through which the intact, self-moving body comes to be: the dignity of the self is the reflective articulation of the moral integrity of the body.

Through socialization, then, we are bodily completed, becoming intact, self-monitoring, and self-moving bodies. If completeness, intactness, and self-movement represent the normative boundary conditions for animal existence, then the same holds for human animals who achieve their bodies. Because we *are* bodies, injuries to our bodies are injuries to the self. In this respect, the pains and pleasures of the animal bodies we are form the minimum ground for ethical self-understanding. Because we *have* bodies, then injuries to the bodies we are *are* injuries to the self; and because some of these injuries are *directed* by others at the self, they are experienced as not merely wounds to the body but as violations of the self. Conversely, because the self is the social elaboration and inscription of the body we are and have, then attacks upon our social selves are forms of injuring or harming. The integrity of the social self, what is meant by the idea of personal identity by Habermas and Honneth, is a symbolic formation of embodiment, and hence subject to violation and harm in a manner precisely analogous to violations of the integrity of the body. The analogy between bodily integrity and the integrity of the person is not accidental but constitutive: personal identity just is the relative completion of organic composition for beings who are born prematurely and whose maturation occurs through socialization rather than natural development.

What these wildly inadequate modes of expression are seeking is a way of articulating what is at stake in Habermas's trenchant claim that the normative regulation of interpersonal relations, relations of recognition (and misrecognition), "may be seen as a porous shell protecting the vulnerable body, and the person incorporated in this body." I understand the notion of "porous shell" as an inevitably metaphoric expression of the fact that the norms regulating interpersonal relations are themselves like the flesh of the living body: violation of them is a source of harm or injury that is analogous to a violation of bodily integrity. Further, persons are "incorporated" in a body in the indissoluble sense that autonomy and agency are always incarnated, always a formation of a vulnerable, living, and mortal being. Unlike the newborn pony, who hours after birth can gambol freely through the fields, humans achieve their bodies socially, and hence both are and have those bodies; as a consequence, we remain radically dependent on our social environment for the sustaining of our personal independence. This dependence signals our constitutive vulnerability.

All this is condensed in Hegel's formulation of structures of recognition being relations of "independence and dependence." What the recognitive constitution of self-consciousness aims to reveal is the internal, conceptual, and empirical connection between *physical vulnerability and social dependence*, and hence, oppositely, how it is only through the "network of legitimately regulated relations of mutual recognition" that "human beings develop" that allows for the maintaining of physical integrity and personal identity—the term "personal identity" again equivalent to, in this context, the presumption about who one is that is directly parallel with that same being's bodily integrity.[24] Hegel uses the morally neutral concepts of independence and dependence because he needs to establish how our animal independence, the independence of the self-moving animal body, is acquired only through and in relation to the independence of the self-conscious agent; and how these forms of independence are jointly purchased through social dependence. As Judith Butler pointedly states the thesis:

> Although we struggle for rights over our own bodies, the very bodies for which we struggle are not quite ever only our own. The body has its invariably public dimension. Constituted as a social phenomenon in the public sphere, my body is and is not mine. Given over from the start to the world of others, it bears the imprint, is formed in the crucible of social life; only later, and with some uncertainty, do I lay claim to my body as my own, if, in fact, I ever do. Indeed, if I deny that prior to the formation of my "will," my body related me to others whom I did not choose to have in proximity to myself, if I build a notion of "autonomy" on the basis of the denial of this sphere of a primary and unwilled physical proximity with others, then am I denying the social conditions of my embodiment in the name of autonomy?[25]

The practical discourse of moral norms and laws regulating interaction between subjects is an elaboration of this recognition of the entwinement of physical and social vulnerability. Moral norms and civil laws are the historically developing social *inventions* through which societies register how bodily integrity and vulnerability are channeled through individual autonomy and heteronomy, making it just as appropriate to speak of bodily autonomy as it is to speak of personal vulnerability.

Against the background of these ideas, we are now in a position to give some precision to the concept of "moral injury," to the relation between moral injury and misrecognition, and to the relation between misrecognition and injustice. The primary goal of moral norms is to regulate social interactions between individuals in a manner that secures *the minimum necessary conditions for physical integrity and individual autonomy*. Because physical independence and autonomy are socially constituted, they are secured only through the continuing recognition of individuals by their social peers. If the recognitive story is right, then failures of recognition return individuals to a state of organic incompleteness; that is, failures of recognition not only bring about a state of affairs that is like the deterioration of the body, since the body is only itself "completed" through recognition, misrecognition "dis-incorporates" the self, ruining physical and moral integrity at once. *Misrecognition entails regression*, and to what one regresses is some aspect of that state of affairs of the brutal and radical incompleteness the infant suffers in its prematurity as it undergoes, or is forced to come to acknowledgment of, separation from its mother. Misrecognition returns the adult individual to the injury that all human beings suffer in their detachment from the maternal whole, the very moment in which prematurity is *suffered* and the recognitive process of coming to have the body it always already is begins. Prematurity and organic incompleteness are not simple facts but complex psychophysical events that infants undergo. In order to take seriously the idea that having a body is an achievement, one must also take seriously the idea that not autonomously having the body one is is suffered—at least in retrospect. The overcoming of that state of suffering is the developmental path that leads from infancy to adult autonomy. If the entire developmental path is equivalent to the coming to be recognized as an individual among equals, then when any of the forms constitutive of adult recognition are violated, the individual is deposited back into a state of fragmentariness and incompleteness corresponding to an earlier moment of its developmental path. When the violation of the minimum necessary norms securing independence is solely the work of one individual against another individual, then the injury to the victim may be termed a moral (or criminal) injury. Moral injuries may be deep or shallow, long-lasting or evanescent. When the violation belongs to a pattern embedded in the life of the community as a whole that systematically blocks one (and those like one) from achieving the independence already available to all others, then the injury suffered is a form of injustice.

If moral and legal norms are social inventions, bound to the historical particularities of a social formation, then to say that injustice is prior to justice is simply to urge that the *demand for recognition*, which is the demand for equal standing in a community of equals, is not exhausted by the positive moral and legal terms available at any time. Since the nonsatisfaction of this demand causes suffering and pain, then social suffering necessarily contains a reflective and a normative dimension: social suffering is a knowledge of the context bringing it about and a negative relation to that context. Just this is implied by Adorno's negative anthropological theorem: "The corporeal moment tells our knowledge that suffering ought not to be, that things should be different."[26]

The Negative Dialectics of Injustice

Honneth contends that the basic concepts for a Critical Theory of society "have to be constructed in such a way that they can grasp the distortions and deficiencies of the social framework of recognition, while the process of societal rationalization loses its central position."[27] If the process of societal rationalization loses its central position, then the deformations of the present become detached from the movement of history—both the fundamental structures and events of history, and their unfolding—leaving Critical Theory precisely where it was when Adorno found it: stranded between social misery and moral ideality. Explaining that those miseries are failures to actualize recognitive ideals gives the problem a higher level of precision, but nothing more. And the reason for this failure is like Habermas's: however delicate, a formal conception of ethical life, even if it does accurately reconstruct the recognitive achievements of modernity, must nonetheless *purify* those achievements, denying both that those forms are implicated in the reproduction of the domination they oppose—as if Marx in *On The Jewish Question* had not emphatically demonstrated that the *duality* between state and civil society, between the ideal and its material base, that continues unmodified to this day, itself perverts the republican end into becoming an instrument serving what should only be the economic means for societal reproduction—and that, in order to comprehend this constant cooptation or perversion, we must assume that what is at issue are historical formations of reason itself. As Adorno repeatedly urged, "The concept of progress is dialectical in a strictly unmetaphorical sense, in that its organon, reason, is one; a nature-dominating level and a reconciling level do not exist separate and disjunct within reason, rather both share all its determinations."²⁸ This duality within reason is found within recognitive reason as much as elsewhere; as Gerhard Schweppenhäuser pointedly states, the historical index that binds the fundamental concepts of morality to their own reverse sides holds even for recognition: "Respect for the other and recognition of the other are never quite separable from the guidelines of behaving through which we learn them: through obedience and fear."²⁹ Or, again, rights are also forms of misrecognition and injury, since they presuppose mutual indifference, formalize that indifference, and abstract from particularity. In modernity, recognition is, also, misrecognition; Honneth's purification of recognition reiterates without shifting the wild hopefulness implied by Habermas's wish to cleanly separate instrumental from communicative rationality.³⁰

Detecting the dirty, repressed history behind and embedded in normative ideality is the materialist procedure Adorno learned from Nietzsche and Marx: behind the equal exchange of commodities is hidden "little less than everything: not only the nature and qualities of the objects involved (their 'use value' as Marx puts it) but also the entire personal and social history which has led up to the exchange, including, crucially, the question of how each partner comes by what is exchanged."³¹ In tracing the miserable history that begins with the violence of primitive accumulation, and proceeds through the exposition of how workers bargain away their labor power in their "free" contracting of their labor power for a specified amount of time, Marx is revealing the objective injustice beneath the surface of just exchange. The priority of injustice over justice in Adorno follows Marx's example, and hence is an elaboration of his commitment to an aporetic materialism that is neither an unswerving method nor a metaphysical doctrine. Dialectics, as Adorno terms his materialism, is the practice of interpreting the contradictions sedimented in the practices and concepts of modern society.

The premise of Adorno's critical theory is that there is not a rose in the cross of the present, neither in Hegel's reflective sense nor in Marx's dynamic sense. Let's say that the priority of injustice over justice is the political face of the priority of object over subject, particular over universal, nonidentity over identity that structures Adorno's thought as a whole: "The more identity is posited by imperious spirit, the more injustice is done to the nonidentical. The injustice is passed on through the resistance of the nonidentical. The resistance in turn reinforces the oppressing principle, while at the same time what is oppressed, poisoned, limps along further."³² Injustice is not the pretheoretical experience of the suffering of self-conscious agents, although such suffering can evince that injustice has occurred, but injury done to the particular through its being misidentified, misrecognized. Moral injury is objective; it can break out in explicit social suffering, or, historically just as surely, via the same social mechanisms that create it, be silenced. Nonetheless, for Adorno the fundamental mechanism of misrecognition is idealizing identification, the recognizing of an object or person as being nothing more than what is stored in the concept through which it is recognized: say, agents freely contracting their labor time. It is by recognizing wage laborers as free and equal that one secures their domination; just as it is by recognizing the table as worth a hundred dollars secures its fetish character. Injustice thus must exceed ideal, established justice because justice's mechanisms of recognition until now simultaneously systematically misrecognize.[33]

If injustice minimally involves the exposition of the misrecognition in each recognition, then Adorno's thesis that "dialectics is the [consistent] consciousness of nonidentity" could just as easily be stated as "dialectics is the consistent sense of injustice." Behind this sense of injustice is a transformation originating in Schiller, namely, the idea "that domination and servitude are, in the first place, part of an ontological distribution (the activity of thought versus the passivity of sensible matter)."[34] Adorno's completion of this thought bears out this hypothesis, since for him the operation of identity thinking is, precisely, conceptual abstraction from material embeddedness: the abstraction of use value from exchange value, the abstraction of labor power from labor time, the abstraction of the corporeal, vulnerable person from the autonomous agent. These abstractions are the source of social suffering, and by their nature objective. It is this that lies behind Adorno's insistence that suffering is objective, that it is an objectivity that weighs upon the subject, and that hence the "need to lend a voice to suffering is the condition of all truth."[35]

It is the soldering together of social suffering with the social pathologies of reason that constitutes Adorno's form of social criticism. Criticism, in the form of negative dialectics, *is* the expression of suffering. Hence, when Adorno argues that Hitler has imposed upon unfree mankind a new categorical imperative, namely, to arrange their thoughts and actions so that Auschwitz will not repeat itself, so that nothing similar will happen, he is not assuming that the truth of this is unmediated or immediate, despite his insistence that to deal with this imperative discursively would be wrong because its authority "gives us a bodily sensation of the moral addendum, bodily, because it is now the practical abhorrence of the unbearable physical agony to which individuals are exposed even with their individuality about to vanish as a form of mental reflection."³⁶ After all, it is the *imperative* that he is discussing, and not the sheer fact of what happened in the camps; and the imperative explicitly connects the diagnosis of Auschwitz as an overdetermined and complex realization of processes of societal rationalization with the unbearable physical agony of the sufferers. So the point of the new imperative is that it means to explicitly move in two opposing directions: revealing the cognitive/rational content implicit in social suffering, and, simultaneously, the affective, somatic content of a moral imperative.³⁷

Of course, Adorno intended that the new categorical imperative should exemplify the primacy of injustice over justice, and hence, since that priority, in binding the authority of universality to particularity, itself involves a transformation in the meaning of reason, then the new imperative simultaneously becomes exemplary for the meaning of the authority of moral norms as such—exemplary of the unavoidability of exemplarity in making moral claims. An important recent essay will help us elaborate this thesis.

In "On the Social Construction of Moral Universals: The 'Holocaust' from War Crime to Trauma Drama,"³⁸ Jeffrey Alexander begins tracing the historical development of the reception of the Holocaust, especially in the United States, from an event about which no one seemed eager to speak, retell, analyze, an event viewed as premised on anti-Semitism and located narrowly within German history, an event routinely labeled simply "atrocities" committed by evil Nazis at the conclusion of the War to, fifty years later, through numerous mediations, becoming the exemplary tragic drama that "challenged the ethical self-identification, the self-esteem, of modernity."³⁹ This transformation follows neither the Enlightenment story, where moral individuals perceive the events for what they are and denounce them in accordance with the belief systems supporting them accordingly, nor the standard psychoanalytic version in which trauma is followed directly by silence and bewilderment, which only after two or three decades eases sufficiently for individuals to begin to talk and allow knowledge of the event to develop. On the contrary, the mediations that transformed the Holocaust from wartime atrocity to moral universal are sociohistorically and cognitively complex. Alexander carefully tracks the steps through which World War II was originally viewed as part of an unfolding story of progress until, by viewing the Holocaust as exemplary trauma drama, the story of progress itself becomes difficult, problematic, nuanced, and we have come to understand precisely the dire proximity between progress and barbarism. So he reminds us of, for example: the impact of Anne Frank's diary; the Eichmann trial itself, and the furor surrounding Hannah Arendt's making of Eichmann not a monster but an ordinary man (her critical effort to deflate evil, to rob it of depth and romantic fervor); America's own descent into barbarity in Vietnam; the consequent drawing of analogical linkages between the Allies (the fire bombing of Dresden; the bombings of Tokyo and Hiroshima) and the Perpetrators, until, via a series of symbolic efforts, both intellectual (the massive growth of research into the Holocaust) and practical (the generation of dozens of museums, memorials, and related efforts of memory), the Holocaust has come to define inhumanity in our time. Once this has occurred, then it can enter into efforts of practical reasoning, both in a wide sense (the setting up of the European Union) and a narrow sense (part of the argument for intervening in Bosnia, and the new international obligations for intervening in cases of "genocide," where the very category of genocide is itself the result of the moral work done around the Holocaust).

As the title of his essay indicates, what Alexander is centrally interested in is how *effective* moral universalism rests upon social processes that construct and channel cultural trauma. It might be complained that this process contains a fundamental dilemma:

> Yet, it was this very status—as a unique event—that eventually compelled it to become generalized and departicularized. For as a metaphor for radical evil, the Holocaust provided a standard of evaluation for judging the evility of other threatening acts. By providing such a standard for comparative judgment, the Holocaust became a norm, initiating a succession of metonymic, analogic, and legal evaluations that deprived it of "uniqueness" by establishing its degrees of likeness and unlikeness to other possible manifestations of evility.[40]

Alexander's riposte seems to me exactly right: the complaint that there is a dilution, that the uniqueness of the Holocaust is being covered over, polluted, fundamentally misunderstands what it is for an event to be exemplary, namely, that the event in question become a "powerful bridging metaphor to make sense of social life."[41] This is not to deny that routinization and forgetting can overcome effective analogical and metonymic generalization; only that we must distinguish between those two eventualities in order that the appropriate kind of memorialization occurs.

Alexander's wider thesis, namely, that moral universals are generalizations from traumatic events, is intriguing. Yet, it is difficult to imagine how this thesis might altogether displace the moral learning processes embedded in the development of the three great monotheistic religions, the transmission of their contents into secular modernity, and the consequent work of moral education carried out by the Enlightenment. This is to acknowledge that there have been alternative paths to collective moral learning. (And these paths overlap. Remember: the trauma of the French Revolution also belongs to the Enlightenment story, while the traumatic experience of slavery and its abolition now belongs to the very constitution of the ideas of liberty and equality in the United States.) Adorno's account of the dialectic of Enlightenment concedes the existence of the traditional path of moral learning but contests the purity of its content and the depth of its authority. What then is significant in the account of the emergence of the Holocaust as a moral universal is, precisely, that it displaces normative justice by exemplary injustice, a progressive narration of modernity with a tragic meta-narrative, and a displacement of the Enlightenment paradigm of the rational, autonomous subject with a universalism premised upon fragility and vulnerability. These displacements are not accidental but go to the very center of the processes that conditioned the Holocaust in the first instance. As Hannah Arendt argues persuasively in *The Origins of Totalitarianism*, the civic republican ideal that was the moral cornerstone of the nation-state always depended on the Janus-faced aid of nationalism in order to provide the social solidarity necessary for political agency.[42] Nationalism's restrictive aspect, making only those who shared a racialized national identity true members of the state, was instrumental in the exclusion of the Jewish people from the protections of the state, and finally, their exclusion from humanity.

In the metonymic chain that finally emerges from the Holocaust—the linking of it to the Gulag, Nanking, Hiroshima, Nagasaki, the killing fields—there is forged a universalism and cosmopolitan sentiment that begins with those who are abused and excluded, those who have lost everything, those who have nothing but their naked humanity, their capacity to suffer. Our post-Holocaust solidarity, what there is of it, turns not on an ideal to be realized, but on the universal recognition of a limit that must not be crossed. Helmut Dubiel summarizes the result: "The idea of the obligation to solidarity with all those who had a human face was formulated in the eighteenth century. It was only after the genocide of the twentieth century however that the idea was validated through living experience."[43]

There are terrible losses involved in a shift from a progressive politics of self-realization to a negative politics of avoiding the worst. Saying something substantive about that will have to await another occasion. My claim here is only that, in effect, Adorno's negativist Critical Theory has been empirically the model that has become the most politically efficacious version of the negative politics of avoiding the worst in the past fifteen years, albeit almost always detached from the particularities of his name and his thought. And hence, the academic renewal of his thought can best be seen as a component of a wider process through which a tragic understanding of modernity is beginning to take effect, however gingerly, however sporadically, however muted. What allows that tragic paradigm to develop are precisely acknowledgments of the orienting theses of Adorno's thought: that moral universality has failed us, and failed us in tandem with the recognition of the way in which, generally, universality squanders particularity; that this pathology of reason requires a renewed attention to suppressed particulars; that suppressed particulars emerge into vision as cases of injustice; that social suffering is a manifestation of this injustice, and hence objective in itself; and hence to orient ethical and political action in relation to this sense of social suffering and injustice is to acknowledge a universality of the living premised upon our mutual dependency on one another as vulnerable creatures. What Adorno offers are the microfoundations for this new negative politics and a model of the form of social criticism through which it can best be promoted. Whatever the case in the academy, in social reality Adorno's Critical Theory has already become its future.

CHAPTER 4

Idiosyncrasies: Of Anti-Semitism
Jan Plug

I

The often brutal condemnation of contemporary society in Horkheimer and Adorno's *Dialectic of Enlightenment* is founded at least in part on their understanding of the devastating consequences of domination, including, but not limited to, that described by the determination of the subject by the economic. Thus, while an interrogation of the status of the subject by the various approaches that have (unhappily) been grouped together under the title of "post-structuralism" is frequently accused of denying any stable ground upon which to make ethicopolitical decisions, and while a strain of contemporary theory increasingly speaks for the "social construction" of the subject (in terms of race, class, and gender, for instance, but not only these), the promise of social theory for Horkheimer and Adorno would seem, paradoxically, to invoke a certain understanding of the individual.[1] For "today the operation of the economic apparatus demands that the masses be directed without any intervention from individuation,"[2] and "[a]ccordance with reality and adaptation to power are no longer the results of a dialectical process between the subject and reality, but are produced directly by the cogwheel mechanism of industry."[3] With even thought taken up in the division of labor and made to work in and for it, "the whole man has become the subject-object of repression."[4]

It would appear from these statements that any possibility of liberation from repression would entail jamming up the cogwheel mechanism of industry. It is a question, then, of the specific historical situation and engagements of *Dialectic of Enlightenment*, of domination as the threat of fascism and capitalism alike. The thrust of Horkheimer and Adorno's response, which is to say the promise their thought holds for an emancipation both in and of that history, necessarily marks the meeting place of conceptuality and politics. But this means that it cannot be a case of an historical determination of philosophical thought or of consciousness more generally, any more than, in a more idealist mode, conceptuality can be said to determine reality. To be sure, the confrontation is fully dialectical. But this is a dialectics that exposes and names itself as such. When it does so, when, in its dialectic of conceptuality and politics, *Dialectic of Enlightenment* thinks itself as dialectic, it exposes its own conceptual mechanisms *as* politics—its movement in and engagement with history.

According to Horkheimer and Adorno's formulations, a relation to history seems to offer the possibility of interrupting the economic, social, and political process of domination to the extent that it allows to emerge an individual capable of being just that, an individual. But would such an individual have to issue from individuality, from a position outside this very totalizing determination of "the whole man"? If so, then this central thesis of *Dialectic of Enlightenment* is caught in the very cogwheel it describes. For if the individual is already fully dominated, then anything he[5] could produce, including a thought that would allow him or others to emerge as individuals, is already inevitably a product and perpetuation of the socioeconomic apparatus. And this means that the thought of individuality, Horkheimer and Adorno's own thought, would itself be in the service of that same totalizing system. If, however, an outside to this system remains a possibility, then the individual is not the determination of economic forces, and the argument for individuation loses much of its force—for the individual has his place as an individual. In this case, Horkheimer and Adorno's call for individuation, in contrast to the cogwheel they describe, serves as evidence for the possibility—and in fact the existence—of an outside to the system of repression.[6] According to the dialectical logic of this scenario, the possibility of an outside to repression is at once a confirmation of the totalizing force of domination (which allows for the outside in order to recuperate it, in effect denying its exteriority) and its negation (the outside is truly outside and remains irrecuperable). Within the historical situation of fascist and capitalist modernism, the economic and cultural forces need not *appear* as totalizing as this logic might suggest. Individuals need not be fully adapted to the economic, but merely enough for the economic to overcome their resistance as individuals. Similarly, not all individuals need be assimilated for the mechanism to function. In each case the totalizing force of modernism is reconfirmed by the part it need never fully eradicate or assimilate.

Adorno takes up the possibility of individuality in a brief section of *Minima Moralia* entitled *Plurale Tantum*. There, he claims that the most faithful model of the social "racket" can be found in "the precise opposite of the collective, namely the individual as monad."[7] Thus, criticism of such a "false society" ought to "consider the organization of divergent drives under the primacy of an ego answering the reality principle as, from the first, an internalized robber band with leader, followers, ceremonies, oaths of allegiance, betrayals, conflicts of interests, intrigues and all its other appurtenances."[8] Social theory, as Adorno thinks it, is thus implicated in the monadic particular because that particular is already social. Whatever resonances such a position might have with current popular (and no less problematic) notions of what is often termed the "social construction of consciousness," Adorno rather relocates the social itself.

> One need only observe outbursts in which the individual asserts himself energetically against his environment, for instance rage. The enraged man always appears as the gang-leader of his own self, giving his unconscious the order to pull no punches, his eyes shining with the satisfaction of speaking for the many that he himself is. The more someone has espoused the cause of his own aggression, the more perfectly he represents the repressive principle of society. In this sense more than any other, perhaps, the proposition is true that the most individual is the most general.[9]

The enraged man is not merely a representative or product of a false society; he *is* false society precisely to the extent that he constitutes himself *as* society. In the most mundane sense, this describes the type of projective attitudes and behavior that can never conceive of anything other than in its relation to one's self.

What is here called repressive society is thus the repetition of the false positing of the self as society. False society is characterized by a so-called individuality that can be the object of social theory precisely because it fails to adhere to itself in all its particularity. If society is to be something other than false (and no matter how utopian the suggestion, the epithet itself implies another, non-false social order), then it will be grounded in the individual—though not because he practices some kind of social benevolence, humanism, or community imperative as conventionally conceived, but because of his self-limitation as an individual. And if the social criticism Adorno practices in this passage, even by refusing social criticism in its conventional manifestations, is to be realized, it will expose the racket of society. But here this means marking the finitude of the individual. It would also mean marking the limits of the individual's self-knowledge and of his attempt to know that he is either determined or not by the cogwheel of industry, for example. One can read this in terms of the resources offered by Kant's philosophy: rather than engaging in transcendental speculation and "wandering among entities we cannot know," as Jameson has put it, what the individual would have to know is the very limit of himself and of his (self-)knowledge.[10] He would have to know where the limits of his knowledge lie, including whether or not he has been determined as part of the cogwheel mechanism of industry. Kantian transcendental speculation becomes the speculation of the subject, speculation *tout court*. The subject can only ever *think* the beyond of this limit, in this case, the socioeconomic forces that might determine it, and in so doing thinks itself.[11] This might not seem to offer any real promise for escaping repression, but the force of limitation in fact offers precisely the possibility of interrupting the (self-)totalization in which repression takes place. If the individual offers some possibility within the cogwheel, then, it is in the first instance not in disrupting the mechanism per se but in marking himself as individual.

II

That in *Dialectic of Enlightenment*, the anti-Semitism chapter in particular, the characterizations of the effects of domination on the individual are similarly accompanied by a corresponding affirmation of the necessity of a thoroughly rethought subject perhaps alone capable of interrupting that system follows necessarily from its psychosocial analysis of fascism and capitalism. The analytic strategy mediates the dialectic between individuals and historical, political, and economic forces. Accordingly, the interpretation of anti-Semitism as a political phenomenon, for instance, as coinciding with the emergence of the nation state, in effect sublates that dialectic under the aegis of politics.[12] Readings focusing on the treatment of anti-Semitism in *Dialectic of Enlightenment* similarly tend toward sociohistorical determinations. For instance, Jameson's characterization of the Nazi anti-Semite and its counterpart, "the seemingly more benign figure of the philistine of the Culture Industry," as the "negative embodiments of the deeper *ressentiment* generated by class society itself," offers a superstructural analysis of the effects of industrialization and modernization that stands as a particularly acute instance of the tenor of much criticism of Horkheimer and Adorno's thought.[13] *Dialectic of Enlightenment* situates itself in such a history, of course. But it does so in a genealogy in which the twin poles of its psychosocial analyses are traced to the development of figuration—both language and mimesis as a particular mode of adaptation to nature. *Dialectic of Enlightenment*, then, articulates the history of figuration in which domination takes place, tracing the politico-economic forces of fascism and capitalism to a mode of representation that is the condition for their emergence as historical possibilities in the first place.

The case of anti-Semitism is exemplary in this history and in the dialectic of individuals and social and cultural forces. As Horkheimer and Adorno explain, anti-Semitism condemns individuals as Jews, in effect denying them their individuality, and yet condemns Jews because of their individuality or particularity. The potential for freedom from anti-Semitism thus lies in a strategic deployment of the position of this particularity.

> The old answer of all the anti-Semites is an appeal to idiosyncrasy. The emancipation of society from anti-Semitism depends on whether the content of the idiosyncrasy is elevated into a concept and becomes aware of its own futility. But idiosyncrasy inheres in the particular. The general, that which fits into the functional context of society, is considered to be natural. But nature which has not been transformed into something purposeful, the grating sound of a stylus moving over a slate, the *haut goût* which recalls filth and decomposition, the sweat which appears on the brow of the busy man—everything which has failed to keep up, or which infringes the commandments which are the sedimented progress of the centuries—has a penetrating effect; it arouses disgust.[14]

Passing off functional society as natural, anti-Semitism posits a generality whose claim to that title will be belied by any particular that has not been similarly naturalized (that is, denaturalized). In the impossibility of its ever finding a place within that order, the idiosyncratic exposes this attempted naturalization of a social and political construct. In the most obvious sense of this formulation, the Jews—though not only they[15]—constitute a particularity that can never be accommodated or assimilated by the social forces of power and domination.

Thus, while Horkheimer and Adorno clearly state that the promise of freedom lies in the self-consciousness of the concept, here of idiosyncrasy, their argument suggests that such a gesture is caught in a double bind and that what is equally at stake is a radicalization of the particular to the point of resisting conceptuality.[16] The general is here constructed not through the subsumption of *a* particular or particular*s* under its rule, but through the exclusion of particularity itself, such that a generality, even generality itself, is constituted by its inability to accommodate particularity as such. Idiosyncrasy would seem to signify the particularity of the particular, what makes it fully itself, what, in other words, constitutes the individuality or identity of a subject.[17] But this same subject is already constituted as the *difference from* an other, this constitution of the seeming immanence of the self through a relation to the other describing the ontology of the subject as community.[18] Further, the conceptualization of idiosyncrasy demands that it forfeit its idiosyncrasy, such that the concept of the idiosyncratic will always belie the very particularity it is meant to think. The concept of the idiosyncratic will necessarily think the idiosyncratic as idiosyncratic even to its own conceptualization and thus necessarily as radical singularity, always irrecuperable, outside the very concept of idiosyncrasy. In *Negative Dialectics*, Adorno will write,

> Though doubtful as ever, a confidence that philosophy can make it after all—that the concept can transcend the concept, the preparatory and concluding element, and can thus reach the nonconceptual—is one of philosophy's inalienable features and part of the naïveté that ails it. Otherwise it must capitulate, and the human mind with it. We could not conceive the simplest operation; there would be no truth; emphatically, everything would be just nothing. But whatever truth the concepts cover beyond their abstract range can have no other stage than what the concepts suppress, disparage, and discard. The utopia of cognition [*Utopie des Erkenntnis*] would be to use concepts to unseal the non-conceptual with concepts, without making it their equal.[19]

Adorno identifies the problem that he and Horkheimer face as striving to transcend the concept by way of the concept.[20] In the context of the radical particularity of the Jews, the unsealing of the nonconceptual is worked out as the necessary interruption of any attempt to formulate a general rule, the interruption, then, of anything like reflective judgment in the Kantian sense.²¹ The concept of idiosyncrasy becomes aware of its own futility, as Horkheimer and Adorno put it, to the extent that it becomes aware of its own impossibility *as concept*.²²

At this point, a more overtly historical reading of *Dialectic of Enlightenment* might attempt to point out the limits of the treatment of anti-Semitism in Horkheimer and Adorno by formulating its own dialectical relation to their thought, showing, for instance, that the particularity that the Jews represent for them, and that should lead to emancipation, can and has been mobilized for far different ends.²³ As valid and illuminating as such a reading would prove, however, it remains caught up in the rhetoric and logic of enlightenment, its dialectical trajectory clearly moving toward a higher—if not absolute—knowledge through the partial historical negation or falsification of Horkheimer and Adorno's thought. In fact, their articulation of the self-consciousness of the concept goes a long way toward warding off this danger. For far from having its liberating effects negated, exposing the impossibility of the concept of idiosyncrasy raises it to the consciousness of its own futility. In other words, the liberatory promise offered by the idiosyncratic is double. On the one hand, its concept will show it to subvert its use in rationalized form by fascism. But, on the other hand, the "content" of idiosyncrasy raised to the level of concept becomes aware of its own futility insofar as it describes the very particularity that can never be assimilated to a concept. The concept of idiosyncrasy thus emerges as the concept of its own impossibility. And yet this impossibility remains an absolute necessity for any possibility of liberating society from anti-Semitism and also for Horkheimer and Adorno's text not to close itself off as a totalizing construct. The concept points to its impossibility and by extension the impossibility of Horkheimer and Adorno's enterprise read as the conceptualization of particularity. It marks the limits, the "Limits of Enlightenment," no doubt, as the subtitle to the anti-Semitism chapter reads, but equally the limits of conceptuality. Thus, it posits an irrecuperable outside, in fact, the idiosyncratic *as* that very outside. The idiosyncratic, then, *demands* its conceptualization (destined to "failure" as it is) in order to posit *itself* as such, as idiosyncratic to that very theorizing.²⁴

Nor is it simply that anti-Semitism's derivation of a *false* generality is brought to light, that a truer, more adequate general term, one that is not naturalizing or anti-Semitic, could be derived. In fact, once ridding the world of anti-Semitism is conceived in terms of a mode of conceptuality, raising the concept to self-consciousness, Horkheimer and Adorno cannot expose the futility of the concept of idiosyncrasy for anti-Semitism without at the same time exposing its futility for conceptuality, their own included. This is not to suggest that Horkheimer and Adorno's analysis is ineffectual or nullified by its operative concept. Rather, it points to a structural necessity of philosophical discourse, according to which the promise of thinking, which is also the promise of freedom, must always also mark the limits of thinking, its futility. The ethicopolitical efficacy of thinking will always at the same time describe the "futility" of thinking and its being made inoperative and radically nonfunctional. It is precisely this structure of self-limitation and self-questioning that withdraws thinking from any possibility of becoming totalizing or losing itself in the self-assurance of its (political) interventions.

Rather than being ahistorical, to disclose the conceptual limits of *Dialectic of Enlightenment* is to point to the historical moment of the text, the point at which conceptuality—and thus a conventional philosophical reading as well—must relinquish its claims upon irreducibly historical particularity. This, then, is to describe the necessity of a thinking that would not fall prey to the most threatening tendencies of enlightenment, for which "[n]othing at all must remain outside, because the mere idea of outsideness is the very source of fear."[25] It can hardly be an accident, therefore, that the formulation of the necessity of a thinking of non-identity here develops out of the articulation of a theory of language that ultimately has everything to do with both philosophical discourse and idiosyncrasy. Not unlike idiosyncrasy, the genealogy of language traces it back to "primitive" experience: "What the primitive experiences . . . is not a spiritual as opposed to a material substance, but the intricacy of the Natural in contrast to the individual. The gasp of surprise which accompanies the experience of the unusual becomes its name. It fixes the transcendence of the unknown in relation to the known, and therefore terror as sacredness."[26] The name will always be the name of the sacred, and language opens the space of a terror that ultimately will extend beyond it.[27]

> When the tree is no longer approached merely as tree, but as evidence for an Other, as the location of *mana*, language expresses the contradiction that something is itself and at one and the same time something other than itself, identical and not identical. Through the deity, language is transformed from tautology to language. The concept, which some would see as the sign-unit for whatever is comprised under it, has from the beginning been instead the product of dialectical thinking in which everything is always that which it is, only because it becomes that which it is not. That was the original form of objectifying definition, in which concept and thing are separated.[28]

To this understanding of the identity and non-identity of language is appended a footnote to Hubert and Mauss's interpretation of "'sympathy' or *mimesis*": "*L'un est le tout, tout est dans l'un, la nature triomphe de la nature*" [the one is the all, all is in the one, nature triumphs over nature].[29] Radicalizing resemblance into a logic of the symbol familiar to both Romanticism and Idealist aesthetics,[30] Horkheimer and Adorno gloss mimesis as a figurative relation that represents the possibility of the part being taken up without remainder in the whole or expressing the whole in itself. Yet what mimesis will come to mean in the chapter on anti-Semitism is precisely the idiosyncratic resistance to totalization. And even in this passage a similar relation is established between the German text and the note and its French citation, thus between the "native" and the "foreign," text and its margins, inside and outside. Horkheimer and Adorno's text never performs the relation it describes, since the mimetic figure for the possibility of totality remains as a kind of leftover expressed in a figurative system that refuses that totality. Mimesis is defined at once as a symbolic totality that expresses nature's self-transcendence and the impossibility of this figuration. Both in the movement between its two formulations—here in the Introduction and later in the discussion of anti-Semitism—and within the attempt to define it as such, mimesis figures the resistance to *its own* formalization as figure of totalization and interrupts its own figuration of the political.

Accordingly, the characterization of language that this note is meant to illuminate speaks to an understanding of nature, language, and the relation of part to whole that will be characterized by a figurative mode that, seemingly closing language off in its self-relation, in fact opens the space for it to emerge precisely as figure.[31] Language here is said to "express" alterity, the relation of identity and non-identity characteristic of nature inhabited or haunted by *mana*, the moving spirit; "language," we are told, "is transformed from tautology to language." How are we to understand the representation of language here? How to understand that language is transformed from tautology to language? How to understand a nontautological model of language expressed in the form of a perfect tautology?

It would seem that for this sentence not to be a mere tautology the word *language* has to change meaning from one instance to the other. Thus, in its first occurrence, *language* is tautology, saying nothing other than itself and only thus, perhaps, establishing a relation to transcendence as such, as the radically other and the outside. With the location of the deity in the tree, *language* takes on a new meaning, the dialectical sense of expressing the simultaneous identity and non-identity of the tree to itself.

Now, then, *language* itself signifies a mode of *expression* in which it says something other than itself, describing a history in which a differentiated language replaces the cries of fear. Yet if the word *language* changes meaning, this would mean that *language* did not mean *language* in the first instance, but rather *tautology*, and that tautology is decidedly *not* language. Language becomes language by putting its tautological past behind it. This conception of the linguistic would overcome the tautology of the phrase "language is the transformed from tautology to language" by constructing itself as a history of language (and of the word *language*) but at the cost of sacrificing one—false—notion of language (as tautology) to another—true—notion (language as nontautological).

If the theory of language implicit here is to assume all its rigor, though, and if the tautological form of this phrase is to be read as something other than a mere slip or instance of the inadequacies of language, then *language* will have to mean nothing less than *language*, every time it occurs. Thus, in the language of this passage, *language* is now identical and not identical, which means not only that it is the "product" of, as Horkheimer and Adorno put it, or *expresses* this dialectical thinking, but that it must itself embody that thinking. Language is simultaneously language and not language. And the only way for that (non)identity of language to be "expressed" is in the form of a tautology in which language performs its own *Aufhebung*, both negating and preserving itself. The transformation describing this becoming-language of language takes place according to the mediation of the deity ("*Through* the deity . . ."). More precisely, the passage from "language . . . to language" marks a transformation in the relation to transcendence. In the first articulation of language as tautology, the transcendent is registered as such, as transcendent, in language's "failure" to say anything other than itself. Language begins to express, to become language, once the transcendence of the deity is transformed, that is, once the deity becomes indwelling and inhabits nature. Language's becoming language and "expression," then, corresponds with the transformation of the deity into something that is no longer, properly speaking, transcendent. What language in this nontautological sense expresses above all is that the deity has been brought down to earth, literally, located in nature. Even as expression, language expresses the loss of transcendence.

Such a conception of language, while it is said here to be the "produce of dialectical thinking," nonetheless necessitates a rethinking of the very terms of the dialectic and of enlightenment.

> But this dialectic remains impotent to the extent that it develops from the cry of terror which is the duplication, the tautology, of terror itself. The

gods cannot take fear away from man, for they bear its petrified sound with them as they bear their names. Man imagines himself free from fear where there is no longer anything unknown. That determines the course of demythologization, of enlightenment, which compounds the animate with the inanimate just as myth compounds the inanimate with the animate. Enlightenment is mythic fear turned radical. The pure immanence of positivism, its ultimate product, is no more than a so to speak universal taboo. Nothing at all may remain outside, because the mere idea of outsideness is the very source of fear.[32]

The dialectic remains impotent as long as it falls prey to a conception of language as duplication or tautology. For dialectical thinking to think otherwise, then, for it not to fall prey to the dual mystifications of enlightenment and myth, it must not merely make room for, accommodate, or express interest in the particular, externality, or the rigorously non-identical—a non-identity that can never be recuperated by identity and that must now be expressed in the un-Hegelian terms of the *non*-identity of identity and non-identity.[33] Even more, the externality of the outside, remaining beyond the limits of dialectical thinking, and inscribing those very limits, will necessarily stand as its condition of possibility, grounding the dialectic upon the very remainder that it can never negate or recuperate for itself.

Thus, it is not that language conforms to the dialectic so much as it is that the conception of language formulated in this phrase stands as the condition of possibility of dialectical thinking and thus as the undisclosed ground for *Dialectic of Enlightenment*. For if language were never transformed from tautology to language, as the most self-evident reading of the language of the phrase would have it, anything like a dialectic of identity and mimesis would be unthinkable. Thus, the very phrase "language is transformed from tautology to language" necessarily discloses a conception of language that, leaving tautology behind, would offer the promise of a relation to the outside of which enlightenment remains incapable. For language becomes language only through the relation to an indwelling deity, and the tautological form of the phrase describes how language achieves its "identity" as language through its relation to something that it is not. And what language is not, this phrase suggests, is tautology, its own tautological past. Language, in other words, becomes language through its relation to tautology. The phrase is no longer "simply" tautological, then, nor does it "simply" express or represent the dialectic of identity. Rather, it enacts language's becoming self through its relation to the pure self-relation of tautology. Language emerges, as signification and the expression of duality, through its relation to its tautological relation to itself, whose form can be reduced to a stylistic device, an oversight, or a mere trifle only at the cost of reducing the historical import of Horkheimer and Adorno's argument. The point, here, is not that there is no historical progression marked in the phrase,[34] that the tautology takes us nowhere, or that history is turned back upon itself in a mode of reversal. Rather, the tautological form of the phrase and the self-relation that it describes are the necessary conditions for the history of language to emerge.

The political engagement of *Dialectic of Enlightenment* can be understood in terms of such a rethinking of language and the relation to externality. For at the same time that they suggest how a notion of a concept dialectically raised to the level of self-consciousness offers the possibility of freedom from anti-Semitism, Horkheimer and Adorno equally posit another language that, if its implications are followed to their logical conclusions, offers a very different approach to ending domination. As they describe it, the emergence of language as a system of signs or as expression signals the possibility, perhaps better, the inevitability, of instrumentalization at the hands of both capitalism and fascism: "When public opinion has reached a state in which thought inevitably becomes a commodity, and language the means of promoting [*Anpreisung*] that commodity, then the attempt to trace [*auf die Spur*] the course of such depravation has to deny any allegiance to current linguistic and conceptual conventions, lest their world-historical consequences thwart it entirely."[35] To be sure, when language is set up as broker, the marketing of commodified thought, a conception of language that would not serve but rather resist any such commodification and the world-historical consequences of the dominant language becomes necessary. What is at stake is nothing less than the language *of* philosophy, what, from Kant to Derrida at least, has been thought as the *popularity* of philosophy.[36] Just as the "dutiful child of modern civilization is possessed by a fear of departing from the facts which . . . dominant conventions of science, commerce, and politics . . . have already molded," so do these "same conventions define the notion of linguistic and conceptual clarity which the art, literature and philosophy of the present have to satisfy."[37]

Horkheimer and Adorno's appeal, then, is to a social and linguistic *deviance*, even an *idiosyncrasy of philosophical language*. Yet such deviance cannot simply depart from the facts if it is to live up to its fundamental responsibility. In fact, the idiosyncrasy, the obscurity, and the stylistic and other difficulties posed by *Dialectic of Enlightenment*, like much of Horkheimer and Adorno's work, will render the conventions and clarity of "the facts." Even by marking itself off from the market conception of language, the language of *Dialectic of Enlightenment* allows those conventions to appear in their difference from its own language. Rather than being brought to light in *Dialectic of Enlightenment* (and thus dialectically recuperating their own language for the conventions they seek to expose), the conventional is exposed in its *relation to* the idiosyncratic, which serves as its defining limit, that point at which conventions institute themselves as such. In this sense, their language not only tracks down, is on the trail [*auf der Spur*] of, language as the marketing of a commodified thought; it follows the traces [*Spuren*] of, it traces, that language, allowing its outline to appear. It is philosophical language's very idiosyncrasy and deviance, its apparent turning of its back upon "the facts" and "conventions," that allow these to emerge in all their facticity and conventionality. Idiosyncratic language must necessarily renounce the promotion or extolling [*Anpreisung*] of the commodification of thought; hence the critical (in the full sense) and even "negative treatment of the facts or of the dominant forms of thought"[38] throughout *Dialectic of Enlightenment*. Yet, perhaps it goes without saying, this very treatment risks being reappropriated by and for the market as just another (negative) mode of promotion. For the deviance of this theory of language to emerge fully and to resist such reappropriation, it would have to be still more idiosyncratic and would have to abandon both promotion and negative treatment. That is, the idiosyncrasy of this language would adhere in its resistance to subsumption to thought or goods in general, such that it could never be made to serve commodification. Language would have to declare its freedom from the intentionality that could always be manipulated into either promotion or bad press.

Taken to its logical limits, the conception of language formulated by Horkheimer and Adorno describes what, in the terms they will elaborate in the anti-Semitism chapter, is a mode of language that would be truly idiosyncratic not only in its particularity but, even more, in its resistance to the subjection, the individual and social education, that characterize the fascist and capitalist subject alike. This mode of language would still be effective to the extent that it resists the processes that characterize the formation of the ego and the history of domination detailed in *Dialectic of Enlightenment*. Not that *Dialectic of Enlightenment* attempts to revert to the "prehistory," both individual and social, that mimesis describes, but that it seeks to deploy an idiosyncratic mode that, prior to the formations that instantiate domination, would resist and interrupt them.[39]

The language of *Dialectic of Enlightenment* can therefore be characterized as a "foreignizing" of philosophical discourse. Adorno's description of a certain language in terms that would, precisely, resist totalization, political and linguistic, by opening it up to an outside should hardly come as a surprise, then. Can it be a mere accident that what emerges as the politicality of language should be articulated in conjunction with "the Jews"?

Anti-Semitism is the rumour about the Jews.

German words of foreign derivation are the Jews of language.[40]

What can this mean? How is one to read the yoking of a racial, ethnic, or religious marker with the linguistic, one that takes place according to a conception of the foreign? Merely *as* yoking, as metaphor? It would seem fairly evident, at any rate, that the phrase articulates how foreign words, precisely because they are perceived as foreign, become linguistic "scapegoats," as Adorno puts it elsewhere,[41] that being the Jews of language puts foreign words in a position of invoking wrath. Yet while such a characterization tells us what foreign words might stand for, it still does little to explain the structure of the phrase or of the workings of the very wrath it characterizes. Simply put, what does it mean to be the Jews *of* language? How is one to read the genitive here?

On the one hand, the phrase denotes the marking of a particular category within the field of language. To be the Jews of language, accordingly, is to be a particular subcategory within language. Thus, German words of foreign derivation, as the Jews of language, are singled out as that part of language that contaminates the purity of language. Even if such purity is not envisaged as a real possibility, it is implicitly posited as the proper, and even original, state of the German language. But, on the other hand, the process of exclusion and purification is perhaps even more radical. To be the Jews of language, in this case, is no longer to be a corrupt and corrupting part of language, but rather that which language itself has designated as infection. Foreign words are no longer even designated as a part of language that must be taken care of, but have already been marked off from language *by* language, which excludes them from itself as nonlanguage, foreign, Jewish. In this sense, language fulfills the sentence pronounced upon foreign words in the first sense above and carries that sentence to its most radical ends. It purifies language of the foreign element, but even more thoroughly, by declaring the foreign nonlinguistic. In effect, this phrase itself constructs an outside, a foreign, and constructs it as *outside language*. Language is purified of the foreign element by positing it as foreign *to* language.

The phrase "Jews of language" therefore designates a process that effectively constructs a nonlinguistic outside to language, still nonetheless consisting of words, no matter how foreign. To be the Jews of language is not only to be impure, a contagion. It is to be outside language, the outside of language, that part of language that is nonetheless outside language and that, while it apparently allows language to close itself off even as the field of language and against the nonlinguistic, simultaneously interrupts that closure, for the nonlinguistic outside, here, is constituted by words, foreign words, but words nonetheless. The particular force of "the Jews of language" is thus to mark a double limit of language: at once the limit between the foreign and the nonforeign within language and the limit between language and what is foreign to it. And since the foreign here is designated by "the Jews," this means marking the boundary between language and race, ethnicity, religion, or culture, in short, a historical configuration. Yet, since they trace that boundary as language's inability to close itself off from a foreign, nonlinguistic outside, the Jews of language mark what might be called the historical or political moment of language, language's necessary and inevitable entry into history in its self-constitution as language. That this site should be designated as the "Jews of language" would suggest that the constitution of language is historical and political (even in marking itself off from, and thus touching upon, history) and functions according to the same processes of exclusion and purification exercised upon the Jews. But by equally suggesting that these same processes and politics of domination are linguistic in the fullest sense, it marks the politicality of language as its resistance to totality, to language's self-constitution as an autonomous entity, and also to the freedom of the political from language. In more concrete terms, the exclusion of the foreign would ultimately rob the "pure" language—and language itself as pure—of its future and destine it to become a dead language, the death of language. Moreover, since the foreign here is not merely another language but the other *of* language, as long as we are in language, and not merely as long as there are words of foreign derivation (without which, by the way, language is unthinkable), there will be Jews. Freedom—from anti-Semitism, for instance—thus necessarily entails deploying the very boundary that refuses to close language and politics off from one another. It entails speaking and writing the foreign, the "Jews of language," a practice Adorno in particular explored continually.

The phrase is relevant to a consideration of anti-Semitism in *Dialectic of Enlightenment* in that it describes the process of exclusion and equally turns this process and that language upon themselves to disclose how a discursive or political "outside" interrupts its own totalizing gesture, even in allowing that field to constitute itself as such. In the terms of the thinking of idiosyncrasy this means that, far from a mere moment in the dialectic, the idiosyncrasy associated with the Jews is what necessarily escapes the dialectic and, thus, makes it possible in the first instance. Idiosyncrasy is that which *Dialectic of Enlightenment* will never be able to raise to the level of a concept, even in raising it to the level of a concept,[42] and that which therefore allows the work to formulate itself as a philosophical discourse—of nontotality and non-identity. Freedom from anti-Semitism therefore cannot reside strictly in the process of a dialectical raising of the concept to self-consciousness, but must rather entail disclosing this very "procedure," the manner in which that derivation is also necessarily impossible. Rather than in the triumph of the concept, the freedom promised by Horkheimer and Adorno's text lies in its disclosure of its impossibility at the moment of its fulfillment.

III

Still, Horkheimer and Adorno's promised freedom is not to emerge from the structure or logic of conceptuality as such, but rather from raising the "content" of the concept of idiosyncrasy to self-consciousness. What is at question in that content is an understanding of the subject, but one that could hardly serve as the ground for a politics of freedom. For while idiosyncrasy as Horkheimer and Adorno understand it involves the history of nothing less than the origin of the subject, no less does it emerge as a particularity so radical and in fact alienating that no subject could ever be derived from it; nor could it function as the basis or ground of subjectivity.

> The motives to which idiosyncrasy appeals recall the ultimate origins. They produce moments of biological prehistory: danger signs which make the hair stand on end and the heart stop beating. In idiosyncrasy, individual organs escape from the control of the subject, and independently obey fundamental biological stimuli. The ego which experiences such reactions— for instance, cutaneous or muscular torpor, or stiffness of joints—is not wholly in control of itself. For a few moments these reactions effect an adaptation to circumambient, motionless nature. But as the animate approaches the inanimate and the more highly developed form of life comes closer to nature, it is alienated from it, since inanimate nature, which life in its most vigorous form aspires to become, is capable only of wholly external, spatial, relationships. Space is absolute alienation. When men try

to become like nature they harden themselves against it. Protection as fear is a form of mimicry. The reflexes of stiffening and numbness in humans are archaic schemata of the urge to survive: by adaptation to death, life pays the toll of its continued existence.[43]

The "biological pre-history" described by mimesis is in fact the condition for history as Horkheimer and Adorno understand and write it.[44] "Civilization" as they conceive it replaces "organic adaptation to others and mimetic behavior proper, by organized control of mimesis, in the magical phase; and, finally, by rational practice, by work, in the historical phase."[45] Civilization and history, as well as the history of the subject, thus arise in the wake of mimesis and attempt to submit it to conscious, functional, programmed control: "Uncontrolled mimesis is outlawed."[46] Civilization and history attempt to submit to consciousness a mimeticism defined precisely as the resistance to all submission to consciousness.

Not only does idiosyncrasy signal an alienation from nature through the approach to nature in mimetic stiffening and numbness, then, but this mimesis, fear as a "form of mimicry," entails the alienation of the subject from itself. As such, the biological mimeticism that takes the name of a radical individuality precedes and anticipates, perhaps even lays the ground for, the social denial of nothing less than that same individuality as it is enacted upon "woman," for instance. "Man as ruler denies woman the honor of individualization. Socially, the individual is an example of the species, a representative of her sex; and therefore male logic sees her wholly as standing for nature, as the substrate of never-ending subsumption notionally, and never-ending subjection in reality. Woman as an alleged natural being is a product of history which denaturizes her."[47] Yet if man denies woman individualization, reducing her to an example of a "species," idiosyncrasy represents a denial perhaps still more radical. The mimesis of the idiosyncratic stiffening of the body in fear is the literal and physical approximation to nature that puts the grounds of individuation itself into question.

> The ego has been formed in resistance to this mimicry. In the constitution of the ego reflective mimesis becomes controlled reflection. "Recognition in the concept," the absorption of the different by the same, takes the place of physical adaptation to nature. But the situation in which equality is established, the direct equality of mimesis and the mediated equality of synthesis, the adaptation to the condition of the object in the blind course of life, and the comparison of the objectified thing in scientific concept formation, is still the state of terror.[48]

Even more than denying it, the mimicry of idiosyncrasy stands in a relation of opposition, and even resistance, to anything like individuation or subject formation. As Horkheimer and Adorno explain it, the adaptation to nature in fact precedes any notional subsumption—of "woman" for instance—to nature, precedes, then, the gendering of the subject. This might merely confirm what a feminist reading of *Dialectic of Enlightenment* already knows—that Horkheimer and Adorno are trapped in the logic they themselves describe, either perpetuating the denial of individualization even in describing it or else belying their own assertions by projecting an individualized "woman."[49] But this is also to suggest a "content" of idiosyncrasy that, while it describes a state of terror, equally exposes the impossibility of ever overcoming that terror by a subject.

What the purported idiosyncrasy of the Jews entails, then, is a mimetic "practice" that refigures the Jews as *anything but* idiosyncratic. The idiosyncrasy of the idiosyncratic is precisely to differ from itself in adapting to nature. The particularity of the Jews is to eschew any particularity that could be said to belong to them proper. The mimesis described by idiosyncrasy thus functions according to what Philippe Lacoue-Labarthe calls a "law of impropriety, which is the very law of mimesis."[50] Mimesis traces a movement in which idiosyncrasy's particularity and specificity is to efface itself as such in a mimetic mode that marks the alienation of and from the self. The alienation of mimesis is the necessary condition for a specificity so radical that it no longer denotes even the identity of the self, conforming to oneself or to the self in general, but rather an idiosyncratic impulse or reaction that would refuse the constitution of the subject as it has been understood since Descartes. It therefore remains to be shown whether or not the out-of-control "ego" that characterizes idiosyncrasy is still an ego properly speaking. Understood in this way, not only as a simple *resemblance* or *adaptation* but as the mechanism by which these are achieved, idiosyncratic mimesis denotes that moment at which the subject is no longer, or not yet, a subject. It marks, at the very least, the body's escape from intentionality, the body's *freedom* and *independence* from subjectivity.

Mimesis therefore describes a certain resemblance, but in a sense much more profound than that of muscular stiffness, to the inanimateness of nature. For mimesis here designates an *adaptation without intentionality*, the approximation of the "subject" to nature in which the will is no longer lord and master. It is precisely this non-intentionality, rather than a form of physical adaptation, that signals the approach to the status of nature. Not only does the subject emerge in resistance to this biological history and the history that follows from it, but what is more, the anti-Semitic subject is the politicized and aestheticized incarnation of that subject as resistance to idiosyncrasy. This is to say that the anti-Semite does not participate in a different "logic" or "structure" from other subjects, but is the politicized mode of the subject.

Imitating the "mimetic ciphers" of the Jews, anti-Semitism effectively imitates that which can never belong to the Jews properly speaking; it seeks to approximate that moment at which the Jews are precisely *not* themselves but rather the approximation, in a physical, bodily, material mode, to something "outside" themselves.

> In the chaotic yet regulated escape reactions of the lower animals, in the convolutions of the sudden swarm, and the convulsive gestures of the martyred, we see the mimetic impulse which can never be completely destroyed. In the death struggle of the creature, at the opposite pole of freedom, freedom still shines out irresistibly as the thwarted destiny of matter. It is opposed by the idiosyncrasy which claims anti-Semitism as its motive.
>
> The mental energy harnessed by political anti-Semitism is this rationalized idiosyncrasy. All the pretexts over which the Führer and his followers reach agreement imply surrender to the mimetic principle—honorably, so to speak. They cannot stand the Jews, yet imitate them.[51]

Horkheimer and Adorno thus describe a kind of mimeticism without reserve, a mimetic impulse that can never be harnessed or destroyed, even in the attempt to submit it to rational control. Yet, for them, this mimeticism can never negate the ontology of freedom,[52] the freedom of matter that ultimately can never be thwarted in any significant way because it is the freedom of being. The political import of this freedom would be not least to call into question the attempt to subject or dominate through mimesis.

What "the Führer and his followers" in fact imitate in the Jews are gestures ("the argumentative movement of a hand, the musical voice painting a vivid picture of things and feelings") and even physical characteristics (the nose—the physiognomic *principium individuationis*, symbol of the specific character of an individual).[53] Yet in each case, in their very imitations they seek to empty that which they imitate of any real meaning. Thus, their imitation of gestures takes place "irrespective of the real content of what is said"[54] and the nose is reduced to the sense of smell. In other words, the fascists do not try to imitate the Jews as such so much as they imitate them as the aestheticized figures of the mimetic impulse. Their imitation of the very figures of their hatred, like their recourse to "carefully thought out symbols . . . skulls and disguises, the barbaric drum beats, the monotonous words and gestures," indeed constitutes the "mimesis of mimesis."[55]

The implications of this second-level mimeticism—implications Horkheimer and Adorno never elaborate fully—are crucial for an understanding not only of anti-Semitism but their project as well. This mimeticism attempts precisely to *formalize* mimesis. It does not imitate a specific, material body or aesthetic, but the mimetic principle. It does so without, of course, being implicated in the hated object, that is, regardless of what might be proper to it, and turning those very characteristics against it. The formalization of the mimetic mode seeks to deny it of any content, which ultimately might prove impossible, condemning the fascists to taking on the materiality of that which they imitate, in this case not only the Jews but mimesis as well. For if imitation "is not entirely independent of the particular content, or substance, of the entity it chooses to represent," if, in other words, it takes on something of the materiality of whatever is imitated, then by definition it would embody an *aesthetic materiality*. And the promise of such an aesthetic would adhere in its resistance to totalization, for one "can conceive of certain mimetic constants or even structures but, to the extent that they remain dependent on a reality principle that lies outside them, they resist formalization."[56] Mimesis thus participates in a materiality that cannot be submitted fully to the totalizing forces of formalization and would not, for example, be formalizable as is the mathematics of which Horkheimer and Adorno are so critical.[57] Its materiality could never be subsumed by consciousness, for instance, and thus could never be reduced to a concept, whether dialectically derived or not. What is more, their mimeticism effectively ensures that the anti-Semites will, in their imitation of Jews as the figures of imitation, imitate alienation. At the very least, their mimeticism ensures that they will never be characterized by anything other than the force of formalization. Thus, while it would certainly seem to be the case that "Fascism is totalitarian in that it seeks to make the rebellion of suppressed nature against domination directly useful to domination,"[58] it is no less true that fascist anti-Semitism is itself caught up in the totalizing power of formalization, in which both fascists and fascism merely stand in as a figure, imitating, substituting for, another figure, but also always substitutable.

The futility of the concept of idiosyncrasy that is to free us from anti-Semitism therefore goes beyond revealing how anti-Semitism imitates the Jews although it hates them. It discloses the act of mimicry itself as *resistance to subjection*—to the formation of the subject and (thereby) of the body to consciousness, but also, therefore, the resistance to the domination of nature. Controlled mimesis, while it attempts to overcome this idiosyncratic mimetic moment, can only ever repeat it in its attempt to bring it under control. The attempt at extermination in fact reproduces what it is to eradicate, producing an excess that could never be negated, in fact producing itself *as excess*.

Horkheimer and Adorno's assertion that "[a]nti-Semitic behavior is generated in situations where blinded men robbed of their subjectivity are set loose as subjects,"[59] like those theories that decry the dissolution (or "deconstruction," as they are often wont to put it) of the subject as politically dangerous or ineffectual, would therefore still need to come to terms with the dangers *of* subjectivity. This would mean, not least, considering how in the rethinking of the subject the body emerges as radically political. In marked contrast to the imperatives of fascism, which cannot bear an idler or even idle nature but must transform them into functional parts in a productive social whole, the body here refuses to do the mind's bidding. Refusing submission, refusing to *work* for the mind or like it, the body resists the movement by which the subject could constitute itself as an autonomous and totalizing entity. It leaves open the space, the very space of a radical mind/body split, that refigures the political space as other than the site of labor or "political" action as it is customarily conceived. This is the space *of* the political, the opening without which political action in this narrower sense could never be thought, the space of the political as the resistance to the logic that allows for the subsumption of body to mind, for subsumption *tout court*.

IV

Horkheimer and Adorno's text remains thoroughly committed to the subject, however, committed to it because it is at risk in contemporary society. But it becomes clear, as the anti-Semitism chapter shifts from the consideration of idiosyncrasy to that of its counterpart, projection, that it is a conception of the subject in terms of reflection that offers the possibility of freedom from anti-Semitism.[60] The danger of anti-Semitism is not simply that of the projection of itself upon the world. It is not "projective behavior as such" that is at issue but "the absence from it of reflection."[61] Necessarily a part of perception, projection for Horkheimer and Adorno characterizes both any possibility of cognition and the formation of the subject.[62] What takes place in perception is the bridging of a gulf between the "true object and the undisputed data of the senses, between within and without."[63] The "subject" in fact "creates the world outside himself from the traces which it leaves in his senses"[64] but is himself equally a creation, since he "constitutes the 'I' retrospectively by learning to grant a synthetic unity not only to the external impressions, but to the internal impressions which separate off from them."[65]

This "subject" that constitutes the "I" retrospectively cannot be named such, properly speaking, insofar as it is this retrospective constitution that allows it to emerge *as subject*. The subject can emerge only as the history of this process, as a retrospective constitution of itself in a past in which it had not yet been constituted. The subject, that is, is what constitutes itself as never yet having been constituted. It can only think itself as the dialectical history formed between the retrospective past and a present in which it exists as subject only by giving itself a past upon which it projects a unity not experienced as such at the time. If the subject must bridge the gap between inside and outside "at its own risk,"[66] then, this is not merely because it risks being lost both in performing that crossing and in *not* performing it. The risk, perhaps even more profoundly, lies in the very "structure" of bridging, a going between poles that discloses the subject as neither here nor there, neither past nor present, but always a between, the movement that refuses to locate it even in itself.

Insisting upon the necessity of reflection for projection not to fall into the kind of abuse of which fascist anti-Semitism is the prime example, Horkheimer and Adorno rely upon a subject who once again must delimit himself and "return to the object what he has received from it."[67] The "false projection"[68] or the "morbid aspect"[69] of anti-Semitic projective behavior resides in this failure, such that the anti-Semite "ceases to reflect upon himself, and loses the ability to differentiate"[70] and thus peoples the world with himself, which is to say, fills it with the void that is the "content" of this "subject."[71] At this point in *Dialectic of Enlightenment* at least, it is still the subject who offers the promise of freedom from anti-Semitism, but in a larger sense freedom as such. And it does so by offering the ultimate promise, in *Dialectic of Enlightenment*, that of a *reconciliation* that, rather than achieving some unity, maintains the "considered opposition" of perception and the object.[72] But the subject here clearly means for Horkheimer and Adorno the constitution of the self in an act of self-delimitation that is at the same time the delimitation of the difference of the "outside" and thus of others, the other.

Yet, perhaps more accurately, locating the promise of freedom from anti-Semitism in the subject as it is conceived here means locating it in the history, even the fiction, of a relation to the past in which one endows oneself with a unity not experienced at the time. A present and, by extension, a future condition of freedom from domination and anti-Semitism thus lies in the continuity of the self created between past and present by projecting that same unity not only on the past but also upon the gap between that past as experienced and as viewed retrospectively. At the same time that Horkheimer and Adorno's understanding of the subject offers the promise of freedom, political and other, it equally opens this gap, the uncloseable gap between experience and retrospect. One might argue that this is the gap that "reflection" would never permit, or at least never permit to be exploited, since the self-conscious subject would always have to be conscious of this exploitation and of his projections upon the world. However, the conception of the subject here can never close off that gap which is its very condition of possibility, a gap which, by granting the "outside" and the "inside" their autonomous unity retrospectively, opens the possibility of ideology, of a further "projection" (as Horkheimer and Adorno themselves call it) that would be the imposition of a present upon a past. What their conception of the subject allows to emerge, then, is precisely that the subject has a history or, even more radically, that the subject emerges as the history of its relation to itself and its own past.

Dialectic of Enlightenment also relates another history, to be sure. It is the history, once again, of freedom, the freedom of thought and the thought of freedom.

> If thought is liberated from domination and if violence is abolished, the long absent idea is liable to develop that Jews too are human beings. This development would represent the step out of an anti-Semitic society which drives the Jews and others to madness, and into the human society. This step would also fulfill the Fascist lie, but in contradicting it: the Jewish question would prove in fact to be the turning point of history. By overcoming that sickness of the mind which thrives on the ground of self-assertion untainted by reflective thought, mankind would develop from a set of opposing races to the species which, even as nature, is more than mere nature. Individual and social emancipation from domination is the countermovement to false projection, and no Jew would then resemble the senseless evil visited upon him as upon all persecuted beings, be they animals or men.[73]

There is, no doubt, little that one would want to find fault with here, since to do so, to argue, for instance, that liberating thought would *not* lead to freedom from anti-Semitism and domination in general leaves the terrifying possibility of there being strictly no way out. The question remains, however, as to precisely how such liberation is to take place. The account of the raising of the concept of idiosyncrasy to the awareness of its futility and that of the necessity of a reflective subject stand as the twin poles of the thinking of freedom from anti-Semitism in *Dialectic of Enlightenment*. But in each case, "thought" can be said to have been freed only at the same time that it is implicated in a history, both of and "before" the subject, that withdraws it from its claims to liberate the Jews into the species, as this passage would have it, which is to say, to liberate the species and nature itself. Yet rather than catching us in the dead-end of thought, perhaps this is to think a thinking that offers the promise of freedom only by renouncing its claims upon that freedom. A thinking, then, that frees not only Jews, all beings, or even nature, but also, necessarily, itself, itself from a thinking of freedom that, as dependent upon thought, would forever remain bound to it.

CHAPTER 5

Adorno's Lesson Plans? The Ethics of (Re)education in "The Meaning of 'Working through the Past'"

Jaimey Fisher

In Germany it is fashionable to complain about political education and certainly it could be better, but sociology already has data indicating that political education, when it is practiced earnestly and not as a burdensome duty, does more good than is generally believed. ... One could well imagine that ... something like cadres could develop, whose influence in the most diverse contexts would then finally reach the whole of society, and the chances for this are all the more favorable, the more conscious the cadres themselves become.

ADORNO, "The Meaning of 'Working through the Past'"

Toward the end of the essay "The Meaning of 'Working through the Past'"—one of his most-cited works and probably his most-cited short essay—Theodor W. Adorno offers this unexpected proposal, one that would seem to contradict his later claim that he never said anything that was "immediately aimed at practical action."[1] It is not only the suggestion of educational cadres that moves the essay in a surprising direction, but also the optimism about "political education," which Adorno contrasts to the skepticism of unnamed critics. Rarely remarked upon in the scholarship on "Working through the Past"—which has influenced sundry fields of study, including, especially, German history—this surprising suggestion for cadres and these unnamed critics points to a subtle, but definitely

---

The epigraph is a slight modification to the translation from Adorno, "The Meaning of 'Working through the Past,'" in *Critical Models*, ed. and trans. by Henry W. Pickford (New York: Columbia University Press, 1998), here 100; the modification is based on the German text "*Was bedeutet: Aufarbeitung der Vergangenheit*," in Adorno, *Gesammelte Schriften* (1986; Frankfurt am Main: Suhrkamp, 1997), 10:569.

discernible subtext to the essay that many readers overlook or do not mention.² In order to illuminate this subtext, I wish to read "The Meaning" within the context of Adorno's 1950s interest in political education and particularly of his response to the "reeducation" imposed on Germany after World War II. Although there have been efforts to link "The Meaning of 'Working through the Past'" to Adorno's later essays on education from five to ten years later—especially in Peter Hohendahl's work—there has been no sustained effort to locate these essays in the public sphere of the late 1940s and 1950s.³ This context includes educational debates of the day, many of which represented continuing fallout from the attempted radical reform of primary, secondary, and higher education after World War II. Citations and even analyses of these essays on education often look forward to his controversial reaction to the student movement of the late 1960s—the beginnings of which he witnessed before his death in 1969—but it is also important to locate these essays in the earlier context that helped produce these educational concerns and against which Adorno was writing.

In approaching this public-sphere context and Adorno's engagement with it, I would like to begin with a text that he wrote in the same year as the well-known "The Meaning of 'Working through the Past,'" an often overlooked work: "Concerning the Democratization of German Universities [*Zur Demokratisierung der deutschen Universitäten*]." This piece underscores how Adorno was engaged with questions of reeducation at the time, such that the terms of the reeducation debates helped to shape his thinking about more general questions he would then address in "The Meaning of 'Working through the Past.'" In the early postwar period, reeducation became a catch-all term, a synecdoche for the occupation as well as for postwar Germany's cultural and psychological struggles.⁴ The widespread and wide-ranging debates about how the Allies and the Germans themselves were to reeducate Germany's complicit citizenry touched nearly all corners of culture and society.⁵ Discussions about reeducation served not only to come to terms with the past, but also to reconstitute German national identity after the war. In fact, coming to terms with the past via the discourse about reeducation simultaneously helped cultural and social elites to select elements of German culture around which national identity could be constituted in the future.

In engaging with and responding to these important, substantive, and sometimes obfuscating debates, "Concerning the Democratization" parallels "Working through the Past" in both its specific themes as well as its general approach: the essays not only underscore Adorno's interest in political education and the politics of education at the time, but also highlight his engagement with the issues that preoccupied intellectuals faced with Allied-imposed, subsequently German-commandeered reeducation. In locating Adorno's work in this context, I do not intend to reduce his work to its historical environment; rather, this framework allows one to appreciate these works in a new way as well as to appreciate Adorno's specific contributions to an issue that preoccupied many Germans at the time. For example, this investigation points to the increasingly prominent place Auschwitz came to play in Adorno's vision for (re)education, but simultaneously underscores how such prominence of place was a fairly unusual approach to (re)education, one that rendered it, like much of his thought, singular in relation to its cultural context and historical moment.

What emerges from this reading is not only a new understanding of Adorno's contribution to thinking about postwar education, but also a sense of the philosopher's underrated public-sphere engagement. While scholars such as Anson Rabinbach have emphasized the remarkable public engagement of postwar German intellectuals like Karl Jaspers, Adorno's interest in and engagement with the political and public-sphere debates of his days are given decidedly short shrift in his Anglophone reception.[6] But addressing this engagement also has important consequences for how we read Adorno's philosophy more generally. A constitutive aspect and consequence of this public-sphere engagement are its unfolding of a positive, if skeptical, normativity not typically attributed to Adorno's work outside of aesthetics. J. M. Bernstein and Judith Butler have focused on Adorno's ethics and the subsequent status of norms and normativity in his theory.[7] In his *Adorno: Disenchantment and Ethics*, Bernstein argues for a positive (if skeptical) ethics in Adorno, what Bernstein terms an "ethical modernism" built on "fugitive experiences." But I want to argue that Adorno also offered positive (if skeptical) norms in educational experience: if one is ruminating on the status of normativity, one should also consider his lesson plans, as offered in this series of essays.[8] Instead of focusing, as many understandably have, on the considered experience of and critical engagement with art—on the normative combination of art's semblance of nonsemblance with dialectical thinking—I would like to augment this conventional line of thinking with another area in which Adorno also offered positive (if skeptical) norms: in the experiences afforded by education and its deliberative approach to both subject and objective conditions.

Rendering Complex the "Democratization of German Universities"

In his biography of Adorno, Stefan Müller-Doohm highlights how, by the end of the 1950s, the philosopher was engaged with questions of education, but few, including Müller-Doohm, have attended to this interest or its context in any substantive fashion.[9] For example, the text "Concerning the Democratization of German Universities," was written in the same year as "The Meaning of 'Working through the Past,'" but has not been juxtaposed to it in any detail. "Concerning the Democratization" reflects how Adorno was thoroughly and productively engaged with some of the prevailing educational themes of the day, most of which had been raised and debated since the end of the war in the context of German reeducation. In "Democratization," he addresses a series of reified concepts about the university that had become common currency at the time, a series of clichés that rendered the university a space away from society and subsequently a space against which a recovering society could define itself as less conservative, less compromised, and less Nazi.[10] The way in which Adorno engages with and then dismantles these clichés not only anticipates, but also lays the foundations for, his later writings about education, which will cast education as an arena in which to confront wider social mechanisms.

"Concerning the Democratization of German Universities" begins with a familiar Adornean approach, namely, by taking up a concept that had grown popular and ossified by that particular historical moment, the "democratization of German universities": "The expression 'democratization of German universities' has several meanings. They are all related, but they must be distinguished if their intertwinement is not to be reflected in pure confusion [*wenn nicht ihre Verflochtenheit in purer Verwirrung sich spiegeln soll*]."[11] In a typically careful and nuanced parsing of an increasingly reified phrase, Adorno divides these familiar words into at least three interwoven meanings often obscured in the popular idiom: the socioeconomic democratization of the students attending the university; the more elusive "democratization" of what he calls the inner spirit of the university (what one might term a democratization of academic culture); and, finally, the democratic tendencies and inclinations of those who graduate from the university. These three interwoven meanings of the catch phrase "democratization of German universities," a typically Adornean complication of an overly simple concept, then structure the essay that follows. In each of these three areas—demographics of the student body, the democratic attitudes of academic culture, and the inclinations of its graduates—it becomes clear that Adorno is responding to an area of topical debate which his own theories subsequently illuminate, dismantle, and recast in a different and, in each case, remarkable light.

Adorno begins the body of the essay by addressing what may seem the simplest aspect of this multifaceted democratization: the diversifying socioeconomic demographics of the student body. This question of which young people went on to higher-education studies had proven hotly contested and nearly intractable in the early postwar period, in all the occupational zones as well as in the early German Democratic Republic and Federal Republic of Germany. Following the war, university admission policies were debated vehemently, since many, especially on the Left, believed that the overwhelmingly bourgeois background of prewar students had made them, as well as the social elites they became, fertile ground for Nazi teachings. Soviet officials had declared early in the occupation that they would admit more students from worker and farming backgrounds, but the numbers of such students had remained relatively small (albeit much higher than in the Western zones).[12] By the end of the occupation, among the thoroughgoing political changes in that year, Soviet and East German officials made a new commitment to reforming the "student-type": officials became more determined than ever to admit more students from such backgrounds because it seemed, increasingly, a mistake to have admitted so many, as Norman Naimark puts it, "representatives of the bourgeoisie and petit-bourgeoisie."[13] Looking enviously to the east, assorted Left-leaning West German officials demanded vociferously that more worker children be permitted and encouraged to study.[14] On the other side of this West German debate, however, many educational officials, teachers, and professors—products, after all, of the old system—defended the traditional admissions process, with its requisite *Abitur* and the *numerus clausus*, which favored those families that could afford the *Gymnasium*.[15] Karl Jaspers, for example, weighed in on the issue of student selection consistently and at considerable length, usually quite conservatively in his series of high-profile essays on the university.[16] All sides of this discussion were aware of the obvious stakes: those allowed to study would inevitably come to constitute the postwar social, economic, and political elites.

In engaging with this important question for the postwar context, Adorno supports, unlike Jaspers, what he characterizes as a "qualitative" change in the admissions policies of the university; there has been, in his opinion, a progressive breakup of the *"Bildungsmonopol"* [educational monopoly] of the upper classes: "Concerning the problem of access, that is, what one has traditionally termed the educational monopoly: according to the institutional requirements, something decisive has changed, unquestionably in a democratic sense."[17] Adorno's stand on this fundamental change in Germany's culture of education—at least in the participants in the culture of higher education—is indisputably progressive in terms of opening up academic study to those Germans who had been traditionally, and emphatically, excluded. On the other hand, however, Adorno is compelled to observe that despite this quantitative change that has culminated in qualitative transformation, the percentage of working-class students is still, proportionally speaking, lamentably low: "Today, as always, the proportion of worker children is extremely small (5%), very disproportional [*ganz außer Verhältnis*] to the number of workers in the total population (around 50%)."[18] He acknowledges that a large part of this underrepresentation is probably due to the economic realities of working-class students—above all, to the need to work to support themselves and their families. But, Adorno goes on to speculate, there is still some resistance to identifying with *Bildung* and the advantages of it for those of the working class.[19] For him, this lack of identification is especially noteworthy because the petty bourgeoisie, whose economic basis does not differ very much from that of the workers, identify with *Bildung* in much greater numbers and in much greater depth. In this argumentative trajectory—moving from statistics and economic motivation to psychological mechanisms—Adorno makes a conceptual move that will recur repeatedly in his writings on education: he shifts from predominantly socioeconomic questions and subsequent reasoning (to which he nominally grants supremacy) to a lengthier citation and description of relevant psychological mechanisms (questions of who identifies with *Bildung* and who acts on such identifications). Many of Adorno's investigations of education will settle on psychological and especially psychoanalytic factors, for example, even in the apparently simple and invitingly empirical area of student demographics.[20]

After this revealing conceptual trajectory in addressing the first of the three definitions of the democratization of German universities, Adorno considers the more opaque issue of the "inner democratization" of academic culture in terms of both the students and the professors. He begins by declaring: "Certainly it can be said that the old talk of the university as a hotbed of the reactionary [*Hochburg der Reaktion*] is no longer accurate. It is also not the last sanctuary of Nazism [*Zufluchtsstätte des Nationalsozialismus*]."[21] This is a far more contentious declaration than it might, at first glance, appear because of the universities' reputation after the war as a holdout for Nazi beliefs. Allied and many German officials considered the problem of denazification of the university even more urgent than repairing the devastating physical destruction facing universities after the war. In fact, one way in which the universities attracted widespread attention was negative: Allied reports regularly regarded education, especially higher education, as the most deficient aspect of the entire military government.[22] As with most educational institutions, the Nazis had been infamously careful to coordinate the universities to the party line, such that a large number of professors were removed in the early phases of Allied denazification.[23] At many universities, moreover, there were also uncomfortably high-level and high-profile problems with denazification. In Heidelberg, for instance, local labor officials attacked the rector of the university, Dr. Karl Bauer, for a 1926 book entitled *Rassenhygiene*.[24] In Munich, it was discovered that professors had formed a "clique" to resist hiring new faculty while any hope remained for rehabilitating denazified and subsequently recently dismissed professors. In essence, they were stalling until the expected liberalizing of the Allies' policies. Horkheimer offered an indictment of precisely such professors, those who had remained in Germany when he returned in 1948.[25]

Concerns about remnant Nazism among university students was even greater: throughout the early postwar period, university students became a particularly complex and important locus for denazification. Labor officials, committed as they were to opening up the university at both the pedagogical and student levels, led a high-profile attack on conventional culture of the academy: one well-known labor leader gave a public lecture provocatively entitled "The Fascist Attitudes of the Youth Admitted to the University" [*"Die faschistische Geisteshaltung der zum Studium zugelassenen Jugend"*]. In another telling episode, one of the most important postwar addresses on the question of guilt—by the pastor Martin Niemöller in an Erlangen church—was rapidly overshadowed by the alleged Nazi-inclined reaction of the student audience. Hermann Glaser, for instance, calls Niemöller's sermon the most important statement on guilt after the war, and Adorno was certainly familiar with it, as he referenced it in a letter to Thomas Mann as a laudable, if powerless, gesture.[26] Pastor Niemöller, a former inmate of Sachsenhausen and Dachau, argued clearly and forcefully that all Germans must acknowledge their participation and guilt for the crimes of the Nazi regime. Newspaper reports on the sermon, however, tended to focus not on the content of this controversial stance—one that seemed very close to the Allies' policy of widespread (if not collective) guilt—but rather on the virulently rejecting reaction of Erlangen university students to Niemöller's sermon. According to the press, as Niemöller argued that all Germans must acknowledge their guilt, he was interrupted multiple times by angry protests from the students; he was able to continue his address only because hosting officials appealed to the sanctity of the venue. A large number of articles speculated on the reasons for this reaction, and most reports, all over Germany, settled on the Nazi inclinations of students, invariably citing the *"Nazi-Studentenschaft."*[27]

The incomplete Allied and checkered German denazification efforts as well as the Niemöller episode underscore how, throughout the postwar public sphere, there was indeed the sense that the university had become a sanctuary of last institutional instance for Nazism. Adorno's clear rejection of this prevailing sense not only proves more optimistic than one might expect, especially as he was concerned, as in "The Meaning of 'Working through the Past,'" with the persistence of fascism and argued forcefully that such persistence posed a danger greater than neo-Nazi groups to postwar society. His engagement with and rejection of these stereotypes about (re)education and the university lays important groundwork for the novel direction in which he will take the question of democratization.

The threat, as Adorno unusually narrates it, is not so much from conventional reactionary or Nazi forces, as many others in the public sphere were claiming, but rather from West German society as it was evolving in the mid- to late-1950s. After dispensing with another stereotype about the university—the idea that the teacher-student relationship continued to be authoritarian, an area in which he (once again, surprisingly positively) credits an Americanization (read: reeducation) of conventional German academic culture[28]—Adorno observes that his relative optimism about the democratization of academic culture at the university does not mean that there is a democratization of consciousness.[29] With the current departure from traditional *Bildung*, there is also the lamentable obsolescence of some positive cultural phenomena associated with it, including what Adorno terms the "resistance [*Widerstand*]" and "autonomy of spirit [*Autonomie des Geistes*]": "The resistance of spirit against those relations in which one has to seek one's own little place in the world, weakens proportionally to the growing power of precisely those relations, and with it the autonomy of spirit itself weakens."[30] The peril here is undoubtedly the pressure to adapt [*sich anpassen*] to existing social relations, a theme to which Adorno will return repeatedly in his essays on education and a theme that ties education to one of the core themes of his philosophy, the intolerance, conceptually and socially, of the non-identical. Much as the simple concepts of identity thinking deny the heterogeneity and historical layering of complex concepts, autonomous individuals are forced to adapt themselves to prevailing social relations. Once Adorno has dispensed with the postwar stereotypes about reeducation, he can make this emphatic point: the real danger to the academy is not, as commonly claimed at the time, remnant conservatism or persisting Nazism, but that it becomes a mere microcosm of society's assault on individual autonomy and undercuts possibility of resistance to its prevailing social relations: "Of course, the contradiction [between "inner-academic" democratic process and the spirit of democracy] to which I draw attention here is difficult to change through the university (through, for instance, its teaching methods and exam structures), but rather points back toward the entire society. But the university represents this like a microcosm."[31] Rather than isolating the university as a singular locus for postwar fascism, Adorno sketches a university thoroughly intertwined and engaged with the society around it. Underpinning this conceptual move and this philosophically inflected observation, however, is a surprising optimism about the university and education to fortify those things that Adorno has subtly celebrated in the heterogeneous notion of *Bildung*: the "resistance" and "autonomy of spirit" as they might be realized in the university.

Adorno subsequently proceeds to address one of the most prevalent reified notions of the postwar public sphere, the notion that students had grown apathetically apolitical, something that he will analyze in a frame that likewise resonates with larger social processes, especially the lack of emotional cathexis with democracy. This public-sphere lament of students' indifference to politics contradicts the ubiquitous image of the Nazi hangers-on or dead-enders, but that did not stop various intellectuals, journalists, even filmmakers from fixating on the issue: assorted figures and media underscored the problem—for a country that is supposed to be democratizing—of an academic elite with no interest or inclination to politics.[32] On this central issue of apolitics, the similarities and contrast to Karl Jaspers are telling. In remarkably similar terms, both Jaspers and Adorno praised the students they encountered as they returned to teaching in postwar Germany, but both also observed how disinclined these students were to (conventional) politics.[33] For Jaspers and Adorno, both pleasantly surprised by the quality of the students in postwar Germany, part of the students' remarkable focus on difficult abstract problems of philosophy had everything to do with their desire to leave politics behind.

In a revealing position on these apolitical students, however, Jaspers celebrated and promoted this kind of anti-politics, a position that seems starkly at odds with Jaspers' own celebrated turn to the public.[34] For Jaspers these apolitical tendencies among students were not to be condemned, but rather lauded.[35] In considering the apolitical tendencies of postwar students, Adorno is taking up an issue that had sustained public-sphere interest and attention, but he takes the topic in an entirely different direction than even a committed liberal like Jaspers. Despite Adorno's well-publicized doubts about the later student movement, the point here is not, as it is with Jaspers, to defend the apolitical inclinations of the student—indeed, Adorno dramatically calls this apolitical tendency the "Achilles heel" of the democratization of German universities.[36] But instead of blaming, as many accounts had, the "new academic youth" themselves, Adorno moves emphatically to contextualize this trend and underscore how this tendency is symptomatic of wider, pernicious social mechanisms. For him, the mechanism emerges because students cannot, like everyone else, chart a politics to which they should engage and commit themselves. Adorno thus revealingly shifts his critical focus from the apolitical students to the situation that the society as a whole offers them as well as the rest of its citizens: as with adaptation or conformity [*Anpassung*], he segues rapidly to another of the recurring themes of his education essays, the way in which people are compelled to assume social roles to the detriment of their own person:

> It is difficult to prophesize how today's students, under the changed economic and political constellation, will behave vis-à-vis democracy. Certainly they have gained in their taste for freedom and for the unregimented life; but, on the other hand, certainly the inclination [*der Hang*] to conformity [*Anpassung*] will not cease where authoritarian orders of whatever variety demand such conformity.[37]

Rather than deliberately apolitical attitudes, Adorno observes in the students what Bernstein has called, in a different context, an "affective skepticism" about the rules and norms of democracy and society, a more general coldness that undercuts the dedicated engagement that a living and democratic polity demands. In her 2002 Adorno lectures, Judith Butler emphasizes a similar challenge to ethics in late modernity: to make them *lebendig* for subjects under different socioeconomic conditions than those under which democracy emerged. For both Bernstein and Butler it is not so much the open contradiction of conventional norms that defines later modernity as the draining of meaning and authority from the existing and still predominating norms, such that they are left cold and lifeless. Adorno thereby casts one of the *idées fixes* of the (re)education debate—the apolitical tendencies of the students—against this widespread affective skepticism toward the norms and practices of democracy. Given this contextualizing approach to the problems of apolitics, it will not be surprising that Adorno will revive, in skeptical and critical fashion, norms within educational institutions.

With this final contextualizing of a recurring topic in the postwar debate about students, Adorno moves to the last definition of "democratization of German universities," the democratic inclinations and/or habits of the graduates of the university. Not surprisingly, because the prevailing and "administered" society put such pressure on the universities and its students, the situation for graduates is very precarious. Once again, it has less to do with the conditions of the universities themselves, which Adorno, in a telling optimism, adjudicates as better than at any time in German history and which he sees as continuing to improve. The trouble is the continuing coordination of postwar German society: what other intellectuals, including Jaspers, have cast in opposition to society is actually thoroughly and detrimentally entwined in its context. Although students have been exposed to freedom and the "unregimented" life, the pressure to adapt, to conform to the authoritarian order, will persist—the mandate of identity thinking disciplines both body and personality—and no one can say for sure whether the time in the democratic environment will allow them to resist. The best defense, Adorno offers in the last line of the essay, is fortification of a critical self-consciousness, an exhortation that will structure his remaining essays on education, which both anticipate and lay the groundwork for the surprisingly normative position that will emerge in this area of Adorno's public engagement.

I have taken time to unfold a detailed reading of this unpublished essay because it lays a critical foundation for the interpretation of Adorno's other essays relating to education, including the now canonical "The Meaning of 'Working through the Past.'" My analysis takes a contextualizing approach because, in "Democratization," one sees how the conceptual constellation with which Adorno was working was thoroughly engaged with central issues in (re)education and educational reform after the war: the agenda of topics, if not the directions in which he took this agenda, was influenced by and imbricated within the debates of the day. Revealing is the way in which that engagement with the public sphere of his day does not, as is commonly argued, focus on the Holocaust, at least not yet; instead, the text concentrates, in a deliberately critical fashion, on reified concepts that had emerged in the debate about reeducation and, typical for Adorno, his philosophical approach aims to render complex these violently simple concepts. He addresses himself to those variegated issues in the heated debate around education—including those who would cast the university as the continuing fiefdom of the upper and middle classes, the last refuge for reactionary and Nazi politics as well as authoritarian relationships, and finally (if contradictorily) the realm of students' emphatically apolitical attitudes—but underscores how these commonly held beliefs have to be seen in the context of a society under rapid transformation: he takes up these public-sphere issues by consistently locating education within larger social, economic, and psychological trends that it is, in turn, necessary to address and, ultimately, resist. Given his reputation, it is surprising how Adorno regards education in the postwar university as not only able to address, but also even to remedy, many of these challenges. This context does not explain every detail of his piece—in fact, it is indispensable not to reduce the text to this historical environment; the context instead makes clear the originality of Adorno's approach. A careful reading leads one to appreciate the way in which these educational notions were interwoven with his other philosophy's central themes, like the resistance and autonomy of spirit against the prevailing pressure to conform to social parameters. These are precisely the kinds of moves Adorno will make in the much-cited "The Meaning of 'Working through the Past'": here again, he addresses a more specific issue in reeducation—one that had also become an *idée fixe* and reified concept—but generalizes its problems and relates them to a society undergoing rapid, radical transformation—an argumentative line that ends up with surprisingly specific engagement with reeducation as well as surprisingly optimistic declarations about its normative potential.

A Reeducational Reading of Adorno's "The Meaning of 'Working through the Past'"

> I'd like to say something general about the question of education. Of course, our education contains something that could be called ideals, although in general I prefer to avoid using the word. We educate people toward the possibility of something better, instead of having them swear an oath to what exists.
>
> THEODOR W. ADORNO in discussion after
> "The Meaning of 'Working through the Past'"[38]

As one of his best-known works, Adorno's "The Meaning of 'Working through the Past'" has mostly been interpreted either for its relevance to the confrontation with the Nazi past [*Vergangenheitsbewältigung*] or, in Adorno's less problematic parlance, *Aufarbeitung der Vergangenheit*, as well as for its elucidation of Adorno's interest in the Holocaust and anti-Semitism.[39] But a close reading of the essay demonstrates how it is well woven into Adorno's interest in educational questions in the 1950s; in fact, it engages the same conceptual constellation as "Concerning the Democratization of German Universities" (also written in 1959), but similarly responds and even recasts these questions from Adorno's singular perspective. This reading underscores how he was fully engaged with one of the most important debates of the postwar public sphere, namely, how Germans were to respond to and then inherit and reorganize the reeducation effort that the Allies had ambitiously instigated, allegedly bungled, and gratefully handed off. Locating the essay in this context, on the one hand, underscores the importance of reeducation questions to intellectuals at the time, and, on the other, illuminates both the general thrust as well as some of the more surprising and challenging conceptual turns in Adorno's text. Some of these curious turns further highlight the normative aspects of education in a decidedly more positive fashion than in "Democratization," which, as we saw, was largely concerned with critiquing the simple concepts and *idées fixes* of the public-sphere debate about reeducation.

Rereading "The Meaning of 'Working through the Past'" in the context of (re)education illuminates a common misunderstanding in analyses of the essay, namely, that postwar Germans repress memories of the past. This common characterization of "working through the past" locates Adorno's essay in an anticipatory line with the Mitscherlich's later, influential study, *The Inability to Mourn*, which, in a self-declared Freudian vein, postulates that postwar Germans (unconsciously) repress traumatic memories of the past. In the first three pages of "The Meaning," Adorno does, indeed, sketch mental resistances to working through the past, including various memory distortions and contortions that culminate in an unmistakable "destruction of memory."[40] But it is crucial to note that he does not understand this destruction of memory as a Mitscherlichian unconscious repression of recent events, but rather as a more conscious, reality-driven and -tested "effacement" [*Tilgung*] of the past: "The effacement of memory is more the achievement of an all too alert consciousness than its weakness when confronted with the superior strength of unconscious processes."[41] This important declaration is not as sudden as it seems: from the essay's very first page, Adorno articulates his skepticism about the putatively unconscious status of these memory-eclipsing mechanisms: "the tendency toward the unconscious and not so unconscious defensiveness against guilt is so absurdly associated with the thought of working through the past that there is sufficient reason to reflect upon it. . . ."[42] Adorno is once again deliberately considering and refiguring common assumptions about the widely cited forgetting in the wake of war, a consideration and recasting that anticipates the later trajectory of the essay.

Given that Adorno has rethought the nature of forgetting itself—not simple repression, but rather the intertwinement of conscious and unconscious processes in a new kind of heterogeneity of forgetting—he dispenses with forgetting as the all-too-simple negation of the past and focuses his text instead on what becomes his central question in "The Meaning": why postwar Germans have only an attenuated attachment to democracy, an attachment that, presumably, should demand a more considered working through the past. In Germany, Adorno underscores, democracy remains only a "working proposition," as he puts it (in English). Adorno underscores here not so much a rational rejection of democracy, but, as with the apolitical students of "Democratization," affective skepticism toward democracy's tenets and practices. This affective skepticism about—that is, lack of emotional investment in or cathexis with—democracy leads him, as a kind of departure point for the entire essay, to theorize what subjective and objective conditions lead to the often subtle persistence of fascism. This question also initiates the section on potential solutions to this persistence, such that the essay seems to attend above all to this question of affective skepticism about democracy, the central problem that Adorno extracted from the debate about reeducation in "Democratization." This question is precisely that at which he arrived near the conclusion, and certainly the culmination, of "Concerning the Democratization," when he considered the ubiquitously cited apolitical tendencies of university students. As I suggested there, Adorno insists on generalizing to a society-wide phenomenon this kind of apolitics that many intellectuals, like Jaspers, were happy to ascribe to students; similarly, in "The Meaning of 'Working through the Past'" the obvious answer of forgetting is expanded to include general trends in society that manifest problematic processes, of which forgetting is only one aspect.

The initial approach to affective skepticism about democracy leads Adorno through a litany of objective and subjective conditions that underscore the persistence of fascism in postwar society. Much as he balances conscious and unconscious processes in the destruction of memory—

unfolding the heterogeneity of forgetting itself—Adorno now focuses on the intertwinement of subjective and objective conditions that allows for the persisting complexes of fascism. In international politics, for instance, the Cold War permits a tenacious fixation on the threats from "The (Russian) East," such that Hitler's obsession with "Bolshevism" did not seem that far off the geopolitical mark. For an example on the subjective side, the collectively narcissistic investments in the national community have persisted beyond the alleged "Zero Hour" and into the postwar period to a degree few are willing to admit. These concerns with the objective and subjective persistence of fascism take up nearly half of the essay, but after reviewing them, Adorno returns to the central question of a lack of cathexis with democracy.

Upon returning to the question of Germany's affective skepticism about democracy—and after offering some of its objective and subjective causes—Adorno is ready to make a series of surprisingly normative, though typically complex, suggestions in confronting it. His suggestions correspond to his approach to forgetting as well as the persistence of fascism: much as Adorno has rendered forgetting heterogeneous, as both conscious and unconscious, and the persistence of fascism both objective and subjective, he will offer a heterogeneous, dialectical solution, namely, a mixture of (re)education and psychology. Reading the essay for these central intertwinements elucidates the curious declaration to which he builds in the last third of "The Meaning of 'Working through the Past'": Germany will require both "teachers and psychologists" to address the lack of commitment to democracy that has undercut its working through the past, a "pedagogical-psychological" combination reiterated in the discussion after the initial lecture. There has been, of course, much more scholarly diligence dedicated to the latter half of this formula, which is only understandable, given the consistent and considerable attention Adorno gives in his work to Freud and psychology more generally.[43] But teachers, the former agents of political change, have of course received much less attention, even though pedagogical questions come to dominate the last four pages of what is probably his most widely cited short piece. I argue that this appearance of the teacher seems not so sudden if one reads the essay in the context of reeducation, which was, as "Concerning the Democratization" demonstrates, very much on Adorno's mind and certainly a key aspect of his public engagement and his positive norms.

Adorno arrives at educational questions after outlining, as a final aspect of problematic objective conditions, the way in which modern economy undercuts the kind of autonomy that democracy demands. Much as modern economy and society subvert a sense of autonomy in political life, they also undercut the sense that the individual is an active agent, a subject, in world history, which, he declares in a rather sudden turn, "refers immediately to democratic pedagogy."[44] Adorno's concern that Germany and the Germans had lost a sense of themselves as political subjects was well documented elsewhere; he, in fact, called this the "decisive" problem of postwar Germany: "The most decisive fact seems to me that Germany has ceased to be a political subject, politics are merely tolerated, and everyone knows it, since they are not exactly dumb."[45] But the reliance on democratic pedagogy and, shortly, on institutions of education explicitly links "democratic pedagogy"—that abstract and highly normative project (in a centralist normative manner, in Bernstein's sense)—to the contingencies of the (re)education debate at the time and the engagement with these contingencies that "Democratization" symptomatized.[46] Adorno is, in fact, careful to position his project as inheriting the initial reeducation work done by the Allies, a positioning that offers a more sympathetic and forgiving interpretation of their work than much of the public-sphere discussion would have offered.

Two aspects of Adorno's focus on education as Enlightenment are particularly noteworthy: first, that education starts where family upbringing stops or, more precisely, fails. After his sudden turn to "democratic pedagogy," Adorno writes: "parents . . . must endure embarrassing questions from children about Hitler and in response, indeed, to whitewash their own guilt, speak of the good aspects and say that in fact it was not so awful. In Germany, it is fashionable to complain about political education, and certainly it could be better, but sociology already has data indicating that political education . . . does more good than is generally believed."[47] This sense of (re)education having to pick up where the conventional family fails was present in the reeducation's basic objectives, which, as did Adorno's own work in *Authoritarian Personality*, tended to highlight how the conventional German family had helped prepare the authoritarian way for the Nazis. In the American "Zook" Report on education, for example, which counts as the formative study for reeducation policy in the Western sectors, education was supposed to pick up where the conventional German family failed to prepare their children for democracy.[48] In both its general turn to "democratic pedagogy" as well as in its specific sketches for educational programs, "The Meaning of 'Working through the Past'" proves to be thoroughly engaged with the very controversial reeducation efforts initiated by the Allies and taken over by the Germans. That this German,

Adorno, otherwise known for skepticism about normativity, would underscore the "better results" of political education demonstrates both his public engagement and unsurprising optimism around these issues.

An even more unexpected aspect of this optimism is Adorno's first specifically institutional suggestion for this essay, those educational cadres with which I opened the essay. He raises this idea as well in "Education after Auschwitz," but his unusual, apparently inscrutable proposal has remained, in that context as well as here, similarly unremarked upon. With these cadres the reeducation context of the essay can help elucidate one of its more curious turns. The oddity of the idea—the peculiarity not only of its militaristic metaphor, but also of Adorno's optimism about such an abruptly practical turn—can be best, or at least better, understood by contextualizing and by comparison, for example, with Friedrich Meinecke's *Goethegemeinden*, a similarly surprising proposal for educational interventionism after the war. In his work *The German Catastrophe*, Meinecke, after sketching an etiology of Nazism, arrives at these *Goethegemeinden*, at this abruptly hybrid form, somewhere between education and religion, where traditional (German) *Bildung* was to be imparted to young people being handed over to (Allied) reeducation. Set against Meinecke's proposal, Adorno's largely similar idea is clearly more progressive: he suggests small, mobile units to offer political education to those, especially in the countryside, who might otherwise have been denied it—there is little, at least in terms of content, of conventional *Bildung* in Adorno's model—but the two notions seem to be both expressions of the context in which intellectuals were charged with proposing inventive (re)education forms; in both cases, the educational and institutional optimism seems considerable, the centralist normativity quite stark.

In the latter part of the essay's (re)education section, Adorno finally turns to a sustained analysis of anti-Semitism and how to combat it. Although many critics, as I outlined above, tend to locate Adorno's work on education in the context of his work on the Holocaust and anti-Semitism, it is noteworthy that he here, as he did in "Democratization of German Universities," tends to generalize the problem of anti-Semitism such that it is a symptom of more general socioeconomic and psychological mechanisms: as Adorno puts it, "if the Jews had not already existed, the anti-Semites would have had to invent them" (102), since the roots of their hatred have nothing to do with Jewish people but rather socioeconomic conditions and the psychologies they spawn. Revealing, here as well as in the first section about education, "The Meaning of 'Working through the Past'" addresses very specific programs that had been introduced as part

Jaimey Fisher

of reeducation, including curricula that emphasized the "great achievement of Jews in the past" (101) as well as exchanges with Israel, in which young Germans and young Israelis are brought together. In an essay ostensibly about *Vergangenheitsbewältiung* or about the Holocaust, Adorno spends the better part of a page criticizing these very specific reeducation programs, suggesting that they only underscore the anti-Semites' insistence that the Jews are, and need to be treated as, a separate group (if no longer "race"). Here again, the essay shows itself to be engaged with reeducation questions: it is after critiquing these programs that Adorno advocates a "turn to the subject," which results in his declaration that these problems "can only be solved by the collaborative effort" of "teachers and psychologists" (102).

This reeducation call to collaboration returns the essay to the series of intertwined, mutually constitutive dualities that structure its entire length: conscious and unconscious destruction of memory; objective and subjective conditions that yield an affective skepticism about democracy; and now—to address these series of conscious/unconscious, objective/subjective conditions—a collaboration of teachers and psychologists. In this fashion, in an essay most scholars see as focusing on questions of working through the past or the Holocaust, Adorno has concluded, in the entire last third of the essay, with very specific (re)education questions and proposals. This reading of the essay in the context of a text written in the same year ("Concerning the Democratization of German Universities"), as well as in the larger context of reeducation, helps illuminates some of the more challenging turns in the essay, including his abrupt raising of "democratic pedagogy" when the family fails; the educational "cadres" he proposes; his criticisms of very specific programs; as well as, finally, this collaboration between teachers and psychologists. Part of what makes these odd turns surprising for readers familiar with Adorno's works like *Dialectic of Enlightenment*, *Negative Dialectics*, and *Aesthetic Theory* is their optimism about institutional engagement, which he generally assiduously critiques. Reading for education demonstrates how Adorno did allow for one realm of collective and institutional optimism, an area that explicitly engages with, but also renders far more complex, the wider reeducation issues of the time.

Toward a Conclusion: "Education after Auschwitz" and "Education to Maturity [Mündigkeit]"

> ... please understand my reflections as a contribution to the attempt to deal with the threat not through fruitless indignation and cosmetic

measures, but rather by comprehending it in its deeper dimensions. Some suggestions for praxis nonetheless may follow, even if one does not imagine the path from insight to action to be as short as so many well-meaning people today seem to believe it to be.

ADORNO, 1962 introduction to
"The Meaning of 'Working through the Past'" (1959)[49]

The last lines of the introduction that Adorno added to "The Meaning of 'Working through the Past'" when he gave the lecture again in 1962 suggest, like the original questions and answers to the lecture, that his mind was very much on the ethics suggested by his lecture, on the norms and praxis it unfolded, even if skeptically.[50] I would like, in lieu of a conclusion, to gesture in the direction of a rereading of Adorno's later essays on education, which I would emphasize grew out of and elaborate Adorno's work on this topic in the 1950s. As Adorno's best-known work about education, "Education after Auschwitz" commences with the conceptual groundwork laid in "Working through the Past," not so much by merely beginning where the latter essay leaves off, but—as "Working through the Past" did with "Democratization"—by extracting specific elements from it and subsequently elaborating them in revealingly different directions. Toward the beginning of "Education after Auschwitz," Adorno takes, as a kind of point of departure, the place where he had arrived on the last page of "Working through the Past": he references the (italicized) "turn to the subject" he had developed in "Working through the Past," but in "Education after Auschwitz," Adorno strongly favors this subjective side over the objective side that he consistently balanced and interwove in the earlier essay. This is one indication of the important differences in the approaches of the two essays, differences that point toward a development away from a critique of the 1940s/1950s education debate and toward a more positive, normative program for postwar education.

In "Education after Auschwitz," instead of the earlier essays' negative catalogue of Germany's affective skepticism toward democracy and then sudden calls for (vague) reeducation, Adorno offers specific elements much more akin to a positive, normative education to be visited upon subjects that might, optimistically, still unfold in productive directions. The greater emphasis on the "turn to the subject" draws the essay, as well as his educational project, closer to Adorno's ethics, which, as are widely noted, tend to focus on the private individual, against the abstract and universal under whose hegemony so much damage has been done to both the subject and the sensuous particular.[51] In "Education after Auschwitz" the most important convergence between his educational and ethical projects is the more central role that Auschwitz (or the Holocaust) has come to play. But it is a convergence that not only demonstrates a development in Adorno's thinking about education by drawing it closer to his ethics; it also suggests a rethinking of those ethics that are usually seen in almost an entirely private frame: in these late essays on education, Adorno elaborates even more specific norms for an institutional setting mostly neglected by the present interest in and analyses of his ethics.

In "Working through the Past," as I argued above, Adorno focused on how anti-Semitism was a symptom of wider social mechanisms; his interest throughout seemed to suggest a more considered engagement with the blockages to democracy, of which anti-Semitism was only one manifestation. Adorno's interest was much more—as was common in the public sphere—with the persistence of fascism, authoritarianism, and passivity, notions he had reframed in terms of affective skepticism toward democracy in society as a whole, not so much with anti-Semitism per se. This conceptual constellation explains the conclusion of "The Meaning of 'Working through the Past'": to educate postwar Germany, the combination of teachers and psychologists should not hesitate to reference the war and its devastating, potentially deterring impact of the air war, as much as Jews and anti-Semitism. By 1966, in "Education after Auschwitz," however, the Holocaust has moved to center stage such that Adorno writes no longer of the vaguer "Working through the Past" and instead can offer the much-cited first line: "The premier demand upon all education is that Auschwitz not happen again. Its priority before any other requirement is such that I believe I need not and should not justify it. I cannot understand why it has been given so little concern until now."[52] The focus in the latter is not so much on merely shaking people out of an admininstered-society torpor—the primary peril in the earlier education essays—as teaching them more specifically, more ethically, and normatively about the subjective and objective tendencies that led to the Holocaust.

The trajectory between the two essays—between "Working through the Past," which was more vested in critiquing (re)education debates at the time, and "Education after Auschwitz," which lays out education more normatively—is a remarkable development for these public debates on education because of its unequivocal emphasis on something quite specific, at a time when far too many reeducation projects offered vague platitudes and nebulous opacity. Some scholars such as Hohendahl have seen a lack of specific educational agenda in Adorno's essays on the topic,[53] while others such as Bernstein generalize Adorno's approach to Auschwitz as an educational mandate to a wider rethinking of normativity and ethics per se: for Bernstein, Adorno's new categorical imperative is exemplary in that it folds the particular, the historical, the contingent back into an ethical thinking that has been hollowed out by instrumental rationality, its relentlessly skeptical inquiries, its denigration of the particular in favor of the universal.[54] But I think it is important to observe, against the deficit that Hohendahl sees as well as against the abstract, if persuasive, trajectory that Bernstein traces, that Adorno does sketch, in this educational context, very specific suggestions, tantamount to lesson plans: he advocates education about folkish traditions, the biographies of perpetrators, and moments of concrete resistance to the Holocaust.

On the last count, it is likewise revealing to locate Adorno's suggestion in the context of the time: self-serving calls to celebrate resistance to the Nazis were not uncommon in a variety of political corners, but Adorno did not highlight the conspirators of July 1944, an important postwar hobbyhorse for conservatives like Ernst Jünger, but rather the resistance to the "euthanasia" killings of the disabled.[55] In this more specific, positive, and normative model for education, Adorno furthermore resumes and elaborates other elements raised seven years before in "Working through the Past": the trajectory of the cadres from "Working through the Past" is telling, as they do indeed reappear here as "mobile educational units [mobile *Erziehungsgruppen*]"[56]; here he suggests that such units should drive into the countryside because that is where Holocaust education is most needed. Even if one finds the conceptual mapping of this constellation problematic, the development of this curious but remarkable model from "Working through the Past" demonstrates how "Education after Auschwitz" has extended his thinking into even more normative formulations, a normativity confirmed by another text, "Education to Maturity [*Mündigkeit*]" (1969) that has received little attention, but that represents another stark intervention in the postwar public sphere.

As a dialogue between Adorno and longtime intellectual interlocutor Hellmut Becker, "Education to Maturity [*Mündigkeit*]" was chosen for broadcast on 13 August 1969, the day of Adorno's funeral. Such a mass-cultural venue confirms Adorno's high-profile engagement in the public-sphere debates about postwar education, an aspect of his intellectual profile that has received somewhat short shrift in Anglophone scholarship. Though "Education to Maturity [*Mündigkeit*]" does not have as specific an educational agenda as "Education after Auschwitz," it does explicitly affirm the kind of positive, even optimistic normativity that Adorno's writing about education—unusual for his writings more generally—manifests. While "Education after Auschwitz" in some ways completes "Working through the Past" by offering more specific details about postwar education, "Education to Maturity [*Mündigkeit*]" underscores the normative subtext to both texts: "Education to Maturity [*Mündigkeit*]" does not elaborate the details of an educational project as much as demonstrate how normativity was indispensable to his thought on the topic.

The dialogue focuses on its eponymous theme: from the first page, Adorno raises the explicitly Kantian concept of *Mündigkeit* in education, the ability to speak (maturely) for oneself, with which Kant famously, in one of his most normative statements, defined the Enlightenment. Taking up this Kantian norm, Adorno argues that such maturity is still a fundamental norm in democracy: "This project of Kant's—which no one, even with the worst will in the world, can accuse of being unclear—seems to remain extraordinarily up-to-date. Democracy is founded on the effective articulation of the will [*Willensbildung*] of the individual, as embodied in the institution of the representative vote."[57] In his original answer to the question "What is Enlightenment?" Kant focused on self-imposed immaturity and subsequently a self-motivated and realized liberation from this immaturity. To achieve this escape from immaturity, he advocates open communication, the public use of reason, to allow for the mature self to emerge. Kant makes little mention of education's assisting in this process; in fact, if anything, the essay seems directed against conventional "guardians," including doctors, the clergy, and even books.[58] But Adorno and Becker speculate on how such maturity can be taught, can be imparted to pupils and to students, certainly a project that is normative both fundamentally and, for the Enlightenment, foundationally. Some of the most interesting passages of the essay focus precisely on the contradictory process by which authority figures can shepherd pupils and students toward autonomy. Although they recognize that such authority is a contradiction—Becker points out and Adorno agrees that authority is necessary but also should make its own superfluity its goal (27)—they advocate it nonetheless as an indispensable aspect of effective and democratic education. Adorno, in fact, justifies it with a strategic deployment of the Oedipal moment: the well-behaved child, the one who internalizes superego from authority figures effectively, is actually the one more likely to achieve autonomy later on.

Both the intervention of the authority figure and the subsequent blossoming of autonomy posited here suggest a very different model for normativity and ethics than is typically the case in Adorno's writings, for instance in Judith Butler's characterization of his ethics as one on the side of reserve, restraint, and *"nicht Mitmachen."*[59] It is telling that, in this normative context, Adorno would suspend a critique not only of strong authorities in family and school, but also his critique of absolute reason:

> I believe that the concept of absolute reason can certainly be criticized philosophically, as can the illusion that the world is the product of "absolute spirit." However, it would be wrong to use that argument to claim that there is any way of defining what should really be done, real praxis, other than by thinking, and, in fact, unwavering and insistent thinking. And the idea that here philosophical criticism of idealism is amalgamated with the denunciation of thought I find to be an atrocious sophism which should be exposed in order finally to put a spark to all this antiquated mustiness, which may even blow it apart.[60]

The concept of absolute reason and spirit is—as much of his work in *Dialectic of Enlightenment* and *Negative Dialectics* testifies—criticizable philosophically, but there are contexts in which the foregrounding of such critique ought to be suspended, at least in terms of "real praxis." While it is important to acknowledge the distinction Adorno is drawing—between the philosophical critique of reason and reason in institutional contexts—it is likewise important to recognize his deliberate and productive engagement in precisely those varied contexts that occasion what, for him, seem markedly unusual arguments. These contexts include areas that have been generally underemphasized in his Anglophone reception: his addressing, conceptually as well as directly, debates in the postwar German public sphere; his affirmation of Enlightenment ideals, like that of *Mündigkeit*, as a cornerstone of his educational project; the latter subsequently representative of a clear engagement with remarkably optimistic normativity and praxis, signs of his unfolding a more normative ethics. The point is not to reduce Adorno's thought to these kinds of contextual engagements, but rather to appreciate the complexity of his work, which includes these kinds of norms and these forms of praxis. Reading "Education after Auschwitz" and "Education to Maturity [*Mündigkeit*]" within the context of Adorno's engagement with (re)education since the 1950s permits us to locate this moment of surprising optimism and emphatic normativity at the end of a long arc of thinking and writing about education and its challenges; such a reading allows us to grasp its normative content and to situate it within a more general portrait of Adorno's multifaceted thought.

CHAPTER 6

Adorno—Nature—Hegel
Theresa M. Kelley

My argument in this essay concerns Theodor W. Adorno's surprising critique of G. W. F. Hegel in *Negative Dialectics*, surprising because for a brief interval Adorno appears to side with nature against Hegel. This is not precisely the move one might have expected of Adorno, for whom nature ought to have been aligned with the material and experimental culture of knowledge that he, like Hegel, opposed to the work of what Hegel called Spirit and the work of dialectic.[1] Yet Adorno charges Hegel with a "rage against nature," and, in the course of a long section of *Negative Dialectics*, he makes that charge stick. According to Adorno, Hegel's "rage" is on behalf of the World Spirit, which seeks to overcome nature, albeit in the guise of enfolding and reimagining nature in a higher mode and understanding—the process in Hegel identified as "sublation" or, in the German, *Aufhebung*. Martin Jay has noted in passing the curiousness of Adorno's phrase. Alexander Düttmann has called attention to *contingency* as that which is for Adorno a key precondition for doing philosophy in our time.[2] I argue here that the contingent, non identity of nature with Spirit provokes and remains the stubborn sign of Hegel's rage. In charging Hegel with forgetting, or foregoing, the non identity of objects and particulars in nature that enables a genuinely negative dialectics,[3] Adorno seeks to revive Hegel's own philosophical commitment to a restless dialectics that would, or ought to, remain ever on the watch for moments of otherness and negativity that keep philosophy from becoming merely abstraction. Adorno's reservation concerns the degree to which Hegel's brief for the World Spirit veers from this dialectical project.

As Hegel well understood, nature is the domain of contingency, and, as such, a threat to the autonomy of reason and spirit. Usually rendered in German as *Zufälligkeit* [from *zufällig*, meaning "by chance," literally "falling" or "stumbling"], contingency marks, many have argued, the modern problem or, if you will, opportunity, of modernity.[4] Precisely because it is a domain where events are often unexpected, where the unpredicted trumps the rule, Nature is for Hegel unstable, unreliable, and in need of spirit's supervision—a supervision so complete as to look more like obliteration. Rather than allow the world of contingent nature to frustrate the work of spirit by repeatedly undoing (or replicating or changing) the particulars that might be taken up by and as spirit, Hegel does what he can to limit nature, by asserting—among other points—that nature has no vitality or life in the sense authorized by spirit. Hegel is hardly circumspect on this point. Indeed, in the introduction to his *Philosophy of [World] History*, he puts the task bluntly: it is the work of the World-historical individual to trample whatever interests do not coincide with one's own. The figure for this task is telling: Hegel says that "so mighty a form [as the world historical spirit] must trample down many an innocent flower—crush to pieces many an object in its path."[5] Not the least of those objects is nature.[6]

My focus in this essay is the shape or architectonics of Adorno's relation to Hegel, of which the dispute about the role of nature is one part. The shape of that relation is profoundly dialectical and at times contentious as well. At issue for Adorno is the very possibility of dialectical thought as he uses it to think with, but also at times against, Hegel. Adorno conveys his shifting yet profoundly committed engagement with Hegelian dialectic in the essay "Parataxis," subtitled "Notes on Hölderlin's Late Poetry" and published in *Notes on Literature* (1974), and in three other essays published together under the English title *Three Studies of Hegel*. The original German title specifies the philosophical importance Adorno assigned to this volume: *Zur Metakritik der Erkenntnistheorie: Drei Studien zu Hegel*.[7] These four essays investigate the problem of reading Hegel in part by exploring the resources of paratactic style, in which lines, figures, sentences, or ideas are presented in a format that does not subordinate any one to any other. That is to say, in these essays Adorno investigates the problem of philosophical metacritique and Hegelian dialectics by invoking a style that is formally antagonistic to the promise of closure or foreclosure that is for Adorno Hegel's dark side. My notice of this rhetorical pattern is evidently guided by Adorno's argument in "Parataxis" that Hölderlin's use of this rhetorical pattern might offer a model for philosophical writing that is also poetic.

Adorno calls the parataxes of Hölderlin's poetry "artificial" disturbances (in the sense that they are rhetorical devices) that "evade the logical hierarchy of a subordinating syntax."[8] As such, they allow him to critique and recuperate Hegelian thought without allowing one task to subordinate the other. But the stakes are in fact even higher. Because Hegelian negativity is so crucial to Adorno's sense of the remaining possibilities for philosophy in late modernity, parataxis becomes, as it were, one element of style (there are certainly others) that Adorno requires to do philosophy, to write philosophically.

The reasons for this return us again to Hegel, or to Adorno's presentation of Hegel in terms of the problem of philosophy. Adorno contends that Cartesian-derived claims for clarity do not suit the task of philosophy because the drive toward "clarity" sacrifices the capacity for philosophical inquiry on the altar of easy meanings, which are clear, without shadows. We should rather insist, says Adorno, that philosophical argument and writing be "intelligible," by which he means capable of being grasped, understood, without reduction.[9] Hegel is for Adorno the modern philosopher whose writing does not (and this is surely evident to us all) aspire to clarity but, at its best, aspires to intelligibility.

It is this aspect of Hegelian thought that Adorno tries to recuperate in Hegel even as he exposes Hegel's lapses from intelligibility into something less, something coercive, something unfaithful, Adorno contends, to Hegel's own negative dialectics. The textual apparatus of that recuperation is slung across the essays gathered together in *Hegel: Three Studies*, and threads of this recuperative project also appear in *Prisms*, elsewhere in the *Notes on Literature* (where "Parataxis" appears), in *Minima Moralia*, and in *Negative Dialectics*. Let me return here to the focus of my present inquiry and restate it slightly with Adorno's project and Hegel's liabilities in mind. It concerns the problem of philosophical style that haunts Adorno's writing: how to make intelligible the form or rather the rhythms of dialectical philosophy, such that one does not crush, like a flower, the particulars that dialectical thinking seeks to preserve. This formulation is admittedly a bit naive about the difficulty that concerns Adorno. For at best preservation is hardly what happens; rather Adorno imagines a philosophical style that would point out the fact that ideas live in "the cavities between what things claim to be and what they are."[10] This phrase from *Negative Dialectics* suggests what I take to be the appeal of parataxis for Adorno: a mode of presentation that insists, by its very awkward unassimilation of one view to the next, that the intelligibility of the truth on offer lies in the cavities [*Höhlen*] between statements, not zipped up inside the seams of the discourse, like the French seam of a fine garment that folds the rough outside edge inside and then seams it shut.[11] In Hegel, this philosophical seam would be the argument that runs smoothly in linked manner from one point to the next, with tidy subordinations that shut off difference, dissimilarity, thus making arguments clear but no longer, in Adorno's view, intelligible. To make Hegel intelligible, Adorno needs a philosophical style that exposes the cavities in Hegel's thinking in order to recuperate the spirit and letter of a still-viable philosophical dialectics.

I turn now to Adorno's "Parataxis," where, it might be argued, Hölderlin's poetic parataxis saves the argument of the essay at precisely the moment when that argument appears to be caught on the horns of an important but stalled discussion of intentionality and meaning. Here, too, what inspires Adorno is a moment in Hegel like those which, to borrow from Blake's poem *Milton*, Satanic reduction cannot find. The moment occurs in the introduction to Hegel's *Aesthetics*. Says Hegel: "it is not what is inexpressible that is highest and best—so that the poet would have a greater inner profundity than would be presented in the work; rather, his works are what is best in the artist."[12] What Adorno wants to find in Hegel and in the philosophy of late modernity is a style that can sustain Hegel's claim, without giving itself over to a reductive clarity. Adorno goes on to specify what he seeks, again by way of the Hegel who offers a "model of immanent analysis" that does not rest within itself "but rather bursts out of the object." On the next page, the same syntax, now constructed using a different verb, describes the way Hölderlin's late poetry "shoots out beyond the mere subjective intention of the poet."[13] Syntactically parallel and unsubordinated, in English and in German, these verbs register Adorno's sense that to get at what Hegel does best one has to allude, paratactically, to what the poet does.

Among the poetic examples Adorno gives is a stanza from Hölderlin's poem "Der Einzige" ["The Only One"]:

> Es entbrennet aber sein Zorn; dass nämlich
> Das Zeichen die Erde berührt, allmählich
> Aus Augen gekommen, als an einer Leiter.
> Diesmal. Eigenwillig sonst, unmässig

Grenzlos, dass der Menschen Hand
Anficht das Lebende, mehr auch, als sich schicket
Für einen Halbgott, Heiliggesetztes übergeht
Der Entwurf. Seit nämlich böser Geist sich
Bemächtiget des glücklichen Altertums, unendlich,
Langher währt Eines, gesangsfeind, klanglos, das
In Massen vergeht, des Sinnes Gewaltsames.

But his wrath is aroused; that, namely,
The sign touches the earth, gradually
Disappeared from sight, as on a ladder.
This time. Self-willed as a rule, immoderately
Unrestrained, that the hand of men
Attacks the living, that the attempt
Goes beyond what is divinely established,
More even, than is seemly for a demigod.
Since evil spirit, namely,
Seizes possession of happy antiquity, there endures
Long since and unendingly, One hostile to song, soundless, and
Perishing in measurements,
One violent of sense.[14]

Adorno argues that the lines in this stanza are linked not by a logical process of judgment, which seeks out evidence of linkage and subordination, but by something that is like music. Commenting on the stanza, Adorno proposes that its "indictment of an act of violence on the part of spirit, which has deified itself and become something infinite, searches for a linguistic form that would escape the dictates of spirit's own synthesizing principle."[15]

The poet Hölderlin, who here speaks a poetic incantation against Hegelian synthesis—that act of violence against nature on behalf of spirit—evidently does so on Adorno's behalf. But the poet does so in order to move on, pursuing the project that also underwrites Adorno's recuperative gesture toward Hegel: to find a form in language that would remain outside the grasp of the spirit's own synthesizing principle. So ventriloquized, Adorno's Hölderlin is the poet who responds to Hegel's praise in his *Aesthetics* for the poet whose works are his "truth" by offering the double truth about Hegel's works: the charge that the drive toward synthesis constitutes an act of violence and the leap beyond that charge that seeks out a form in language that would resist the grasp of synthetic closure, however brilliant its hidden and stitched seam.

Toward that end, what Adorno finds in Hölderlin's lines are "constructions [that] strain . . . away from what fetters them.[16] The music-like connectivity of Hölderlin's German belongs, Adorno argues, to the poet's late style, where certain paratactic patterns recur, among them "the split-off *'Diesmal*' ['this time'],'' the rondo-like associative linking of the sentences, and the twice-used particle *'nämlich*' ['namely'].''[17] *Parataxis* refers, then, not only to the "micrological" constructions of Hölderlin's mature poetics and, in a later essay, to Hegel's own writing, but also to the way larger structures in music, like the rondo, make possible a mode of repetition or seriality without subordination. It is symptomatic of the paratactic energy of Adorno's own writing that he goes on to consider Hegel's comment on another of Hölderlin's poems and then turns to Beethoven's late style. At each of these turns, it is the paratactic advantage of structures in which repetition or seriality continues without subordination that attracts Adorno, even as the trajectory of his argument mirrors such structures.

I offer here an overview, stitched together from different locations, of Adorno's parataxes of Hegel to show how they seek to accomplish for Hegel what Hölderlin's late style accomplishes—a presentation of Hegel that suspends, with the full force of rhetorical artifice, the formal Hegelian tendency to use spirit to trump and thus to subordinate everything else. The excerpts that follow, taken from Adorno's remarks about Hegel in different essays, can be read as *stychomythia*, that is to say, like dialogue in Greek drama in which alternate lines embody a sharp disputation between distinct views. The excerpts themselves exemplify a fairly pervasive tendency in Adorno's style, a tendency that is especially marked when the subject is Hegel. Like the Hölderlin stanza that Adorno discusses in "Parataxis," a serial pattern of repetition and difference knits these statements together such that the "cavities" between them can be read as Hegel's ideas saved from the kind of "rage" Hegel directed against nature and, more generally, from the rage that Hegelian spirit directs against those unruly, contingent particulars that disturb spirit's takeover. I offer this schematic, admittedly artificed, stitched-together group of excerpts to make explicit a philosophical and stylistic project that occupies a good deal of Adorno's thinking about writing in the last decades of his life and career.

Adorno's philosophical project is, then, to put so much rhetorical and therefore stylistic pressure on Hegel's writing that it bursts out of the seams and subordinations it nonetheless creates, like a Blakean Urizen roaming the dens of nature: dividing, suturing, tying up those loose contingent ends. In the seriality of Adorno's re-presentation of Hegel, logical logjams and end points must yield, or be burst through, blasted out. Or to make this point another way: to counteract the late Hegel of the *Logic*, which so often closes off the negativity of his earlier *Phenomenology of Spirit*, Adorno needs the poetry of late Hölderlin to show how the poetic work of parataxis might underwrite a poetic philosophy that would render Hegel as he couldn't render himself. Then too, Hegel would seem to be the shadow figure for Adorno himself as the philosopher who seeks to craft a philosophical style that might be not precisely adequate to the project of a negative dialectics (again, the term "adequacy," like "preservation," falsifies the difficulty Adorno wishes to sustain), but available to that project.

What follows is, then, a sample, not a full census, of Adorno's efforts to read Hegel into a series of parataxes. I begin with two sets of quotations from *Negative Dialectics* that appear in the second part of this work, entitled, probably with some irony, "Concepts and Categories," rather than, as one could imagine a less critical follower of Hegel might do, "The Categories of the Concept."

Criticizing Hegel for his reliance on method in a paragraph that is billed as a "farewell to" or "emancipation from" ["*Lossage*"] Hegel,[18] Adorno counters that dialectics is

> not a pure method nor a reality in the naive sense of the word. It is not a method, for the unreconciled matter [*unversönte Sache*]—lacking precisely the identity surrogated by the thought—is contradictory and resists any attempt at unanimous interpretation. It is the matter, not the organizing drive of thought, that brings us to dialectics. Nor is dialectics a simple reality, for contradictoriness is a category of reflection, the cogitative confrontation of concept and thing [*Begriff und Sache*]. To proceed dialectically means to think in contradictions, for the sake of the contradiction once experienced in the thing, and against that contradiction. A contradiction in reality, it is a contradiction against reality. But such a dialectics is no longer reconcilable with Hegel.
>
> Keine Methode: denn die unversöhnte Sache, der genau jene Identität mangelt, die der Gedanke surrogiert, ist widerspruchsvoll und sperrt sich gegen jeglichen Versuch ihrer einstimmigen Deutung. Sie, nicht der Organisationsdrang des Gedankens veranlaßt zur Dialektik. Kein schlicht Reales: denn Widersprülichkeit ise eine Reflexions-kategorie, die denkende Konfrontation von Begriff und Sache. Dialektik als Verfahren heißt, un des einmal an der Sache erfahrenen Widerspruches willen und gegen ihn in Widersprüchen zu denken. Widerspruch in der Realität, ist sie Widerspruch gegen diese. Mit Hegel aber läßt soche Dialektik nicht mehr sich vereinen.[19]

In the original German key terms like thought [*Gedanke*], contradiction [*Widerspruch*], thing [*Sache*], dialectic [*Dialektik*], real and reality [*Reales; Realität*], and their cognates create a sound shape that depends not on repetitions that convey identity or unity, but on a pattern of repetition in which difference and contradiction are the outcome. For example, words like "contradiction" and its cognates [*Widerspruch*] gather forces of opposition that are serially deployed in other words like "confrontation," the "unreconciled" state of matter itself, and above all "dialectic" to insist that Hegel's dialectics, in which matter is made to knuckle under to concept, mistakes the real work of the dialectic, whereas what is unreconciled in matter prompts thought and resists being taken up in and by thought. Only by way of such inner contradictions, Adorno will always contend, can the dialectic continue.

Another pair of statements—the two are noncontiguous, although they appear in successive paragraphs in *Negative Dialectics*—offers a more sharply counterpointed rhetorical shape. The first reads: "Nonidentity is the secret *telos* of identification. It is the part that can be salvaged; the mistake in traditional thinking is that identity is taken for the goal."[20] Next Adorno invokes, then rebukes the formal tendency in Hegel, by aligning it with Kant's thing-in-itself: "To define identity as the correspondence of the thing-in-itself to its concept is *hubris*; but the ideal of identity must not simply be discarded. Living in the rebuke that the thing is not identical with the concept is the concept's longing to become identical with the thing. This is how the sense of nonidentity contains identity." Note here how the Greek terms *telos* and *hubris* help to organize the axis along which identity and nonidentity exfoliate into cognate terms and get reassigned in value. Then Adorno takes one more step, moving inside that "rebuke" to recognize how its passional nature, its longing for identity, is the filament of identity that nonidentity knows.

I read this moment of Adorno's sympathy for identity-thinking as a deep sign of his effort to undo or not do what the older Hegel insisted that the world-historical individual must do: make the passional life of particulars pay for being subordinated to the plot of a philosophical argument. I refer here to the last sentence in Hegel's statement about the world-historical individual with which I began this essay. That sentence reads: "the idea pays the penalty of determinate existence and of corruptibility, not from itself, but from the passions of individuals."[21] Instead of using longing *against* the drive toward identity, Adorno here uses it to recognize in that drive a desire for what is outside identity, a desire for what is other that insures the life of the dialectic as he specifies its operations and as he claims Hegel's deepest dialectical impulse would also require.

Yet Hegel himself, and most evidently Hegel on the subject of nature, stands in the way of Adorno's dialectical project. David Krell has argued that what turns the young Hegel from nature is precisely what attracted his Jena colleagues, Schelling and Goethe, to nature: its availability to contingency [*Zufälligkeit*], its variability, and its vitality. Urging the use of violence against nature lest, Proteus-like, it slips out of one's grasp, Hegel enacts a categorical violence by remaking nature's availability to contingency [*Zufalligkeit*, from *Zufall*, "accident"] into the related but harsher *Abfall*, the trash that spirit and idea cast off as merely external, merely matter, nothing or at least nothing to them.[22] As the middle term in Hegel's tripartite division of nature into mineral, plant, and animal, plants trouble this account because they are evidently organic and, among *Naturphilosophie* writers, vital. Minerals are, after all, dead structures, mere crystal skeletons; animals have the capacity for inner-directed, conceptual life. Only plants occupy an uneasy middle place in Hegel's system: their spiral vessels act, as Hegel's contemporaries never tired of observing, like a circulatory and respiratory system. And yet, despite efforts to systematize plants into a stable taxonomy, they are endlessly available to variation, the monstrous deviations from known types. As such, Hegel argued, their contingency leads not to freedom but to a cycle of repeated collapses into different forms, an endless profusion.

Hegel's solution for the problem of plant nature is, Elaine Miller observes, death, an outcome that carried his sharp disavowal of *Naturphilosophie* arguments about plant vitalism and his wariness of Goethe's more complex understanding of an explicitly mechanical vitalism in the plant's metamorphosis from seed to leaf to bud to blossom to fruit. Precisely because Goethe describes this process in terms of plant agency and inner direction, Hegel found this more scientific and experimental view of plant development equally problematic. Gesturing silently to Goethe's analysis of the life cycle of a single annual plant in *Versuch die Metamorphose der Pflanzen*, Hegel insists that plants grow not into individuals but as many particulars (seed, leaf, bud) that never form a unity.[23]

Hegel, in short, knows what plants are for. Disorganized to the last, plants are to be consumed by animals or cast off as the externalization or alienation [*Entäusserung*] of spirit because they lack conceptual life, which is the only life that counts. In fact, Hegel paradoxically implies that plants also know what they are for when he asserts that "the goal of nature is to kill itself [*sich zu töten*]" in order to be "rejuvenated as spirit."[24] Although the capacity a seed has to germinate prompts Hegel's admiration for this "mystical, magical act," he insists that "the plant's capacity to actualize this potential is limited."[25] As such, plants are like women and animals like men. Miller notes that the middle position Hegel gives plants in this system of gendered analogy parallels that given to Christ in Hegel's history of religion, where Christ enacts the spirit's version of the plant's self-sacrifice and externalization of an implicit concept. The difference between them is succinctly Hegelian: whereas Christ is reanimated, nature remains the corpse. For Miller and for Georges Bataille, Hegel's path for spirit as for plant nature is death, except that for the plant it is permanent.

So ends the loose, undisciplined proliferation that plants share, in Hegel's philosophy of history, with "oriental" civilization.[26] And yet, as this last fillip in the figural likenesses of Hegel's writing suggests, the problematic middle of his philosophy of nature is uncannily exhumed in the "oriental," whose evocation of the symbolic makes it the compelling middle term between the classic and the romantic in Hegel's history of art. Thus for (or despite) Hegel, nature (especially plant nature) has more staying power than one might expect, despite its sensuous, contingent, and oriental alienation from the (dialectical) work of spirit. I speculate further that it is precisely this lingering, sensuous alienation that Adorno's negative dialectics seeks to retain, despite Hegel's efforts to kill it off.

In the three essays published in 1963 as *Hegel: Three Essays*, Adorno attempts, as Nicholsen and Shapiro put it in their introduction to the English translation, to show why Hegel was "the true revolutionary thinker," truer even than Marx.[27] To make this case, they note, Adorno must recuperate "the negative and dialectical core" he finds in Hegel's thought in order to open a way toward a "revised conception of the dialectic."[28] The first essay, "Aspects of Hegel's Philosophy," which Adorno delivered in 1956 on the occasion of the 125th anniversary of Hegel's death, is the most recuperative of the three Hegel essays. Yet even here, and even for such an occasion, Adorno insists on what he calls the "*skandalon*" of Hegel's thought. The literal translation for this Greek term, "a snare or a trap or a stumbling block," specifies why Adorno uses the term rather than its English equivalent to call attention to Hegel's style as a writer and a lecturer:

> The quintessence of the conditioned, according to Hegel, is the unconditioned. It is this, not the least of all, that gives rise to the hovering, suspended quality of Hegelian philosophy, its quality of being up in the air, its

permanent *skandalon*: the name of the highest speculative concept, that of the absolute, of something utterly detached, is literally the name of that suspended quality. The Hegelian *skandalon* cannot be ascribed to any confusion or lack of clarity; rather, it is the price Hegel has to pay for absolute consistency, which comes up against the limits of consistent thought without being able to do away with them. Hegelian dialectic finds its ultimate truth, that of its own impossibility, in its unresolved and vulnerable quality, even if, as the theodicy of self-consciousness, it has no awareness of this.[29]

Paying the price here refers not to the con game in which the World Spirit or world-historical individual gets particulars to pay the price for their own demolition, but to the necessary philosophical payment that is both the scandal or stumbling block of the Hegelian dialectic and the enterprise that saves that dialectic from getting closed down.

In the second of the Hegel essays, entitled "The Experiential Content of Hegel's Philosophy," Adorno sharpens his notice of Hegel's serial performance of dialectical thought. The first passage reads as though it were presenting Hegel at his most philosophical. It begins:

"The dialectic expresses the fact that philosophical knowledge is not at home in the place where tradition has settled it, a place where it flourishes all too easily, unsaturated, as it were, with the heaviness and the resistance of what exists. Philosophical knowledge begins only where it opens up things that traditional thought has considered opaque, impenetrable, and mere products of individuation."[30] Further down, still in the same paragraph, Adorno lets the arrow fly, seeking like Apollo's arrow its hidden and vulnerable hidden target: "no doubt there is a secret positivist impulse at work in Hegel's deification of the quintessence of what is." When saturated with the heaviness and resistance of what is, including existing political regimes, Hegel is, as Adorno says still more emphatically in this essay, "on the side of the big guns."[31]

With another turn, again in this same paragraph, Adorno presents Hegel on the French Revolution as Benjamin's (and Adorno's) man, the one who sees history as dialectics at a standstill: "What most shocks the innocent reader of the *Phenomenology*..., the sudden flashes of illumination that link the highest speculative ideas with the actual political experience of the French Revolution and the age of Napoleon, is what is actually dialectical."[32] Even when Adorno reckons with the deepest untruths of Hegel's thought, among them the claim that the real is rationality,[33] what he finds in Hegel is someone whose deepest experiential truths find him out: "Even when Hegel flies in the face of experience, including the experience that motivates his own philosophy, experience speaks from him."[34]

The last of Adorno's essays on Hegel, "Skoteinos," reads Hegel's style as a writer and lecturer. This essay provides, as it were, the sound and music for the paratactic style that Adorno imagines for philosophy in the essay of that name. The essay begins with a line from the poet Rudolf Borchardt: "Ich habe nichts als Rauschen" ("I have nothing but murmuring"). Adorno's editors note that the verb *rauschen* refers to "the murmuring of a brook, the rustling of the wind in the trees, or the surging of waves on a beach" and, figuratively, to a kind of intoxication.[35] For Adorno it is Hegel's murmuring, his inaudible as well as audible speaking and writing, that specify, in the language of the old philosopher's body, how to do philosophy, but also how to listen or strain to hear philosophy as a way of proceeding, not a specific goal.

As if to reintroduce the labor and physicality into philosophical thought that, he had once argued, Hegel sought to put beyond that thought, Adorno quotes at length from an account of Hegel lecturing his students during his Berlin years:

> Exhausted, morose, he sat there as if collapsed into himself, his head bent down, and while speaking kept turning pages and searching in his long folio notebooks, forward and backward, high and low. His constant clearing of his throat and coughing interrupted any flow of speech. Every sentence stood alone and came out with effort, cut in pieces and jumbled. Every word, every syllable detached itself only reluctantly to receive a strangely thorough emphasis from the metallic-empty voice with its broad Swabian dialect, as if each were the most important. . . . Eloquence that flows along smoothly presupposes that the speaker is finished with the subject inside and out and has it by heart, and formal skill has the ability to glide on garrulously and most graciously in what is half-baked and superficial. This man, however, had to raise up the most powerful thought from the deepest ground of things, and if they were to have a living effect then, although they had been pondered and worked over years before and ever again, they had to regenerate themselves in him in an ever-living present.[36]

For Adorno, the laborious, even clumsy physicality of Hegel's lecturing style appears to convey two related points. First, doing philosophy isn't an out-of-body experience; rather it is the body, precisely because of its hesitations, its stumbling with words, with the process of getting up, finding notes, sitting down, that is the *skandalon* of the philosopher's systematic: the very reality that insures, as Adorno's source puts it, that what

Hegel has to offer will not be half-baked or overbaked. It will be intelligible—capable of being thought about and thought through—if not always clear or easy to hear. Second, it is Hegel's particularity as an individual and a physical body that gives truth to the Hegelian dialectic, not the impulses within Hegel's body of work that work hard to shut the individual up or out, to rid itself of particulars even as it makes those particulars pay and pay for their banishment.

As Adorno's interest in this anecdote makes clear, Hegel's style matters. The "microstructures" of that style sustain Adorno's attention throughout the essay. As he had noted before, he remarks again on the suspended quality of Hegelian thought.[37] He characterizes Hegel's published writing as "antitexts,"[38] both because of their inner spirit of dialectic and because they were not produced as books, but from the collection of students' lecture notes that editors have used, together with Hegel's manuscript notes, principally in the form of sketchy outline, to construct Hegel's "books." That body of published work is for this reason "more like films of thought than texts" because "the untutored eye can never capture the details of a film the way it can those of a still image."[39] Here too Adorno's dialectical rendering of Hegel requires that the seeming admiration of this statement be paid back into the truer, sharper work of seeing Hegel serially, paratactically:

> This [the filmic quality of Hegel's writing] is the locus of the forbidding quality in them, and it is precisely here that Hegel regresses behind his dialectical content. To be consistent, that content would require a presentation antithetical to it. The individual moments would need to be so sharply distinguished linguistically, so responsibly expressed, that the subjective process of thought and its arbitrary quality would drop away from them. If on the contrary the presentation is assimilated without resistance to the structure of the dialectical movement, the price that the speculative concept's critique of traditional logic has to pay to the latter is set too low. Hegel did not deal with this adequately.[40]

To do so on Hegel's (and his own) behalf, Adorno keeps his eye on the cavities, the holes, the moments that don't add up in Hegel's thought and style:

> This man who reflected on all reflection did not reflect on language; he moved about in language with a carelessness that is incompatible with what he said. In presentation his writings attempt a direct resemblance to the substance. Their significative character recedes in favor of a mimetic one, a kind of gestural or curvilinear writing strangely at odds with the solemn

claims of reason that Hegel inherited from Kant and the Enlightenment. Dialects are analogous, like the Swabian with its untranslatable "Ha no," repositories of gestures that literary languages have given up. The romanticism that the mature Hegel treated with contempt, but which was the ferment of his own speculation, may have taken its revenge on him by taking over his language in its folksy tone. Abstractly flowing, Hegel's style, like Hölderlin's abstractions, takes on a musical quality that is absent from the sober style of the romantic Schelling.[41]

Adorno illustrates this tendency with Hegel's use of "but" [*aber*] to signal merely connection without contrast or comparison:

> Now because in the absolute, the form is only simple self-identity, the absolute does not determine itself; for determination is a form of difference which, in the first instance, counts as such. But because at the same time it contains all differences and form-determination whatever, or because it is itself the absolute form and reflection, the difference of the content must appear in it. *But* [emphasis added by Adorno], the absolute itself is absolute identity; this is its determination, for in it all manifoldness of the world-in-itself and the world of Appearance, or of inner and outer totality, is sublated.[42]

From dialectics to dialect to a musical style that evades Hegel's own plans for its schematization, Adorno tries to find a style and figure for what he calls in Hegel, after Walter Benjamin, "dialectics at a standstill," which is, says Adorno, "comparable to the experience the eye has when looking through a microscope at a drop of water that begins to teem with life; except that what that stubborn, spellbinding gaze falls on is not firmly delineated as an object but frayed, as it were, around the edges."[43] That fraying is strangely musical, a series in which reprise and reincorporation lead, as Adorno says they do in the late Beethoven, to a mode of development that is "heard multidimensionally, forward and backward at the same time."[44]

By way of conclusion, I want to move forward and backward between Hegel and Adorno one more time. I do so now to think about how Adorno replies to a famous Hegelian phrase, "Die List der Vernunft," usually translated as the "ruse" or "cunning" of reason in the *Philosophy of History*. My conclusion is itself by way of reprise, since this phrase appears in the section of Hegel's introduction to his *Philosophy of History* which begins with the advice that the world-historical individual crush plants and other unruly individuals, with which I began this essay. The passage is well known. Reinhard Koselleck quotes it to argue that Hegel, among others, tries to exclude contingency even as its role in history becomes difficult to ignore.⁴⁵ Hegel's text reads, in part:

> This may be called the *cunning of reason*—that it sets the passions to work for itself, while that which develops its existence through such impulsion pays the penalty, and suffers loss. For it is *phenomenal* being that is so treated, and of this, part is of no value, part is positive and real. The particular is for the most part of too trifling value as compared with the general: individuals are sacrificed and abandoned. The Idea pays the penalty of determinate existence and of corruptibility, not from itself, but from the passions of individuals.⁴⁶

Cunning indeed: reason's highly creative and lucrative system, in which individuals pay for their own loss, may have prompted Adorno's rhetoric of paying up front or on credit. It is also the likely occasion for Adorno's own rage against Hegel, for the question of redirecting or making something else out of the passions of individuals is a reiterated motif in Adorno's critiques of Hegel. And yet, in a passage that I find shocking in Adorno's "Aspects of Hegel's Philosophy," delivered on the occasion of the 125th anniversary of Hegel's death, Adorno lets Hegelian cunning off the hook: "Hegel introduced the cunning of reason into the philosophy of history in order to provide a plausible demonstration of the way objective reason, the realization of freedom, succeeds by means of the blind, irrational passions of historical individuals" and further, that "This concept [in Hegel] reveals something about the experiential core of Hegel's thought."⁴⁷

How to grasp why Adorno would seem here to admire in Hegel what outraged him at other moments? Adorno goes on to suggest that in overpowering what is blind and irrational in individuals, including, I surmise, particulars in nature, Hegel creates the engine of his dialectic. That engine, Adorno adds, is the one that the "slave" can finally use to overthrow the "master" in the section of Hegel's *Phenomenology of Spirit* that tracks this possibility as the project of Hegelian dialectic, which Adorno here glosses admiringly as "the organized spirit of contradiction."⁴⁸ So, the spirit does to an (apparently) dominant, powerful nature what the dialectic allows the slave to do, eventually, to his master, at least in the realm of absolute, ideal freedom of spirit. Left out of Adorno's account here is the heaviness, the materiality of the condition of being a slave or servant to one's master or lord, the heaviness of being just a particular that is finally of no consequence to the rule of abstraction or spirit that masters all.⁴⁹ Here Adorno's wariness of what he calls in "Skoteinos" the bourgeois tendency to hypotastize the "blinders of the particular, the belief that its contingency ['*Zufälligkeit*'] is its law"[50] suggests something like an affinity for Hegel's brief for concept over against particulars.

When Adorno returns, in his own voice, to the matter of philosophical ruses or cunning in a short piece in *Minima Moralia*, he gestures toward a way of reading, from Hegel forward to late philosophical modernity and after Auschwitz, that is hauntingly about, once again, saving particulars. My argument begins by joining Hegel's phrase "*Die List der Vernunft*" to what I take to be Adorno's elliptical parsing of it in the short piece about two rabbits and a song, quoted in full below:

> As long as I have been able to think, I have derived happiness from the song: "Between the mountain and the deep, deep vale": about the two rabbits who, regaling themselves on the grass, were shot down by the hunter, and, on realizing that they were still alive, made off in haste. But only later did I understand the moral of this: sense [*Vernunft*, that is reason] can only endure in despair and extremity; it needs absurdity, in order not to fall victim to objective madness. One ought to follow the example of the two rabbits; [who] when the shot comes, fall down giddily, half-dead with fright, collect one's wits and then, if one still has breath, show a clean pair of heels. The capacity for fear and for happiness are the same, the unrestricted openness to experience amounting to self-abandonment in which the vanquished discovers himself. What would happiness be that was not measured by the immeasurable grief at what is? For the world is deeply ailing. He who cautiously adapts to it by this very act shares in its madness, while the eccentric alone would stand his ground and bid it rave no more. He alone could pause to think on the illusoriness of disaster, the "unreality of despair," and realize not merely that he is still alive but that there is still life. The ruse of the dazed rabbits ["*Die List der ohnmächtigen Hasen*"] redeems, with them, even the hunter, whose guilt they purloin.[51]

Although the standard English translation, reproduced here, gives "sense" for *Vernunft* as in "good sense" or "smarts," meaning perhaps peasant or rabbit cunning, the whole passage urges both its relation to Hegel's phrase and style and to the kind of reason that Adorno wants to offer as true for Hegel and for the work of philosophy more generally. This reason is akin to the rabbits' willingness to profit from their unexpected survival and to the eccentric's decision to accept the world's madness and grief and then go on living. Both recognize in the contingent, the unexpected an opportunity for swerving, in a kind of eccentric path, away from those ready to take life from the world. The rabbits' ruse or cunning is their eccentric, dazed, yet effective flight, which teaches the lesson reason needs to learn from contingency and, indeed, that reason needs to learn from contingency. For the fact that the rabbits happen to still be alive is an occasion they should and do profit from by running away. In the case of the dialectic as Adorno understands its capacities, one can profit from what is contingent, in nature, in the eventness of the world. Philosophical style should thus be at the ready to recognize in the "turnings intricate" of paratactic style opportunities for dialectical reading and speaking. Indeed, the last sentence of the piece marks Adorno's own swerve back to Hegel's repeated claims that particulars take on projects that save Hegelian spirit at no cost to itself. As Adorno Workshop colleagues have reminded me, after Auschwitz Adorno is the rabbit-particular whose survival redeems the hunter who would have had him dead.

The exchange, if we can call it that, is that Adorno, like those rabbits, steals the hunter's guilt and assumes it, much as particulars in Hegel's scheme for the World Spirit pay the price for their own loss. Adorno's sympathy with those particulars would, then, take him this far, or necessarily this far after Auschwitz, years after Hegel and years after learning the song about those rabbits. Here, in a way that is perhaps more subtle than his rescue of Hegel in "Aspects," Adorno assents to the structure of the work of Hegelian spirit, but understands from inside it how incriminating, how damaging that structure can be to particular beings when, in this case, it lets the hunter off the hook on the grounds that his intention misfired. To be blamed for that misfiring seems to urge too that Adorno blames himself for others that don't survive, in the random luck that distinguishes those who live from those who do not in and after Auschwitz. Adorno's (via the rabbits') assumption of guilt may also register his resistance to "working through the past," a program that he rejects in the essay with that title because it appears to sanction forgetting the Nazi era. Only by incorporating its mechanisms, over again, will its presence remain at issue, at large.[52] In the *Minima Moralia* text, then, Adorno embodies the passional understanding of what it means to be a particular, alive or dead, that takes on the suffering, the loss without recompense, which is the consequence of holding the position given to nature and its contingent particulars in Hegel's dialectic on behalf of the World Spirit. It may be absurd for the rabbits to have escaped with their hides and lives intact, but in that absurdity lies a logic that might at least recognize the cunning of Hegelian reason not as a cost to be borne, but as one to try to outrun, elliptically. Here the elliptical gesture is to side with those rabbits and to understand, in the strata of his own time and philosophy, the cost as well as the unexpected outcome entailed by doing so.

I close this essay with one more vignette, which presents itself as a pendant portrait to Adorno's of the older Hegel at his lectern and suggests the oblique dialectical presence that Adorno engages, by siding with the rabbits and against the Hegelian economy in which nature is mastered and the spirit is triumphant. In the early years when the Frankfurt School existed in exile at the Institute for Social Research at Columbia University, Adorno participated in Tuesday evening seminars at which Max Horkheimer in effect presided. Unlike the lectures delivered as part of the Horkheimer Circle, which were intended to present social and theoretical research to the American students, the Tuesday evening seminars were intended to more directly satisfy the intellectual needs of the members of the research group, which included Adorno, Friedrich Pollock, Herbert Marcuse, Franz L. Neumann, Leo Lowenthal, Henryk Grossman, Otto Kirchheimer, and Arkady Gurland. Nonmembers who attended could comment, but all recognized that the seminars belonged to the Horkheimer Circle. As Daniel Bell recalled these gatherings, they exhibited the structure of paternal authority that Horkheimer insisted on, seated at the center of the table, surrounded by members of the seminar in a fixed seating arrangement, with a fixed order of presentation. Horkheimer never smiled and Pollack sat "in a state of perpetual solemnity." Those who were consigned to speak last had little left that they could say and so were often provocative or wildly speculative, such that they inevitably laid themselves open to their colleagues' scorn. The only exception to the physical entrapment and authoritarian regime of the Tuesday evening seminar table was Adorno, who would move constantly about the room because he was "unable to contain his intellect or excitement," choosing instead to "flit . . . about the room like a hummingbird constantly conversing with people."[53] As I read this vignette, it stages Adorno's willingness to work obliquely across a magisterial discourse and system, even one that Adorno himself found attractive, whether Horkheimer's or Hegel's. In the corporeal, passional manner Adorno uses to cut across systemic imposition lies the negative, because other-directed, impulse of his dialectics.

CHAPTER 7

The Idiom of Crisis: On the Historical Immanence of Language in Adorno
Neil Larsen

I

"The whole is the untrue."[1] This phrase, one of the signatures of Adorno's most unmistakable work, *Minima Moralia*, points to an irony that perhaps not even its author could have discerned. Notwithstanding the truth of its bitter rebuke to the Hegelian dialectic as apology for capitalist modernity, as a philosophical dictum in its own right it would itself have to be judged false, fatal to any aspiration to dialectical thought. To that much, of course, Adorno himself also testifies, both in practice—for neither *Minima Moralia* nor any other of his works reflect any doubt that critical theory, as part of its own conceptual movement, must strive for the totalization of its object—but also in theory: one need look no further than to *Minima Moralia* itself than to have this confirmed: "Dialectical thought opposes reification in the ... sense that it refuses to affirm individual things in their isolation and separateness: it designates isolation as precisely a product of the universal."[2] A refusal to isolate means a commitment to totalize, albeit a non-Hegelian one. The alternative would be to succumb to the reified consciousness of the object in its sheer immediacy. The "whole" may be the "untrue," but that does not make the part the truth. *Both* become false, at least from the immediate standpoint of "wrong life" reflected, consciously and without apology, by *Minima Moralia*.

The less conscious, perhaps inadvertent, irony in these words, however, is how true they become in relation to Adorno's own formal mode of self-presentation—that is, as a reflection on the relationship of his thinking to the language and style in which it is conveyed. With only a few exceptions, this is a language that, outwardly at least, resists its own mediation by any *formal* standard of systematicity or argumentative blueprint. Any reader of Adorno, from the newcomer to the initiate and academic exegete, experiences this, for example, in the great difficulty one has in summarizing—and also at times in retaining—his arguments. As I can confirm from my own experience in teaching Adorno's works and assigning my students to produce such summaries, this can seem to be a virtually impossible task. The end result is often little more than a list of citations, almost always a sampling of Adorno's aphoristic and dialectically tensed sentences. Consider for example—taking Horkheimer's coauthorship as moot in this regard—the chapter on the Culture Industry in *Dialectic of Enlightenment*. How is one to outline or condense the logic of its argument as a whole? One can attempt a gloss, or look up one of the reasonably good ones already published, but sooner or later, if the text itself is followed closely, the conclusion seems inevitable that this logic, though everywhere in force, does not so much develop by stages as it reiterates itself continuously and in shifting empirical and polemical contexts. From its opening statement—"Culture today is infecting everything with sameness. Film, radio and magazines form a system"[3]—the "whole" is, in essence, already expounded, and, although someone not immediately persuaded by it might in the end succumb to the sheer thrust—almost a kind of fury—of its will to truth and to its sociological sweep, nothing in *Dialectic of Enlightenment* that follows can be said to take on the burden of *proving* it, or any other in the series of emphatic, unrelentingly indicative-mood sentences that follow it and that, in effect, make up the entire text of chapter and work themselves. Here, as, to one degree or another throughout Adorno's corpus, the "untruth" of the "whole" can only be eluded through constant exertions to wrestle the latter into virtually every lexical predication. That Adorno's thinking at any given point in its development and formal presentation forms a coherent, exquisitely reflective, and mediated whole, supple and adaptive, is in no way contradicted by this. But the movement of thought through language is at the same time an inward, condensing movement of language within itself, a movement toward what is, for the logical organization of Adornean critical prose, a fusion of dialectics and *style* at the level of such language's smallest moving part: the sentence or short, aphoristic sequence of sentences. So, for instance, a sentence taken almost at random: "There is laughter because there is nothing to laugh about."[4] Or another: "What is offered [in photographic images] is not Italy but evidence that it exists."[5] Or again: "The consumer becomes the ideology of the amusement industry, whose institutions he or she cannot escape."[6] The last of these sentences, somewhat more theoretically explicit, is probably a better choice than the former for the would-be précis of "The Culture Industry," but the essay's claim to truth, and its corresponding power of conviction, seems to weigh equally in each of them. All such sentences or *dicta* appear to elaborate, in an iterative or serial structure, on a logic that is virtually identical and whole in each of them.

No one, of course, was more aware of this than Adorno himself, and one can find reflections on this form of presentation throughout his writings.[7] But nowhere is the latter more poignantly evoked than in one of the centerpieces of *Notes to Literature*, "The Essay as Form."[8] What Adorno observes there—essayistically—of the essay—e.g., that it "allows for the consciousness of nonidentity, without expressing it directly"; that it "is radical in its non-radicalism, in refraining from any reduction to principle, in its accentuation of the partial against the total, in its fragmentary character"[9]—not only provides the elements for a general theory of the essay-form but is as good an account as any of what Adorno's readers should, ideally, experience if form remains true to its intention.

But such reflections on what amounts to Adorno's fundamental formal principle, the node at which style and theoretical aim merge in what we might refer to schematically here as Adorno's *dialectical minimalism*, are not the end of the story. Even if Adorno is right about the cognitive and critical powers of the "methodically unmethodical"[10]—and, as could be argued, his dialectical minimalism has succeeded, probably beyond Adorno's wildest dreams, in generalizing itself as a kind of (ironically) popular-cultural voice of critical-theoretical authenticity, a voice that no one striving for such authenticity, including the author of these lines, can resist trying to imitate—there remain the questions both of the deeper, historico-genetic origin of such language and of what might be its own ideological limitation, its own possible moment of "untruth." At the very least we are faced with a theoretical and formal paradox staring back at us from virtually every page of Adorno's work as a critical theorist: *namely, why has the "whole" become the "untrue" for the formal, expressive tendency of a thinking that, in relation to any given object, knows—and ultimately reflects this knowledge in its own content and movement—just the opposite?* This is the question I want to discuss, however speculatively, in these pages.

II

One way to attempt to illuminate this paradox is to consider how Adorno's dialectical minimalism compares to the inevitable model for all modern, critical-dialectical prose, namely the language of Marx, and above all that of *Capital*. Even if, philosophically and, in a sense, philologically speaking, the most visible debt of the Adornean dialectic is to Hegel, Adorno's rethinking of the *form* of critical theory in relation to totality and system is unquestionably mediated by Adorno's own positive theoretical relationship to Marx, however problematic this relationship and however reluctant he seems to have been to address it explicitly. Consider, in this light, one of Marx's most distinctive and enigmatically dialectical *mots* from the concluding, fourth section (on the "fetishism of commodities") of the first chapter of *Capital* I: "Value, therefore, does not have its description branded on its forehead. It rather transforms every product of labor into a social hieroglyphic."[11] This two-sentence sequence contains the dialectical chiasmus or inversion typical of Marx as a dialectical stylist: the objective, reified surface of the capitalist social formation *appears* as something self-evident, as transparent. The value-form is socially tacit, its own logic apparently already given in universal social practice. But it is just this apparent self-evidence, this objective transparency, that *conceals* the essence, the fundamental synthetic principle of capitalist society. The value-form is a fetish-form, not because it is mysterious (a "hieroglyphic") per se, but because it is an objective social nexus that itself turns its products into fetishes and its own social "bearers" into fetish-worshippers. The truth of the value-form is *hidden* in its own transparent self-evidence, both practically and theoretically. To decipher value one first must understand how value converts the social totality itself into a cipher.

Adorno, more than most Marxists of his day—and thanks, clearly, to being as much the student of Hegel as was Marx himself—knew how to read *Capital*, and, down to the sentence level, could reproduce the same dialectical, logicostylistic movement evident there, often in the same inverted or chiasmic form. Thus the Culture Industry, as theorized in *Dialectic of Enlightenment*, does not dominate its consumers by hectoring or lulling them into subservience. It does this precisely by making them *free* to consume its products, that is, by virtue of already having taken on a social objectivity existing "behind the backs" of consumers who, say, even when switching off the television, continue to reproduce the essence of its "message" in their own heads. The Culture Industry, like value, represents the outward, objective form of what the subjects of the dominant, reifying social relation already *are* qua subjects.

But the *position* of Marx's "social hieroglyphic" dictum within the whole that is *Capital* is in no way arbitrary. Marx could not have opened the chapter on the commodity with it because the truth that it condenses, here in a quasi-aphoristic style, about the object of Marx's critique—the value-form—must already have been shown by means of the rigorously theoretical argument that precedes the concluding, fourth section of the chapter on the commodity. The seemingly objective transparency of value has already been *proven* by Marx to disclose, within its own *immanent* terms, its mysterious, fetishized essence. That the value-relation self-evidently *exists* and just as self-evidently rests on an equation of qualitatively different kinds of labor and use-values serves as the unshakeable *premise* here from which it follows that value must appear as a paradoxically "social substance" residing in commodities as their seemingly material, thing-like property. And *that result*, judged by the *same* standard of objective self-evidence furnished by the value-relation itself, must be deemed false. The classical political-economic theory of Smith and Ricardo succumbs to the commodity-fetish, convicting itself, ultimately, on its own, immanent terms. The incomparable critical force of Marx's chiasmic dictum on the value-form and of his mode of presentation generally in *Capital* rests on this proof, and the remainder of *Capital* proceeds to extrapolate from it and to build a theoretical system on its rigorous foundation.

Not so the dialectical sentences of "The Culture Industry." In Adorno's defense, it must doubtless be acknowledged that his own thinking also, even if only implicitly, strives consistently to follow through on this theoretically rigorous point of departure, or at least to keep its radical truth constantly in view. Moreover, insofar as the objects of Adornean critique are cultural or ideological in form, the standards of proof themselves become considerably more difficult to meet, far more complexly mediated. But that should not, in principle, have prevented Adorno—much less prevent his contemporary readers and students—from attempting to hold critical theory and immanent critique to this same, rigorous standard. The abjuring of systems and "false" wholes, whether in the name of the "individual" or the "non-identical," may begin to look like little more than theoretical abdications in light of the systematic, logical standard set by *Capital*. Yet, already in *Dialectic of Enlightenment*, Adorno appears to require of his readers that they somehow learn to overcome the expectation that the logical articulations and truth-claims of immanent critique *could* meet such standards of proof. Ironically, given what is on one level its uncompromising philosophical tenor, nothing in Adorno's thinking is proven—unless, that is, one is willing or able to share Adorno's evident suspicions that anything not already reified and turned into a piece of "positive" knowledge *could* be proven, or that proof could count any longer as anything more than the perpetual, emphatic disclosure of the object's sheer negativity. The movement of what *would* count as proof for Adorno, if one were (or perhaps when one is) possible, appears to coil itself within the dialectical springs of style and language themselves, in the intuitive hope, if not faith, that the critically theorized object in its own worldly course will shine through the words themselves when the moment is right. But in the meantime, a possible moment of self-apology has to be acknowledged in Adorno: for surely it is not the essay, as Adorno (self-referentially) describes it in "The Essay as Form," that constitutes the "critical form par excellence."[12] The form of *Capital*—a form regarding which one might indeed speculate (to what *genre* does *Capital* belong?) but that is certainly not that of the essay—sets this standard, and sets aside and humbles any claims lodged on behalf of a "methodically unmethodical" flux of quasi-Nietzschean aphorisms, however dialectically charged and true such sentences may be, in their particularity, to their Marxian point of origin.

Marx, it will be useful to recall, reflects on the methodological question of the whole in a widely read section of the introduction to the *Grundrisse* subtitled "The Method of Political Economy."[13] There he acknowledges the seemingly more obvious method of "beginning with the real and concrete"—in economics, population—and then moving "analytically towards ever more simple concepts (e.g., class, exchange, division of labor) from the imagined concrete towards ever thinner abstractions until [arriving] at the simplest determinations."[14] This method he contrasts to the inverse, less spontaneous one of beginning with such simple determinations—with abstract concepts—and ascending from these back to the level of the concrete whole: "Along the first path the full conception was evaporated to yield an abstract determination; along the second the abstract determination leads towards a reproduction of the concrete by way of thought."[15] The latter is, according to Marx, "obviously the scientifically correct method" (ibid.). Although one should stipulate here that, on this plane of generality, the "scientifically correct method" is still that of the classical political-economic systems (Smith and Ricardo primarily) that Marx takes as his own immanent object of critique, it is clear that, formally, *Capital* too adheres to this method by starting with the commodity, or value-form, and deriving from it the structured sequence of theoretical categories (e.g., exchange, money, capital, surplus-value) that leads, theoretically, to the "concrete totality" that is the capitalist mode of production itself. Marx diverges—*critically*—from classical political economy by insisting on the historical, specifically bourgeois origin of the conceptual abstractions themselves.[16] While retaining their abstraction, however, their systematic interrelation or structure in the methodological context of *Capital* is *itself* made possible by a historically evolved whole—a concrete totality—whose own structure and "laws of motion" *Capital*'s theoretical structure, in a sense, now comes to embody directly, i.e., to which it now becomes *immanent*. The simple determinations or conceptual abstractions *work* as abstractions without succumbing, as they do in classical political-economy, to their own reified, naturalized form because they have become, in *Capital*, historically grounded *moments* of a totality that is *not* abstract. Thus the proof that value, in its social form of appearance, conceals the social whole that generates it is, on one level, a (theoretically) straightforward matter of showing that this whole is historical, that it has not always been and will, necessarily, become other than what it is. *Capital*'s "mode of presentation" (its *Darstellungsweise*, in the terms of Marx's postface to the second edition of *Capital* I) does not coincide with its "mode of investigation" (*Forschungsweise*) because only the former can reflect the immanent motion of the historical whole and set forth the theoretical system within which a rigorous proof of this historicity—a proof that does not revert to the reified, tautological form of classical political economy—is possible.[17]

Considered from precisely this vantage point, Adorno's dialectical minimalism, his idiosyncratically dialectical dissidence in relation to the logic of the system and to rigorous theoretical method, at least on the level of his own *Darstellungsweise*, betrays neither a reversion to the naïve empiricism governed by the "chaotic concrete" nor a Hegelian-idealist equation of the whole with the concept itself. It bespeaks rather an *adherence* to the method of *Capital* in which, paradoxically, what should be the concrete, historical whole has itself undergone a kind of collapse back into abstraction. It is as if the "concrete totality" immanent to and thus mediating the theoretical abstraction and systematicity of *Capital* had inexplicably lost its historical source of motion and come to a halt. Concepts, in Adorno, retain their dialectical, nonreified form—thus evading their "bad" abstraction in, say, the theoretical poverties of positivism—but seem to resist their own methodological deployment on the level of a theoretical system. This is because the only concrete totality that could possibly ground a "totality in thought" already appears, to Adorno, to have falsified its own historical concept. Method itself, without ceasing to be sensed as necessary, grinds to a stop. There is no mediated, logical way to arrive at a whole that no longer, as in *Capital*, situates itself in thought as both the premise and the *result* of theoretical reasoning, because this whole now confronts theory as a "bad" abstraction, as a given, as soon as its concept is invoked.

Thus the "whole," in this case, turns out to be "untrue" in still another sense—as the historical totality that, recalling but simultaneously annulling its own methodological basis in *Capital*, mediates the conceptual abstractions of theory and method, only here with the apparent risk of *stripping* them of their truth. Mediation seems to turn back on itself, resulting in the paradoxical need for a dialectical *immediacy*. Faced, that is, with such a monolithically "false" whole it follows that only a dialectic that never for a moment turned its back on it, that denounced it and its absolute positivity incessantly—a dialectic that had bound itself, like Odysseus before the Sirens, to its own immediate surface as form—could hope to survive.

III

Yet even if the thought positing it could somehow manage to preserve its own dialectical consistency and configuration, the problem here is that such a whole would not *itself* be dialectical and would work just as incessantly to annul the dialectical movement of its own immanent, critical reflection. This is, in effect, the argument advanced by Moishe Postone in *Time, Labor, and Social Domination* against Horkheimer's "critical pessimism," but it would appear to apply with equal force to Adorno.[18] Observing the key influence of Friedrich Pollock's theory of state capitalism on Horkheimer's thinking, Postone notes a "theoretical turn taken [by the Frankfurt School] in the 1930s, wherein postliberal capitalism came to be conceived as a completely administered, integrated, one-dimensional society, one that no longer gives rise to any immanent possibility of social emancipation."[19] This is a charge often made by "orthodox" Marxists and "revolutionary" theory generally against Critical Theory, and against Adorno in particular—one recalls Lukács' famous quip about Adorno's having taken up residence in the "Grand Hotel Abyss"—but what lends particular force to Postone's argument is its careful demonstration that Horkheimer's was not merely a conjunctural but a "necessary pessimism" concerning the "immanent *possibility* that capitalism could be superseded."[20] This paradoxically *immanent* historical necessity, ascribed by Horkheimer to stagnation and paralysis rather than to internal crisis and social transformation is clearly a model for the paradoxically 'orthodox' but paralyzing adaptation of the dialectical methodology of *Capital* evident in Adorno's thinking. Postone, that is, attributes such "critical pessimism" not to a deviation (as per Critical Theory's "revolutionary" detractors) but precisely to an unquestioned, uncritical *adherence* to "traditional Marxism" and especially to the latter's identification of the revolutionary, critical standpoint with that of the proletariat, or "labor."

Postone's general critique of this standpoint is too far-reaching to summarize adequately here, but its gist is that labor in its historically specific, dual abstract/concrete form in capitalism, no less than the commodity- or value-form in which it is objectified, is a 'real abstraction' immanent to the relations of capitalist society. As such a 'real abstraction,' labor itself, and not merely the market or exchange social nexus, is the objective form of social mediation that actively constitutes these social relations.[21] The counter-posing of labor to capitalism as if the former represented a positive, spontaneous and necessary pathway to social emancipation is inconsistent, according to Postone, with a theoretical discovery already formulated in *Capital* and the *Grundrisse*: that the abstracting of 'labor' from the general form of purposive social activity already conforms to the logic, specific to capitalism, that counts as socially valid only activity that takes on commodity form. Take away the commodity- or value-abstraction, however, and the logic of isolating 'labor' as a correspondingly abstract form of social mediation from concrete social praxis and reproduction falls with it.

Making "labor" the revolutionary subject thus, according to Postone, only reproduces the Ricardian standpoint that directly counterposes the relations of production to those of distribution, effectively reasoning as though value in its subjective active form as labor could somehow negate itself merely by abolishing its own form as a given object or product capable of being appropriated and distributed. Thus the danger clearly arises that, in the wake of a conjunctural, political defeat of the proletariat as the representative of "labor," a "pessimistic" theory might interpret this crisis as merely the eclipse of the subjective factor, leaving the objective side of "labor"—value—and the neo-Ricardian distortion of *Capital* firmly in place. This is the apocalyptic, "negative" reaffirmation of "traditional Marxism" that Postone attributes to Horkheimer:

> We have seen that Horkheimer's theory of knowledge had been based upon the assumption that social constitution is a function of "labor," which in capitalism is fragmented and hindered from fully unfolding by the relations of production. He now begins to consider the contradictions of capitalism to have been no more than the motor of a repressive development, which

he expresses categorically with his statement that "the self-movement of the concept of the commodity leads to the concept of state capitalism just as for Hegel the certainty of sense data leads to absolute knowledge." Horkheimer has thus come to the conclusion that a Hegelian dialectic, in which the contradictions of the categories lead to the self-unfolded realization of the Subject as totality (rather than to the abolition of the totality), could only result in the affirmation of the existing order. Yet he does not formulate his position in a way that would go beyond the limits of that order, for example, in terms of Marx's critique of Hegel and of Ricardo. Instead, Horkheimer reverses his earlier position: "labor" and the totality, which earlier had been the standpoint of critique, now become the grounds of oppression and unfreedom.[22]

Adorno was, to be sure, a more subtle and consistently radical thinker than Horkheimer, as apt to question the latter's increasingly liberal positions on late capitalism as he was to share Horkheimer's generally pessimistic view of the possibility of social emancipation. But the underlying connection between such pessimism and Horkheimer's continued, ironic adherence to a traditional Marxist privileging of 'labor' as disclosed by Postone has the potential to explain certain basic problems in Adorno's thought as well. That an inverted, pessimistic, but still implicitly labor-centered Marxism likewise suffuses and delimits the theoretical content of *Dialectic of Enlightenment* has, in fact, been argued recently and in detail by the German critical theorist Norbert Trenkle.[23] While acknowledging the path-breaking contribution of Horkheimer and Adorno to a radical critique of Enlightenment, Trenkle—along with Robert Kurz, Ernst Lohoff, and Roswitha Scholz one of the leading representatives of the critical school known as *Wertkritik* in German-speaking, left-wing circles—finds in the text of *Dialectic of Enlightenment* itself "the document of a critique always partially recanted out of fear of itself. Its argumentative movement is at least in part one that does not base itself in the dialectic of the thing itself but that is derived in opposition to it."[24] This "dialectic of the thing itself," Trenkle argues, resides in "a historically specific social relation, fully constituted by commodity and value-form."[25] Although Adorno and Horkheimer clearly grasp and allow for this inner, dialectical connection of Enlightenment to value-form (to that extent showing their unmistakable debt, shared by virtually all Frankfurt School Critical Theory, to Lukács' *History and Class Consciousness*), they reduce it in turn to a far more generalized, abstract, and anthropologized "abortive separation from Nature" ["*misslungene Ablösung von der Natur*"][26] lying, apparently, at the threshold of primordial societalization. But by the very fact of this "reverse-projection" ["*Rückprojektion*"][27] of the value-abstraction—an abstraction from *all* qualitative content, issuing in what for Kant becomes the pure, ahistorical formalism of Reason itself—back to the origins, so to speak, of "species-being," *Dialectic of Enlightenment* reproduces the ideology of bourgeois Enlightenment itself, as the standpoint that (like the classical political-economic systems critiqued in *Capital*) regards all previous history as merely the incomplete working-out of itself, i.e., of the value-abstraction and its rationalist, philosophical sublimation. What distinguishes the teleology underlying *Dialectic of Enlightenment* from its bourgeois Enlightenment variant is not, finally, any substantive critical-theoretical break but the former's "turn to resignation" ("*resignative Wendung*"):

> What is described is no longer the glorious triumphal march of progress but the gloomy tread of fatality. Liberation from domination is never more than a flickering possibility, rendered groundless and no longer, in any case, the end-point of history. As correct and important as the critique of the idea of progress clearly is [in *Dialectic of Enlightenment*], it remains caught up in the latter's idea itself. Insofar as it merely rejects the optimism of the idea of progress (the supposed necessity of liberation), it reproduces the historico-philosophical construct that forms its basis.[28]

Trenkle traces the same "negative" Enlightenment-teleology, the same tendency to recoil from the full, *historical* implications of a crisis of capitalist modernity only imperfectly glimpsed, to Adorno's later works as well, specifically to *Negative Dialectics*.[29] Here he criticizes Adorno's attempt to "rescue" Kantian ethics as well as his ambiguous stance vis-á-vis the exchange abstraction: an abstraction accurately grasped (following Alfred Sohn-Rethel) as the underlying, social-form basis of "identity thinking" but simultaneously and paradoxically projected as the possibility of a utopianized, purportedly reciprocal and noncapitalist form, freed from the fetters of surplus-value extraction, as if a kind of Kantian "ethics" of exchange could point beyond its own social and historical determination.

But Trenkle's fundamental critical insight here—that Adorno initiates a fundamental break with a "traditional Marxist" reduction of critical standpoint to class standpoint only at the cost of a dehistoricizing, abstract-universalization of this break itself—could, I think, be developed still further and help to unravel the more troubling aspects of Adorno's aesthetics. This is the subject for a study of its own, exceeding the immediate limits of this essay. But its argument would run as follows: Adornean aesthetic theory can be considered to rest on a paradoxically dual conception of formal abstraction as a negative principle both 1) qua mimesis: i.e., formal abstraction as the true, negative rendering of the "positive" reifications of late capitalism; and 2) qua emancipation: i.e., the modern, abstract work of art as itself the only remaining historical line of flight or negative standpoint from which to oppose or resist said reification. Following Trenkle, and *Wertkritik*, one might see in this duality yet another working out of the logic of "fractured negativity" ("*gebrochene Negativität*"): *that* artistic form is inexorably driven to comprehend the equally inexorable tendency of the value-abstraction to negate, even to the point of self-annihilation, all social content, aesthetic included, ultimately follows from the historical specificity of capitalist crisis itself. But *that* such a *mimetic* negativity should double as a kind of social transcendental, that the aesthetic should, in some mysterious way, step in to redeem a lost social negativity, removes us once again to a plane of abstraction outside the historical specificity of the crisis of value-form. The abstract work of art suddenly takes up a position with respect to the value-abstraction essentially congruent with that of 'labor' in traditional Marxism: such a work becomes the "subjective" negation of an object that, as part of this same, pseudodialectical movement, expels from its own theoretical consciousness any and all principles of *immanent* negativity or contradiction. That 'labor' falls away and the abstract work of art steps in to take its place thereby furnishes the 'real abstraction' of value with a kind of historical alibi in the face of its real, and terminal, historical crisis.

IV

But if, theoretically—that is, on the level of *system*—Adorno fails to integrate into his thinking the real, concrete specificity and scope of capital's historical crisis as a crisis of the value-form itself, it could, I think, be argued that he anticipates the virtual implications of such a crisis when his thinking takes as its objects the cultural, aesthetic, and ethical particularities of his own historical moment. Might it not be that when Adorno looks back at the "false" whole through its parts—when it is conceptually and formally the parts that mediate the whole—the tendency to historical abstraction in his thinking begins to be reversed? At least, might this not be so when the "parts," as they almost invariably do, take on the form of immediacy of culture, the ethical and, especially, the aesthetic itself? Such might be a hypothetical conclusion to the above, sketched here only in rough outline.

This is a possibility intriguingly suggested by, among other things, the fact that Adorno's least explicitly systematic work, the one that most closely adheres to the Benjaminian organizing principle of constellation—*Minima Moralia*—is also in many ways his most richly historicized. The inward, self-condensing movement of Adorno's thought-form, at its apogee in *Minima Moralia* but detectable everywhere in his opus, would thus be provisionally explained by the fact that, when experienced through and at the level of its cultural particularities and immediacies, the fully historical truth of late-capitalist crisis, its reality as an absolute internal limit, no longer appears strictly as something that must (but cannot) be proven theoretically and must therefore be projected back into falsely primordialized "abortive separation from nature." On the level of culture and "wrong life" it is the objective immediacies of crisis—however under-theorized the latter category was to remain in Adorno's thinking— that, so to speak, have already taken upon themselves the "burden of proof," and the task of the critic then limits itself to assessing such truth-claims on their own, immanent terms. Adorno's "minimalist" and stylized dialectic might then be understood as the form that, because it imitates the accidental, fragmentary form of its objects, permits him to render the historical truth of crisis to which such objects point without needing to have already worked out its theoretical critique—in advance, so to speak, of having formulated its concept. The movement toward totality, toward dialectical mediation and synthesis, a movement that takes place for Adorno *within* sentences as much or more than it does between them, could be seen, in this sense, as a direct way of giving provisionally conceptual shape to the historical mediation of aesthetic, cultural, and ethical immediacies that do not yet, for him, add up to a historical whole. Such sentences might thus be said to constitute an *idiom* of crisis in lieu but also in anticipation of the rigorously theoretical formulation of what would be the latter's theoretical concept.

But what, then, might explain in turn the anticipatory, *idiomatic* reflection of a terminal crisis of capital that perhaps only now, in the wake of the demise of Fordism and of the advent of capital's "third" (microelectronic) industrial revolution, becomes a possible object of theorization? From the critical standpoint worked out by contemporary critical theorists such as Postone and Trenkle—from the standpoint of the historical unity-in-crisis of capital *and* labor[30]—the answer I propose here points us again to the ironic fact that, in the "minimalist" Adorno, it is, above all, the aesthetic object, not the political or economic (or philosophical) one, through and in relation to which his thinking seems to take on its richest, most concrete historical mediacy. Adorno would thus be understood as equipped, in essence, to think the crisis of capital immanently through the form of the aesthetic even while failing, in the end, to do so in the direct, systematic categories of philosophy and theory *tout court*. But this, surely, would reflect equally what is, for Adorno, the still fundamentally intuitive understanding of the aesthetic as what is directly negated, not merely by the "false" whole of the Culture Industry or by bourgeois "Enlightenment," *but by the value-abstraction itself. The social logic of the value-relation, of the "real," fetishized abstraction of the commodity form, is, inexorably, to annihilate all aesthetic content and experience.* (The same, perhaps, might be said as well of the negativity of ethical content in relation to the value-abstraction—such at least would appear to be an unspoken but absolute premise of *Minima Moralia*.) The more explicitly philosophical categories of Adorno's thinking—such as "negative dialectics"—remain far more ambiguous and historically impoverished in this sense, erecting themselves in a negative relation not to the value-abstraction itself but to categories—such as "Enlightenment" or "identity"—that eventually, because of their own "bad" abstraction, find their way back, as Trenkle has observed, into Adorno's philosophical standpoint itself. One should be careful to add here that the more explicitly philosophical arguments of Adorno's aesthetic theory, above all that artistic abstraction (e.g., "serious music" in the essay on jazz) somehow manages to exempt itself from the reifying, essentially nihilistic logic of the value-abstraction, suffer the same historical impoverishment. But when engaged by and situated within the mediate space of aesthetic, cultural, and ethical objects *in their particularity*, Adorno guides himself unerringly by the historical truth that these objects themselves also, unconsciously, sense: that the terminal crisis of the society governed by abstract labor and the logic of self-valorizing value, *and the historical possibility of its negation*, are all that now warrant their existence.

CHAPTER 8

Aesthetic Theory and Nonpropositional Truth Content in Adorno

Gerhard Richter

Readers of Theodor W. Adorno's texts, especially those devoted to philosophical aesthetics, can hardly fail to be struck by their chiastic structure. The aesthetic theory that Adorno develops constitutes not only a theory of the aesthetic but also a theory that is itself aesthetic, hence a theory of literature that exhibits qualities associated with literary texts, and a theory of music that harbors within itself traces of musical composition. The rhetorically self-conscious tropes of his posthumous *Aesthetic Theory*, the stylized literary studies of his *Notes to Literature*, his musically inflected meditations on musicological questions from Beethoven to Arnold Schönberg, and so many of his other texts perform this provocative inversion in a variety of registers and conceptual modulations. In *Aesthetic Theory*, for instance, Adorno insists that the aesthetic dimension of philosophy and the philosophical dimension of art are not merely dimensions among so many others: "Aesthetics is not applied philosophy but philosophical in itself."[1] What does it mean for an aesthetic theory itself to become aesthetic, for a literary theory itself to become literary, aside from the conceptual conflation of two otherwise independent spheres? This question is encrypted, in a different context, in Martin Heidegger's intuition, expressed with regard to Friedrich Hölderlin's hymns, that "thinking is almost like a poeticizing along [*das Denken ist fast wie ein Mitdichten*]."[2] Yet given the inherent epistemological difficulties, would such a self-conscious intervention not blatantly violate the requirement that theoretical thinking and writing—expected to be sober, vigilant, and rigorous—remain unaffected by the rhythms and rhetorical movements of its object, along the lines of a public sign displayed in Vienna opera houses around the turn of the twentieth century declaring: "*Mitsingen verboten!*" (No singing along)?[3] Well aware of this problem, Adorno records, in his fragments on Beethoven, the cautious but resolute reminder from his friend Max Horkheimer that "philosophy should not be a symphony."[4] How can an aesthetic theory that thematizes, among other things, the dialectic of Enlightenment and the remote, yet thinkable, possibility of transgressing the requirements of the irrational and misguided mimetic structures that dominate a remainderlessly administered world, justify the instrumentalization of the very structures that are the object of its critique to achieve this transgression without itself succumbing to those structures?

Contrary to the suggestion of some of his readers, the mature Adorno's interest in what he called a *Verfransung*, or interpenetration of philosophy with modernist strategies of art, literature, and music characterized by a gradual dissolution of the generic and material boundaries that have been staples of Western avant-gardes at least since surrealism, cannot fully explain this chiastic structure.[5] After all, the self-conscious conceptual density and aberrant figural rigor of his language inform even minute details of individual sentences, such as when Adorno's diction, grammar, and syntax enact principles theorized in his meditations on what is German and on the philosophical significance of punctuation marks. The crystalline sentence fragments, apodictic metaphors, and the notoriously deferred reflexive pronoun *sich* are only some of the best-known examples of this singular and idiosyncratic discourse.

To be sure, Adorno's experimental co-articulation of the philosophical and the artistic, of logic and rhetoric, is not unfamiliar to modernity's intellectual trajectory. Readers may think, for instance, of Friedrich Schlegel's and Novalis's poetic investment of the philosophical fragment in Jena Romanticism, Friedrich Nietzsche's aphoristically lyrical philosophy in such works as *Human, All Too Human* or, more recently, Claude Lévi-Strauss's unconventional structuring of his main scholarly work to accord with the principles of musical form, and Jacques Derrida's self-conscious use, in *Glas*, of interactive and competing columns of side-by-side text, one for literary readers, the other for philosophers. Each of these chiastic experiments of thought and form—of thought in and as form, and of form in and as thought—has provoked resistance from readers who, reenacting the primal scene in Plato's *Republic* when poetry is banished, are disturbed by such border transgressions. But in the case of Adorno, for reasons that have yet to be reconstructed, this readerly unease assumes special urgency. It is, after all, no secret in Adorno studies that the self-consciously aesthetic quality of his aesthetic philosophy has always troubled some of his readers—among them some of his most perspicacious explicators. The philosopher Rüdiger Bubner, a kind of unofficial representative of these perturbed readers, complains that in Adorno's work "all these complications would be avoidable if philosophy finally parted with the dream of being itself and yet something else." Demanding precisely the kind of philosophical self-identity that Adorno's project sought to dismantle, Bubner warns that aestheticizing theory places a theory of the aesthetic in danger of becoming "entangled in a semblance which is not the one of which it speaks" and that it would be well advised finally to disown "the attempt to allow theory to become aesthetic" that only can end badly, that is, "with the confusion of a semblance of theory with a work of art."[6] There is little use in constructing such readers as straw men for the cheap thrill of substituting a putatively erroneous reading with an ostensibly correct one, especially when the knotty relationship between the philosophical and the aesthetic in Adorno remains far from resolved. Yet from a broader perspective it is nonetheless instructive to consider not only why Adorno's aesthetic project upsets even those readers whose erudition and analytical depth are beyond reproach, but also to consider to what end Adorno writes the way he does.

I wish to suggest here that the chiastic structure of Adorno's aesthetic theory must not be thought in isolation from his conviction that "art stands in need of philosophy that interprets it in order to say that which it cannot say, whereas art only is able to say what it says by not saying it."[7] Adorno here puts his finger on the predicament at the core of the relation between speculative commentary and aesthetic production. On the one hand, art—at least the high modernist variety of Schönberg, Alban Berg, and Samuel Beckett that Adorno so often championed—requires philosophical discourse to bring to the fore as a graspable, cognitive, and propositional structure the *Wahrheitsgehalt*, or the speculative truth content, that, in the absence of critical commentary and elucidation, lies latent. On the other hand, the very thing that philosophy claims the artwork says, that on behalf of which philosophy acts as a kind of conceptual translator, can be said by the artwork only when it remains silent about it. If the artwork actually said what it says in a transparent cognitive proposition, shorn of the mediations and aberrations of its imaginative flourishes and its singular expression of beauty and form, then it would cease to be an artwork. It would simply be a philosophical treatise on a conceptual content that now no longer could claim membership in the domain of art. Yet if the artwork can be itself only by not saying what philosophy claims it says, if the cognitive propositional content on which philosophy focuses cannot be verified in the articulations and inscriptions of the artwork itself—lest it abdicate its status as a work of art—then how can one clarify and verify philosophy's claims about the content and meaning of artworks? And, by extension, why does art continue to stand in need of philosophy's translational services? These questions are inflected by Adorno's far-reaching insistence on what he calls his "model," that is, the supposition "that artworks unfold in their philosophical interpretation."[8]

Adorno's conception of the vexed but necessary relation between philosophical commentary and the work of art is brought into further relief when we relate it to a specific rhetorical figure: allegory. As the literary critic J. Hillis Miller reminds us, allegory "means to say it otherwise in the marketplace, in public, as an exoteric expression of an esoteric wisdom. As in the case of parable, for example the parables of Jesus in the Gospels, this is a way of revealing it and not revealing it. If you have the key to the allegory, then the esoteric wisdom has been expressed (otherwise), but then you would not have needed to have said it otherwise." And he continues: "If you do not have the key, then the allegory remains opaque. You are likely to take it literally, to think it means just what it says. If you understand it you do not need it. If you do not understand it you never will do so from anything on the surface. A paradox of unreadability is therefore built into the concept of allegory from the beginning."[9] If allegory resides in the space of an unreadability predicated upon both its resistant opaqueness and the straightforward transparency that would make it superfluous, then the relays that Adorno forges between philosophical commentaries on artworks and the artworks themselves behave in a similar fashion.[10] If the meaning of an artwork remained sealed off from all logical comprehension, then no philosophy could ever truly speak to this meaning. But if the meaning of an artwork revealed itself readily, then no artwork would be needed—since its "content" could have been stated more easily in prosaic, discursive language that would require no philosophy to expound it.[11]

The poetic work of Friedrich Hölderlin, whose writings serve as a constant touchstone for Adorno's aesthetic meditations, provides a case in point for the predicament of allegorical or figurative reading. In "Parataxis," Adorno claims that while "Hölderlin's poetry, like all rigorous poetry, requires philosophy in order to bring to light its truth content, any recourse to a philosophy which merely appropriates the truth content in this or that manner is unusable."[12] While no poetic truth content can emerge in the absence of philosophy, it is equally the case that no philosophy can do justice to poetic truth while making claims to the stability of its meaning. In this context, we may recall the admonition that prefaces Hölderlin's epistolary novel *Hyperion* (1797–1799): "I would like to promise to this book the love of the Germans. But I am afraid that some will read it like a compendium, too much concerned with its *fabula docet*, while others will take it all too lightly, and both groups will fail to understand it. He who only smells my plant does not know it, and he who plucks it merely in order to learn from it does not know it either. The dissolution of dissonances in a certain character is neither a matter of mere reflection nor one of empty pleasure [*leere Lust*]."[13] It is therefore not enough to say that artworks afford pleasure, even though the most rigorous and beautiful ones certainly do, a point of which Adorno himself is keenly aware. As we learn in *Aesthetic Theory*, "whoever enjoys artworks concretistically is a philistine; expressions such as 'a feast for the ears [*Ohrenschmaus*]' give him away. Yet if the last traces of pleasure were extirpated, the question as to the purpose of artworks would be an embarrassment."[14] But, beyond the pleasure principle, what is at stake for Adorno's aesthetic theory in thinking through the relation between philosophical speculation and the work of art is the truth that expresses itself, in that very relation, not only otherwise but also as the singularity of a particular form that, while resistant to verification by logic alone, still offers a mode of complexly mediated insight that is unavailable to the conceptual terms of conventional speculative discourse. If this other kind of truth is merely an illusion, then it is an illusion that itself exhibits, as a negative capability, something other than mere garden-variety illusion, the very illusion of the illusionless. This is why for Adorno, "truth has art as the illusion of the illusionless."[15]

Insofar as truth "has" art in this way, the relationship between the philosophical and the aesthetic cannot but have epistemopolitical implications. As Christoph Menke and others have persuasively demonstrated, Adorno's so-called aesthetic negativity cannot be reduced to the kind of neo-Marxian interventionist aesthetic that his friend Herbert Marcuse advocated any more than it can be assimilated into a purely aestheticist impulse that would elide the artwork's politically charged relation to the material situatedness that first sponsored it. As a determinate and necessary negation of any attempt at hermeneutic understanding, Adorno's project stresses the processual character of the aesthetic by casting aesthetic negativity as a perpetual provocation to all normative discourses of reason and transparent understanding.[16]

Yet if it is true, as Adorno and Horkheimer argue in *Dialectic of Enlightenment*, that the advent of the modern form of rationality has banished from the admissible realm of reason any form of cognition that does not conform to a series of narrowly defined scientific assumptions, then the artwork, if it is to offer any truth at all, even the truth of its untruth, is compelled to reconceptualize the relation between logic and rhetoric, science and art, theory and praxis. To put it in the terms of Simon Jarvis, Adorno, in his desire to exhibit art's cognitive truth-content, conceives of "art as having a cognitive content with a non-propositional character."[17] Here, I wish to explicate these propositions in relation to the singular idiom of Adorno's actual language and, in so doing, to examine the particular ways in which Adorno's praxis as a writer responds to a desire to remain faithful to the difficulty of the uneasy and nonpropositional elective affinity between philosophy and art. Specifically, I attempt to read the notorious one-page thought-image "Zum Ende," entry 153 in *Minima Moralia: Reflections from Damaged Life*, in light of these concerns. It is not only because "Zum Ende" constitutes the final entry in *Minima Moralia* that it is the allegorical sum and summary of all of Adorno's previous thought-images and their speculative concerns; rather, as an aberrant aesthetico-methodological commentary, it also is the instantiation and radicalization of the kind of thinking, mediated by a consideration of the relation between philosophy and art, that Adorno calls for and himself performs throughout his writings. Although often cited, "Zum Ende" has received relatively little sustained commentary because of the overly charged relays that crisscross it. Even a new Suhrkamp anthology entirely devoted to readings of individual thought-images from *Minima Moralia*—by such formidable literary critics and philosophers as Bernhard Böschenstein, Hans Ulrich Gumbrecht, Wolf Lepenies, Gerhard Neumann, and Slavoj Žižek—brackets "Zum Ende" as though it were the absent center that needed to be honored by remaining silent about it.[18] Adorno's sentences read:

> *Zum Ende.*—Philosophie, wie sie im Angesicht der Verzweiflung einzig noch zu verantworten ist, wäre der Versuch, alle Dinge so zu betrachten, wie sie vom Standpunkt der Erlösung aus sich darstellten. Erkenntnis hat kein Licht, als das von der Erlösung her auf die Welt scheint: alles andere erschöpft sich in der Nachkonstruktion und bleibt ein Stück Technik. Perspektiven müßten hergestellt werden, in denen die Welt ähnlich sich versetzt, verfremdet, ihre Risse und Schründe offenbart, wie sie einmal als

bedürftig und enstellt im Messianischen Lichte daliegen wird. Ohne Willkür und Gewalt, ganz aus der Fühlung mit den Gegenständen heraus solche Perspektiven zu gewinnen, darauf allein kommt es dem Denken an. Es ist das Allereinfachste, weil der Zustand unabweisbar nach solcher Erkenntnis ruft, ja weil die vollendete Negativität, einmal ganz ins Auge gefaßt, zur Spiegelschrift ihres Gegenteils zusammenschießt. Aber es ist auch das ganz Unmögliche, weil es einen Standort voraussetzt, der dem Bannkreis des Daseins, wäre es auch nur um ein Winziges, entrückt ist, während doch jede mögliche Erkenntnis nicht bloß dem was ist erst abgetrotzt werden muß, um verbindlich zu geraten, sondern eben darum selber auch mit der gleichen Entstelltheit und Bedürftigkeit geschlagen ist, der sie zu entrinnen vorhat. Je leidenschaftlicher der Gedanke gegen sein Bedingtsein sich abdichtet um des Unbedingten willen, um so bewußtloser, und damit verhängnisvoller, fällt er der Welt zu. Selbst seine eigene Unmöglichkeit muß er noch begreifen um der Möglichkeit willen. Gegenüber der Forderung, die damit an ihn ergeht, ist aber die Frage nach der Wirklichkeit oder Unwirklichkeit der Erlösung selber fast gleichgültig.

Toward the End.—The only kind of philosophy for which, in the face of despair, responsibility could be assumed, would be the attempt to contemplate all things the way that they would present themselves from the standpoint of redemption. Cognition has no light other than the one that shines onto the world from redemption: everything else exhausts itself in reconstruction and remains a piece of technique. Perspectives would have to be manufactured in which the world similarly displaces and estranges itself, revealing its tears and cracks, as it at some point will lie there, needy and disfigured, in the Messianic light. To gain such perspectives without arbitrariness and violence, wholly from one's contact with the objects—this alone is what matters to thinking. This is the easiest of all because the condition irrefutably calls for such cognition, indeed, because completed negativity, once fully captured by the eye, shoots together to form the mirror-writing of its opposite. But it also is the entirely impossible, because it presupposes a standpoint removed, even if only by the most minuscule degree, from the sphere of the spell of being, whereas every possible cognition, in order to become binding, not only must first be wrested from what is, but, for this very reason, is itself struck with the same disfiguration and neediness from which it intends to escape. The more passionately thought seals itself off from its conditionality for the sake of the unconditional, the more unconsciously and, therefore, the more disastrously, it falls toward the world. It must grasp even its own impossibility for the sake of the possible. But, faced with the demand that thereby is issued to it, the question concerning the reality or unreality of redemption is itself almost irrelevant.[19]

Given its position at the end of *Minima Moralia*, "Zum Ende" seems to be appropriately titled. Yet the preposition "zum" is of importance here, an importance elided by the published English translation, which simply gives us "Finale," as though Adorno had written "Ende," rather than "Zum Ende." "Zum" here can mean either "toward," describing a movement toward the end, or "on the occasion of," placing the text that follows in the position of delivering a commentary on something *other* than itself, namely the end. A third possibility is that "zum" here means "with regard to," in which case the reflections that follow could also be understood as commenting on the philosophical question of "Ende" as "Zweck," the end as goal, that is, in terms of the problematized means-end relationship at the core of Walter Benjamin's 1921 essay "Critique of Violence," an issue in which Benjamin was still deeply immersed when Adorno first met him in Frankfurt in 1923.[20] While Adorno's language leaves us suspended in the realm of undecidability among these three readings, what unites them is that in each case they are *something other* than the end itself. The relationship of the title to that which it names, the end, is not one of identity but one of alterity and even radical *non-identity*, a category so crucial to Adorno's *Negative Dialectics*. In this way, what seemingly had announced itself as the end is rather one more deferral, one more erratic suspension, in non-identity, of the finality that would foreclose any future thought or inspired act of reading.

For the narrating poetic voice of *Minima Moralia*—can we be absolutely certain that this is in fact the author's voice, rather than an invented and highly stylized poetico-philosophical narrator's voice whose model is the ironic gesture of Nietzsche's confession that "my books are one thing, I am another"?—the kind of philosophy that could still be practiced responsibly in the face of despair would attempt to read the inhabitants of the object world "the way they would present themselves from the standpoint of redemption." This gesture implies a doubly figurative or allegorical stance. First, philosophy is called upon to regard things in terms of another, as what they are not. To enter a responsible relation to the object world, that is, to do justice to the objects, also is to depart from their unmediated manifestation; in order to remain faithful and responsible to them, we must break with them and see them *otherwise*. Second, the standpoint from which they are to be regarded, that of redemption, has itself not yet been attained, as the conditional mood of Adorno's grammar indicates ("*sich darstellten*")—after all, the standpoint of redemption is a homeland to which no one has ever been. This means that philosophy is called upon to assume a perspective on the object world that not only departs from the objects' manifestations as phenomena but that also stands in a figurative or allegorical relation to the perspective that is to be substituted for the perspective of the object world as it conventionally presents itself. Adorno's sentence thus encrypts the radically figurative and doubly allegorical relationship that philosophy is asked to assume vis-à-vis the world in which it occurs.

Our understanding of the speaking and thinking otherwise that constitutes Adorno's allegorical relation to the world in which thought occurs is intensified when, in the sentence that follows, we are told that "cognition has no light other than the one that shines onto the world from redemption." That Adorno is not at all triumphalist about the weak possibility of that redemption is suggested by the fact that redemption itself does not shine a light on the world (as the published English translation misleadingly states: "shed on the world by redemption") but, rather, it is only from the province of redemption that a light is cast, a light that has no agency other than its own self-reflexivity—"kein Licht, als das von der Erlösung her auf die Welt scheint." It is as if the metaphor that seems to depict redemption as a light shining onto the world also undid itself by depicting that light as emanating from *the site of* redemption rather than identifying the light with redemption itself. This double gesture, in which a promise simultaneously is extended and withdrawn, can be read as an instance of the non-identical, a reading that adds a new interpretive dimension to Adorno's conviction in *Negative Dialectics* that "what would be different has not yet begun."[21]

But how, one might well ask, can Adorno claim that this is the *only* light that cognition has at its disposal ("kein Licht, als das von der Erlösung") in its efforts to achieve knowledge and insight? Could one not imagine other forms of cognition that would be independent of such a highly mediated shining? Moreover, does not this general truth claim also undermine the singularity and idiom of the individual act of cognition that may fasten upon this or that object and that may be facilitated by variegated modes and conditions of possibility? In this same vein, the part of the sentence following the colon extends this general truth claim when it states that "alles andere," everything else, exhausts itself and remains insufficient. Adorno here wishes to emphasize the universal applicability of this kind of thinking about philosophy in a time of despair. If, for him, everything else exhausts itself in reconstruction (*Nachkonstruktion*) and remains merely technique or technics (*Technik*) his sentence gives us other, alternative forms of thinking and writing to think. When viewed in the larger context of Adorno's work, his word *Nachkonstruktion* is negatively charged in that it conjures a form of mimesis that he generally abhorred: the direct, reflective, and reproductive kind. As he argues throughout *Aesthetic Theory*, what he wishes for in the work of art as well as in philosophy is in fact a different kind of mimesis: a mimesis of what does not yet exist, the negative traces of a futurity that can be neither predicted nor programmed in advance but that nevertheless inscribes itself into the artwork, and into the philosophy that enters a relation with that artwork, as a non-identical and negatively charged otherness.

The philosophy at stake here sponsors perspectives "in which the world similarly displaces itself, estranges itself [*sich versetzt, entfremdet*]." Notably, it is the perspectives themselves that cause this displacement and estrangement; they enable, as a condition of possibility, a movement that the world itself performs, as emphasized in Adorno's notorious use of the reflexive "*sich*." If, however, with the aid of these new perspectives the world is capable of displacing and estranging *itself*, presumably with an eye toward the kind of allegorical philosophical thinking that is yet to come, then that capability always already must have been latent in the world. In this sense, an allegorical thinking of the future is not an external intervention, mobilized by some autonomous standard of measurement or insight independent of that world, but rather an activation or liberation of what always already was at work, silently and invisibly, within the figures of the world itself. This figurative thinking thus works to actualize and radicalize, through a close and caring reading, the hidden movements and structures that become visible, if only in the blink of an eye, when the world has entered a course of displacement and estrangement that thinks and says things *otherwise*.

Clearly, when under the gaze of the allegorical perspective the world performs the defamiliarizing gestures of self-displacement and self-estrangement—that is, reveals itself, in the messianic light, as "bedürftig" (needy) and "*enstellt*" (disfigured)—it also reveals, in its need for redemption, the condition of possibility for the issuance of any messianic intervention. Adorno likewise extends his emphasis on an engagement with the internal logic and structure of the object, a gesture that refrains from externally mobilized interventions—which, for him, can only lead to "Willkür" (arbitrariness) and "Gewalt" (violence)—by stressing a "Fühlung mit den Gegenständen," a felt contact with the objects. Yet why does he emphasize that "darauf allein kommt es dem Denken an" ("this alone is what matters to thinking")? Here it is instructive to return to the published English translation, which gives us "this alone is the task of thinking," as if Adorno had written "das allein ist die Aufgabe des Denkens."

The difference here could not be more crucial: Adorno's text implicitly refuses to assign a task to thought not simply because "Aufgabe" in German means both a task and a final giving up, but also because the very idea of a task inscribes the radical kind of thinking that he imagines into the language and logic of instrumental reason, the target of much of *Dialectic of Enlightenment*. The new thinking here is not to be instrumentalized as a task whose aim is to locate objects and to assume contact with them according to an entirely rational, preplanned program, because such a program would only repeat one more time the rational structure of a too-narrowly-conceived notion of reason that already has led to such disastrous consequences as the current needy and disfigured state of the world (Adorno writes these lines in 1946–1947, amidst the debris and trauma left behind by German fascism). Rather than enlist a thinking to come that places itself in the service of instrumental reason, even with the best of intentions, Adorno initializes a thinking that is on the way *elsewhere*, its restless strivings born of an inner dynamic rather than in response to the assignments issued by a task whose aim it does not yet know.

The actualization of this movement of thought, however, can never be taken for granted or perfunctorily installed as an administrable program, even as it remains both necessary and "das Allereinfachste," the simplest thing of all. This is so because the precondition for the "vollendete Negativität," or perfected negativity, to delineate, explosively, the "Spiegelschrift ihres Gegenteils," the mirror-writing of its opposite, can never be fully present: just as negativity can never be fully perfected or completed ["vollendet"], it can never be "ganz ins Auge gefaßt," fully captured or completely faced. Thus, while Adorno's metaphors give the impression of supplying the figures of a possible redemption, even the redemption that is lodged in negativity, his diction also withdraws that promise by retreating from a full actualization of the goal toward which it strives. It is no accident that this retreat is linked performatively to language, since it is the allegorical or figurative domain of language itself that draws the contours of redemption while at the same time undoing its triumphant endorsement. It is for this reason, too, that the metaphor of "Spiegelschrift," mirror-writing—erroneously rendered as "mirror-image" in the standard English translation, as though Adorno had written "Spiegelbild ihres Gegenteils"—is significant here. "Spiegelschrift" retains an emphasis on the idea that what is visible is not what is immediately accessible, a gesture that decouples perception from cognition. To read "Spiegelschrift" as "Spiegelbild" implicitly surrenders the status of the negatively contoured representation to the domain of an image in which visibility so often is mistaken for comprehensibility.

Further complicating the promise of, and retreat from, redemption in allegorical language, Adorno concedes that what he had called "the simplest thing of all" is also, dialectically, "das ganz Unmögliche," the wholly impossible. This impossibility stems from the fact that the thought that thinks otherwise, that is, strives toward the *other* perspective that the text has worked to define, itself is lodged in the space in which the transformation of that very perspective is articulated and therefore also emerges as needy and disfigured. Adorno's sentence here stages the ways in which what hopes to depart from a given situation or problematic is also conditioned by it and that, by extension, a transgressive breaking-away from something on the way to something else is always also in part a tacit perpetuation of the same. The "afterness" of the after, we might say, remains in what Adorno here calls the "Bannkreis des Daseins," which is not merely the "scope of existence," as the published English translation claims, but also the tenacious spell and authoritative domain of existence from which thought had hoped to depart. Adorno here allegorizes a point made at greater length in the contemporaneous *Dialectic of Enlightenment*, that if an enlightened and putatively progressive thought fails to take account of its own residual attachment to that which it strives to overcome, if it fails to consider its own situatedness and conditionedness within the regressive forces it hopes to conquer, then this thought will, in a hardly perceptible dialectical reversal, revert to the very darkness that it had sought to illuminate. This fate is especially inescapable for the thought that "passionately" and relentlessly "seals itself off from its own conditionality [*gegen seine Bedingtheit sich abdichtet*]," with an eye toward escaping the unreliable and aleatory constraints of its multiple contingencies in favor of the universal transcendental aspirations of "das Unbedingte," the unconditional unmarred by the conditions and contingencies of thought and experience. But for Adorno, this is a mistake, a dangerous aberration. The more thought strives to shuck the aleatory traces of its own contingency and conditionality, the more it returns to and reproduces the world's insufficiencies ("fällt er der Welt zu"), while believing itself to innovate and to transgress.

Adorno's maxim, situated somewhere on the far side of instrumental reason and the delusion of regarding afterness as a clean and absolute break, therefore is that thought should "grasp even its own impossibility for the sake of possibility." If there is to be possibility at all—and we never can be quite certain that there is—it first must travel through the aporia of the impossible. This is the future-directed negativity that Adorno, a few years later in "Cultural Criticism and Society," will designate as a movement of thought that follows the "logic of [an object's] aporias, the impasse contained within the task itself [*Logik seiner Aporien, der in der Aufgabe selber gelegenen Unlösbarkeit*]."[22] Indeed, a relentless thinking through of thought's impossibility is the condition of possibility for striving toward what is possible. Yet, if thought is impossible, how can it think its own impossibility with an eye toward the possible? Would this thinking and grasping of the impossible not be a sign that thought in fact is possible, as evidenced by its capacity to think something, namely, its own impossibility? Much hinges on Adorno's verb "muß" [*"muß er noch begreifen"*], "it must at last grasp." What kind of command is being issued here? By whom? Situated where, if not precisely in the needy and disfigured world and therefore tinged by its shortcomings and aberrations? Is this "muß" a description of the current state of affairs, of what thought actually does—a possible reading, given the indicative present tense form—or is it the call from an unnamed otherness that a subject receives and henceforth is required to act upon without quite knowing how—which is another possible reading, given that German often uses the present tense indicative to refer to an obligation or intention to be acted upon in the future?

The final sentence of Adorno's thought-image—or, in light of our discussion of the piece's title, perhaps we should say the sentence that unfolds on the occasion of or toward the end?—suggests that we are to imagine a command being issued to thought from an unnamed elsewhere, an absent other: "But with regard to the demand that thus is issued toward thought [*die damit an ihn ergeht*], the question concerning the reality or unreality of redemption itself is almost irrelevant [*fast gleichgültig*]." Rather than assuming, as the published English translation does, that the difference between the reality and the unreality of redemption "hardly matters," Adorno suggests the opposite. Even though the demand that is issued to thought by an unnamed, absent otherness may be privileged over the unpredictable outcome of what it has set in motion—that is, the "that" of the demand is more strongly felt than its "what"—what remains at stake is still the thinking of a possible redemption, as the engine and arbiter of undeconstructable concepts such as freedom and justice, even if these have not been achieved and even if they remain the property of a negative otherness that is the homeland where no one has ever been.

If thought thinks its own impossibility in the name of a possibility that refuses to remain unthinkable even while presenting itself as impossible, then the movement of thought that enables this thinking is facilitated by the hypothetical idea of redemption. From the standpoint of the thought-enabling function of redemption, its actual manifestation or "reality" would not seem to matter: it works to set thought into motion, even when that thought seems to have been arrested for good. Almost. After all, Adorno refuses simply to write that the reality of redemption is irrelevant—he writes that it is *almost* irrelevant—*fast gleichgültig*. What literally is equally valid (*gleich-gültig*), is cast into disequilibrium and asymmetry by the qualifying adverb. That this *almost* remains perpetually open, that it is never the last word but, literally and figuratively, the second-to-last word, not *das letzte Wort* but, as in *Minima Moralia*, precisely *das vorletzte Wort*—this names the fragile promise of any negative dialectics.

The language of this negative dialectics registers, in a diction at once poetic and philosophical, the injury but also the hope that resides in the very world in which it unfolds. The violence and injustice of this world cannot be thought in isolation from the rhetorical structure of any language that wishes to interact with them. "That the violence of the facts," Adorno writes in his Bar Harbor notebook, "has become such a horror, that any theory, even the true kind, looks like a ridicule of that horror—this is burned as a sign into the very organ of theory, language."[23] The language of theory therefore not only turns to the world of objects and ideas but also perpetually takes stock of the burned sign whose scar remains. Therefore, Adorno suggests in his "Theses on the Language of the Philosopher" that the philosopher's "decomposed language [*zerfallene Sprache*]" is compelled to construct a kind of writer whose "materials are the ruins of words to which history binds him."[24] For Adorno, as for Benjamin in his theses on the ruins of history, there can be no philosophical language that does not remain faithful to this difficulty. Here, the "intended comprehensibility of philosophical language today is to be uncovered in all aspects as a delusion. It is either banal, that is, naively assumes words to be pre-given and valid whose relation to the object-matter, in truth, would be problematic; or it is untrue, in that it works to dissimulate this problematic, using the pathos of words that appear to have been extrapolated from the dynamics of history in order to bestow upon these words non-historical validity and at once comprehensibility."[25] The language of the writer who strives to remain aware of these difficulties therefore would follow the poetic and philosophical paths of a certain melancholia of negativity, a careful and caring probing, a provisional yet steadfast searching, a non-anthropocentric yet deeply responsible engagement with what remains non-identical.

To say that Adorno's project of "philosophical modernism," which radicalizes the formal claims of Kant's third *Critique* and furthers the Jena Romantics' abiding insistence on the reflective judgments of art in the very space in which self-reflexive, fragmented writing embodies both philosophy and art,[26] also is to say that, for Adorno, no conjunction of philosophy and art even would be needed if it did not also, in the alterity of its own negativity, point to an elsewhere that has not abandoned a structure of promise, prayer, and the thinking of an unknown, and potentially worthwhile, futurity. What Adorno's project therefore shares with the Marxian transformation of Kantian aesthetics and of Hegelian dialectics is a certain oppositional spirit that allows aesthetic form to provide an elusive space in which the potential of the concept no longer is hampered by its rigid attachment to a purely logical system of reason that polices the legality and admissibility of a concept's movements and qualities.[27] As Adorno articulates this oppositional impulse in *Negative Dialectics*, the "utopia of cognition would be to use concepts to unseal the nonconceptual by means of concepts, without making it their equal."[28] The "almost" of thought, the otherness inscribed in works that, like "Zum Ende," embody both philosophical and aesthetic elements, both logic and rhetoric, is charged with the passionate insight through which we "strive, by way of the concept, to move beyond the concept."[29] While Adorno here echoes Heidegger's admonition against the pursuit of a thinking that "fails to recognize that there is a thinking more rigorous than the conceptual,"[30] he also departs from Heidegger in that he wishes to orient his remarks not with an eye toward the requirements of a new fundamental ontology but rather toward what within the artwork both embodies and radicalizes a thinking of non-identity and of a negative dialectics that at any given moment deserves to be thought as the condition of possibility for a futurity that has not yet been foreclosed. To be sure, for Adorno the overconcretization of that futurity, what he prefers to call a mere *Auspinseln*, dooms even the dialectically charged artwork to endorse yet another humanism and to repeat the failure of what already is. But Adorno's faithfulness to a perpetual engagement with the radically opposed yet interdependent requirements of philosophy and art, enabled by the aesthetic form, continues to be a thorn, that is, a-*Dorn*, in the side of those ideologies of the end of history that have resigned themselves to mere mimesis and a tireless affirmation of self-identity. Today, a half century later, such ideologies amount to perpetuating, in mind and checkbook, geopolitical empire-building, the mindless diversions of our consciousness industry, daily worldwide ecocides, the suburban banalities of a globalized simulcast, and their attendant lack of affect. As a miniature artwork that possesses a negatively charged aesthetic cognitive content with a nonpropositional character, "Zum Ende," therefore, only ever will have been a beginning.

CHAPTER 9

The Homeland of Language: A Note on Truth and Knowledge in Adorno

Mirko Wischke

In section 50 of *Minima Moralia* Adorno states that it would be wrong to demand an author to "show explicitly all the steps that have led him to his conclusion, so enabling every reader to" immerse him- or herself in the world of the writer's imagination.[1] But why should writers refuse to give readers insight into their thoughts? What should stop them from having some degree of consideration for the reader? Do they not wish to be understood? This seemingly trivial question follows from Adorno's criticism of the expectation that writers make their train of thought as explicit as possible—that is, comprehensible—in order to enable the reader to follow their thought process. What, then, might have led Adorno not only to deny that this is a reasonable demand, but also to deem it a false presentational principle arising from the "fiction" of the communicability of each and every thought? Each and every thought? Do thoughts exist that cannot be communicated?

If "language is by its own objective substance social expression," as Adorno argues in *Minima Moralia*, then his reference to the fiction of the communicability of all thought could be understood as follows: one must distance oneself from the banal everyday use of language in which communication usually takes place in order to avert the risk of robbing complex thoughts of their detail and substance.[2] Adorno appears to proceed from the premise that every object requires a linguistic presentation peculiar to it alone. This poses a significant challenge to writers in that they acquire their material from the meaning assigned to words in linguistic communicative practice. Adorno addresses this issue in the section of *Minima Moralia* entitled "Morality and Style" by observing that unfamiliar articulation appears foreign and abrasive and requires getting used to. Language is an expression of the course of daily life to which writers would appear to be bound if they are to be understood. Should they distance themselves from this practice, they reduce the risk of their conceptual workshop becoming cluttered with colloquial and disfigured linguistic forms. Such a renunciation comes at a price, however, for "regard for the object, rather than for communication, is suspect in any expression: anything specific, not taken from pre-existent patterns, appears inconsiderate, a symptom of eccentricity, almost of confusion."[3] The earliest formulation of this objection dates back to the 1930s. He counters the position that philosophical language must be comprehensible and "socially communicable" in that he remains attached to the "signifying character" of language; the other position is not tenable, he argues, because in language "objects . . . cannot adequately be given."[4]

The trajectory of Adorno's assertion becomes evident when he emphasizes in *Negative Dialectics* that the object of language is neither a "pure facticity" nor a mere product of thought. The language theory Adorno develops with Horkheimer in *Dialectic of Enlightenment* calls attention to this dimension; it centers on the thesis that language is "reified" and "reifying" in the same measure to which it begins to converge with the designation and classification of what remains identical to itself. What thoughts seek to express by way of language is obstructed by an insurmountable barrier. It is not the arbitrariness of human subjects, however, that stands in the way of adequate articulation. Rather, gaining full knowledge of things seems to falter due to the nature of language itself. In addressing this, Adorno asserts that "to want substance in cognition is to want utopia"; a "cognitive utopia" would be to "unseal the non-conceptual with concepts."[5]

Is the implication of this declaration for our initial question that thoughts are actually not communicable because words cannot adequately capture what they seek to express? The reference to the nonconceptual of the concept would seem to indicate that which evades the conceptual imagination and can only be defined negatively—in other words, as that which exceeds the concept and lies on the far side of what is known and accessible through concepts. This conclusion is found wanting, however, when confronted by the premises of the language theory of *Dialectic of Enlightenment*. If no exact correspondence exists between a word and the object in question, then it remains unclear how we can use concepts to understand that which is nonconceptual in nature.

Or should the conclusion instead state that thoughts cannot be easily captured in words because they possess a vacillating range of meaning, rendering the attempt to make a thought communicable a reckless endeavor? This seems to be suggested by the reference to the *content of knowledge, as opposed to the linguistic-conceptual form* of knowledge, insofar as language precedes our thought. A subject uses language to create a conception of the world "which it ratifies as an opinion *about* the world as soon as the subject speaks and thinks in language."[6] If no exact correspondence can be assumed between word and object, however, it remains unclear by which criteria an intellectual insight might be measured at all. Adorno's determination that a concept hypostasizes "its own form against the content" is reminiscent of Hegel's postulation of an opposition, frozen by reflection, between the concept and the matter at hand as respectively autonomous realms.[7] Likewise, it is similar to Plato's observation of an inner tendency toward reversal by which the word, the concept, the insight, and the illustration attempt to express themselves, rather than disappearing behind that which they are meant to make present. This difference provides an explanation for Plato, as for Adorno, as to why the labor of conceptualization does not consist in creating access to things as they really are. Other thinkers, such as Gadamer, draw the conclusion that in language, where the word—unlike a sign—does not refer to something else, the attempt to recognize things as they really are is not what is truly at stake.[8]

Adorno does not draw a conclusion similar to that of Hans-Georg Gadamer, nor does he share Nietzsche's conviction that language always bars us from recognizing things as that which they are in and of themselves. According to Nietzsche, the choice between mere "considering to be true" and actual knowledge is, in this respect, not truly an alternative, as one must proceed from the assumption that there can be no knowledge of the truth as such.[9] Humans have no access to things as they really are—a dilemma that, according to Nietzsche, they cope with via language; within it, however, terms and objects do not fully correspond. Language, it follows, represents something just as little as it illustrates it; what it designates is solely the relation between humans and things.[10]

Adorno does not consider perspectivism as a possibility. Rather, his embrace of Nietzsche's critique of the metaphysics of that which remains misconstrues Nietzsche's approach, which is not in fact concerned with the (temporal) presence of things in contrast to their "true" being. Instead, it centers on the way in which the metaphoricity and the anthrocentrism of language serve human self-assertion, though in the most elementary fashion. Nietzsche believes that humans' only access to the world is through language. Without it, they could neither orient themselves in relation to the world, nor make themselves accessible to it.[11]

Though neither Nietzsche's perspectivism nor his approach meet with Adorno's approval, these ideas are at least not unfamiliar to him. This becomes clear when he expresses epistemological doubt that a position could be assumed outside of language practice from which things could be perceived as they really are, beyond the realm of linguistic disfiguration. Likewise, Adorno's thinking converges with Nietzsche's at the point at which Nietzsche states that only language provides us with access to the surrounding world. Adorno also assumes that language must be understood as the "organon of thought," that the formation of concepts primarily serves the purpose of dominating nature, and that concepts refer to the "non-conceptual" to which we have no real access.[12] However, Adorno does not consider Nietzsche's perspectivism to be sufficient to declare that concepts can have a relation to things when the correspondence itself is actually quite dubious. Unsatisfied, he not only outlines perspectivism's negative aspect, but also finds that concepts, because they are "emphatically non-conceptual," "mean" beyond themselves.[13] Convinced that, as two distinct realms, the conceptual and nonconceptual cannot be fixed in their separation, Adorno considers it less problematic than Kant that an insurmountable divide separates language from that which lies beyond it. Along with Nietzsche and Gadamer, Adorno also assumes that we can only gain access to the world in language, and even when concepts tend to conceal this access, "dissatisfaction with their own conceptuality is part of their meaning, although the inclusion of nonconceptuality in their meaning makes it tendentially their equal and thus keeps them trapped within themselves."[14] This insight explains an apparent reversal in Adorno's critique of the demand for the communicability of thought. This comes when he emphasizes that the writer, to the degree that he or she attempts to express him- or herself more precisely, conscientiously, and appropriately—in order to dissolve the distinction between object and expression—will have the unpleasant experience that the literary result will be considered nearly incomprehensible. Is there really any way to eliminate this difference? And does it make any sense to attempt it in the first place?

In the section of *Minima Moralia* that I am concerned with here, the answer to these questions is imbued with a certain melancholy. How can language come close to that which is thought, if language determines thought and thereby prevents its legitimation, if not crippling it or even rendering it impossible?

Starting from the assumption that all knowledge is "knowledge through concepts," Kant made the well-noted qualification that concepts never directly relate to an object, although thought is nothing other than this knowledge through concepts.[15] Hegel not only concurs with Kant that concepts construct their own reality, but in the *Phenomenology of Spirit* he radicalizes this view into the assumption that immediate being cannot be expressed by language, since the concept exists in something other than sensual reality. Adorno and Hegel both hold to this epistemological premise, according to which we differentiate between sensual being and sensual reality. However, Adorno does not consider Hegel's premise to generally apply to language as such, but rather to describe the phenomenon of the objectification of non-objectifiable things through language. Just as Nietzsche's and Gadamer's theorizations of language depart from an ontology of presence in the conviction that the existence of a word is *not* to be equated with the existence of the matter to which it refers, Adorno adheres to the position that the *use* of language is not to be equated with that which is actually meant to be articulated within it: the nonconceptual. In contrast to Gadamer, for whom the question of how close or far from reality things are brought to language is not actually the problem, and in contrast to Nietzsche, for whom the pragmatic aspect of language is ultimately the most significant, for Adorno language possesses a real epistemological significance—even if in his view the being of a word is not subsumed by its meaning.

What Nietzsche sees as an anthropologically necessary evil, Adorno directs to the question of whether language could be used to break through its own barriers in order to reveal what the apparent identity of concept and thing denies, an identity that had been cast in doubt as early as Plato's "Kratylos." Denied is, namely, that which language does not say, although it precedes it and language refers to it: the nonlinguistic, nonconceptual, and non-identical. The question is how object and expression can converge by linguistic means, if the operating principle of language is supposed to be the way in which it becomes independent in relation to that which is to be expressed. Specifically, in regard to the section of *Minima Moralia* I am examining the question reads: How can something true be recognized by that which is incommunicable, nonlinguistic, or nonconceptual, if the form of knowledge (and communication) is of a nonconceptual nature?

One might think that an adequate answer to this question could be found in Adorno's assertion of an inner transcendence of the concept, which is particular to it through its relation to the nonconceptual. Yet how can something be representable in concepts, to which the concepts refer, without its being able to represent itself through its own power? The preliminary answer is: Through a presentation that is not a presentation in the sense of a cognitive notion, but instead an individual form, which yields something that both author and reader have a part in. It still remains unclear, however, which criteria the presentation has to fulfill in order to be able to transform the nonconceptual into the conceptual. The question could be posed in the following way: How is it possible to overcome the tendency of concepts to place themselves before that which they are actually supposed to express? How can the concept and the thing minimize the difference between them without shedding it entirely?

Bound up in the respective language of the presentation, concepts become fluid, as it were, in that they cluster into constellations in order to make visible what their conceptual schemata conceal. Solely the presentation in the form of such conceptual constellations represents "what the concept has cut away within: the 'more'" of the concept.[16] As early as in the "Theses On the Language of the Philosopher" from the 1930s it is stated that one can read that the configuration of words is not to be identified with the intention of "explaining" new truths through conventional words; rather, Adorno sees configurative language representing a practice that is meant to spare the unbowed dignity of words.[17] Adorno not only adopts Benjamin's notion that the truth can, in principle, only be represented in language, but also the distinction between knowledge, concept, and presentation. Adorno follows Benjamin in the assumption that the concept does not directly refer to an object, but through mediation, inasfar as the concept is dependent upon other conceptions of the object. This peculiarity to which Kant repeatedly referred should undermine Benjamin's distinction between method and presentation: "For knowledge, method is a way of acquiring its object . . . for truth it is self-presentation, and is therefore immanent in it as form."[18] This conception of form can be misconstrued in that Benjamin did not wish to think of the relation between presentation and truth as the relationship between form and content, but instead conceives of configurative presentation as the presentation of phenomena. Such a presentation requires a reintegration of conceptions in language.

Adorno's notion, informed by Benjamin, that truth is in principle only representable in language leaves the question open of how to conceive of the return of concepts to language. Evidently, in equating language with presentation, Adorno means that the relation which the form of the constellation establishes between concepts in presentation in order to train them on an object should itself be considered language.[19] In various groupings focused on a factual content, concepts are supposed to reclaim the linguistic ambiguity they have as that which is spoken in the performance of language. The reclamation of linguistic ambiguity is, however, just a first step. In approaching the spoken word, the concept is not only supposed to recover the ambiguity that is only lessened by the position it occupies in the context of this or that speech act. The conceptual principle of identification, too, is meant to be cracked open in order to cognize the nonconceptual meaning of the concept that the form of the constellation is meant to give over to preliminary presentation. The reintegration of concepts into language, the remembrance of a concept's linguistic from, is the attempt to make usable, for the written word, the mimetic potential of language, its nonconceptual moment of expression, which objectifies the act of presentation. As a (re)transformation of previous linguistic forms of expression, in the dissolution of existing referential contexts and forms of words' relations, presentation is supposed to enact the plurality of meaning of individual linguistic elements so that concepts can be made to speak, the "language of things"[20] can be made audible, and the "creative act" in which the concepts have acquired their meanings can be restaged once again.[21] Here Benjamin would argue that the "languages of things" are not only "imperfect," but also "mute." Things are denied the "pure formal principle of language," namely sound.[22] How then are things to accede to language?

According to Benjamin, the "incomparable feature of human language" is that it has a "magical community with things."[23] In other words, language is the mental being of things. If the mental being of man is language, Benjamin argues, then he can only express himself within it: "The quintessence of this intensive totality of language as the mental being of man is the name.... All nature, insofar as it communicates itself, communicates itself in language.... Only through the linguistic being of things can he [man] get beyond himself and gain knowledge of them—in the name."[24] What consequences does Adorno draw from Benjamin's observations?

Presentation is the expression of a new composition of concepts for the purpose of releasing them from established contexts of meaning; as the non-identity of a concept with experience, the difference between object and expression is not to come to rest in presentation, but instead to continually prompt the formation of new constellations. In *Aesthetic Theory* Adorno states that expression is "the antithesis of expressing something," because its "character of eloquence" [*Sprachcharakter*] distinguishes itself from "communicative language," namely through its "mimetic consummation" of language.[25] This reference provides us with a further answer to the initial question of why Adorno deems the communicability of each and every thought to be a fiction. Then the question of to what degree that which is thought seeks to make itself communicable, that is capable of being communicated, is undermined by the distinction between expression and object, makes Adorno dependent upon the recovery and participation in the eventful execution of language, which loses the "spoken language" to the extent that it takes place in the form of relations of signification, sentence structures, and contexts of meaning. That concepts or words, by developing a life of their own, should retrieve some part of that which they once had is an ambivalent assertion. After all, expression does not stand in opposition to the concept because it has not yet emancipated itself from the performance of language; rather, as such a performance, the expression transforms the concept back into that which is encoded within it, namely by way of the incomplete, the polyvalent, and the ambivalent, which breaks open the signification of "communicative" language, making it "incommunicable," or to be more precise, partially incommunicable. Mimetic, artistic linguisticality emerges less from the complete negation of established linguisticality, but rather through the gradual divergence from familiar contexts.[26]

In this way expression as linguistic form can initially only be characterized negatively, that is, in its difference from an ordinary "language of words."[27] This initially only allows for a negative characterization of expression as a linguistic form, that is, in its difference from a conventional "language of words"—even if it includes the destruction of the meaning of that which is represented—that is the break from a preexisting notion of the form and meaning of that which is represented, through which the presentation is to acquire transcendence.[28] This practice does not allow thought to become incommunicable. Similar to modern art, literary presentation finds an audience, but no understanding, because it does not direct its language to others, but instead establishes form as something that appears to contradict its (ordinary) content. No matter how convincing it might sound when Adorno points out that the paradoxes and contradictions of form testify to the possibility of deciphering concepts, serious difficulties emerge when one considers that the expression of the presentation, which only speaks of that which it intends to communicate, is heard and answered.

This leads us back to our initial question: Do thoughts exist that cannot be communicated? Indeed, for Adorno there do seem to be incommunicable thoughts, at least in the sense that it is beyond the author's powers to convincingly convey his or her thoughts. As a performative form of rhetoric, expression, language, and composition, presentation makes up for this difficulty, according to Adorno, insofar as "the persuasiveness of communication" is the "determination of presentation as such." This persuasion is dependent upon the "compelling element" of the construction of presentation.[29]

Such a formulation calls to mind those critiques that interpret the definition of rhetoric as the art of persuasion in such a way that the listener, overwhelmed by the speaker's flow of words and blinded by the perspicuous analysis, does not arrive at a clear understanding of what was said. It appears as if Adorno assumes this understanding when he suggests that presentation should convince the reader and critic to allow him take part in the performance of language, from which he feels excluded through presentation's turn away from "communicative" language and the linguistic and hermetic introversion of presentation. In Adorno's discussion the never-permanently-realized aim of rhetoric to make something believable does not originate in mere persuasion, but rather in the dilemma of wanting to give up "communicative" language without being able to do without it. Adorno appeals to the traditional notion of rhetoric, yet in a way that shows its apparent weakness to actually be its strength: His recourse to rhetoric does not assume the possibility of an alternative insight, but rather the plausibility that one does not possess. Ultimately, this is by and large the context in which Adorno's discussion of incommunicable thoughts is to be understood. The reclamation of the ambiguity of words and the rupture of the identity principle of concepts can illuminate by way of presentation, yet they cannot be proved. There are thoughts, such as the non-identical, that cannot be conveyed like other things, because the reference "to its object . . . forgoes the full transparency of its logical genesis," should the individual object only be partially expressed in the form of the general and the extant. This is the site of a profound "inadequacy," which cannot sacrifice the help of the rhetorical art of persuasion, whose equation with coercion belongs to the conventional prejudice about rhetoric, because only agreement can be seen as the ever-revocable result of persuasion.[30]

Benjamin's premise that truth as presentation never appears as that which is to be represented is not only adopted in Adorno's rehabilitation of rhetoric, it is also expanded upon, in that the rhetorical technique of the transformation of language into an associative "serialization," whose elements intertwine in a manner different from the subsumption under that which is given and known, provides a corrective to the appearance that the subject forms its image of the world on the far side of language itself. For in the futile search for suitable words it experiences in the transformation of language—by which it first becomes a subject—it itself changes as well.[31] In this sense Adorno stresses that "he who thinks" makes himself the stage of a mental "experience,"[32] in which the attempt to provide an account of this scene in linguistic terms inevitably leaves behind certain gaps—such is the title of the section of *Minima Moralia* on which I have been commenting—that are not caused by subjective inconsistencies of thought, but instead result from the way in which the subject expressing itself in language is "feigning a relevance that was withdrawn from it," because it limits that which "accedes to language."[33] With this assertion in *Aesthetic Theory* not only does Adorno shift the emphasis from the opposition of the word and that which is to be expressed to the persistence of objective experience in linguistic expression; he also gives the impression that he ultimately could relinquish neither the belief in the world-encompassing power of language nor the possibility of cognitive access to the "language of things," in whose possibility, if not Hegel then Hegel's insight, must have made him skeptical that language and thought converge in the synthetic form of the concept.[34]

Translated from the German by Eric Jarosinski

CHAPTER 10

Of Stones and Glass Houses:
Minima Moralia as Critique of Transparency

Eric Jarosinski

To mark the centennial of Theodor W. Adorno's birth, in September 2003 the city of Frankfurt erected a monument in his honor on the university campus. Designed by the Russian artist Vadim Zakharov, the installation consists of a transparent glass cube housing a representation of Adorno's study, including a section of wooden flooring, a chair, and a heavy wooden desk, upon which lie an early edition of *Negative Dialectics* and several corrected manuscript pages. The desk is illuminated at night by a small lamp and accompanied by the steady ticking of a metronome. Surrounded by citations from *Minima Moralia* engraved in the paving stones, the work invites inspection by visitors who are sometimes found peering into the glass, squinting to read the typescript on the desk within.

The fate of the crystalline monument since its unveiling provides an interesting allegory, if not a parable, of the promises and perils of transparency, an aesthetic that has become of central significance to Germany's current confrontation with its past. The most visible incarnation is Sir Norman Foster's highly acclaimed cupola atop the Reichstag in Berlin, a glass dome that seeks to demonstrate the putative access and accountability of post-Wall German democracy. Transparency has come to enact a fantasy of renewal and immediacy that Adorno himself criticized decades before its widespread deployment in the embassies, ministries, and other government and commercial buildings dotting the landscape of the "New Berlin." His work criticizes transparency in asserting that the potential promise of insight is only to be realized, if ever, through a recognition of reason's own limitations and the coercive influence of social relations upon critical perception. In this essay I will trace this critique in the thought-images of *Minima Moralia* and in Adorno's essay "Functionalism Today," in which he brings much of his critique of aesthetics and politics to bear on architecture. Within "damaged life" the greatest knowledge available is that of one's own complicity with a system that is structured to deny experience, to stunt critical capacities, and to prohibit change. Any chance of renewing the vitality of a critical view upon life is predicated upon an examination of its corruption—not in that it has become more opaque, but more transparent.

Indeed, to return to the Adorno monument, we can see that the installation itself points to the ambiguous status of transparency as an aesthetic of access. It has set off an intense local debate about the appropriateness of the transparency metaphor, as well as the practical considerations of the use of glass in a public space. Zakharov, the work's creator, describes it as a "monument to creative thought," situated in a "space of public commentary."[1] The installation, he explains, challenges the traditional monument in its openness, connection to the everyday, and commemoration of thought itself rather than the great thinker placed high upon a pedestal. It is a "portrait of Adorno" in which he himself is absent, though the unfinished manuscript pages and the lit lamp suggest he could return at any moment.[2] As a testament to Adorno's work and its extension into the public sphere, the monument's outdoor campus setting is of great significance to the work, representing for Zakharov both a challenge and a provocation: "I allowed myself to do the unthinkable by bringing the private sphere out into the open."[3] The gesture was meant to transcend boundaries and make Adorno's thought visible in a wider public sphere; yet it has brought a great deal more to the surface as well, as the chain of events marking the last few years demonstrates.

Since the monument's unveiling, the public has reacted less than enthusiastically, with critics calling it everything from a "foreign body" to an "absurdity," likening the square itself (Adorno-Platz) to more of a "hangman's square" than a site of remembrance. (Curiously, the monument is located but a stone's throw from the Bockenheimer Warte, a medieval guard tower and campus landmark that served as the setting for one of the many execution scenes that mark the "protocols" Adorno kept of his dreams; on the day he was to be crucified, the surrounding area "resembled a village on a Sunday, quiet, as if under glass."⁴) Others have referred to the work as "Adorno's dollhouse" and question whether such a vehement critic of reification would be honored by a monument of any sort. And inevitably some simply think of the installation as a scandalous waste of money—220,000 euros—in a city struggling with a financial crisis. Yet what has generated the most debate is the material used in the monument itself, as the plate glass walls of Adorno's office have become the target of both critics' complaints and vandals' stones.

What Zakharov sees as a dissolution of borders through the transparency of the work has been read by some as quite the opposite; they view the 350-kilo, two-centimeter-thick sheets of glass surrounding Adorno's office as more indicative of a barrier or hermetic seal. As one newspaper report comments: "Critics find that the bullet-proof glass that is supposed to protect Adorno's study is not particularly well-chosen, for the co-founder of the Frankfurt School was always concerned with maintaining a closeness to his students."⁵ Too much "proximity" has itself proven to be a problem, however, as the monument has been damaged repeatedly by "unidentified rowdies" who have smashed the glass several times since its unveiling. Surveying the damage, one commentator has concluded that the monument's glass walls "prove not to be thick and heavy enough to establish a respectful distance."⁶ Walter Grasskamp, of the *Münchener Akademie der Bildenden Künste*, saw this coming. In a panel discussion debating the future of the monument, he stated that he was against the see-through design from the start, "and not because of artistic concerns, but rather because of the material; using glass in a public space simply cannot turn out well. I asked myself if the jury was naive or if it deliberately wanted to conduct an experiment."⁷ In attempting to understand why the work was being repeatedly damaged, the city of Frankfurt called in an expert: Dario Libero Gamboni, a Swiss art historian who has studied vandalism to public works of art. His analysis of reactions to the monument that were e-mailed to the city showed the following: "The attacks on the glass cube are the 'aggressive attempt to rescind distance.' Residents attempted to 'enter into [the monument] even if only in the form of a thrown stone.' E-mails continually criticized the 'ivory tower' in which the artwork is situated."⁸ Here the artist's intention of creating access is read as distance, and the intended extension of intellectual life into the public sphere is seen as a colonizing gesture on the part of the ivory tower. To further protect the monument, it was shielded behind sturdy steel fencing, and might be relocated to a location "which allows for better social and police control."⁹ In the meantime, it has been proposed that the fencing be replaced by twenty-four-hour video surveillance, a move thought to provide greater security for the monument: "Anyone who attacks the monument 'will know that he's on camera.' "¹⁰ In the end, an installation that sought to mobilize the aesthetic of transparency in the name of openness and access might well contribute to tighter control and monitoring of public space, an issue of some concern for civil rights and privacy advocates in Frankfurt and other major cities worldwide.

For Adorno, an astute critic of art's complex relations to society, perhaps nothing could be more fitting than such a dialectical reversal, whereby the intentions and practical effects of an aesthetic are so squarely at odds. For the moment, Adorno-Platz remains more of a place-holder; his see-through but now highly fortified and carefully monitored study awaits the day when his desk might be cleared and the utopian ambitions of the monument realized. In the meantime, we might do best by simply considering the complexities of something as seemingly straightforward as transparency, asking how Adorno's own work would have us consider this aesthetic as anything other than natural or self-explanatory. In the introduction to an essay collection written for the Adorno centennial, the editors address the relevancy of Adorno today by posing the question "What can one see using [*mit*] Adorno and what not?"¹¹ The most productive way of engaging with this question in examining transparency would not be to instrumentalize Adorno, to *use* his work as an optical prosthetic, but to join him in a careful reading of his work, to see *with* Adorno as he does so himself. This is what I propose to do here in my examination of *Minima Moralia*.

In upholding the principle of non-identity, the fundamental disjunction between concepts and objects, Adorno bases his mode of negative and immanent critique on tracing the cracks within "the cellophane of modernity," a deceptive sense of clarity within a society characterized by reified relations and the coercion resulting from the domination of nature.¹² For Adorno, "society's crystal-clear order" offers a promise of insight that fails to deliver anything more than ready-made enlightenment, blocking out a more engaging vision of change that is still to come.¹³ The urgent task of critical thought is to question the authenticity of that which might seem the most self-apparent and natural. This is a moment of resistance to a "society of glass houses where every hiding place has been smoked out" and a departure from the belief that insight is to be found in the absence of mediation—the truth claim of the conventionally transparent—toward an examination of mediation itself.¹⁴ As he writes in *Minima Moralia*:

"Wherever immediateness posits and entrenches itself, the bad mediateness of society is insidiously asserted. The cause of immediacy is now espoused by only the most circumspect reflections."[15] In offering his own reflections in *Minima Moralia*, Adorno offers us a model of perception and critical reflection that departs from the "cellophane shamelessness" of a valorization of immediacy in favor of a radical reassessment of the incomprehensible.[16] In this work and others, he defines illumination, of writing in particular, not in terms of its clarity, but rather its porous and material nature, a quality that might also be known by the name transparency but of a rather different order.

We are challenged to join him in an intense process of scrutiny that puts into question much of the accepted, the rational, and ultimately a great deal of traditional philosophical practice itself. In so doing we are faced with the task of privileging ongoing criticism over notions of fixed understanding, departing from abstraction in favor of the analysis of the concrete and the minute, and subjecting assigned meaning to an analysis of the power structure behind it. If we seek to arrive at any notion of truth, it is only to be located in the force field of a constellation of negative critiques put in motion through dialectical thinking, defined in *Minima Moralia* as "an attempt to break through the coercion of logic by its own means."[17] Such an attempt implies a questioning of the current order and a serious challenge to notions of fixity, permanence, and rationality that govern not only cultural, economic, and everyday social practices but also their study. Adorno is careful to situate the position of the critic within the larger social dynamics he critiques. Critics have indeed noted that the subtitle of *Minima Moralia* is, significantly, "Reflections from Damaged Life"—*from*, not *on*.

Of most significance in examining transparency, and indeed the potential of Adorno's work as a whole, is the relationship between power and rationality, representation and reflection. The truth claim of transparency is that it delivers insight at first glance, while Adorno sees it as an aesthetic that reveals more in its staging than its putative revelations. Glass appears in his work as a figure of that which would seem to create a connection, but instead enforces established separations, be it of objects from concepts, thought from imagination, or of human beings from each other. This is an image of "Isolation by Communication," as a fragment from *Dialectic of Enlightenment* is titled, a separation and division brought about through transparency as a mechanism of control:

> Progress keeps people literally apart. The little counter at the railroad station or the bank allowed the clerks to whisper to their colleagues and share

their meager secrets; the glass partitions of modern offices, the huge rooms in which countless employees sitting together can be easily supervised both by the public and by their managers, no longer countenance private conversations and idylls. Even in offices, the taxpayer is now protected from wasting of time by wage earners, who are isolated in their collective.[18]

As a technology of surveillance, transparency diminishes personal freedom and stunts the potential to develop capacities yet to be realized. This is as true for the lives of people as it is for their study. The gesture of making visible within the context of empirical sociological research provides for no insight if it freezes its object in the process. Adorno examines this problem in the essay "Reason and Revelation," in which he again mobilizes a figure of the transparent:

> In contrast to the richly and concretely developed religious imagination of old, the currently prevailing opinion, which claims that the life and experience of people, their immanence, is a kind of glass case, through whose walls one can gaze the eternally immutable ontological stock of a *philosophia* or *religio perennis*, is itself an expression of a state of affairs in which the belief in revelation is no longer substantially present in people and in the organization of their relationships and can be maintained only through a desperate abstraction.[19]

Here the figure of a transparent glass box is equated with the reifying gaze, that which falsifies by making eternal and immutable. This is of course the focus of Adorno and Horkheimer's attack in *Dialectic of Enlightenment*, which proposes a model of cultural development based on the premise that the search for enlightenment, defined broadly as demystification and mastery of nature through reason, has itself become irrational. In developing this theory into then-contemporary sociology, Adorno seeks a new understanding of sociology itself, one that would reflect an increasing self-awareness of the constructed nature of its own methodology and ultimate social function. Questioning the transparency of empirical social science, Adorno seeks a similar radical potential in his metacritique of cultural analysis in his essay "Cultural Criticism and Society" in the 1955 volume *Prisms*. In it he ascribes an essentially affirmative role to its dominant mode, a practice that evaluates individual manifestations of "culture" without scrutinizing their relation to a larger political economy of cultural production. The critic fails to recognize his or her own positionality and is either unable or unwilling to trace cultural production back to its own material conditions. Adorno is raising questions of epistemology, but also, and perhaps most importantly, the issue of ethics. First, to the position of the critic, Adorno writes: "The cultural critic is not happy with civilization, to which alone he owes his discontent. He speaks as if he represented either unadulterated nature or a higher historical stage. Yet he is necessarily of the same essence as that to which he fancies himself superior."[20] Epistemologically, this implies an irrationality of the critic's critique, a myopia that skews any attempt at interpretation. The question that follows is, of course, why? Here is where questions of power and ethics arise. As Adorno writes: "When the critics in their playground—art—no longer understand what they judge and enthusiastically permit themselves to be degraded to propagandists and censors, it is the old dishonesty of trade fulfilling itself in their fate. The prerogatives of information and position permit them to express their opinion as if it were objectivity. But it is solely the objectivity of the ruling mind. They help to weave the veil."[21] Creating a clear and neutral depiction of society, to make its dynamics transparent, is to overlook reification and veil its more nebulous workings. Further, he criticizes a false sense of freedom on the part of the critic, resulting from his lack of reflection and willing blindness to his instrumentalization. Thus, what is often thought a critical mode is in fact the replication of domination, implying guilt not only through association but also the complicity of self-deception. That such a transformation should occur is tied to the recognition that the image of the culture industry's false utopia does not preclude the realization that another, more liberating sense of freedom and democracy could still emerge. Adorno situates this hope in the tiny "gaps" in the "administered world" that might still allow imagination to shine through, though ever so faintly. He offers a fleeting glimpse of this possibility in *Minima Moralia*, which, to take one of its section headings, is a "picture-book without pictures," an outline of that which might still be to come, sketched not by illustration or example, but by the movement and tension of thought itself.

In *Minima Moralia* Adorno enacts more than depicts a nonmimetic philosophical critique through a collection of thought-images in which truth is not revealed but only hinted at through his critique of untruth. It is put forth as a critical gesture, a movement in thought. As he writes in the reflection "I.Q.": "Thinking no longer means anything more than checking at each moment whether one can indeed think. Hence the impression of suffocation conveyed even by all apparently independent intellectual productions, theoretical no less than artistic. The socialization of mind keeps it boxed in, isolated in a glass case, as long as society is itself imprisoned."[22] The text is dedicated to "Max in gratitude and promise," signaling both an acknowledgment of the work's past as well as the promise it may yet realize. Indeed, in the work's very title, an inversion of Aristotle's *Magna Moralia*, Adorno plots a new course for philosophy, a path beginning with the careful scrutiny of the minute and expanding into larger conceptual constellations. For Adorno, philosophy cannot simply start over again, however, but has to come to terms with its past. Thus we see him working not to postulate an entirely new system, but rather to proceed through a largely immanent critique of existing philosophical systems.

Adorno's task in *Minima Moralia* leads to the emergence of thought not easily simplified, passively consumed, or prone to paraphrase. As he writes in the dedication, following his critique requires a departure from the truth claims of the transparent and the challenge to develop a new critical vision: "He who wishes to know the truth about life in its immediacy must scrutinize its estranged form, the objective powers that determine individual existence even in its most hidden recesses."[23] Critical insight hence becomes a difficult process of recognition of the deformed, of acknowledging that life itself has taken on a new shape under the dynamics of capitalism and been damaged in the process. Indeed, reading *Minima Moralia* is to actively engage with Adorno's notion of the non-identical, or the remainder he posits in the incomplete identification of a concept with its object. The work of such thought, as Adorno writes, is the critical disruption of transparent truths. As he writes in the section "Finale" ["Zum Ende"]: "Perspectives must be fashioned that displace and estrange the world, reveal it to be, with its rifts and crevices, as indigent and distorted as it will appear one day in the messianic light. To gain such perspectives without velleity or violence, entirely from felt contact with its objects—this alone is the task of thought."[24] We might also see this as the task informing Adorno's own mode of representation in his attempt to give voice to the non-identical in a performative, figurative language, whose metaphors enact the nuanced and contradictory relation between concepts and objects, the universal and the particular. As Samuel Weber, one of the most adept translators of Adorno's work, writes:

> Like *Dichtung*, the specificity of Adorno's thought is inseparable from its articulation. If conceptual concreteness may be measured by the density with which thought and articulation permeate each other, then Adorno's style can be characterized by the constant striving to be concrete. . . . Whatever the historical causes of this empirical orientation might have been, contemporary English does not tolerate the notion that what is nearest at

hand may in fact be most abstract, while that which is invisible, intangible, accessible only to the mind may in fact be more real than reality itself."[25]

Further, Adorno's paratactic style refuses conceptual hierarchy and places ideas within constellations and force fields that highlight tensions and contradictions.[26] That which readily presents itself as the authentic, the self-evident, or the natural is for Adorno that which is in need of greatest mediation in order to arrive at its truth-content. Departing from the insistence on stable, immediate modes of thought and communication, Adorno writes in the section "Gaps" that "knowledge comes to us through a network [*Geflecht*] of prejudices, opinions, innervations, self-corrections, presuppositions and exaggerations, in short through the dense, firmly-founded but by no means uniformly transparent medium of experience."[27] It is only in deferral, through distance and mediation, that the work of critical thought—the weaving and unraveling of contradictions—can take place. This necessitates the thinking subject to "keep one's distance," as one of the reflections is headed, to estrange oneself in order to not succumb to the false presence of transparent truths. Adorno challenges subjective reason to take on a negative "monogram" that denies self-identity and recognizes that "true thoughts are those alone which do not understand themselves."[28]

Such thinking can only be communicated through an exploration of opacity, a "second harvest" [*zweite Lese*], as the aphorism's title implies, available to those readers who wait for the seemingly incomprehensible to bear fruit and labor for its harvest. As Adorno writes, this explains the critical afterlife of a text: "The transparency and simplicity of a text bears [*sic*] no direct relation to its capacity to enter tradition. It may be its very impenetrability, demanding constant renewed interpretation, that confers on a sentence or a work the authority which dedicates it to posterity."[29] Attempts at *Sachlichkeit* or "matter-of-factness," he argues, come at the expense of both matter and fact. For Adorno this point is critical, because the language of a text is inseparable from its engagement with concepts and materiality, making the stakes high for the use and abuse of language. Engaging with, or at least acknowledging, the difficulties of representation is to engage in an ethics of reading in which mediation is recognized and carefully scrutinized, even if this should render any transparent certainties untenable. As Adorno writes in the reflection "On the morality of thinking": "Mediately to affirm immediacy, instead of comprehending it as mediated within itself, is to pervert thought into an apologia of its antithesis, into the immediate lie."[30] In a dialectical maneuver so characteristic of

Minima Moralia, here again what is purported to be truth and revelation is instead positioned as its opposite. Comprehending [*begreifen*], literally the grasping of the materiality of representation and mediation, is privileged over "affirming" [*behaupten*], the assertion of communicable truths. Failing to engage with the text but not the texture of reading is to deny the mechanics and context of representation, an oversight or deliberate overlooking that stunts critical perception: "This perversion serves all bad purposes, from the private pigheadedness of 'life's-like-that' to the justification of social injustice as a law of nature."[31] Accepting injustice as natural, Adorno suggests here, is likewise an acceptance of an ideology of transparency, the naturalization of the constructed, that would conceal its staging of representation as an absence of mediation.

Charting a landscape of mediation, the topography of language's twists and turns in *Minima Moralia*, takes us "Over the hills," the heading of a section later in the text. Here Adorno relates thought and perception to a study of melancholy, expressed nowhere as aptly as in Snow White and the figure of the queen. Looking out into the snow through the "black mourning of the window-frame," she mourns her daughter, "who lies as if asleep in the glass coffin."[32] Reading is to join in this sorrow, which is at once a powerless hope: "All contemplation can do no more than patiently trace the ambiguity of melancholy in ever new configurations."[33] This is an arduous task, requiring patience, the making of difficult decisions, and a tolerance of ambiguity in the face of crisis, yet it is also the only way to gain a glimpse of any possible salvation: "Truth is inseparable from the illusory belief [*Wahn*] that from the figures of the unreal [*Schein*] one day, in spite of it all, real deliverance [*Rettung*] will come."[34] The way in which this hope manifests itself is indeed through an engagement with "figures," the reading of the *Schein* of the *scheinlos* and the material reality of apparition.

One of the most important meditations on reading and transparency in *Minima Moralia* is found in the section "Memento" [*"Hinter den Spiegel"*]. This thought-image takes us to the far side of mimetic perception and reflection, behind the mirror, offering what might be a new way of thinking transparency. Once arrived, however, we do not stay there, as indicated by the accusative article *den*; we are to remain in motion, following the movement of language as it passes through and bears the traces of a complex web of social relations and aesthetic conventions. Here Adorno reflects on illuminating writing not in terms of its clarity, but rather its porous, material nature. Inscription that entangles language, concepts, and arguments, that binds them to their object, is that which offers the hope of communication of something beyond banal, affirmative reflection. He writes: "Properly written texts are like spiders' webs: tight, concentric, transparent, well-spun and firm. They draw into themselves all the creatures of the air. Metaphors flitting hastily through them become their nourishing prey."[35] Here the transparent is a figure of mediation itself, rather than its denial. It does not seek to conceal its material existence, but insists upon it, sucking in matter with a magnetic, predatory force. In so doing, the transparent web clings to its object, winding it in its folds, and offering up a faint illumination: "It proves its relation to the object as soon as other objects crystallize around it. In the light that it casts on its chosen substance, others begin to glow."[36] With the possibility for insight lodged in the tangles of a web between gaps in concepts and objects, Adorno's text conveys a fragile hope and an urgent demand. Readers must proceed slowly, dialectically, but must also act quickly, before illumination, *Beute*, falls prey to the spider minding its traps, the tangled condition of its own possibility. The figure of the net also appears in the essay "Why Still Philosophy?" in which Adorno examines the role of philosophical investigation within reified relations: "The more reified the world becomes, the thicker the veil [*Netz*] cast upon nature, the more the thinking weaving that veil in its turn claims ideologically to be nature, primordial experience."[37] Following the tangle of these threads makes every new reading an *Urerfahrung*, a fresh interpretation based on the specific materiality of the evolving context at hand. Tracing these new formations requires a critical perception and an ability to think in figures and abstractions that allow for recognition of that which is as yet unseen. As Adorno writes in the section "Picture-book without pictures," however, this is exactly the capacity most threatened: "Amid the network [*Netz*] of now wholly abstract relations of people to each other and to things, the power of abstraction is vanishing."[38] Without a recognition of this web, the ties that connect become those that restrain, as the allure of immediacy, the promise that seeing is believing, erase the relays that are the text to be read. As Adorno writes in the section "Struwwelpeter":

> Estrangement shows itself precisely in the elimination of distance between people. For only as long as they abstain from importuning one another with giving and taking, discussion and implementation, control and function, is there space enough between them for the delicate connecting filigree of external forms in which alone the internal can crystallize.[39]

The consequence of this supposed immediacy is not greater openness, but less humanity: that which is laid bare is also made coarse. Putative immediacy only leads to increased reification, and the estrangement from oneself.

Doing away with ornament, the explicit conventions of ideology, promises transparent communication—free of hesitation, divagations, or reflections—but also absent of the substance that makes us most human: the capacity for that powerless hope for something more than the circumstances at hand. Hence, the promise becomes a command; the "direct word," a "silence." In turning to Adorno's essay "Functionalism Today" we will see how he interprets this same promise and command of transparency into the aesthetics and implicit politics of transparency in architecture. Here the stakes are just as high, as Adorno pleads for the reinvigoration of imagination through an acknowledgment of and critical engagement with the materiality of the aesthetics of architectural projects and programs.

"Functionalism Today" is Adorno's most explicit treatment of architecture, presenting an extended meditation on the relationship between material and design and the interplay of architectural visions and physical constraints. In it he examines the paradoxes of Adolf Loos's famous attack on architectural symbolism, "Ornament and Crime," and argues for the creation of human dwellings that are themselves humane. The essay targets immediate postwar construction in Germany in particular, but can be generalized as a commentary on a larger relationship between architectural aesthetics and human needs and hopes. "A critical analysis of the mediocre modernity of the style of German reconstruction by a true expert would be extremely relevant," he writes: "My suspicion in the *Minima Moralia* that the world is no longer habitable has already been confirmed."[40] Indeed, if the assertion made throughout *Minima Moralia* is that life itself is damaged, Adorno asks here how the built environment might offer some potential, if not for redemption, then at least for temporary shelter or the rudimentary framework for a more humane form of dwelling in the future.

Much of the essay revolves around the question of ornament versus function. While Le Corbusier and other proponents of *"Das Neue Bauen"* and later Functionalism would set the two in opposition, Adorno looks to the relays between them, arguing that both notions are highly contingent categories. Dividing them is a question of legitimation, that which is deemed fitting in a certain historical moment. This opens up the opposition to the indeterminacy of change and draws attention to the interests served in the solidification of the binary. "Criticism of ornament means no more than criticism of that which has lost its functional and symbolic signification," he writes: "Ornament becomes then a mere decaying and poisonous organic vestige."[41] Indeed, in dismantling the opposition between the "purpose-free and the purposeful arts," he determines that no form is determined solely by its function, even those that seem the most "pure." Instead, the aesthetic is always already implicated:

> The belief that a substance bears within itself its own adequate form presumes that it is already invested with meaning. Such a doctrine made the symbolist aesthetic possible. The resistance to the excesses of the applied arts pertained not just to hidden forms, but also to the cult of materials. It created an aura of essentiality about them.[42]

Neglecting these tensions and contradictions leads to a fetishization of form over truly humane function. For Adorno the "sharp edges, bare calculated rooms, stairways, and the like" are "sadistic blows" and "barbaric traits" of functionalist aesthetics.[43] In the name of rejecting style, it has itself incorporated the worst aspects of that which it criticized, leading to further damage to the human: "Virtually every consumer had probably felt all too painfully the impracticality of the mercilessly practical. Hence our bitter suspicion is formulated: the absolute rejection of style becomes style."[44] A greater potential exists in activating the surplus that these materials contain, that is, the way in which they have been used in the past and how they might still take shape in the future. This is a shift from the ontology of material to its malleability and contingency. There is something more to building than materials and form, Adorno writes: "Imagination means to *innervate* this something. This is not as absurd a notion as it may sound. For the forms, even the materials, are by no means merely given by nature, as an unreflective artist might easily presume. History has accumulated in them, and spirit permeated them."[45] To engage with material, to arrange and shape it in new constellations, is to encounter its past and point toward new configurations. Yet Adorno cautions against seeing this as a "positive law," but rather as the possibility of critical engagement. This is likened to a slow and patient dialogue with the materiality of expression: "Artistic imagination awakens these accumulated elements by becoming aware of the innate problematic of the material. The minimal progress of imagination responds to the wordless question posed to by the materials and forms in their quiet and elemental language [*Dingsprache*]."[46] Engaging with questions posed in a language as material as it is potentially unfathomable means fostering an attentiveness to the potential as well as the limitations of the material. Likewise, it requires the recognition of the connection between aesthetics and the larger network of relations with which it is always engaged. To attempt to deny this connection is to retreat into the "cult of materials" that is in actuality a denial of the material aspect of architecture itself. As Adorno writes:

> On the one hand, an imagined utopia, free from the binding purposes of the existing order, would become powerless, a detached ornament, since it must take its elements and structure from that very order. On the other, any attempt to ban the utopian factor, like a prohibition of images [*Bilderverbot*], immediately falls victim to the spell of the prevailing order.[47]

Any attempt to revolutionize architecture, to make it part of a larger project of liberation, must acknowledge social and material constraints. In addition, thought itself takes on a material aspect; its traces are found within the history of forms and materials. "The object at hand demands the kind of reflection which objectivity [*Sachlichkeit*] generally rebuked in a clearly non-objective manner. Thought has its own coercive impulse," writes Adorno, "like the one you are familiar with in your work with your material."[48] To engage with the history of materials is also to examine the various discourses in which they have been imbricated. It is also to recognize the shadow side of all creative construction, the ruins upon which the new is built. As Adorno writes: "The heavy shadow of instability bears upon built form, the shadow of mass migrations, which had their preludes in the years of Hitler and his war."[49] To build in a truly humane fashion is to engage with this history and its contradictions, not to conceal them: "Art, in order to be art according to its own formal laws, must be crystallized in autonomous form. This constitutes its truth content; otherwise, it would be subservient to that which it negates by its very existence."[50] Here to "crystallize" is to become solid, to take on form and materiality in a way that incorporates a material's past as much as its future.

In the essay "Culture and Administration" Adorno again takes up the figure of glass houses, writing: "Constructivism and greenhouses [*Glashäuser*] can be conceived only under conditions of warmth and within psychologically protected dwellings—and this is not to be understood only in literal terms."[51] Here he once again articulates the necessity of thinking through the limitations of an aesthetic as much as its promises. At stake are life and thought themselves. As the passage continues, "the equalization of the tensions felt today between culture and its objective conditions threatens culture with spiritual death by freezing."[52] In facing this threat, Adorno issues a challenge, calling on us to critically examine the transparent, to become able to recognize mediation in what might appear the most immediate. Doing so is the work of the imagination, the ability to visualize that which is not yet or no longer present; "should it be driven out," Adorno writes in one of *Minima Moralia*'s most melancholy reflections, "*Intellectus sacrificium intellectus*," "judgment too, the real act of knowledge, is also exorcised."[53] Its loss would be a "castration of perception" resulting in the inability to change.[54]

We are challenged as readers to maintain a position both "inside and outside," to cite another section heading from *Minima Moralia*. "Between delight in emptiness and the lie of fullness, the prevailing intellectual situation allows no third way," Adorno warns.[55] The urgent task, however, is to assume this third position, to incorporate a criticism of the staging of perception into perception itself, to combine image with imagination. Despite the damage inflicted on the human capacity for critical perception, Adorno writes, "a gaze averted from the beaten track, a hatred of brutality, a search for fresh concepts not yet encompassed by the general pattern, is the last hope for thought."[56] His critique of the transparent in *Minima Moralia* would have us question the self-identity, self-certainty, and self-constructed redemption of the epistemological promise of the transparent and in its political mobilization, be it in contemporary government architecture, crystalline office buildings and shopping centers, or elsewhere. We are charged with scrutinizing what the transparent conceals as much as that which supposedly reveals.

CHAPTER 11

The Polemic of the Late Work: Adorno's Hölderlin

Robert Savage

What does it mean to conceive of philosophy, in an essential and not merely incidental sense, as polemical? What is at stake when a philosopher polemicizes on behalf of poetry in order to salvage a polemic deemed to be proper to poetry itself? I want to explore these questions in this essay through a selective reading of "Parataxis: On Hölderlin's Late Poetry," an address to the Hölderlin Society delivered by Adorno on 7 June 1963, the 120th anniversary of the poet's death.[1] Polemic and rescue [*Rettung*], it will be argued, are the twin poles between which "Parataxis" oscillates and that delimit its field of argumentation. Their relationship generates a ferment in which each term passes imperceptibly into the other. On the one hand, the polemic figures a kind of loving hate that mortifies in order to save: no resurrection without the stench of death. In Gnostic terms, the polemic affords a glimpse of divine truth through its absolute negation of the fallen world of the demiurge, anticipating the rescue of the particular in the universal envisaged by Adorno's regulative "utopia of knowledge."[2] On the other hand, as an unrelieved negativity that resists being swept into the speculative movement of *Aufhebung*, the polemic equally designates the rescue of the particular *from* the universal. Adorno explains how in his *Philosophy of Modern Music*: "The absolute liberation of the particular from the universal renders it universal through the polemical and principal

172

relationship of the universal to the particular."³ The polemic becomes the marginalized placeholder for a good universality through the intransigence of its opposition to a bad one. It permits Adorno to think reconciliation without giving up on contingency, and to uphold the claims of the non-identical without saturating it in the light of the idea. Yet because a refusal of communication is also a refusal of media(tiza)tion, Adorno's theoretical domestication of the polemic, while allowing it to be perceived as such, also threatens to downgrade it into just another discursive turn. The challenge lies in enduring the tension of polemic and rescue without dissolving it in favor of one or the other. Three interrelated questions need to be posed here:

1. How do polemic and rescue belong together in Adorno's reading of Hölderlin's late work? By what law can something fallen, attacked, negated, and repudiated be simultaneously raised, transcended, affirmed, and fulfilled?

2. How is their co-belonging structurally articulated in the essay? What does the form of "Parataxis," as "sedimented content," reveal about the polemic?[4]

3. What is the relationship between this oxymoronic polemic, this rescue without armistice or amnesty, and the polemic as it is commonly understood, which certainly does not intend the rescue of its target?

I will address these questions in reverse order, moving from a consideration of Adorno's decidedly nonredemptive polemic against the Hölderlin interpretation advanced by Martin Heidegger, which takes up the first half of his address, to a discussion of "late style" as the self-reflection of the polemic in the medium of art, the focus of its second half.

Polemical Semblance

To ground these questions, a brief recapitulation of Adorno's concept of aesthetic rescue is called for. This concept receives its most comprehensive treatment in *Aesthetic Theory*, where Adorno decrees "the rescue of semblance" to be "central to aesthetics," adding that "the emphatic right of art, the legitimation of its truth, depends on this rescue."[5] For Adorno, art requires the intervention of philosophy in order to transform its semblance character, the stigma inflicted upon it by a bad social totality and the mark of its impotence, into utopian *Vor-Schein* or pre-semblance, the source of its minimal discrepancy from the realm of means-ends rationality and the sole guarantor of its truth. While an artwork is the product of human activity, hence subjectively willed, it can only instantiate a form of cognition to be found nowhere else if its truth content transcends volition. Art justifies itself as art, rather than as a sugarcoating to make otherwise unpalatable religious, political, or philosophical messages easier to swallow, when it reflects upon its semblance character, the agent of its categorical distinction from all other spheres of a fully rationalized, disenchanted society. By virtue of its semblance character, the autonomous artwork appears as a thing in and for itself, obeying none but its own formal law and supremely indifferent to the onlooker; yet its production, reception, and artifactuality all tie it back to the universe of consumption and exchange. Adorno therefore writes: "The question of the truth of something made is indeed none other than the question of semblance and the rescue of semblance as the semblance of the true."[6] The rescue of semblance does not imply its overcoming as *dissemblance* or *illusion*, nor the discursive explication of a truth content for which the artwork would be the mere *appearance*, but the demonstration of a discursively inexhaustible truth-claim bound up with the modality and processuality of aesthetic *appearing*.[7]

Adorno's rationale for a philosophical engagement with art underwrites his argumentative strategy in "Parataxis," which maintains a twofold relation to the polemic. First, the rescue of semblance he undertakes there is designed to release in Hölderlin an implacable antagonism toward the status quo left unheeded by philology, and transmuted by Heidegger into the myth of the founder-poet. This antagonism, however, is void of any determinable political content. The semblance character of art makes it the refuge for a form of cognition—mimetic, nonsubsumptive, and sensuous—that has otherwise been banished from modern life. Consequently, although Adorno has a clear eye for Hölderlin's philosophical and affective attachment to the ideals of the French Revolution, he holds that the politicization of art, expressed in the demand that its always particular truth-claims become legislative for a community, amounts to its false sublation. As J. M. Bernstein comments, "to politicize art is to employ the rationality it refuses for the sake of the rationality it enjoins."[8] Adorno's adamant aestheticism, which marks his distance from the post-1968 reception of Hölderlin on the Left, makes it difficult to say where the specific polemical thrust of Hölderlin's poetry lies, beyond the mere fact of its being art. A number of passages in *Aesthetic Theory* do indeed suggest that art is polemical a priori, insofar as it formally constitutes itself through the determinate negation of social reality.[9] Philosophy's task would then be to recognize that art's refusal of communication, its monadic imperviousness to external demands, is itself a form of communication, and so to realize it *as* polemical. This is exactly what Adorno sets out to do in "Parataxis." Second, this polemicization of Hölderlin's work follows from an interpretative comportment that itself operates polemically. The difference between "polemical" and "ontological" understandings adduced by Adorno[10] would thus be one between an approach that locates art's latent critical force in its constitutive distance from other domains of the social, and an approach that attempts to abolish that distance by interpretative fiat: "Heidegger glorifies the poet supra-aesthetically, as a founder, without reflecting concretely on the agency of form."[11]

A further, equally intimate connection between rescue and polemic in "Parataxis" becomes apparent once the historical dynamic discerned by Adorno in the afterlife or *Nachgeschichte* of an artwork is taken into account. For Adorno, the truth content of an artwork has a temporal core. Among other things, this means that the truth of a poem depends upon its bearing witness, in however mediated a fashion, to the time of its creation. Adorno takes Heidegger to task for violating this maxim through his obsession with the poet's heroic individuality, which allegedly leads the philosopher, "all his perorations about historicity notwithstanding," to catapult Hölderlin into the timeless firmament of genius.[12] The "historical core of the truth content itself" dictates that no poem has a guarantee of immortality.[13] Once-celebrated works shed meaning as they age, grow silent, and sink into the footnotes of literary history. Others, all but ignored at the time of their appearance, patiently await a posterity equipped to unlock their secrets; like Heidegger, Adorno reckons Hölderlin to this latter category.[14] In "Parataxis," the relationship between a poem and its afterlife is described as a process of self-realization, almost of revelation: "What unfolds and becomes visible in the works, the source of their authority, is none other than the truth manifested objectively in them."[15] But this confident claim, which makes history the final arbiter of aesthetic value, is in fact ambiguous. It is compromised by a further postulate, according to which the changes undergone by an artwork over the course of its evolution invest it with meanings that were not merely concealed at its conception, lying ready to be stumbled upon by future generations, but that cannot even be said to have existed before the moment of their belated "discovery." Thus Adorno argues in the *Introduction to the Sociology of Music* that a "history of the critique of Beethoven could demonstrate how with every new layer of critical consciousness, new layers of his work itself were uncovered, *in a certain sense first constituted themselves through that process* [my italics—R.S.]."¹⁶

Once history is no longer conceived as the stage upon which the truth content of an artwork comes to blossom before an ever-more-discerning audience, once it is conceded the power to precipitate changes in the artwork's inner development, such that work and temporal reception reciprocally condition one another, the discomforting possibility arises that even a misinterpretation may cause a previously unknown stratum in Hölderlin's poetry to crystallize, demonstrating a potential for misuse that will haunt each subsequent reading. Adorno moves to limit the damage by insisting that only a particular form of reception he calls *critique* is of any consequence for a poem's truth content. Critique registers, as upon a seismograph, the tremors issuing from the artwork as it grows older, using knowledge of the most "advanced" compositional techniques of the day to pick up reverberations too faint for the ordinary ear. Yet if "history has retroactive force," as Adorno insists against the historicist endeavor to know the past "as it actually happened," does not the exoteric, one is tempted to say "inauthentic," reception of a poet—in this case, the sinister popularity whipped up for Hölderlin during the Second World War—also prove relevant for critique, as the index and catalyst of a subcutaneous transformation?¹⁷ And if that is correct, might not the scandalous violence with which Adorno takes to Heidegger, whose interpretation he explicitly (and controversially)¹⁸ assimilates to the nationalist orgy that marked the centenary of the poet's death in 1943, betray a residual doubt as to the purity of the poet for whose sake he was fighting? From this angle, Adorno's offensive public relations campaign is to be understood as a defensive reflex calculated to prevent his self-implicating theory of interpretation from sliding into self-incrimination.

The problem may be clarified by means of a detour to another speech delivered by Adorno in the same year, 1963, on a similarly solemn commemorative occasion, that of the 150th anniversary of Kierkegaard's birth. While the speech rehearses many of the arguments from his *Habilitationsschrift*, the tone is much sharper than thirty years earlier, and for reasons not unrelated to the catastrophe that had transpired in the interim. Adorno begins by drawing attention to a contradiction between Kierkegaard's distrust for the worldly success of a doctrine and the dubious influence exerted by his writings upon the theological seminaries and philosophical seminars of the early twentieth century. "By the measure of his own writing, Kierkegaard may not be victorious,"¹⁹ yet the same uncompromising individualism that drove him into isolation during his lifetime and harried him to an early grave has since degenerated into an intellectual *mode du jour*: "From that individual has arisen the mendacious chatter which proclaims the others to be inauthentic and themselves fallen to chatter. That was sealed in Germany when, before 1933, the Nazi Emanuel Hirsch took out a general lease on him: victory as defeat." Adorno leaves no doubt that Kierkegaard would have turned away in horror from his posthumous fame. Nonetheless: "The trajectory of such a victory is that of a self-unfolding untruth of Kierkegaard's doctrine."[20] The parallel to his interpretative strategy in "Parataxis," which likewise uses a review of its subject's afterlife as a point of entry into the work, only underscores the startling divergence in Adorno's evaluation of the evidence. The travesty suffered by Hölderlin at the hands of Heidegger reflects nothing more than the latter's philistinism, that inflicted upon Kierkegaard by Hirsch nothing less than the former's involuntary complicity. On what grounds, then, does Kierkegaard's misappropriation by the Nazis cast a retroactive judgment upon his work, whereas Hölderlin, whose writings proved incomparably more amenable to their evil ends, escapes scot-free from the tribunal of history? Why do Heidegger's commentaries, which Adorno rightly or wrongly makes representative for the entire National Socialist reception, take hold of Hölderlin as their helpless prey, rather than revealing a potential in his poetry that can now be seen to have inhered in it from the first? Why was Kierkegaard partially responsible for his historical fate, Hölderlin the victim of a crude falsification that leaves the truth content of his poetry intact?

However convincing the arguments leveled against Heidegger in "Parataxis" may be, in themselves they cannot suffice to answer such questions, just as the most compelling textual refutation of Hirsch's claims does nothing to alter the fact that they were in some sense authorized by Kierkegaard. This is where the polemic comes to the rescue. The opening line of "Parataxis" drops the hint: "There is no question that understanding of Hölderlin's work has grown along with his fame since the school of Stefan George demolished the conception of him as a quiet, refined minor poet with a touching life story."[21] Tellingly, Adorno recasts the George Circle's messianically tinged "discovery" of Hölderlin in polemical terms, reminding his audience—whose stated aim, after all, was to further the poet's "fame" and "understanding"—that a moment of radical discontinuity or necessary violence is sometimes required to set in motion the tranquil dialectic of intellectual progress. In retrospect, Adorno's words read like a veiled apology for the bad manners that would soon leave his listeners gasping. But they also offer a way out of the cul-de-sac into which

Adorno's thinking of the historicity of artworks had led him. The conventions of academic debate notionally adhered to by the Hölderlin Society, as by every other such organization, presuppose both the reasonableness of the participants and the respectability of their positions. Regardless of whether they are actually observed in day-to-day practice, such conventions operate under the normative assumption that consensus can be reached through the noncoercive force of the better argument. Once an interlocutor has shown himself to be immune to reason, however, they become a cumbrance rather than an aid to the common search for truth; Adorno probably had something like this in mind when he remarked that it is not possible to have a conversation with a fascist.[22] From a discourse-theoretical perspective, the polemicist violates the rules of the game for the sake of the outcome, his principal objective being to ostracize a member of the language community who had hitherto enjoyed full rights of speech. "Ideology critique," writes Peter Sloterdijk with reference to Adorno, "signifies the polemical continuation of a broken-down dialogue with other means."[23] The opening words of "Parataxis" justify the coming attack on Heidegger, whose philosophy Adorno branded in the same year as being "fascist to its innermost cells,"[24] by presenting it, against all appearances, as an indispensable moment in the process of enlightenment. Heidegger's obscurantist arguments may prove to be irrefutable, but they can nonetheless be *disabled* by creating discursive conditions under which they will no longer be heeded.[25]

For all its rhetorical force, Adorno's war of words ultimately depends for its effectiveness upon the (polemical) rescue of (polemical) semblance that follows and informs it. Only such rescue can show that the fight will have been worthwhile. Without it, any argument about Hölderlin descends into a puerile and meaningless squabble for ownership of one of the countless scraps on the trash-heap of culture "after Auschwitz." The rescue of semblance undertaken in "Parataxis" offers Hölderlin the chance, refused to Kierkegaard, of a precarious sanctuary from the vicissitudes of his reception. Not by exempting his poetry from history—art's semblance character is historical through and through—but by polemically intervening in history, and demonstrating through the event of interpretation what Adorno's own theory of reception could not: that Hölderlin's poetry is not what Heidegger has made it (out) to be. The appropriate theoretical response to "the right-wing German cult of Hölderlin" is an eminently practical one.[26]

The Sundered Whole

"Parataxis" is divided into roughly equal halves—in the printed version, they take up twenty-one and twenty-three pages, respectively—the first of which corresponds to Adorno's polemic against Heidegger, the second to his interpretation of Hölderlin (or, as we can now specify, to the rescue of semblance in Hölderlin's late work). Of course, this schematic division cannot be taken as absolute, given that Adorno's sense of how Hölderlin is to be read inevitably colors the polemic against Heidegger; given, too, that the shots discharged there continue to ricochet in the immanent reading that ensues. Each half of "Parataxis" maintains numerous connections with its counterpart. Yet the bar of white space that juts between them should not be bridged too hastily in our eagerness to apprehend the essay as a whole. The unity of the essay is the product, not the encompassing ground of its inner dislocation. If indeed the first half stands under the sign of the polemic, the second under that of rescue, and if polemic and rescue name two aspects of the same state of affairs, then the suspicion arises that an X-ray picture of "Parataxis" might provide the clearest possible indication of the difference *and* identity of these terms.

This suspicion is confirmed by a comment Adorno made toward the end of his life. Rolf Tiedemann and Gretel Adorno, as reliable witnesses as any, report it in their afterword to *Aesthetic Theory*: "he noted of his own method that it had the closest affinities with the aesthetic texts of the late Hölderlin."[27] The editors cite the remark in drawing attention to the paratactic organization of Adorno's posthumous work, which eschews the linearity of expository argument to circle, in ever-varying approaches, around the same constitutive aporias of art. Applied to "Parataxis," the only text he devoted to the poet,[28] Adorno's admission effectively collapses the distinction between what he says about Hölderlin's late work, the essay's thematic content, and how he says it, its form. The proximity acknowledged by Adorno substitutes the sense of detachment with which the professional critic usually approaches the literary object for the intimacy of communion. As the convergence-point of Adorno's late philosophical method and Hölderlin's late work, "Parataxis" enacts the critical confluence of interpretation and self-description.

Thus emboldened to search "Parataxis" for statements that communicate subterraneously with Adorno's own formal procedure, one comes across the following reading of "Hälfte des Lebens" ["Half of Life"], Hölderlin's best-known paratactic structure:

In a manner reminiscent of Hegel, mediation of the vulgar kind, a middle element standing outside the moments it is to connect, is eliminated as being external and inessential, something that occurs frequently in Beethoven's late style; this not least of all gives Hölderlin's late poetry its anticlassicistic quality, its rebellion against harmony. What is lined up in sequence, unconnected, is as harsh as it is flowing. The mediation is set within what is mediated instead of bridging it. As Beißner and more recently Szondi have emphasized, each of the two stanzas of "Hälfte des Lebens" has an inherent need for its opposite. In this regard as well, content and form are demonstrably one. In order to become expression, the antithesis of sensuous love and being cast out, an antithesis of content, breaks the stanzas apart, just as conversely it is only the paratactical form itself that produced the caesura between the halves of life.[29]

Adorno's observation, that each strophe in "Hälfte des Lebens" requires its opposite, holds just as true for the two massive discursive blocks that make up "Parataxis," whose architecture he may well have modeled on this very poem. The relation between the idyllic landscape of the first strophe and the wintry world of the second mirrors in reverse that between polemic and rescue in "Parataxis." Rescue is the unspoken yearning of the polemic, which in turn acts as the plenipotentiary and executor of rescue, yet their solidarity demands absolute discretion if it is to avoid betrayal. Were polemic and rescue to declare their union through the good offices of "a middle element standing outside the moments it is to connect"—one is reminded here of the marriage-meddling Mittler from Goethe's *Elective Affinities*—then they would fall victim to the same extorted reconciliation from which the polemic had resiled in the first place.

According to Adorno, Hölderlin exposes such mediation as the logical equivalent to the subjugation of nature, insofar as he demonstrates that the copula through which synthesis is effected remains indifferent to whatever it happens to be synthesizing.[30] Rather than forcing the halves of life into the Procrustean bed of identity ($A = B$), Hölderlin leaves them juxtaposed without commentary (A/B), such that their "harsh jointure"[31] insinuates synthesis in the painful absence of synthesis. The abrupt cry of *"Weh mir"*[32] ["Alas"] at the beginning of the second strophe, which shatters the blissful image evoked by its predecessor, advertises and exacerbates the wound in life that a hypotactic transition, be it even a *yet* or *but*, would presume to suture. Like the antithetical moods to which each strophe gives voice, the opposition of polemic and rescue in Adorno's essay is not to be overcome by flattening them into synonymity, but by driving their contrast to an extreme. Their relationship is itself polemical. "Parataxis" (and parataxis, the formal correlate of this process of distension and dissociation) may accordingly be characterized as the (dis)union of polemic and rescue under the preponderance of the polemic. Just as Hölderlin's poem rends a mythic wholeness of life into disconnected halves, so Adorno's aptly named essay submits to paratactic diremption the virtual unity of polemic and rescue that can only be inferred, never posited as such: here the brutally insensitive publicist, there the hypersensitive literary critic; here a refusal of communication, there a communion that has no need of it; here the sound and the fury of the polemic, there the redemptive calm of Hölderlin's "intention to cast aside synthesis and trust to pure passivity in order to completely fill the present."[33] What nonetheless allows one to speak of dissociation and diremption, rather than an insignificant side-by-side of unrelated elements, is the fact that in both cases the burden of mediation comes to be transposed from the suspended copula to "within what is mediated." The polemic against Heidegger generates of itself the need for the rescue of semblance, while that rescue, far from leaving the polemic behind as its mere prelude, bestows upon it the greatest possible epistemological dignity.

The striking parallels between the subject matter of "Parataxis" and its formal constitution—"in this regard as well, content and form are demonstrably one"—by no means end there. In "Hälfte des Lebens," the structural *symmetry* of the two strophes is offset by the *dissymmetry* of the stylistic principles that organize them. The language of the first half flows in a continuous movement over the course of a single sentence, beginning with the description of the yellow pears, rising to the apostrophe to the loving swans that occupies the middle line of the strophe, before subsiding at the end, along with the swans' drunken heads, into the holy-sober water. The form reproduces the ripple effect on the surface of the lake that emanates from *"Ihr holden Schwäne"* ["You loving swans"] (both the line and the swans themselves). The next strophe, by contrast, is broken into two sentences, the first a despairing question, the second not so much its answer as a paratactic recognition that no answer will be forthcoming: *"Die Mauern stehn / Sprachlos und kalt, im Winde / Klirren die Fahnen"* ["The walls loom / Speechless and cold, in the wind / Weathercocks clatter"]. The form seems to buckle and collapse here under the weight placed upon the suffering, isolated subject, which only now makes itself heard in a series of strongly alliterative, staccato-like phrases: *"Weh mir, wo nehm' ich, wenn / Es Winter ist, die Blumen . . . ?"* ["Alas, where shall I find when / Winter comes, the flowers . . . ?"][34] What Adorno calls the "antithesis of sensuous love and being cast out, an antithesis of content" is thus matched *and* unbalanced by a formal antithesis of smooth hypotaxis and disturbed parataxis within a paratactic (always already sundered) whole.

Similarly, a crude overview of the structure of "Parataxis" reveals that each of its halves entails a different mode of presentation that militates against their synthesis in an overarching whole. The first half is composed of eight enormous paragraphs. The opening pair, recognizably the introductory section of the essay, establish philosophy's prerogative to concern itself with Hölderlin, while the remaining six are taken up with showing how Heidegger has abused that right. The first sentence of the third paragraph ensures an unruffled transition: "While Hölderlin's poetry, like everything that is poetry in the emphatic sense, needs philosophy as the medium that brings its truth content to light"—this the result of the argument so far—"this need is not fulfilled through recourse to a philosophy that in any way seizes possession of the poetry"—this the omen of things to come.[35] Each of the following four paragraphs then sets out to denounce a particular weakness of Heidegger's reading: its anti-aesthetic celebration of the poet (§3); its fixation on the late work's gnomic sayings at the expense of their contextual significance (§4); its barely-concealed allegiance to certain fascist topoi (§5); and its willful disregard for the collective historical experience from which Hölderlin's poetry draws (§6). The penultimate paragraph preempts the obvious retort—if Heidegger got it so wrong, how is one to explain Hölderlin's attractiveness to him?—with reference to the role of abstractions in the hymnic work. There follows a last, emphatic attempt to liberate Hölderlin once and for all from the clutches of ontology: "[Hölderlin's] distant phantasmata of the nearby cannot be hoarded up in the treasury of *Heimatkunst*."[36] The well-defined tripartite structure of this essay within the essay—the preparation, execution, and *coup de grâce* of the polemic, as it were—articulates the relentless momentum driving the argument toward its goal. This is, essentially, that of "smashing Heidegger," a plan hatched out decades earlier by Benjamin and Brecht,[37] but first carried out by Adorno during the early 1960s.[38]

The second half consists of nine paragraphs, again of colossal dimensions. The first (§9) proposes that the corrective to Heidegger's procedure be sought in the relationship of form and content in Hölderlin's late work: "What philosophy can hope for in poetry is constituted only in this relationship; only here can it be grasped without violence."[39] Sections 10 to 13 go on to view this relationship through the prism of form, paying special attention to Hölderlin's paratactic technique and his use of correspondences, then §14 to §17 through that of content, thematizing the poetry's explicit critique of synthesis. The unity of form and content in the "poetized" [*Gedichtete*], a term Adorno borrows from Benjamin's early essay on Hölderlin,[40] makes their disentanglement a consciously heuristic measure. To study one in isolation from the other is justified only if their partition annuls itself over the course of the interpretation, which is what Adorno's approach evidently intends. Yet he also insists that the unity of form and content does not precede its critical elaboration: "But there is scarcely any aesthetic object that demonstrates more forcefully than Hölderlin's work that the assertion of an unarticulated unity of form and content is no longer adequate. Such a unity can be conceived only as a unity across its moments; the moments must be distinguished from one another if they are to harmonize with the content and be neither merely separate nor passively identical."[41] Each paragraph in the second half must therefore be understood as performing a function that is at once analytic and synthetic; each examines an integral part of a whole that first emerges through its reconstruction; each explicates the same matter of thinking from a different vantage point; and each refers, by virtue of its fragmentariness, to the aggregate of the parts. Benjamin's description of the tractate in his *Origin of the German Play of Mourning* is apposite to that book's most avid reader: "Tirelessly the process of thinking makes new beginnings, returning in a roundabout way to its original object. This continual pausing for breath is the mode most proper to the process of contemplation."[42] The moments when Adorno's argument snatches breath before taking another tilt at Hölderlin—and what else is signified by a paragraph break?—stand in the same relation to the form of the essay's second half as does parataxis to a compound sentence.

The pronounced contrast between the polemical, progressive ductus of the first half and the constellative, cyclical procedure of the second finds its strict analogy, and perhaps its model, in the stylistic dissymmetry of "Hälfte des Lebens." What is the import of this split between polemical and redemptive presentation, and how does it further our understanding of "Parataxis" as a (paratactic) whole? A letter from Benjamin to Adorno, dated 19 June 1938, provides the germ of an answer. Adorno had invited him to comment on his recently completed manuscript on Wagner. In accord with later critical opinion,[43] Benjamin identified what he took to be a polemical motivation behind the book, and went on to contrast the polemic qua literary form with rescue:[44]

> A polemical engagement with Wagner by no means has to exclude illumination of the progressive elements in his work, as you yourself show, and

especially if these cannot simply be separated from the regressive ones like the sheep from the goats. But yet—and here, dear Teddie, you must allow me to surprise you in body and soul with your own favourite image from Indian Joe about unearthing the hatchet and provoking a fight[45]—it seems to me that any such rescue, undertaken from the perspective of the philosophy of history, is incompatible with one undertaken from a critical perspective that is focused upon progress and regress. . . . I hardly imagine you will wish to contradict me if I say that the philosophical project of such rescue requires a form of writing which . . . has a particular affinity with musical form itself. Rescue is a cyclical form, polemic a progressive one. . . . The decisive element in such rescue—am I not right?—is never simply something progressive; it can resemble the regressive as much as it resembles the ultimate goal, which is what Karl Kraus calls the origin.

It is impossible not to recall here the fourteenth of the theses on the concept of history, committed to paper shortly afterward, which takes as its epigraph the same Karl Kraus dictum cited by Benjamin at the end of his critique. Thesis XIV opposes the "homogeneous, empty time" of progress, which is also the time of social democracy, to the "now-time" of revolutionary upheaval.[46] The latter blasts open the "continuum of history" to redeem possibilities that had been neglected by the inexorable march of progress (which, as Benjamin's letter makes clear, is equally that of regress; expressed in the language of the "Theses," there is no document of civilization that is not also one of barbarism).[47] Accordingly, polemic and rescue are the concomitant formal principles to the "perspective[s] of the philosophy of history" of progress and messianic rupture. They are irreconcilable because the rhythm and manner of their unfolding are dictated by radically different temporalities. The polemic operates within the unilinear time of history, deriving its legitimacy from a telos that makes possible the identification, if not the segregation, of pro- and regressive tendencies. The literary form of rescue, on the other hand, interrupts history to present its object in the undiminished actuality of the day of creation. Benjamin's reference to music makes clear that this process is not to be conceived as the abstract negation of transitoriness—music, after all, is the art most closely wedded to time—but as the fulfillment of the transitory in recurrence, the renewed coming to be of what had long since passed away and had apparently missed its moment. For Benjamin, whereas the polemic occupies the profane time-space of evolution, rescue anticipates the *kairos* of revolution (the indifference of origin and goal in "cyclical form"), and there can be no congress between the two.[48]

As Benjamin foresaw, Adorno showed no inclination to contest his insightful comments on the musical technique proper to *Rettung*. He also conceded the justness of Benjamin's central criticism regarding the monograph's polemical conception.[49] In the guise of an "attenuating circumstance," however, he averred that he "did not relate the idea of 'saving' Wagner solely and unconditionally to the progressive features of his work, but rather attempted everywhere to emphasize the entanglement of the progressive and the regressive moments."[50] While this somewhat muted defense might seem merely to reiterate the inseparability of progressive and regressive elements already acknowledged in Benjamin's original letter, it actually points to a key divergence in their respective philosophies of history. For in relating his attempted rescue of Wagner to the "entanglement of the progressive and the regressive moments" accentuated throughout the book, Adorno commits what Benjamin must have regarded as an illegitimate incursion into the exclusive province of the polemic. Between the lines, Adorno is arguing that polemic and rescue can no more be separated than progress and regress. To be sure, his assent to Benjamin's comments on the literary form appropriate to each indicates that he does not dispute their opposition. But whereas Benjamin withdraws that opposition from mediation, so proclaiming it to be absolute, Adorno sees it as the polarized function of a *single* historical-philosophical perspective, just as he grasps the antithesis of "Hälfte des Lebens" as the diremption of a life that must at least be thinkable in an undirempted state. In other words, the noncommunication of rescue and polemic correctly identified by Benjamin is to be understood as being polemical in nature, hence tenuously communicative. The circumstance referred to by Adorno is "attenuating" in the precise sense that it mitigates the finality of their severance: "And perhaps it is also indicative of this fact that the work possesses more of a cyclical form in your own sense than you are ready to credit."[51]

The debate played out between Benjamin and Adorno in 1938 repeats itself exactly twenty-five years later as an immanent conflict between the stylistic opposition of polemic and rescue, on the one hand, and their operative entwinement and speculative identity, on the other. This conflict cannot be resolved in "Parataxis," nor is such a resolution attempted; instead, the essay bears out and dramatizes, it *is* this conflict. Or to paraphrase Adorno: in order to become expression, the antithesis of rescue and polemic breaks apart the essay, just as, conversely, it is only the paratactic form itself that brings about their scission. Paradoxically, this cut in the text is the stitch that holds it together, the binding that prevents it splitting down the middle into Benjamin's utterly disparate spheres. It is to this

Schnittstelle, this empty yet perilously fraught caesura, that we must now turn.

The End of the Polemic

Adorno's concept of the caesura has its prehistory. From its humble origins in prosody, where it designates a division in a metrical foot indicating a pause in delivery, the caesura first rises to theoretical prominence in Hölderlin's poetological reinscription of a poetics of tragic effect. The basic problem addressed in the notes to *Oedipus* displays a marked resemblance to the constitutive dilemma of "Parataxis": through what technique or *mekhanē* can the violently conflicting drives that constitute the proper subject of tragedy—Hölderlin names them the boundless copulation and boundless separation of man and god—be brought together, bound, in a beautiful work of art?[52] Hölderlin's answer is audaciously speculative: "Thereby, in the rhythmic sequence of the representations wherein *transport* presents itself, there becomes necessary *what in poetic meter is called caesura*, the pure word, the counterrhythmic rupture; namely, in order to meet the onrushing change of representations at its highest point in such a manner that very soon there does not appear the change of representation but the representation itself."[53] Two points need to be noted here, however briefly. First, the caesura delimits and protects the work by bringing to a halt the catastrophic oscillation that threatens to derange the presentation. It *takes the measure* of the tragedy; that is to say, it moderates the work's excessive drives by determining their proportions and relative weighting within the tragic poem as a whole. It thereby guarantees the continuing relatedness of the opposing poles that are flung apart, with tremendous velocity, at the height of the tragic transport.[54] Second, as a pure word eviscerated of meaning, the caesura marks the hiatus around which the entire play is structured. It is an absence—nothing happens at the caesura; it is not the peripeteia[55]—but it is an absence that reveals the conditions of presence and presencing in the play, and as such is "the liberation by default—but a non-negative default—of meaning itself or of the truth of the work."[56]

We can already surmise that the caesura of "Parataxis" functions in much the same way, and it comes as no surprise that Adorno twice introduces the concept into his interpretation. Yet although Adorno was familiar with Hölderlin's theory of tragedy,[57] neither of these references makes any mention of it, just as the essay in general shows scant regard for the poet's protracted meditations on the genre. Of more immediate relevance to Adorno's use of the term is Benjamin's study on the *Elective Affinities*. In that text, thought by Adorno to be the finest he ever wrote, Benjamin extends the range of the caesura far beyond the bounds of tragedy by bringing it into connection with what he called "the expressionless," which is "a category of language and art and not of the work or of the genres." The expressionless "is the critical violence which, while unable to separate semblance from essence in art, prevents them from mingling."[58] For Benjamin, the expressionless power of language cannot be translated without remainder into appearance—it does not tarry in the medium of language, awaiting release from the poet—nor does it transcend appearance, floating in a languageless ether accessible only to intuition. Rather, the expressionless communicates itself in the caesura as the spiritual form of an artwork, which otherwise lies submerged in the means of its expression. The "occidental Junonian sobriety," which Hölderlin considered the greatest achievement of Greek art, "is only another name for the caesura, in which, along with harmony, every expression simultaneously comes to a standstill, in order to give free reign to an expressionless power inside all artistic media."[59] The organic flux of the harmonious work of art must momentarily be transfixed in order that the expressionless, punctuating appearance, appear as such; for caesuras, as Winfried Menninghaus points out, are "partitioning cuts, which precisely as lacunae . . . indicate the position of the knife itself."[60] The Benjaminian caesura brings the expressionless to expression without delivering it over to language, pointing the way to the truth content of the work, that region in which the distinction between appearance and essence is both articulated and resolved into a higher unity.

Much more could be said about the caesura in both Hölderlin and Benjamin. Its significance for Adorno, however, clearly lies in his own elaboration of the concept. To convey a sense of how he refashions it, I cite the first and more explicit of the two references in "Parataxis."[61] The context is a discussion of "Friedensfeier" ["Celebration of Peace"], the great hymn discovered and published only a few years before Adorno delivered his speech: "The fact that the keyword [*Stichwort*] 'thanks' follows the word 'fate' at the end of these lines, mediated by the word 'but,' establishes a caesura in the poem; the linguistic configuration defines gratitude as the antithesis of fate, or, in Hegelian terms, as the qualitative leap that in responding to fate [*auf es antwortend*] leads out of it."[62] Because a caesura is, literally, an incision (from the Latin *caedere*, to cut up), one might expect it to manifest itself as a tear in the close-knit fabric of the poem. Yet unlike the caesura of "Hälfte des Lebens," which coincides with the unmediated break between the strophes, the cut that disrupts Hölderlin's celebration of peace is not paratactic; on the contrary, it follows upon a mediating particle, a "but." Adorno locates the caesura instead in a *Stichwort*, a word whose polemical associations he points out elsewhere[63]: "the keyword 'thanks,'" which cuts itself free from its antithesis in cutting into it. Rephrased in the discourse-theoretical terms suggested by the rhetoric of the passage, "thanks" represents a conversational counter-turn—"responding to fate"—which in the same stroke cuts short the conversation. Its *Antwort* or answer to fate, a constative utterance, can only prevent fate having the last word because it is equally a *Stichwort*, a performative utterance. Thanksgiving is the polemical riposte to fate, the cutting rejoinder that leaves fate speechless.

Adorno now attempts to explain how "thanks," this most improbable of combatants, overcomes its almighty adversary: "In its content, gratitude is purely and simply antimythological; it is what is expressed at the moment when eternal variance is suspended. While the poet praises fate, the poetry, on the basis of its own momentum, opposes gratitude to fate, without the poetry having necessarily intended this."[64] If "myth is catastrophe in permanence,"[65] as Adorno remarks in a speech on Wagner from the same year, then thanks is antimythological because it signals that the catastrophe has been averted or brought to a (provisional) close: Hölderlin composed "Friedensfeier" upon receiving news of the Treaty of Lunéville, which promised to put a stop to the bloodshed in Europe. As the eternal return of the same, the catastrophe of history stands for the attack that never fails to draw a counterattack, the crime interminably perpetuated through its punishment. Thanksgiving is premature unless all arms have been laid to rest. The immobilization of myth therefore seems to require that one refrain from aggression, even when incited by an enemy. At times, notably whenever he comments on the "docility" or "supreme passivity" characteristic of Hölderlin's spiritual bearing,[66] Adorno holds out the prospect of such a general ceasefire, envisaged in idealist terms as a peace with nature: "Metaphysical passivity as the substance of Hölderlin's poetry is allied, in opposition to myth, with the hope for a reality in which humanity would be free of the spell of its own entanglement in nature, an entanglement that was reflected in the conception of absolute spirit."[67] But because the caesura that leads out of mythic fate is a *Stichwort*, because the counterrhythmic interruption that suspends the cycle of violence is itself violently polemical, rescue assumes the guise of a catastrophe to end the state of permanent catastrophe. In an irredeemably fallen world, all hope gravitates toward the apocalypse, the ultimate circuit breaker.

The harbinger of the apocalypse in which it would come to term, the polemic stands for—and stands in the way of—the universal amnesty invoked by Hölderlin. The polemic works toward a state in which it would become superfluous, a state whose advent it thereby indefinitely postpones. Its fate replicates the historical fate of art, whose polemical effectiveness against instrumental rationality hinges upon its social effectlessness, the fact that it changes nothing; this is why the work of art becomes the privileged locus and agent of the polemic in Adorno's thought. In the same book on Wagner whose polemical conception had been criticized by Benjamin, Adorno detects a conventional happy ending lurking behind the Schopenhauerian façade of the world-conflagration at the end of the *Ring*. The negation of the bourgeois world celebrated by Wagner, transfigured too quickly into the positive, forfeits its negativity and results in a false *Erlösung* or redemption.[68] The conclusion is unavoidable that for an authentic rescue, for a rigorously polemical *Rettung*, Wagner's catastrophe is *not catastrophic enough*.[69] In the smooth roundedness of its construction, in the perfect arc with which it falls back upon its origin, the *Ring* lacks a caesura to rupture and complete it.[70] Through its destruction of aesthetic totality, the caesura transforms the "bad" catastrophe of history—fate—into the "good" catastrophe of (the truth content of) art. Catastrophe is the ineluctable remnant of myth in rescue, which is always rescue from myth. Like the subject in Hölderlin's poetry, myth thus survives its own demise: "There is a mythic layer inherent in the substance of Hölderlin's work, as in any genuine demythologization."[71]

While the Benjaminian provenance of this concept of the caesura is unmistakable, I want to argue that it owes its specific inflection in "Parataxis" to its affiliation with "late style." The caesura in "Friedensfeier" is not just one example among others, such that the analysis of a different caesura might have yielded an entirely different interpretative conclusion. Rather, what Adorno says of the *Stichwort* "thanks" holds true of the caesura in general: it is "purely and simply antimythological." Adorno calls works that are punctured by a caesura "late works." The late work is intrinsically antimythological because it is self-reflexively polemical, that is, it polemicizes against, and strives to redeem, that which constitutes it as a work of art: its semblance character. For Adorno, the caesura, itself semblance because itself an aesthetic category, is the redemptive (catastrophic) cut in semblance that refers art to what would be more or other than semblance. To demonstrate this claim, I will turn to Adorno's writings on Beethoven, which contain his most detailed accounts of late style. This move is justified, indeed necessitated, by the frequent comparisons of Hölderlin's late work to Beethoven's drawn in "Parataxis" and elsewhere, for which the concept of late style serves as the *tertium comparationis*.[72]

This concept requires some preliminary clarification. The term resonates with the mellow wisdom of a ripe old age, yet the poetry analyzed in "Parataxis" is that of a man barely over thirty, with half his life still before him. (Hölderlin philology has had to resort to the clumsy epithet "very late work" to deal with the poems of madness.) At the very least, "late style" suggests the final stage in a process of maturation through early and middle styles, yet Adorno denies Beethoven's ninth symphony the title of a late work, which he nonetheless accords to much of the chamber music composed before it. Late style is thus a qualitative ascription, not a chronological one. We come a little closer to Adorno's meaning when we recall that lateness also carries overtones of tardiness, of the *too* late, hence of dis-appointment. The late work misses the moment when the creative will fused part and whole, particular and universal into the harmonious work of art, intruding instead upon a scene of abandonment: a heap of lifeless, used-up material on the one hand; an insubstantial, listless subjectivity on the other.[73] The word "style" is also problematic here, given that it ordinarily designates the signature of an irreducible individuality, that indefinable, unreproducible X that permeates every phrase and stamps it as belonging to Beethoven and no one else—the mark, that is, of an authentic and sovereign subject. How, then, can Adorno claim that Hölderlin and Beethoven, but also such wildly dissimilar artists as Rembrandt, Michelangelo, Goethe, and El Greco,[74] have a style *in common*?

This is the point at which Adorno takes up his analysis. For Adorno, the subject that has attained an absolute mastery of its craft is precisely what the late work deconstructs; late style is the autocritique of the concept of style. I quote from the 1937 essay "Late Style in Beethoven," Adorno's most compressed statement on the matter: "The usual view explains [the dissonance peculiar to late works] with the argument that they are products of an uninhibited subjectivity, or, better yet, 'personality,' which breaks through the envelope of form to better express itself."[75] Adorno proposes instead that the proximity to death which the late work radiates so powerfully, far from reflecting the experience of the composer, lies in its incommensurability with the category of individual experience. The brittle hollowness that pertains to the fragmentary hymns of Hölderlin or the last quartets of Beethoven is legible as the shell of an evacuated interiority, the anorganic residue of an organic middle period. Such texts are the barren site from which the expressive subject has taken leave, a process sketched by Adorno in the notes to his unfinished monograph on Beethoven: "[W]hereas the 'classical' style sublates [the individual element] within the totality and gives it the *semblance* of significance . . . , now the insignificance of the individual element emerges as such and makes it the 'accidental' bearer of the universal. In other words, the style is the self-consciousness of the nugatoriness of the individual, the existent. Therein lies the relationship of late style to *death*."[76] And in "Late Style in Beethoven" he asserts: "The power of subjectivity in late works of art is the irascible gesture with which it takes leave of the works themselves. It breaks their bonds, not in order to express itself, but in order, expressionless, to cast off the semblance of art."[77]

Late style's expressive affinity to death derives from art's struggle to transcend expression, to cast aside its semblance character and become knowledge. This task is Sisyphean because art's knowledge of itself in the late work confronts it with the impossibility of its self-transcendence unto knowledge: "Late style would mean that the music becomes aware of the *limit* of this movement—the impossibility of cancelling its premises by force of its own logic."[78] Much as the thoughts of the inmate desperate to escape come to be dominated by the bars of his prison cell, so the late work's effort to overcome its semblance character throws it all the more forcefully upon semblance, which is now revealed to be the fatal admixture to *all* art. The appearance of vitality with which the classical work captivates its audience was just that: appearance, and the late work exposes such appearance as ideological. Arriving *post festum*, the late work retroactively ruins the party. But because it cannot claim exemption from its polemic against semblance, it also attacks its own foundations. When Adorno, once again adopting a terroristic vocabulary, calls Hölderlin's poetry an "assassination attempt on the harmonious work of art," the image of a suicide bombing aimed at the explosion of appearance is more pertinent than that of a sniper's bullet aimed at its liquidation.[79] As art and anti-art alike, the late work foreshadows the achievement and predicament of the European avant-gardes since around 1910, rehearsing the same aporetic scenario laboriously played out in *Aesthetic Theory*, defined by the exhaustion of latency and the liberation of dissonance.[80] Adorno's somewhat forced coupling of Hölderlin and Beethoven to Beckett and Schönberg, respectively, establishes late style as the ontogenetic prefiguration of art's phylogenesis in modernity—a genealogy of modernism that allows him to rescue a tradition of, and from, the irreversible dissolution of tradition.

What role does the caesura play in the late work? The concluding lines of "Late Style in Beethoven" provide a cryptic answer:

> [Beethoven] no longer gathers the landscape, deserted now and alienated, into an image. He lights it with rays from the fire that is ignited by subjectivity, which breaks out and throws itself against the walls of the work, true to the idea of its dynamism. . . . It is subjectivity that forcibly brings the extremes together in the moment. . . . The caesuras, the sudden discontinuities that more than anything else characterise the very late Beethoven, are those moments of breaking away; the work is silent at the instant when it is left behind, and turns its emptiness outward. Not until then does the next fragment attach itself, transfixed by the spell of subjectivity breaking loose and conjoined for better or worse with whatever preceded it; for the mystery is between them, and it cannot be invoked otherwise than in the figure they create together. This sheds light on the *Widersinn* that the very late Beethoven is called both subjective and objective. Objective is the fractured landscape, subjective the light in which—alone—it glows into life. He does not bring about their harmonious synthesis. As the power of dissociation, he tears them apart in time, in order, perhaps, to preserve them for the eternal. In the history of art late works are the catastrophes.[81]

I will not endeavor to undertake an exhaustive analysis of this passage, which gathers together all the central motifs of the much later essay on Hölderlin. The key term is perhaps *Widersinn*. Susan H. Gillespie offers the following translation of the sentence in which it appears: "This sheds light on the nonsensical fact that the very late Beethoven is called both subjective and objective."[82] According to this rendition, Adorno's enlightening explanation enforces the hermeneutic directive that where nonsense was, there sense shall be. In translating Adorno's *Widersinn* into prospective meaning, however, Gillespie misses the polemical thrust of the passage. For according to a distinction that Adorno may have picked up from Husserl,[83] *Widersinn* is not *Unsinn*, a complete absence of meaning to be dispelled in the light of interpretation; nor is it *Gegensinn*, an alternative meaning that could exist amicably alongside its counterpart, as if the subjectivity and objectivity ascribed to late Beethoven were two sides of the same coin. Rather, *Widersinn* is meaning inimical to meaning: polemical meaning. The question as to whether *Widersinn* polemicizes against meaning as such, and is itself meaningless, or whether it polemicizes against particular meaning, and is itself meaningful, is not to be decided one way or the other. In the first case, *Widersinn* would be converted into a privative form of meaning and then ignored; in the second, it would be neutralized into a potential source of meaning and then interrogated. Either way, the polemic, which feeds off the tension between its overtly totalizing hostility to meaning-making and its covert meaning as rescue, would be silenced through its redirection into a semantic economy.[84]

Adorno's interpretation of late style is caught in the same dilemma. How is one to understand polemical meaning without betraying it to the enemy? And if polemical meaning repels every attempt to understand it, where does that leave the interpreter? In "Late Style in Beethoven," Adorno's solution is to *shed light on Widersinn*, that is, to make the recognition that the late work is contrasensical, *widersinnig*, the spur to further interpretation rather than its defeat. The critic's task is to embrace this resistance to meaning without trying to circumvent or surmount it. I take this to be the strategy common to all of Adorno's writings on late style, including "Parataxis." In the opening pages of that essay, Adorno admiringly enumerates Beißner's philological elucidations to Hölderlin's "Winkel von Hardt"—"Beißner's explanation of the mention of something '*übrig*,' 'left over,' as the place that remained is illuminating"[85]—but goes on to argue that philology is ill-equipped to fathom the poem's "disturbed character": "It will be understood only by someone who not only ascertains the pragmatic content, the content which has its locus outside the poem and which is manifested in its language, but also continues to feel the shock of the unexpected name Ulrich, someone who will be troubled by the 'far from mute'. . . ."[86] To understand "Winkel von Hardt," in other words, is to learn through the experiences of shock and irritation that it withdraws from our attempts to understand it, however illuminating such attempts may be. Hölderlin's residual site, which Beißner neatly relocates outside the poem, remains within the poem itself as the unidentified, unidentifiable no-man's-land from which it launches its campaign against meaning. Indeed, Wolfgang Binder inadvertently corroborates Adorno's respectful critique when he proposes that the line "*an übrigem Ort*" ["at the place left over"] be read as meaning "not here or there, but somewhere as such."[87] By seeking to assign poetry a clearly delimited space determined by a set of externally imposed coordinates, Beißner's topographical reading leaves no room in the poem *übrig*, unaccounted for. Like Heidegger, Adorno suggests that Hölderlin's poetry founds its own place; but for Adorno, that place is unsettled, unsettling, and completely unsuited to "beautiful dwelling." It is the desolate, uninhabitable, and apocalyptic landscape of the late work, and if Adorno remarks that Beethoven no longer gathers this landscape into an image, then this is because he well knows that no map could possibly accommodate it.

As the site of *Widersinn*, the caesura is the reader's portal to that hostile landscape, the interface between art's narrowly circumscribed social, historical, and institutional situation and a utopia that is neither here nor there, "but somewhere as such." The caesura precipitates the catastrophe of meaning in the late work while promising rescue as the meaning of catastrophe. This promise is of course *widersinnig*, and from the outside must even appear to be nonsensical. Common sense tells us that it is absurd to hope for rescue from destruction. But such is the price and risk of the caesura, which has nothing more than a *perhaps* to justify its attack on semblance: "As the power of dissociation, it tears them apart in time, in order, perhaps, to preserve them for the eternal." The grammatical subject of this sentence is late Beethoven. Its true subject is the caesura, that same caesura that Adorno elsewhere calls "the contrasensical [*widersinnige*] caesura that brings hope into existence through its collapse."[88] Polemic would be its other name.

CHAPTER 12

Twelve Anacoluthic Theses on Adorno's "Parataxis: On Hölderlin's Late Poetry"

David Farrell Krell

What follows is a transcription of notes from a seminar devoted to Theodor W. Adorno's "Parataxis: On Hölderlin's Late Poetry."[1] The notes, themselves tentative, were presented tentatively at the time of the seminar, albeit in thesis form.[2] I have decided to preserve the somewhat anomalous thesis form here, opting for clarity of exposition, at the risk of appearing to suppress the notes' tentative quality.

1. Adorno would love to join Walter Muschg's condemnation of the "metaphysical" (that is to say, Heideggerian) reading of Hölderlin's late hymns, and in fact he does join in the condemnation, does relish his revenge. At the same time, however, he realizes that the good philologists are far too confident about their ability to uncover Hölderlin's "intentions" by aligning bits and pieces of the late poems alongside one another. Such an adroit, well-informed, and yet entirely unreflective recursion to textual "meanings" and authorial "intentions" will not suffice. For the ostensibly firm ground of philology has in the meantime been shaken (447–48). To put it formulaically, in language Adorno borrows, by his own admission, from Benjamin and Heidegger alike, *Das Gedichtete nötigt zur Philosophie*, what is poetized compels us to philosophize (450).

2. Behind every philological procedure and decision stand philosophical commitments, inevitably so, whether these commitments are

expressed or remain tacit. The commitment behind all appeals to authorial "intention" is that the artist-subject "owns" the work of art as an expression of his or her *ownmost* individuality and subjectivity, his or her ownmost *genius*. That commitment has been in place since the age of Kant and Goethe. As opposed to that, Adorno favors a dialectical approach to all subject-object relations, including the relation between genius and work of art: artists themselves are "in the meantime instructed by their experience of how little their own [*ihr Eigenes*] belongs to them," which is to say, of the extent to which they are always merely heeding "the compulsion of the configuration" of the work, *in welchem Maß sie dem Zwang des Gebildes gehorchen* (448). Adorno offers a long quotation from Hegel's *Lectures on Aesthetics* in order to present a work-centered, "objective" conception of the work of art. He might also have pointed to the despised Heidegger's "Origin of the Work of Art," which, arguably, moves beyond both an "objective" and a dialectical subject-object conception of work and artist. One should perhaps also note that a far more telling critique of "ownness" or "propriation," that is, of all the *eigen, eignen* words, than Adorno's self-cited *Jargon der Eigentlichkeit*, which never manages to rise above the level of polemic, is to be found in the work of Jacques Derrida, from "The End(s) of Man," in *Margins of Philosophy*, to *The Post Card from Socrates to Freud and Beyond* and *Of Spirit: Heidegger and the Question*.[3]

3. The philosophical theme that pervades Hölderlin's late hymns—if there is one, and if it can be distinguished from the "metaphysical" or Heideggerian theme of being—is what Adorno calls "an allegorical history of nature" (449). Later in "Parataxis" Adorno will describe this theme as resistance to the will to dominate nature, resistance to the compulsion to *Naturbeherrschung* (482–83). Yet here too Adorno rejoins the scorned Heidegger, whose resistance to the essence of technology arises from his analysis of the will-to-will that expresses itself preeminently in the drive to subdue beings as a whole.[4]

4. One cannot, however, simply bypass Adorno's critique of Heidegger. In brief, Adorno accuses Heidegger of confiscating Hölderlin's late poetry for his own history of being—*Beschlagnahme* is Adorno's word for it. Poetry can never be reduced to an assertion [*eine Aussage*], inasmuch as such reduction ignores the nature of the poem as a simulacrum and as radiant semblance—what Adorno calls poetry's *Scheincharakter* (453). Heidegger's confiscation betrays certain anachronistic traits from the history of art: Adorno refers to the *gespensterhaft wiederkehrenden Geist des Jugendstils* in Heidegger's style, the ghostly recurrence of the spirit of *Jugendstil*.

(One might rather say, in keeping with the literary and artistic movements that were so powerful in shaping Heidegger, his *Expressionism*.) The anachrony of the style violates Hölderlin in its very paraphrasing of his poems. (Before any discussion of *parataxis*, then, Adorno descries in Heidegger a *periphrasis* that is in fact a *paraphrasis*.) To be sure, Heidegger is not entirely at fault: Adorno argues that a certain sententiousness creeps into Hölderlin's late style, which therefore tempts readers to reduce the hymns to their meaning-content. Both Hölderlin and Heidegger, writes Adorno, are "ultimately products of the identical philhellenic tradition" (455). Later in "Parataxis" Adorno will try to find traces of the prophetic and even messianic tradition in Hölderlin, though not in Heidegger (459, 489). What Adorno deplores in Heidegger is the tendency to reduce Hölderlin's utopian side—which is the side that is open to the foreign—to something all-too-familiar. With Heidegger it is always a matter of—in Heidegger's own words, from the *Erläuterungen zu Hölderlins Dichtung*, citing Hölderlin's own words from his famous first letter to Böhlendorff—*eine künftige Aneignung des Eigenen* (457), an imminent appropriation of what is one's own. Whereas Hölderlin's move to the alien stresses the foreignness of what is one's own, that is, the unmastered elements of one's so-called "national gift," Heidegger's move is always to colonize and confiscate by reduction to a nationality that is stolidly self-possessed and parochial. Whereas Hölderlin, in the final version of "Bread and Wine," exhorts us—Adorno refers to Hölderlin's *parænesis*, "exhortation," before raising the theme of *parataxis*—to test ourselves so that we may come to believe that spirit is not at home in the beginning, not at the source, Heidegger never tests his faith, never doubts his intimacy with beginnings and origins—especially the national ones of fatherland and motherland. Whereas Hölderlin loves the adventure of colony, Heidegger loves colonization. Whereas Hölderlin wishes he could strike out for Tahiti, Heidegger would prefer to stay in the provinces of his homeland. A particularly droll example of Heidegger's tendency to appropriate and colonize—droll, even though drollery seems hard to associate with this fraught issue, and also quite revelatory, even if some may find it simply embarrassing—is the way in which Heidegger tries to distract his students and readers from Hölderlin's vision of the "brown women" of southern France by bringing to their attention the homey virtues of *der deutschen Frauen*. Adorno unmasks Heidegger's Schillerian moralizing tendency in matters of sex and gender as an attribute of the authoritarian personality, for whom the erotic poses the threat of a foreign invasion. Adorno's comment on Heidegger's transmogrification of Hölderlin's "brown women" of the Gironde into the virtuous women of southern Germany is that Heidegger's subtlety is nothing less than Neanderthal: *Sie* [that is, the women of Germany] *werden an den Haaren herbeigeschleppt* (458), they are dragged in by the hair. It may well be that brothers, sisters, and lovers are always handled this way in Heidegger's thought.[5]

5. It is futile to go into any detail concerning the neo-Hegelian and Kojèvean concepts that Adorno would like to oppose to the Heideggerian reading, if only because Adorno himself refers to them in "Parataxis" merely in passing. Neither "the aesthetic medium of the truth-content" (455), nor "the position of consciousness toward objectivity" (460), nor "the collective force that first of all engenders intellectual individuation" (461); neither Adorno's vague references to the *Weltgeist* and to the supposed parallels between the Hegel who is advancing toward the *Phenomenology of Spirit* and Hölderlin (462 and elsewhere) nor the appeal to Adorno's much-loved "immanent dialectic" (485) and "theater of dialectical reversal" (486)—none of this, I say, gets us any closer to Hölderlin's late hymns than any other philosophical discourse, including the Heideggerian.[6]

6. What does get us closer to the later Hölderlin is something that Adorno identifies first of all as the difference between *naming* and *meaning*, that is, between nomination and any given *Sinn* that such nomination might conjure up (464). In Hölderlin's late hymns, traditional symbolism is surpassed by a concrete naming of persons and places. Such naming grants to every signification "a second life" (465), albeit a life that is "saturated with mourning" (467). In nomination, meaning submits to mourning, *Trauer*. "Patmos" and "Mnemosyne" are prime examples here. Recall, from the latter, these lines: "*Am Feigenbaum ist mein / Achilles mir gestorben, / Und Ajax liegt / An den Grotten der See. . . .*" "My" Achilles, named and appropriated only in broken lines, invoked beyond all conceptual meaning, abandoned to his tears at the water's edge, is dead to "me."

7. After a double paragraph break—the only such break in "Parataxis"—Adorno catches his breath and makes a new start, as it were. He asserts that there is only one way to resist the Heideggerian reading, and that is to heed more carefully than Heidegger does the *form* of the late poetry, precisely at those points where Heidegger breaks away from Hölderlin's text in order to shift the focus to this or that *seinsgeschichtliche* theme. The first impact of the form, however, is one of estrangement or alienation, the fact that Hölderlin's language transports us to a far remove, *daß die Sprache fernrückt* (469). Adorno now borrows a word from Heidegger's reading of Trakl (whether wittingly or not is impossible to say), the

word Heidegger uses to name the locale of Trakl's singular poem, namely, *Abgeschiedenheit*, "apartness." Adorno discerns such apartness, prior to Trakl, already in Hölderlin. Borrowing a word now from Maurice Blanchot (again, whether wittingly or not), a word Blanchot invents in order to write about the caesura or counter-rhythmic interruption that Hölderlin discusses in his *Anmerkungen* to the Sophocles translations, Adorno defines the Hölderlinian form as *hiatus*.[7] "First of all through the hiatus, that is, through the form, the content becomes import [*wird der Inhalt zum Gehalt*]" (470). An example—really a prime instance—of form-as-hiatus is the abrupt *questions* that suddenly obtrude in the otherwise elevated diction of the late hymns, those *Swabian* questions, one might say, that displace and even derange the poetic diction. Adorno uses the word *zerrüttet* to designate derangements such as these in "Mnemosyne": *Wie aber Liebes?* and *was ist diß?* At the moments when these questions obtrude and interrupt, the poetry appears to collapse into prose. Admittedly, it is the sort of prose, says Adorno, without citing Benjamin directly, that one would find in a sacred text.

8. Adorno now makes his most paradoxical move. (Before *parataxis*, then, *paradox*.) From poetry and prose he turns to music, first by referring to the *sonata form* that according to Beißner structures the late hymns, then by alluding to the *refrain* of *hin* and *fernhin* in "Patmos." He now arrives at the notion of *parataxis* proper, and he does so in the context of music, perhaps even the music of the tone row, or of seriality (*Reihe, Reihung*). Parataxis? The lexicon says: placing words or phrases alongside one another without hypotaxis or syntaxis, i.e., without logical subordination or grammatical ordering. Parataxis may occur with or without conjunctions, i.e., either syndetically or asyndetically. Especially in the asyndetic form ("They run, rescue themselves, flee"), the impact of parataxis is such that each word or phrase is given equal force and weight. Parataxis is often used to indicate speed of motion or, paradoxically, the stillness that reflects the inner tension of a situation; in any case, it represents not a rationally articulated assertion but a passionate outburst. But to return to Adorno's text, this time to quote him at length:

> Große Musik ist begriffslose Synthesis; diese das Urbild von Hölderlins später Dichtung, wie denn Hölderlins Idee des Gesangs streng für die Musik gilt, freigelassene, verströmende Natur, die, nicht länger im Bann von Naturbeherrschung, eben dadurch sich transzendiert. Aber die Sprache ist, vermöge ihres signifikativen Elements, des Gegenpols zum mimetisch-ausdruckhaften, an die Form von Urteil und Satz und damit an die synthetische Funktion des Begriffs gekettet. Anders als in Musik, kehrt in der

Dichtung die begriffslose Synthesis sich wider das Medium: sie wird zur konstitutiven Dissoziation. Die traditionelle Logik der Synthesis wird darum von Hölderlin zart nur suspendiert. Benjamin hat deskriptiv mit dem Begriff der Reihe diesen Sachverhalt erreicht: "So daß hier, um die Mitte des Gedichts, Menschen, Himmlische und Fürsten, gleichsam abstürzend aus ihren alten Ordnungen, zueinander gereiht sind."[8] Was von Benjamin auf die Hölderlinsche Metaphysik als Ausgleich der Sphären der Lebendigen und der Himmlischen bezogen wird, nennt zugleich die sprachliche Verfahrungsweise. Während, wie Staiger mit Recht hervorhob, die Hölderlinsche, an der griechischen gestählte kühn durchgebildeter hypotaktischer Konstruktionen nicht enträt, fallen als kunstvolle Störungen Parataxen auf, welche der logischen Hierarchie subordinierender Syntax ausweichen. Unwiderstehlich zieht es Hölderlin zu solchen Bildungen. Musikhaft ist die Verwandlung der Sprache in eine Reihung, deren Elemente anders sich verknüpfen als im Urteil. Exemplarisch eine Strophe aus der zweiten Fassung des "Einzigen." Von Christus wird gesagt:

> Es entbrennet aber sein Zorn; daß nämlich
> Das Zeichen die Erde berührt, allmählich
> Aus Augen gekommen, als an einer Leiter.
> Diesmal. Eigenwillig sonst, unmäßig
> Grenzlos, daß der Menschen Hand
> Anficht das Lebende, mehr auch, als sich schicket
> Für einen Halbgott, Heiliggestztes übergeht
> Der Entwurf. Seit nämlich böser Geist sich
> Bemächtiget des glücklichen Altertums, unendlich,
> Langher währt Eines, gesangsfeind, klanglos, das
> In Maßen vergeht, des Sinnes Gewaltsames.

Die Anklage gegen die Gewalttat des sich zum Unendlichen gewordenen und sich vergottenden Geistes sucht nach einer Sprachform, welchen dem Diktat von dessen eigenem synthesierenden Prinzip entronnen wäre. Daher das abgesprengte "Diesmal"; die rondohaft assoziative Verbindung der Sätze; die zweimal verwendete, vom späten Hölderlin überhaupt begünstigte Partikel "nämlich." Sie rückt folgerungslose Explikation anstelle eines sogenannten gedanklichen Fortgangs. (471–72).

In English translation:

> Great music is synthesis without concepts; this is the prototype for Hölderlin's late poetry, just as Hölderlin's idea of song holds strictly for music: a liberated, freely flowing nature that transcends itself precisely by having escaped from the spell cast by domination of nature. Yet by virtue of its

significative element, the opposite pole to its mimetic-expressive element, language is fettered to the form of judgment and proposition—and thereby to the synthetic form of the concept. In poetry, unlike music, nonconceptual synthesis turns against its medium; it becomes constitutive dissociation. Hence Hölderlin merely suspends the traditional logic of synthesis, and he does so gently. Benjamin captures this state of affairs descriptively in the concept of the series: "So that here, at the center of the poem, human beings, divinities, and princes are arranged serially, plunging, as it were, from their old orderings." What Benjamin links with Hölderlin's metaphysics as a balancing of the spheres of the living and the divine also names Hölderlin's linguistic technique. While, as Staiger correctly pointed out, Hölderlin's technique, tempered by his experience of the Greeks, is not lacking in boldly formulated hypotactic constructions, the parataxes are nevertheless striking—artful disturbances that evade the logical hierarchy of a subordinating syntax. Hölderlin is irresistibly drawn to such constructions. The transformation of language into a serial order whose elements are linked differently than in the judgment is reminiscent of music. A stanza from the second version of *Der Einzige* ["The Only One"] is exemplary. It is said of Christ:

> But his wrath is aroused; so that, namely,
> The sign touches the earth, having gradually
> Vanished from sight, as along a lightning-rod.
> This time. Otherwise, headstrong, immoderate
> And boundless, the hand of men
> Attacks the living, and also, more than is proper
> To a demigod, going beyond what the holy establishes,
> This project. Since, namely, an evil spirit seizes
> Possession of felicitous antiquity, and infinitely so,
> One long endures that is hostile to song, soundless,
> Transgressing massively, violent of sense.

The indictment of an act of violence on the part of spirit, which has deified itself and become something infinite, searches for a linguistic form that would escape the dictates of spirit's own synthesizing principle. Hence the split-off "This time," the rondo-like associative linking of sentences, and the twice-used particle "namely," favored by the late Hölderlin generally. The particle puts explication without deduction in the place of a so-called train of thought.[9]

9. The philosophical theme of liberation from the spell of *Naturbeherrschung*, that is, emancipation from the compulsion to dominate nature,

such liberation resulting in what Benjamin identifies as a higher form of *passivity* in Hölderlin's poetry, will occupy the final pages of Adorno's text. For the moment, let us remain with more formal considerations. Adorno writes: "Renunciation of predicative assertion brings the rhythm into approximation with a musical sequence . . ." (472). Parataxis applies not only to the line but also to entire stanzas, as in "Hälfte des Lebens."

> HÄLFTE DES LEBENS
>
> Mit gelben Birnen hänget
> Und voll mit wilden Rosen
> Das Land in den See,
> Ihr holden Schwäne,
> Und trunken von Küssen
> Tunkt ihr das Haupt
> Ins heilignüchterne Wasser.
>
> Weh mir, wo nehm' ich, wenn
> Es Winter ist, die Blumen, und wo
> Den Sonnenschein,
> Und Schatten der Erde?
> Die Mauern stehn
> Sprachlos und kalt, im Winde
> Klirren die Fahnen.[10]

In English translation:

> HALF OF LIFE
>
> With yellow pears hangs
> And full of wild roses
> The land in the lake,
> You fair swans,
> And drunk with kisses
> You dip your heads
> Into sacred sober water.
>
> Alas, where shall I find, when
> Winter comes, flowers, and where
> The sunshine,
> And shadows of earth?
> The walls stand
> Speechless and cold; in the wind
> Banners clang like steel.[11]

Here, as in Beethoven's late compositions, all interstitial tissue is cut away. The liberated rows of tones and words both flow smoothly and halt abruptly: *Das Gereihte ist als Unverbundenes schroff nicht weniger denn gleitend* (473). The words both glide and bump. Norbert von Hellingrath, and after him Peter Szondi, Beda Allemann, and many others have described Hölderlin's late style in terms of what ancient rhetoric calls *harte Fügungen*, hard jointures. "Patmos," in its seemingly endless versions and rewrites, might serve as the best example of this:

> ... daß nirgend ein
> Unsterbliches mehr am Himmel zu sehen ist oder
> Auf grüner Erde, was ist diß?[12]

> ... that nowhere any longer
> Do we see immortal things in heaven or
> On the green earth, what is this?

And yet these hard rhythmic joinings, these sudden hiatuses, caesurae, and collision-course questions are actually signs of a certain *flexibility* and even *docility* in Hölderlin. *Harte Fügungen* express nothing less than *Fügsamkeit* (475). To be sure, such docility is transformed into autonomy and even a revolutionary audacity. Adorno writes: *Die Sublimierung primärer Fügsamkeit ... zur Autonomie ist jene oberste Passivität, die ihr formales Korralat in der Technik des Reihens fand* (475). "The sublimation of primary docility ... toward autonomy is that supreme passivity which found its formal correlative in the technique of seriality."

10. We may understand the paratactic paradox of *harte Fügung / Fügsamkeit* more clearly when we think of it as a certain giving-over to language, very much in the manner of Novalis's *Monolog*—although Adorno does not cite Novalis's remarkable text.[13] Adorno writes: *Mit dem gesetzgebenden Subjekt wird dessen Intention, der Primat des Sinnes, an die Sprache zediert* (477). "Along with the legislating subject, the subject's intention, the primacy of meaning, is ceded to language." Adorno is here very close to the Heideggerian appeal to an un-speaking correspondence with language, *das Ent-sprechen der Sprache*. Adorno, for his part, invokes the *sinnleere Protokollsätze* of Samuel Beckett, in which Hölderlinian parataxis may be said to culminate (479). One might also think of what Blanchot, reading Nietzsche, calls *fragmentary writing*, in which meaning is not abandoned, although the sense of direction [sens, *Sinn*] is often lost. Adorno notes the "fragmentary character of the great hymns," which are in fact "constitutively uncompletable" (480). Hölderlin's repeated use of connective particles, such as *denn* and *nämlich*, as though desperately trying to impose

hypotaxis on an irreducible parataxis, are signs of an impossibility at the innermost core of Hölderlin's hymns. Adorno refers—mysteriously, cryptically—to Hölderlin's "theology" in this regard. No doubt, the theses of such theology would be closer to the atheses of an atheology, closer perhaps to what Philippe Lacoue-Labarthe in *Métaphrasis* calls an unforeseen and unheard-of *theophany* in Hölderlin's Sophocles translations and notes: the god becomes present, says Hölderlin, *nur in der Gestalt des Todes*, only in the figure of death.[14]

11. Nature, for its part, retains its power, far beyond any and every human project. Adorno is no doubt thinking of what Hölderlin in his essays surrounding *The Death of Empedocles* calls *das Aorgischere*, the more savage, more untamable force of nature. If we may interpret "the orgic," by contrast, as the "organizable," and thus as a tendency at least reminiscent of *Naturbeherrschung*, then it is not difficult to understand what Benjamin and Adorno (and perhaps the later Lévinas) mean by supreme passivity. Adorno writes of the "remarkable derangement" of several lines of "Mnemosyne," third version; he identifies there the rhetorical figure of *anacoluthon*, ακολυθία, inconsequence (in its primary sense) or anomaly, in which what is to be thought stretches syntax to the breaking point, defies logic, and metonymizes metaphor—all for the sake of supreme passivity.

> Und immer
> Ins Ungebundene gehet eine Sehnsucht. Vieles aber ist
> Zu behalten. Und Noth die Treue.
> Vorwärts aber und rückwärts wollen wir
> Nicht sehen. Uns wiegen lassen, wie
> Auf schwankem Kahne der See.[15]

> And ever
> Into the unbounded goes a longing. Yet much is
> To be retained. And fidelity needed.
> Yet forward and backward we will not want
> To see. Let ourselves be cradled, as
> On the swaying bark of sea.

Such cradling—better, such allowing oneself to be cradled, endlessly rocking—such supreme passivity, flexibility, docility, and giving oneself over, is the eminent *anacoluthon* of Hölderlin's late poetry. The tendency of that poetry is utopian, resisting the violence and will-to-dominion [*Gewalt*] that animate the West.

12. Adorno cites Benjamin's account of Hölderlinian passivity as "the oriental, mystical principle, which passes across boundaries" (489). Oriental, inasmuch as Hölderlin loves Ionia and Asia. We recall Hölderlin's desire to make his translations of *Oedipus the Tyrant* and *Antigone* "livelier" by releasing the Greek from its tendency to suppress its own Oriental past. Hölderlin's hymns therefore exhibit an unmistakable messianic quality. That quality envisages in the most ancient myths the desire for reconciliation, peace, nonviolence, celebration—in short, a different destiny for the West.[16] The late hymns, even those featuring Christ, are written under the sign of Zeus's thunderbolt, within earshot of the thunder of the Napoleonic wars. Yet it is a thunder that eventually succumbs to the carillon of peace, a thunder *übertönt von Friedenslauten* (490). That does not mean that some sort of "otherworldly" spirit dominates the hymns. Their nonviolent utopia is destined for mortals alone, mortals who have shaken off all the illusions of absolute spirit, mortals who have embraced what one might call *the tragic absolute*. Adorno closes (491) with Heidegger's favorite lines from "Mnemosyne," in its first version entitled "The Nymph." These lines are reminiscent of those equally famous lines of the Rhine hymn:[17]

>   Denn nicht vermögen
> Die Himmlischen alles. Nämlich es reichen
> Die Sterblichen eh an den Abgrund. Also wendet es sich, das Echo
> Mit diesen.

>   For the celestial ones cannot do
> Everything. Namely, it is the mortals who make it
> All the way to the abyss. So it turns, the echo
> With these ones.

CHAPTER 13

The Ephemeral and the Absolute: Provisional Notes to Adorno's *Aesthetic Theory*

Peter Uwe Hohendahl

Adorno's *Aesthetic Theory*, initially shunned or attacked when it was posthumously published in 1970, has become increasingly his most widely and carefully read work. While the interpreters are still in disagreement about the appropriate reading of the text, there is largely consensus about its significance as the culmination of Adorno's œuvre and its importance for the contemporary aesthetic debate. More controversial, however, is the value assigned to Adorno's contribution to the contemporary discussion. Briefly put, three positions can be distinguished. First, among the interpreters of Adorno there still exists a core of more or less orthodox readers for whom Adorno's *Aesthetic Theory* represents the most advanced articulation of the aesthetic problematic.[1] For them, competing theories are either theoretically inferior or historically less relevant; therefore, they deny the need for a reassessment of Adorno's theory in light of more recent experiences and theoretical developments—a need suggested by the second position. Here we find readers who acknowledge the significance and value of Adorno's writings, but insist on analyzing them in the context of later theories, such as those of Habermas or Luhmann.[2] This second position foregrounds the historical relevance of Adorno, but also the task of going beyond Adorno's theory. With the third position, the emphasis shifts from a positive historical assessment to a more critical or even negative one.

Here, Adorno's theory is perceived primarily as outdated and therefore in the way of new perspectives.[3] Some of the more familiar objections concern Adorno's resistance to popular art and his rigid emphasis on aesthetic autonomy, defined in terms of the sovereignty of the artwork. Of course, the rejection of Adorno's understanding of art can be articulated in different theoretical terms, ranging from a Foucauldian denial of aesthetic autonomy to a reconsideration of the aesthetic in Bourdieu and Luhmann.

The recent polemic against the Adorno orthodoxy has highlighted two moments of his theory: on the one hand, it has challenged Adorno's philosophical assessment of modern art, in particular his conception of the end of art and the impossibility of returning to a stable and unquestioned concept of art; on the other, it has foregrounded the narrow parameters of Adorno's theory, i.e., its Eurocentric nature and its failure vis-à-vis the contemporary global art scene. His more hostile critics focus on the failure of Adorno's most central claims and therefore call for no less than a replacement of Adorno's aesthetic theory. The problem with this type of critique is its theoretical foundation. It tends to share an unacknowledged common ground with more orthodox interpretations. Put differently, the rejection of Adorno is grounded in the very kind of interpretation that orthodox Adorno critics have put forward to defend his work. I suggest that it is time to reexamine this discourse, which needs to be challenged; therefore we may want to review a set of notions and ideas that have guided the reading of *Aesthetic Theory* since 1970. They have defined the parameters of the discussion and thereby also the character and the limits of criticism. Those who have called for an overdue revision or an outright rejection of Adorno's theory operate on an assessment of Adorno's writings that claims the authority of the author. Hence they can speak in the name of Adorno, whose self-representation they use for their own purposes. The purpose of this essay is to break away from this approach, whose historical legitimacy is by no means denied. Instead, I want to explore the possibility of an alternative understanding of *Aesthetic Theory* in which key concepts receive a different interpretation, thereby changing the configuration of the theory and by extension the dogma. The point of this exercise is not confrontation and polemic but opening up a different perspective that will show Adorno's work in an unexpected light. While Adorno has served in contemporary discourse mainly as the voice of aesthetic autonomy, I want to show that this interpretation has overlooked or downplayed those passages in which the authority of the artwork is radically questioned, and in which the highly problematic status of art is foregrounded. Seen in this light, Adorno appears to undermine his own defense of art in a late-capitalist society.

In order to unfold this perspective, we have to take seriously the theological moment in Adorno's late writings, not as a defense of positive religion, to be sure, but rather as a way of defining the Absolute that determines the aesthetic realm.[4] Of course, this approach could easily lead us to a romantic reading of Adorno in which the religious and aesthetic spheres are ultimately merged. It should be noted that this is not the route that Adorno meant to take. His insistence that art can be understood in terms of a truth content does not mean that it can be treated as a stable object. The truly radical element of Adorno's theory comes to the fore in the emphasis on the enigmatic nature of the artwork and its fleeting character, which is threatened by failure and ultimate *Überflüssigkeit*. In *Aesthetic Theory* these radical elements are balanced by the more familiar moments, namely the philosophical sublation of art, i.e., the process in which the artwork can be rescued through its philosophical interpretation, which is admittedly both necessary and violent insofar as it is fixated on the use of concepts.

The articulation of a precarious balance between the enigmatic nature of art and its philosophical interpretation has been the hallmark of understanding Adorno's late work. In an exemplary manner, J. M. Bernstein has recently (2004) demonstrated how Adorno's concept of the artwork can be integrated into the philosophical discourse. This goal is clearly stated in the remark that "in Critical Theory [including Adorno], philosophical aesthetics is about reason and only about reason."[5] By drawing a strong line from Marx to the first generation of Critical Theory Bernstein emphasizes both the rational and critical intent of the project in which the aesthetic finds its appropriate place. On the one hand, Bernstein points to the critique of instrumental reason in the work of the Frankfurt School; on the other, he defines aesthetic theory as a specific philosophical discourse concerned with traditional categories of aesthetic experience, but now "as reformed in the light of the practices and experience of artistic modernism."[6] For Bernstein, it is the historical configuration (modernism) that redefines the discourse, i.e., the way traditional concepts such as the beautiful and the sublime or style, genre, and form can be used. The rigid division between the sensible and the rational realm, clearly stated by Kant, is reinterpreted as the result of disenchantment and repression. In this constellation, as Bernstein argues, art preserves what is lost in the sphere of reason. Hence aesthetic theory must be about reason or, to be more precise, about the fate of reason in modernism. This claim has two consequences: First, it reinstates the priority of the philosophical discourse (as a critical intervention) vis-à-vis the artwork; second, it provides a mode of functional integration for art into the larger social context (modernity and advanced capitalism). The discussion of a social context, however, raises the question of the autonomy of art. The idea of autonomy is indispensable for Bernstein's reading, since it allows him to both separate and connect the aesthetic and the realm of reason. On the one hand, the artwork is acknowledged as different from rational discourse; on the other, it can be understood as part of a larger sociocultural constellation, in which it takes over a critical function. In short, "the double character of art entails that the affirmative and negative aspects of art's autonomy mutually refer to one another, and that hence, generally, for all aesthetic phenomena there will be a purely aesthetic or internal way of regarding them and an external, social characterization."[7] By highlighting the double character of art, Bernstein stresses a specific moment of Adorno's concept of autonomy, namely, the hiatus between the aesthetic and the social, the resistance of the artwork to its social context, but at the same time also the link and thereby negative social function defined as the "return of the repressed."[8]

On the basis of this interpretation of the concept of autonomy in *Aesthetic Theory*, Bernstein develops a reading around four themes. He emphasizes the dialectic of form and content, specifically the negativity of the artwork vis-à-vis its social context. Second, he focuses on the peculiar status of the artwork in the economy, i.e., its commodity status, which it articulates through its own fetishism of form against the fetishism of the commodity. Third, he underlines the possibility of artistic progress in the world of commodities as the radical pursuit of form leading to an abstractness analogous to the abstractness of the social structure. And fourth, he points to the aporetic moments of Adorno's concept of autonomy and emphasizes the vulnerability of the artwork quoting Adorno's statement: "The shadow of art's autarchic radicalism is its harmlessness."[9] Yet even this crucial moment is read as a consequence of the social dialectic, in which the vulnerability of the artwork is due to the threat of a commodity-driven society. In his ensuing discussion of the concept of truth content Bernstein returns to his main theme, i.e., the centrality of reason for aesthetic theory, by contrasting instrumental reason ("the villain of the piece"[10]) and art. In this binary opposition the truth of art is determined by its resistance to the process of rationalization that has characterized human history. In other words, Bernstein proposes to read *Aesthetic Theory* as a continuation of *Dialectic of Enlightenment*, which means that aesthetic theory becomes a historically inflected theory of rationality applied to art. In this constellation the concept of autonomy is the crucial bridge between aesthetic production and social construction.

Toward the end of the essay Bernstein suggests that the truth content of the artwork as a philosophical construct negates the work of art and quotes Adorno's statement: "Each artwork, as a structure, perishes in its truth content" (*AT* 131–32). Worth noting is his conclusion that neither a communicative nor a pragmatic notion of truth would support Adorno's theory. This is one of the few places where the essay steps outside of Adorno's theory and at least suggests the possibility of another approach to the question of reason, and by extension to the question of art. Yet this move remains without consequences, for Bernstein decides to remain strictly with Adorno's thought. Since for him Adorno's philosophy and his understanding of art are identical, one cannot escape from the rigor of the system. Had he decided to give greater prominence to the structure of Adorno's late work, specifically to the moments of anti-systematic thought, the understanding of the aesthetic sphere and the place of the artwork in it might have been different.

In contrast to Bernstein, I want to suggest that in *Aesthetic Theory* Adorno follows two separate tendencies: on the one hand, Adorno presses the ultimate importance of art in light of the failure of philosophy; on the other, he emphasizes the problematic nature of art to such a degree that its autonomy is in danger of vanishing. The result is a theological perspective that is absent from Adorno's earlier work. This moment comes to the fore especially in the discussion of the ultimate failure of aesthetic reconciliation [*Versöhnung*]. Insofar as Adorno, possibly as an implied critique of Heidegger, rejects the notion of an ultimate mediation of metaphysical meaning [*Sinnvermittlung*], he opens up a space beyond the aesthetic, although, as we will see, this space cannot be entered or controlled by the means of philosophical discourse.

Hegel's claim that in the work of art aesthetic appearance transcends the sphere of the sensuous, that it offers a *Durchscheinen der Idee*, is certainly present in *Aesthetic Theory*, but its claim is under duress. Not only has the relationship between the work of art and its truth content become considerably more complex and ambiguous, it seems that, in the final analysis, Adorno is no longer prepared to rescue the artwork, to give it the prominent place that both German Idealism and European modernism assigned to it. Since as a critic Adorno himself was part of European modernism and a passionate interpreter of avant-garde music who defended the significance of modern art, this cautious hesitation deserves special attention. In the posthumous text those elements that undermine the trajectory of a modernist defense of art come to the fore. They stand side by side with more familiar arguments, for instance in the long section on society and art (*AT* 225–61), not to mention the old introduction, which Adorno later discarded as no longer adequate. These sections continue to argue for a social dialectic of art in which the meaning of the artwork is established through its determined negation, as Adorno had already argued in his essay "Rede über Lyrik und Gesellschaft." This approach then goes hand-in-hand with a theory of the artwork that emphasizes the concepts of material, technique, and process. These parts affirm the philosophical relevance of the advanced artwork (as opposed to the production of the culture industry) precisely by denying its positive function. Yet its significance as a critical intervention in a totally administered society is upheld. For this reason Bernstein can sustain his interpretation of *Aesthetic Theory* by referring to these parts of the text, paying due respect to the complexity of Adorno's argument. When we turn to different sections, however, this reading is more difficult to uphold, since here Adorno seems to push the limits of his theory and thereby undermines the more familiar negative dialectic.[11] The result is the abandonment of art as a critical counterpoint.

Using the example of fireworks, Adorno points to the extreme vulnerability of the artwork. Its brief appearance as a form of mere entertainment offers a completely different perspective, since its obvious lack of deeper and lasting meaning problematizes the search for significance or relevance. Adorno uses the term "apparition" and comments: "They [artworks] appear empirically yet are liberated from the burden of the empirical, which is the obligation of duration; they are a sign from heaven yet artifactual, an ominous warning, a script that flashes up, vanishes, and indeed cannot be read for its meaning" (*AT* 81). It is telling that the example is taken from the sphere of entertainment, yet a form that cannot be mass-produced, that remains unique in its fleeting appearance. It is also worth noting that Adorno reads the phenomenon as a form of writing asking to be decoded and thereby to receive meaning [*Bedeutung*]. Yet the apparition does not give an answer, not because the answer is hidden or esoteric but rather because there is no meaning. The autonomy of the aesthetic sphere, its "afunctionality" (*AT* 81), claimed by idealism, is taken out of its familiar context. By using fireworks as a model for entertaining art he deliberately undercuts the synthesis of form and content [*Gehalt*] and forcefully reduces the artwork to the moment of "apparition" and expression that cannot be stabilized. This move, however, is not to be taken as a denial of the spiritual element of the artwork, which Adorno later asserts; rather, it must be seen as a form of questioning meaning as a secure property of the artwork, as an element that can be rescued in a larger cultural context. While

Adorno, following the tradition of modernist aesthetics, calls attention to the moment of transformation of the empirical material, he refuses to define this moment in terms of significant meaning. Transformation remains open-ended: "In each genuine artwork something appears that does not exist" (*AT* 82). Art promises, Adorno suggests, something it cannot deliver. Hence he distances himself from aesthetic idealism: "Idealist aesthetics fails by its inability to do justice to art's *promesse du bonheur*" (*AT* 82). Romantic theory attempted to apprehend this moment by underlining the *Unendlichkeit* of the artistic process, which still proposes a notion of truth in the form of *Ahnung*. By contrast, now looking back at the practice of artistic modernism, Adorno faces the negative moment with greater clarity: "Even radical art is a lie insofar as it fails to create the possible to which it gives rise as semblance" (*AT* 83). There is no guarantee that artworks will actually keep their promises, that the act of transformation will lead to a new and qualitatively different life world.

If even radical art cannot be trusted, if it cannot be assumed to contain, although in mediated form, a moment of truth beyond its mere appearance, what can be hoped for? Is there a path that leads to a recognition of significance and importance? As we might expect, Adorno's response is highly ambiguous. In certain ways he holds on to an understanding that takes seriously the *promesse du bonheur*, i.e., the possibility of reconciliation, even if this moment remains presently unfulfilled, as Adorno states: "For artworks it is incumbent to grasp the universal—which dictates the nexus of the existing and is hidden by the existing—in the particular" (*AT* 84). By evoking a universal Adorno suggests that there could be meaning in the emphatic sense of the term. But this claim is almost immediately taken back, modified, and restricted. According to Adorno, recent art, especially radical works, moves in the opposite direction. They create shocks by exploding their own aesthetic form. "Art today is scarcely conceivable except as a form of reaction that anticipates the apocalypse" (*AT* 85). It is not accidental that Adorno invokes an apocalyptic scenario, the notion of an end that swallows prior promises of history and human progress. "Equilibrium" (*AT* 85) has become impossible; instead we are confronted with loss of meaning (explosion). It is for this reason that Adorno opposes the notion of mythical images as grounding forces proposed by Klages and Jung. Instead, Adorno emphasizes the moment of artistic illusion both at the level of "*Erscheinung*" [appearance] and the level of cultural significance.

Given the radical questioning of the aesthetic sphere and the artwork, can the notion of aesthetic truth be mentioned at all? Put differently, can Adorno still make use of the Hegelian tradition that claims a strong link between the idea and the artwork? Adorno's answer is ambiguous. While he acknowledges the importance of Hegel's philosophy as a major step beyond Kant's formalism, a step that allows us to consider the truth content of art, he is highly critical of locating the truth content in the idea. First of all, there is the criticism that the philosophical discourse by its very nature misunderstands the artwork: "Even idealism's emphatic concept of the idea relegates artworks to examples of the idea as instances of what is ever-the-same" (*AT* 128). The philosophical discourse is unable to articulate the specificity of the artwork. Yet Adorno's critique seems to go further. The very notion of a truth content, a notion that is at the heart of Adorno's theory, comes under investigation, since it appears to clash with Adorno's radical concept of the artwork. Hence Adorno continues: "The content [*Gehalt*] of art does not reduce without remainder into the idea, rather, this content is the extrapolation of what is irreducible" (*AT* 128). The crucial term is "extrapolation" as a way of dealing with the relationship between the artwork and truth content. Adorno suggests in this formulation that the elements that defy "*Auflösung*" [unbinding or dissolution] block the transition from the work of art (its structure) to the realm of the philosophical idea. As it turns out, the blockage is more than a methodological question; rather, it points to the deeply enigmatic character of the artwork. Hence only by closely examining Adorno's understanding of the enigma of art can we comprehend his unexpected radical departure from the philosophical tradition.

Adorno's concept of the enigma challenges traditional hermeneutics, which operates with the assumption of possible disclosure of meaning. What appears strange to the uninitiated reader becomes apparent and meaningful in the process of interpretation. Adorno holds against this process a more fundamental recognition of the artistic enigma. "The better an artwork is understood and the more it is unpuzzled on one level, the more obscure its constitutive enigmaticalness becomes" (*AT* 121, modified). Put differently, the enigmatic nature of the artwork is part of its constitution rather than a specific element of its structure that the hermeneutic process can dissolve. For this reason, as Adorno underlines, ultimately the hermeneutic process will always fail. The metaphor of the *Vexierbild* is used to explicate this fundamental difficulty. "Every artwork is a picture puzzle, a puzzle to be solved, but this puzzle is constituted in such a fashion that it remains a vexation, the preestablished routing of its observer" (*AT* 121). Of course, it is possible to establish through a process of reading the formal structure as well as the thematic configuration of the individual artwork, but this process, as Adorno points out, misses the fundamental hiatus between the work and the act of reading. The failure of understanding at the level of the constitution of art (as opposed to the level of the structure of artworks) is caused by a disregard of the nature of aesthetic experience, its fleeting character that Adorno finds in the image of the rainbow. Any attempt to get close to the phenomenon in order to grasp it destroys the phenomenon. Under these conditions the question of truth in the artwork becomes not only difficult to answer but problematic in the sense that possibly there may not be an answer. As Adorno notes: "Ultimately, artworks are enigmatic in terms not of their composition but of their truth content" (*AT* 127). The search for the truth content as the ultimate exploration challenges the artwork as much as the enigmatic artwork challenges and potentially defeats the quest for the truth content. Nonetheless, Adorno tries to rescue the idea of a truth content as a solution to the enigma. This sudden and unexpected reversal deserves special attention. He notes: "The truth content of artworks is the objective solution of the enigma posed by each and every one" (*AT* 127). The enigma previously seen as insurmountable for aesthetic theory is now perceived as open to a solution [*Auflösung*]. How is this revision possible? How can thought overcome the extreme hiatus?

A sufficient and appropriate answer requires a more extensive discussion of the enigmatic nature of art and, secondly, a closer examination of the conception of the truth content, specifically its relationship to the artwork. When Adorno claims the convergence of philosophy and art through the truth content he states the official program of *Aesthetic Theory*: "The progressive self-unfolding truth of the artwork is none other than the truth of the philosophical concept" (*AT* 130). This line of argument remains obviously rather close to German idealism, for instance to Schelling's theory, as Adorno readily admits. Yet the way he develops the thought places the emphasis more on the failure of idealist systems than the nature of artworks. These are, as it were, compromised by the overstatement of idealism. Hence Adorno concludes that the search for meaning in the artwork legitimized by idealism has to be suspended and ultimately replaced by a different and more radical understanding of truth outside the concept of meaning. But this step is actually not prepared in the following passage, which leads to a tentative but crucial definition of the truth content. Adorno writes: "The truth content of artworks is not what they mean but rather what decides whether the work in itself is true or false, and only this truth of the work in-itself is commensurable to philosophical interpretation and coincides—with regard to the idea, in any case—with the idea of philosophical truth" (*AT* 130). It is worth noting that Adorno shifts the question of truth from the consideration of meaning [*Bedeutung*] to the assessment of a more fundamental issue, namely the question of whether a work of art is true or not. The compatibility of art and philosophy is measured in terms of a truth that is intrinsic to art (unlike an idea imposed from the outside). There can be no doubt that in this passage Adorno insists on the possibility of a philosophical explication of the artwork by emphasizing the transformation of aesthetic experience into philosophical thought ("Aesthetic experience is not genuine experience unless it becomes philosophy" [*AT* 131]). For this reason he asserts the moment of universality [*Allgemeinheit*] as a link between art and philosophy, a universal element that is, by the way, conceived as collective. But we have to remind ourselves that Adorno has not explicated what he understands by the truth of art. Does he refer to a specifically aesthetic truth (defined in terms of form and structure) or does he mean the truthfulness of the expression?

At this point we have to return to the enigmatic nature of art and the denial of reconciliation. In the section on the enigmatic character of art Adorno radically questions the status of art and foregrounds its unreliability and ambiguity. Artworks are relatively safe only in the context of an established cultural tradition in which radical doubt is not permitted. The value of art, Adorno suggests, always depends on the cultural presupposition that art should be assigned value. Yet when this taboo is broken, art remains without protection and is potentially exposed to complete devaluation. Moreover, since artworks are nondiscursive, they are unable to defend themselves, a task that is assigned to philosophy, but the procedure of philosophy is extrinsic to art. And, on the other hand, as we have seen, the intrinsic approach by way of hermeneutics fails as well. As mere apparition the value of the artwork is seriously in doubt. Therefore the convergence of art and philosophy stipulated by Adorno seems to be an impossible task, since the universal element, supposedly contained by both, must not be imposed on art by philosophy. In other words, the redemption of the artwork has to come from the inside. The radical doubt must be overcome with the help of the very fragility that characterizes the artwork. This is the task that Adorno pursues energetically, and by doing so he is forced to revise both the concept of art and the idea of the truth content, as well as their relationship. In a nutshell, the path that Adorno follows leads him to the concept of *Vergeistigung* at the expense of the artwork, which has to be sacrificed. As Adorno notes, "Artworks stand in the most extreme tension to their truth content. Although this truth content, conceptless, appears nowhere else than in what is made, it negates the made. Each artwork, as a structure, perishes in its truth content; through it the artwork sinks into irrelevance, something that is granted exclusively to the greatest artworks" (*AT* 131). Hence the transformation of the artwork to the level of its (immanent) truth content is the ultimate telos of art. Again, we have to note that for Adorno the truth content through which the artwork can be redeemed must not be confused with ideas. Rather, the authenticity of the artwork is enclosed and articulated within the sphere of semblance [*Schein*]; yet at the same time, semblance points beyond itself, suggesting through its formal organization that there is truth. But Adorno does not assign a content to this concept of truth; there is only the moment of negation of empirical (social) reality and the element of *Sehnsucht*, the suggestion of the "possibility of the possible" (*AT* 132).

If one follows these reflections, one is led to familiar Adornean territory, i.e., the utopian aspect of art through rigorous negation. By foregrounding the category of negation Adorno arrives at a critical function of art in which the refusal of thematic engagement and the radical formal organization of the work of art are the only legitimate avenues for this critique. In this context the radical notion of the sacrifice of the artwork is toned down, while the compatibility of the aesthetic and the critical philosophical discourse are more strongly emphasized. Along these lines Adorno notes: "Whereas art opposes society, it is nevertheless unable to take up a position beyond it; it achieves opposition only through identification with that against which it remonstrates" (*AT* 133). The specification of art as social opposition returns to a functionalist-dialectical understanding of art and moves away from the radical split between the enigma of art and the rational discourse of philosophy. However, in those parts of *Aesthetic Theory* where Adorno takes this hiatus most seriously, where he stresses the fundamental deficiency of the artwork, he is contemplating a different outcome in which the moment of spiritualization [*Vergeistigung*] plays a central role, to which the notion of the *Vergänglichkeit* of the artwork provides the logical contrast ("This was not contested until art began to experience itself as transient" [*AT* 179]).

Adorno's concept of Spirit [*Geist*] in the context of the definition of art must be kept separate from general notions of spirit in German idealism. In Adorno's discussion spirit appears as a supplement. He writes: "What appears in artworks and is neither to be separated from their appearance nor to be held simply identical with it—the nonfactual in their facticity—is their spirit" (*AT* 86). This definition underlines the paradox of the concept. While the spirit cannot be separated from (aesthetic) appearance, it is at the same time distinct from appearance. Again and again, Adorno points to the blindness of the artwork, which relates to its status as a thing in the world. This blindness is overcome through the spirit, which provides, to extend the metaphor, the eyes that allow the artwork to see. But it is important for Adorno that spirit is not imposed on the artwork from without. Instead, the spirit is a self-produced moment of the artwork, responsible for the animation [*Beseelung*] of the work as well as the interior force of objectivization. Hence Adorno defines the spirit of artworks as an immanent mediation between the work as thing and the work as expression of truth. It is the moment of transformation that Adorno wants to address and contrast to an approach that derives the truth of artwork from the realm of ideas. While Adorno readily acknowledges the decisive advance of Hegel's aesthetic theory over older models (including Kant), he clearly and firmly differentiates his understanding of spirit. He criticizes Hegel for his "apology for immediacy as something meaningful" (*AT* 90), and suggests that radical spiritualization is its opposite. The phrase that Adorno chooses to articulate his own understanding is anything but self-evident: Spirit is "the mimetic impulse fixated as totality" (*AT* 90). Spiritualization can be achieved neither by mimesis [*Abbildung, Nachahmung*] nor by the mere use of the material (colors, stone, tones). For Adorno it seems to be the process leading to an organization of the material that becomes the basis for spiritualization. He uses the term "configurations" (*AT* 91) in order to describe the outcome of the process, yet he is obviously less interested in the outcome than the process itself ("something in a process of development and formation" [*AT* 91]).

As much as Adorno distances himself from Hegel, he follows the latter in historicizing the concept of spirit and its use in the history of art. Not unlike Hegel, Adorno conceives the emphasis on spiritualization as a specifically modern aspect of art. With modernism the pressure on the artwork to transform itself spiritually has become inescapable: "Only radically spiritualized art is still possible, all other art is childish" (*AT* 92). This verdict creates a narrow path for artistic production, a path that not only enhances the significance of the artwork as a bearer of spirit but also its constitutive problems. Adorno discusses them as the danger of abstractness, the separation of spirit from the sensual side, which becomes mere material, and a delight in barbarism as an unreflected gesture of refusal. On the whole, however, Adorno sees the process of increasing spiritualization since 1850 as a positive moment, as a necessary form of intellectual opposition against a life world that has become almost uninhabitable [*verhärtete Welt*]. Again, we note that the turn to a historical discussion, i.e., the examination of the link between the spiritualization of art, on the one hand, and the process of increasing reification of the social world, on the other, encourages Adorno to emphasize the legitimacy of the artwork and art in general, although he is aware of the pitfalls of this development. By the same token, he avoids the more radical question that he posed in his discussion of the enigmatic and fleeting nature of the artwork, an examination that subverts the very ground of art. Yet the radical articulation of spirit in the modern artwork, especially its abstract character for which the concept of the symbol is inadequate, creates an internal tension that threatens to destroy the artwork, not only because of the deprivation of the material but also because of the abstractness of the spirit, which turns into a mere rational concept. As Adorno reminds us: "the work itself does not make judgments" (*AT* 99). While the work may contain rational judgments, it remains itself outside a rational discourse.

As we have seen, Adorno's historical analysis, with its focus on modernism, provides a conditional form of legitimization for the artwork, but it keeps open and undecided the question of whether the artwork can be redeemed in absolute terms. But this question implies another, more fundamental question, namely the quest for an absolute that can provide meaning to our lives. Adorno's attitude toward the theological dimension is highly ambivalent. On the one hand, he fully acknowledges the process of secularization that has weakened an older, theologically defined metaphysical world order. The emancipation of the modern subject, he suggests, has undermined the legitimacy of this order, but also, as he adds, any notion of a positive frame of meaning (*AT* 152). On the other hand, he retains the notion of a meaningful absolute that also informs the definition of art. In his discussion of *Jugendstil* [art nouveau] this moment comes unexpectedly to the fore when Adorno asserts that the aesthetic principle of form implies meaning, even when the content of the work opposes the idea of meaning. Therefore, "to this extent, whatever it wills or states, art remains theology" (*AT* 271). This sentence from the *Paralipomena* must be read together with a passage from the chapter "Towards a Theory of the Artwork," where Adorno establishes a link between the concept of the sublime and theology: "The sublime marks the immediate occupation of the artwork by theology" (*AT* 198). For Adorno it is the sublime artwork—he may think of Beethoven—that not only changes the limits of the aesthetic experience but also the degree of (spiritual) meaning that artworks are able to articulate. Deliberately Adorno refers in this passage to Kant's concept of the sublime, which its author restricted to the perception of nature. While Adorno does not accept this limit, he acknowledges Kant's motivation, namely the intent to keep art within the realm of beauty. Yet it is precisely this attempt of setting borders that blocks the connection between art and the absolute. The following formulation highlights both Adorno's insistence on the link and his skepticism with regard to the substitution of religion by art: "Even the hubris of art as a religion [*Kunstreligion*], the self-exaltation of art as the absolute, has its truth content in the allergy against what is not sublime in art, against that play that is satisfied with the sovereignty of spirit" (*AT* 197). Still, the absolute outside the aesthetic sphere, which theology would examine, is by no means dismissed out of hand. Rather, it is retained as a figure of alterity, the other to which the advanced artwork strives without reaching it. As we have noted, the artwork stands on the side of *Vergänglichkeit* just as human beings are seen as marked by the "fragility of the empirical individual" (*AT* 198), which starkly contrasts with the eternity of the spirit.

The inevitable question, then, is this: How serious is Adorno in his pursuit of a theological grounding of art and where would it lead him?[12] Clearly, Adorno would reject a line of reasoning that places art in the service of religion. The central concept of aesthetic autonomy forbids a dogmatic religious legitimization of art. Although he recognizes the religious function of premodern art and thereby its link to mythology, he stresses the moment of autonomy even in very early examples of artistic production (the example of Paleolithic art). Adorno's theological interest enters *Aesthetic Theory*, as it were, through the backdoor. First of all, there is the distinction between theology and myth, a distinction that contrasts spirit as a force of emancipation and nature as a form of unfreedom. But moreover, the theological element provides a sphere of radical transcendence against which the aesthetic sphere can be judged. Adorno argues in favor of a metaphysics of art as radically separate from religion (*AT* 138), as a form of methexis (participation) of the artwork. The artwork can articulate truth, although it is and remains blind. Yet it is necessary to grasp that the moment of participation is paid for by death: "Their own life preys on death" (*AT* 133). Through its death or dissolution the artwork shares the fate of "an autonomous entity" (*AT* 1), *das Seiende*, its *Vergänglichkeit*.

Within the Marxian tradition the contrast to Lukács' aesthetic theory could not have been expressed in stronger terms. Where Lukács understands art as the representation of a reality that is on its way to a historical telos, Adorno discovers only glimpses of hope in a radical spiritualization of art that leaves both the social reality and its aesthetic representation behind. Occasionally this outlook has been called the fundamental pessimism of the first generation of the Frankfurt School, a pessimism that according to this reading was primarily motivated by the lessons of World War II. Yet this assessment, I believe, does not do justice to the theoretical configuration as such, for it overlooks the basis in Adorno's thought, in particular the theological aspect that has remained a largely unacknowledged element. As long as Adorno's aesthetic theory is read as part of his social theory, as long as the concept of critique has been foregrounded, the theological aspect has been hidden.[13] Put differently, the process of secularization, which plays such an important role in Adorno's diagnosis of the modern world, has also deeply impacted his own thought. Unlike Bloch or Benjamin, Adorno's thought remains committed to the demands of rigorous conceptual work. This commitment, however, especially in his late work, resists political practice and interprets thought as a form of political resistance in a world that has completely hardened (totally administered). In part, *Aesthetic Theory* formulates a response to this condition in which the artwork takes up a central place as a locus of resistance. Art's lack of conceptual rigor (compared with philosophy) comes across as an advantage, since it can point to a truth content beyond the realm of rational discourse. But the articulation of the truth content goes hand-in-hand with the sacrifice of the artwork. In order to highlight the moment of transcendence Adorno also emphasizes the *Vergänglichkeit* of the artwork, the fact that it is part of the world. This structure seems to exclude reconciliation. The hope that the world can be redeemed through art is denied. Unlike Herbert Marcuse, who holds on to the revolutionary potential of the aesthetic program of German Classicism, Adorno rejects this solution and presents a strict dualism. Already in the *Philosophy of Modern Music*, this structure is clearly prefigured when Adorno writes: "The shocks of incomprehension . . . undergo a sudden change. They illuminate the meaningless world. Modern music sacrifices itself to this effort. It has taken upon itself all the darkness and guilt of the world."[14] Michael Pauen is correct when he notes that Adorno is attracted by eschatological ideas. The Other to which art refers (without being it) cannot be contained in the concept of a "historical reconciliation of world-immanent contradictions."[15] The absolute, while not present in the artwork, is invoked. Accordingly, Adorno differentiates between "epiphanies" (*AT* 103) and the expectation of the presence of the absolute in the artwork. This means that the aesthetic sphere, although not equal to a religious epiphany, evokes the absolute as a necessary but hidden dimension of art.

For the attuned and focused recipient, therefore, the approach to art not only demands attention and concentration but also a moment of exstasis [*Betroffenheit*], loss of control, and opening up. The affinity to Gnostic thought becomes apparent. The ecstatic experience turns into a moment of liberation, a moment of leaving behind the hardened social world. "What connects [Adorno] with Gnostic thought is the insistence on the difference between aesthetic experiences and sensual elements; therefore there is not only the characteristic reservation towards the sensual but also the notion that the sensual realm is linked to the powers of evil."[16] When Pauen concludes that Adorno, in close affinity to Gnostic thought (there is never the question of influence), strives for a moment of redemption he overstates his case, since, as we have seen, the aesthetic experience, insofar as it remains necessarily connected to the sensual realm, can only point to the truth content, which stands outside the work of art. However, cognition of the truth content through the process of rigorous interpretation offers a perspective to liberation. Yet the destination of liberation cannot be articulated in positive terms, for the absolute is accessible neither to rational discourse nor the artwork. Epistemologically the artwork has an advantage compared with philosophy: through the truth content it can transcend itself and at least move toward the absolute. This advantage is paid for by its own epistemological blindness, which can be compensated only by the intervention of philosophy. The act of comprehending the complete alterity of the absolute (in contrast to organized religion, which defines the absolute as God and the path to redemption in terms of God's intervention) describes the ultimate limit of human intervention. The pessimism that Adorno's critics have noted more than once is epistemologically grounded in the structure of his thought and specifically in his theory of art, which follows a tension-ridden double trajectory. On the one hand, it strongly emphasizes the exceptional status of art, its autonomy vis-à-vis social reality; on the other, it contrasts the value of art with the unknown and hidden absolute, stressing art's vulnerability and *Vergänglichkeit*. This means reconciliation cannot be found in the artwork itself; at best it can be hoped for in an intense aesthetic experience.

In *Aesthetic Theory* historical analysis and theological (Gnostic) thought patterns enter into a complex relationship that is not free of contradictions. They converge in a radically negative position toward empirical history and its contemporary outcome. If one takes the theological figure seriously and not only as a metaphor for an immanent process, one has to come to terms with the status of the absolute and, more specifically, with the relationship between the absolute and history. It would be difficult to read Adorno's theory as an extension of Hegel's phenomenology of the spirit. In contrast to Hegel, Adorno's theory of history recognizes its dialectic (in the wake of Marx), but does not acknowledge its positive value.

Therefore the concept of progress takes on a highly problematic meaning. In *Aesthetic Theory* it can be rescued only as a moment of the immanent process of the development of art. Progress is linked to the historically inflected organization of the artistic material in the artwork, representing the most advanced and most differentiated procedures. Aesthetically the concept of progress operates through negation: it involves "a negative canon, a set of prohibitions against what the modern has disavowed in experience and technique" (*AT* 34). Applied to social history, the concept has become, as Adorno reminds us again and again, part of a technocratic ideology. Hence the invocation of an absolute cannot arrest the historical process, but redirects our attention. It creates a counterpoint that enables Adorno to demarcate the boundaries of art, specifically its fundamental limitations as man-produced and part of the temporal realm. The theological figure therefore functions critically as a way of distancing Adorno's aesthetic theory from the *Kunstreligion* of the nineteenth century, that is to say, from a celebration of the aesthetic as a form of immanent reconciliation. Hence *Aesthetic Theory* is not, as some critics of Adorno have claimed, characterized by an overemphasis on the importance of art. While Adorno insists on the need of radical spiritualization when he discusses modern art, the concept of spirit is, as we have seen, part of the temporal sphere, although it is clearly distinct from the sensual. As a counterpoint, the absolute remains pure transcendence.

Where does this leave us? The emphasis on the theological moment in *Aesthetic Theory* could well be used as a basis for criticism. In his final assessment of Adorno's Gnosticism, Michael Pauen, for instance, makes the theological trope responsible for Adorno's increasing pessimism vis-à-vis the post-war development. Since the Gnostic sees the temporal world in terms of enduring catastrophe, there is no room for political change.[17] More generally, the hiatus between theory (knowledge) and empirical world cannot be overcome, which means for Pauen that Adorno's theory, left to its own devices, becomes ultimately self-absorbed and blind.[18] It is worth noting that Pauen's criticism, which echoes that of a number of previous critics, is primarily focused on Adorno's social theory without much attention to Adorno's philosophy of art. Would the theological figure have the same disabling consequences in *Aesthetic Theory*? Recently critics have asked this question with greater rigor, emphatically rejecting a more historicist approach to Adorno's thought, demanding instead a response inflected by the contemporary problematic. These charges can be summarized in the following way: First, Adorno's theory remains locked in negativity based on a self-grinding dialectical reflection. Second, Adorno overrates the force of art and the aesthetic and thereby overburdens contemporary art. Third, Adorno's rigid opposition to questions of practice is no longer reasonable (if it ever was). Fourth, his critique of capitalism, while well-intended, is out of touch with the globalization of capitalism. Fifth, Adorno's dialectical method has to be replaced by a form of praxis-oriented pragmatism. The test for a new aesthetic theory is its usefulness rather than its complexity. Unlike Pauen's objections, this critique connects a general negative assessment of Adorno with a sharp criticism of his aesthetic theory, which comes across as outmoded and solipsistic. Yet closer scrutiny of the five points reveals that this characterization of Adorno is not without problems. The charge of overemphasis on the aesthetic sphere makes an interesting point in the context of the debate about mass culture, but fails to grasp Adorno's intent to limit the importance and value of art through the theological figure. If we understand this criticism as a refusal to buy into a reading of *Aesthetic Theory* that focuses on art as social criticism through aesthetic negation, the charge of overloading the artwork might be more plausible. In the end, the claim that *Aesthetic Theory* is outdated both in terms of method (dialectics) and content (understanding of art) is most difficult to handle, since it is historically obviously true but theoretically by all means an open question that cannot be foreclosed by an abstract and extrinsic claim of outdatedness. In this regard it is worth noting that Frederic Jameson turned the tables around and argued for the relevance of Adorno's thought precisely because it was "outdated" and therefore still contained a critical edge that later theory lost.[19] The fact that *Aesthetic Theory* was written in the 1960s and first discussed in the early 1970s in the context of the politics of the New Left has left its marks on the text, but does not necessarily exhaust the meaning and the truth content.

The call for a "return to Adorno" of the 1990s, in part an implied critique of the later Frankfurt School and in particular of Habermas, will be least successful as an attempt to restore the work as a dogma or a plan to defend Adorno's position of the 1960s. Instead, what is significant and important for the present can be revealed only in a process of reading that takes note of the tensions and contradictions of the text. For this reason, I focused on the theological figure that the mainstream interpretations dealing with *Aesthetic Theory* have considered as marginal. This deliberate one-sidedness brought to the fore the serious skepticism of Adorno's theory with regard to the status of art and his strong resistance to any form of *Kunstreligion*, i.e., any attempt to assign art the place once occupied by religion. While Adorno openly acknowledges a metaphysical framework, he clearly rejects a form of aestheticism that brushes aside ethical concerns. One might even argue that he puts the advanced work of art, by way of its formal organization, in the service of ethical concerns, filtered through the concept of authenticity. In a radical formulation he calls for the end of art after Auschwitz. In his most famous verdict Adorno questions the justification of aesthetic production in light of the ethical demands of the Holocaust. This call is clearly not meant as, and should not be confused with, the intrinsic fate of modern art, namely its ultimate self-negation, its wish to come to an end.[20] This fate only radicalizes the status of art in general. It is therefore not altogether surprising that, seen against the absolute, the otherwise sharply marked opposition between genuine art and the culture industry breaks down. The logic of critical resistance through the artwork, which dominates much of *Aesthetic Theory*, is superseded by the theological figure. In this light art and mass culture are allowed to show their similarities, the latter as the parody of the former, a parody that throws its shadow over the presumed purity of the artwork.

The Holocaust seems to pull art into its force field. The horror of suffering and the weight of the dead have created a caesura that cannot be eliminated or dialectically sublated. Hence the actual survival of art, the continuation of aesthetic production after World War II, must be understood as an act of *Gedankenlosigkeit*, a lack of reflection that violates ethical obligations. To be sure, Adorno was correct to point out that these obligations would not be addressed by an authoritarian order but needed to find their own immanent response. As Adorno notes: "Radical art today is synonymous with dark art; its primary color is black" (*AT* 39). Adorno's rejection of *"heitere Kunst"* is closely connected with the weight of the dead. "The injustice committed by all cheerful art, especially by entertainment, is probably an injustice to the dead; to accumulated, speechless pain" (*AT* 40). The continuation of this sentence deserves our full attention, since Adorno gives his radical assessment an unexpected turn: "Still, black art bears features that would, if they were definitive, set their seal on historical despair, to the extent that change is always still possible they too may be ephemeral" (*AT* 40). Adorno suggests a logic of historical despair articulated in "black art," yet this logic is suspended in view of the mere possibility of change. We have to note that the German phrase *"es immer noch anders werden kann"* is even more indecisive than Robert Hullot-Kentor's translation *"that change is always still possible."* This weak indication of something different affects the artwork insofar as it alters the rigorous seriousness, its blackness, and gives it an ephemeral aspect. Thus the ethical demand leads to a paradoxical situation. The very intention of the artwork to include the horror of mass death in its structure, the intention of absolute seriousness leads away from absolute seriousness to an ephemeral act of artistic production, based on pleasure, i.e., on a sensual moment that is fundamentally inadequate to the suffering of humankind. The paradox is the appearance of happiness emanating from the artwork in the context of complete darkness. Put differently, art is by its constitution unable to live up to rigorous ethical demands, yet this very inability, the fact that it is bound to the sensual, provides the happiness that is at least the *Vorschein* of redemption. The ethics of the artwork becomes (or always was) "the capacity of standing firm" (*AT* 40) in a situation where standing firm is the most unlikely response.

Given the problematic nature of art, its critical negativity (opposition) on the one hand and its ephemeral character on the other, the status of the theological figure becomes imperative, since both aesthetic and ethical concerns are determined by this question. Undoubtedly Adorno (and Horkheimer) never contemplated a return to religion as a system of dogmas supported by a social institution. His critique of Christianity as a regression to forms of magic makes that quite clear.[21] Yet even the concept of a negative theology might still be too closely linked to notions of a religious return. What we have to explore and grasp is Adorno's translation of religious language for purposes that are analogous to but not identical with religion.

In the last thought image of *Minima Moralia*, entitled "Zum Ende," Adorno reflects on the fate of philosophy in the face of despair [*Verzweiflung*].[22] The figure of redemption, taken either from messianic Judaism or Christianity, provides Adorno with a structure to contemplate the future of thought when institutional philosophy has demonstrated its failure to make sense of the world and "exhausts itself in reconstruction and remains a piece of technique."[23] The alternative would be, Adorno suggests, a philosophy that contemplates things "the way they would present themselves from the standpoint of redemption."[24] While the perspective of redemption is suggested as the only one left, Adorno also undermines any expectation of a certain delivery. It is not the vision of the new philosophy that is difficult to grasp; in fact, Adorno calls this "the easiest of all because the condition irrefutably calls for such cognition,"[25] but the actual practice, anticipating redemption as a way of thinking. The actual practice, Adorno reminds the reader, remains captured by the very conditions it wants to escape. Philosophy's intention to reach the absolute [*Unbedingte*] through abstract consciousness must fail precisely because it is unconsciously part of the world it wants to escape. Thus the figure of redemption offers an alternative perspective but no certainty. As Gerhard Richter correctly observes, Adorno gives the impression of evoking the hope of redemption and simultaneously withdraws this promise.[26] The possibility of redemption depends on the insight that it is actually impossible. But for Adorno the recognition of this paradox does not result in intensified despair. Instead, the passage concludes with the statement that the question of whether redemption is real or not (the decisive moment in theology) is almost unimportant. In view of the demand [*Forderung*] the philosopher faces, we have to note that the actual fulfillment of the promise is unimportant. Philosophy persists by accepting its own impossibility as the challenge of its uncertain future. However, this prolongation also contains a break: It must open itself to a theological perspective without affirming an actual content.

As we have come to realize, the theological figure, while clearly not to be taken literally, is decisive for Adorno's thought. It provides both the perspective (which is not to be confused with a goal) and the task. Aesthetic theory stands under this sign as well. Thinking about artworks as linked to an undefined absolute spells out the ultimate stakes: the need to take them seriously as a form of condensed "*Spiegelschrift*" [mirror writing] that through its negation points to the unattainable other and the impossibility to take them seriously, since they are part of the temporal world in which they lack ethical responsibility.

APPENDIX

Who's Afraid of the Ivory Tower?
A Conversation with Theodor W. Adorno

*Translated, Edited, and with an
Introduction by Gerhard Richter*

"Philosophy, which once seemed passé," Theodor W. Adorno's *Negative Dialectics* begins, "remains alive because the moment of its realization was missed" ["*Philosophie, die einmal überholt schien, erhält sich am Leben, weil der Augenblick ihrer Verwirklichung versäumt ward*"].[1] This perspective encrypts the double movement of a simultaneous resignation or lament and a productive, enabling force. It is only because the philosophy of which Adorno speaks—negative dialectics—was not realized that its actualization is yet to come. That it once existed without becoming an actuality means that it still remains to be thought, both as a failure and a promise. The erratic traces of this double movement not only name but also *enact* Adorno's notion of a negative dialectic. The movement of the negative dialectic of failure and promise has strongly marked the reception of the English translations of his writings. After all, Adorno's German, and the thought that it enacts, is rigorously and infamously resistant to translation. His writing is both strange and foreign—*fremd*—even in its "original" German.

To acknowledge this strangeness is also to acknowledge that what Adorno says cannot be separated from how he says it. As Samuel Weber, one of Adorno's earliest translators, so apodictically and incontrovertibly puts it in his 1967 "Translating the Untranslatable," the "specificity of

Adorno's thought is inseparable from its articulation," so that "conceptual concreteness may be measured by the density with which thought and articulation permeate each other."[2] For this reason, any translator who, in spite of these difficulties, attempts to translate Adorno's sentences runs the risk of constructing an Adorno who, in the words of translator Robert Hullot-Kentor, appears "dubbed rather than translated."[3] Thus, as Hullot-Kentor points out, while many admirable English translations of Adorno's texts exist, others deserve to be retranslated.[4] The process is now well under way, with, for instance, the re-translation of *Aesthetic Theory*, which replaces the British version of 1984.

The following interview with Adorno has not received the attention that it deserves. It originally appeared on 5 May 1969, three months before the philosopher's death, under the title "Keine Angst vor dem Elfenbeinturm" in the widely circulating German weekly news magazine *Der Spiegel*.[5] Shortly after it appeared in Germany, an English translation, which has been virtually ignored in the American context, was published in a British journal.[6] In a very real sense, then, the "moment of its realization was missed." To present this important document today in an entirely new translation means to take seriously—with a bit of Blochian nonsynchronicity—the critical potential that it still may hold for readers interested in the relation between aesthetics and politics. But the re-presentation of the document today also requires an explanation of historical contexts and political references, glosses that culturally aware readers in 1969 may not have required and that were provided neither in the British translation nor by Adorno's German editors, who later included the text in his collected writings [*Gesammelte Schriften*].[7] I have therefore provided explanatory notes to clarify historical references for today's readers.

To appropriate the conceptual content of the discussion with Adorno for our time also requires some contextualization in the tensions of its own time. The immediate occasion for the highly visible interview was Adorno's cancellation of his University of Frankfurt lecture course "Introduction to Dialectical Thinking" during the summer semester of 1969, following confrontations with student activists who disrupted his lectures with heckling. During the previous semester, Adorno's decision to involve the police in clearing student occupiers from the Institute for Social Research (the Frankfurt School's departmental unit at the University of Frankfurt) had caused controversy. While some regarded Adorno's reliance on the authorities as a betrayal—a siding with the enemy against the common cause of social progress—others tended to agree with Adorno's assessment of the radical activism of some students as misguided or even, in the words of his former research assistant Jürgen Habermas, as a form of "left-wing fascism."[8] On the day that the *Spiegel* interview appeared, Adorno writes to his friend and Frankfurt School colleague Herbert Marcuse: "One should refrain from ... demonizing the police wholesale. I can only repeat that they treated the students much more gingerly than the students treated me. That was beyond description." He continues: "The other day I was told by Mr. Cohn-Bendit during a departmental town meeting that I only had the right to call in the police if people actually wanted to beat me up with metal rods. I answered that then it would be too late."[9]

The irony of the tensions between Adorno and some student activists are legible enough. On the one hand, his theories had contributed to the establishment of the first general waves of political activism in West Germany after Word War II and to a general critical engagement with the legacies of German fascism, a subject that had largely remained taboo after 1945. Examples of Adorno's theoretical interventions that were especially significant in this regard included his and Horkheimer's analysis of the culture industry, his dissection of the authoritarian personality, his subversive reflections on what it means to be German, his meditations on education "after Auschwitz," and his anti-fascist reflections, among many others. But on the other hand, more concrete signs of solidarity were expected of Adorno after December 1966, especially on the part of the "APO." "APO" stands for "*Außerparlamentarische Opposition*" ["Extraparliamentary opposition"], the collective name of the West German student and New Left movements, along with a variety of smaller oppositional groups that were not presented in the West German parliament. The APO came into existence in 1967, in response to the "Grand Coalition" formed between Kurt Georg Kiesinger's conservative CDU/CSU and Willy Brandt's social-democratic SPD on 1 December 1966—that is, when almost no opposition remained within the West German parliament itself. Many in the Frankfurt APO now looked to Adorno and other members of the Frankfurt School for practical political leadership, often in vain.

In a patricidal reversal that pitted parts of the Student Protest Movement and the New Left against one of their theoretical fathers, Adorno was subjected to a series of institutional and personal attacks at least since 1967, and leaflets proclaiming that "Adorno as an institution is dead" ["*Adorno als Institution ist tot*"] were circulated during his lectures. For instance, when he was invited by Peter Szondi and Wilhelm Emrich on behalf of the departments of German and Comparative Literature at the

Free University of Berlin to deliver a lecture in July 1967 on "The Classicism of Goethe's *Iphigenie*," a meditation that was later included as an essay in his *Notes to Literature*, Adorno was greeted with heckles on the part of some. Adorno had earlier refused to write a letter of support exculpating the activist Fritz Teufel, whose controversial handouts and leaflets had been read by his accusers not as a satire but as a concrete incitement to arson and violence. Because Adorno refused to conduct a political discussion instead of delivering his lecture as planned, his detractors regarded his decision to speak on Goethe as a retreat from political intervention into classicist aesthetics.

But the most notorious incident was yet to come. During an April 1969 assault, an instance of "planned tenderness," which has come to be known as the "breast action" [*Busenaktion*], three female sociology students wearing long leather jackets invaded the lecturer's podium, sprinkled rose and tulip petals over Adorno's head, attempted to plant lipstick kisses on his cheeks, exposed their naked breasts to him, and provoked him with erotic pantomimes. Adorno, attempting to protect himself with his briefcase, proceeded to exit *Hörsaal V* ["Lecture Hall V"]. This attempt to embarrass Adorno publicly was a sign of the larger structure of misunderstanding between Adorno and those student activists who had grown increasingly impatient with their theoretically minded teacher's reluctance to engage in street interventions and other forms of political activism.

The tension and misunderstanding between Adorno and some of the student activists was by no means universal. Indeed, many found the public provocations of Adorno by a minority of students misplaced and embarrassing. Those critical of the activities to which Adorno was subjected must have recalled not only their indebtedness to the theoretical apparatus for a critical analysis of society and culture that he had supplied, but also Adorno's general interest in being a public intellectual open to discussion and to a sustained engagement in concrete political causes. For instance, after the so-called German-American friendship week had been marred by severe street violence and clashes between protesters and the police in May 1967, Adorno, along with his colleague Max Horkheimer and others, on 12 June 1967 engaged in a public discussion with students and activists regarding the relationship between Critical Theory and political praxis. Similarly, Adorno spoke out publicly against the West German *Notstandsgesetze* ["Emergency Laws"]. These Emergency Laws were to enable the West German government to suspend certain basic democratic citizens' rights when protests and concrete opposition threatened to destabilize the basic order of the state. The constitution that would make Emergency

Laws legal was passed on 30 May 1968. Two days earlier, Adorno had made a last-minute effort to derail the passing of these laws, formulating a firm rejection of these curtailments of civil liberties in an address entitled *"Gegen die Notstandsgesetze"* ["Against the Emergency Laws"] in the *Große Sendesaal* of the *Hessischer Rundfunk* [Hessian Broadcast Service].[10] And as Adorno reveals in a November 1968 letter to the writer Günter Grass, he maintained friendly relations with the Social Democratic politician Gustav Heinemann—then West Germany's minister of justice and later, from 1969 through 1974, president of the Federal Republic—whom he closely advised regarding West Germany's progressive criminal law reform. Similarly, Adorno was instrumental in helping to work out a compromise agreement between the *IG Metall*, West Germany's metal workers' union, and their companies. But while he supported these and other political causes, such as then Foreign Minister and Vice Chancellor Willy Brandt's concrete attempts to loosen the iron collar of Cold War ideologies through a new political relationship with countries to West Germany's East, he remained suspicious of certain "aporias of the politics of reconciliation" [*"Aporien der Versöhnungspolitik"*]. These included the politics that he feared would disguise the ways in which the Soviet Union's gestures of political reconciliation with its satellite states could also be read as attempts at even greater domination of these states. Here, he feared, the questionable and deeply problematic political interests represented by both Washington and Moscow found a possible way of supplementing one another in their expansivist quests for world domination. Rejecting what he often denounced as "forced reconciliation" (*"erpreßte Versöhnung"*), Adorno confesses to Grass his "mounting aversion to any kind of praxis in which my natural disposition and the objective hopelessness of praxis in this historical moment may meet each other."[11] Between the writing of these lines and his death some ten months later, this aversion may have grown ever more pronounced in light of the heightening intensity with which the personal attacks against him were carried out.

In the interview that follows, Adorno explains, in more lucid and conversational terms than is characteristic of his formal writings, his conceptualization of the political relevance that his theoretical work may have. For him, the political impact of his work is not to be measured by the extent to which it enables unmediated social praxis but rather by the extent to which it effects a broad change in consciousness. Here, the oppositional pair of thought and action itself is suspended. The text belongs in the general orbit of similar meditations that Adorno devoted to this subject in the late 1960s, such as his texts "Resignation" and "Marginalia on Theory and Praxis," and his conversation regarding Critical Theory and the Protest Movement with the *Süddeutsche Zeitung*.[12] Indeed, there is no sentence in Adorno's mature work that is not touched by the political implications of the thoughts that he expresses in the *Spiegel* interview.

In my English translation, I have attempted to capture some of the informal conversational tone of Adorno's sentences, a tone that may strike some readers as belonging to a surprisingly different register than that found in the formal and rigorous precision of his written works, where his German prose, in its persistent self-reflexivity and performativity, often appears, quite strategically, to resemble no living language. The sinewy lucidity of Adorno's spoken and improvised language in this interview cannot be explained fully by *Der Spiegel*'s editorial practices, as listeners to the recently published collection of five compact disks containing a variety of his speeches and interviews can attest.[13] Adorno's fluid style as an interlocutor and public speaker—especially as he developed it for his various radio, television, and mass print appearances soon following his return to Germany from American exile in 1949—should be placed into a dynamic constellation with his written language to assess the shifting contours of his imagined relationship to the audience.

I wish to thank Petra Hardt of Suhrkamp Verlag as well as Adorno's German editors, Christoph Gödde and Henri Lonitz of the Theodor W. Adorno Archive at the *Institut für Sozialforschung* in Frankfurt, for permission to publish it here.

> *Spiegel*: Professor Adorno, two weeks ago, the world still seemed in order. . . .
>
> Adorno: Not to me.
>
> *Spiegel*: You said that your relations with the students were not strained. In your courses, you said, discussions were fruitful, sober, and untainted by personal disturbances. But now you have cancelled your lecture.
>
> Adorno: I did not cancel my lecture for the entire semester, but only until further notice. I hope to start up again in a few weeks. All colleagues do this when their lectures are so massively disrupted.
>
> *Spiegel*: Were you subjected to violence?
>
> Adorno: Not physical violence, but so much noise was made that my lecture would have been drowned by it. That was obviously the plan.
>
> *Spiegel*: Are you repulsed only by the manner in which students today take action against you—students who once were on your side—or did their political goals also disturb you? After all, it is fair to say that there used to be agreement between you and the rebels.

Adorno: That is not the dimension in which our differences play themselves out. Recently I said in a television interview that, even though I had established a theoretical model, I could not have foreseen that people would try to implement it with Molotov cocktails. This sentence has been cited numerous times, but it requires substantial interpretation.

Spiegel: How would you interpret it today?

Adorno: In my writings, I have never offered a model for any kind of action or for some specific campaign. I am a theoretical human being who views theoretical thinking as lying extraordinarily close to his artistic intentions. It is not as if I had turned away from praxis only recently; my thinking always has stood in a rather indirect relationship to praxis. My thinking has perhaps had practical consequences in that some of its motifs have entered consciousness, but I have never said anything that was immediately aimed at practical actions. Ever since the first bedlam was organized against me in 1967 in Berlin, certain student groups have time and again attempted to force me into solidarity, demanding practical actions of me. I have refused.

Spiegel: But Critical Theory does not wish to keep conditions as they are. The SDS students learned this from you.[14] You, Professor Adorno, now refuse practical action. Are you not cultivating a mere "liturgy of critique," as Dahrendorf claims?[15]

Adorno: In the case of Dahrendorf, a tone of fresh and cheerful conviction reigns supreme: If only you change little things here and there, then perhaps everything will be better.[16] I cannot accept this presupposition. But among the APO, I always encounter the compulsive pressure to deliver oneself, to join in; this is something I have resisted since my earliest youth. And in that area nothing has changed in me. I attempt to put into words what I see and what I think. But I cannot predicate this on what will be done with it or what will become of it.

Spiegel: Scholarship in the ivory tower, then?

Adorno: I am not at all afraid of the term "ivory tower." This term has certainly seen better days, as when Baudelaire employed it.[17] But since you bring up the ivory tower: I believe that a theory is much more capable of having practical consequences owing to the strength of its own objectivity than if it had subjected itself to praxis from the start. Today's unfortunate relationship between theory and praxis consists precisely in the fact that theory is subjected to a practical pre-censorship. For instance, people wish to forbid me to put into words simple things that show the illusionary character of many of the political goals that certain students have.

Spiegel: But these students apparently have a large following.

Adorno: A small group of students succeeds time and again in enforcing loyalty, something which the vast majority of leftist students may not fully resist. But I wish to emphasize again the following: They simply cannot refer to models of action that I allegedly gave them in order then to place me at odds with these models. There are no such models.

Spiegel: Yet it is the case that students refer, at times very directly, at other times indirectly, to your critique of society. Without your theories, the student protest movement might not even have developed.

Adorno: I do not wish to deny that. Nevertheless, it is difficult for me to assess this connection fully. I would like to believe, for instance, that a critique of the manipulation of public opinion—which I consider legitimate even in its demonstrative form—would not have been possible without the chapter on the culture industry in the *Dialectic of Enlightenment* by Horkheimer and myself. But I think that one often conceives the connection between theory and praxis too reductively. If one has taught and published for twenty years with the intensity that I have, it does enter into general consciousness.

Spiegel: And thus also into praxis?

Adorno: Possibly, but not necessarily so. In our writings, the value of so-called individual actions is delimited by an emphasis on societal totality.

Spiegel: But how would one go about changing societal totality without individual action?

Adorno: This is asking too much of me. In response to the question "What is to be done?" I usually can only answer "I do not know."[18] I can only analyze relentlessly what is. In the process, I am reproached in the following manner: "If you criticize, you have to say how to do better." But I consider this a bourgeois prejudice. Historically, there have been countless instances in which precisely those works that pursued purely theoretical intentions altered consciousness and, by extension, societal reality.

Spiegel: But in your writings you have set Critical Theory apart from other kinds of theory. It should not merely describe reality empirically, but also should consider [*mit bedenken*] the proper organization of society.

Adorno: Here, I was concerned with a critique of positivism.[19] Note that I said *also consider* [*mit bedenken*]. In no way does this sentence suggest that I would be so presumptuous as to tell people how to act.

Spiegel: You once said, however, that Critical Theory should "lift the rock under which barbarism breeds." If the students are now throwing this rock—is this so incomprehensible?

Adorno: Certainly not incomprehensible. I believe that their actionism [*Aktionismus*][20] can essentially be traced back to despair, because people sense how little power they actually have to change society. But I am equally convinced that these individual actions are predestined to fail; this also proved to be the case during the May revolt in France.[21]

Spiegel: So if individual actions are pointless, is not the "critical impotence," of which the SDS has accused you, the only thing that remains?

Adorno: There is a sentence by Grabbe that reads: "For nothing but despair can save us."[22] This is provocative, but not at all dumb. I cannot fault someone living in our world today for feeling despairing, pessimistic, and negative. Those who compulsively shout down their objective despair with the noisy optimism of immediate action in order to lighten their psychological burden are much more deluded.[23]

Spiegel: Your colleague Jürgen Habermas, also a proponent of Critical Theory, has now conceded in an essay that the students have developed an "imaginative provocationism" and have really managed to change some things.[24]

Adorno: I would agree with Habermas on this point. I believe that the university reform, of which we incidentally do not yet know the outcome, would never have been set into motion without the students.[25] I believe that the general attention to processes of dumbing down, which are prevalent in our present society, would never have crystallized without the student movement. And furthermore, to mention something very concrete, I believe that it was only through the investigation, led by Berlin students, of the murder of Ohnesorg that this horrifying story penetrated public consciousness at all.[26] With this I wish to say that I in no way close myself off to practical consequences as long as they are transparent to me.

Spiegel: And when have they been transparent to you?

Adorno: I participated in demonstrations against Emergency Laws [*Notstandsgesetze*], and I have done what I could in the area of criminal law reform. But there is a decisive difference between doing something like that and taking part in the half-crazed activity of throwing rocks at university institutes.

Spiegel: How would you determine whether or not an action is worthwhile?

Adorno: For one thing, this decision depends in large measure on the concrete situation. For another, I have the strongest reservations against any use of violence. I would have to disown my entire life—my experiences under Hitler and what I have observed of Stalinism—if I did not refuse to participate in the eternal circle of using violence to fight violence. The only meaningfully transformative praxis that I could imagine would be a non-violent one.

Spiegel: Even under a Fascist dictatorship?

Adorno: There certainly may be situations in which things would look different. To a real Fascism, one can only react with violence. I am anything but rigid on this point. But I refuse to follow those who, after the murder of countless millions in the totalitarian states, still preach violence today. That is the decisive threshold.

Spiegel: Did students cross that threshold when they attempted to prevent the delivery of Springer newspapers through sit-down strikes?[27]

Adorno: I consider this sit-down strike legitimate.

Spiegel: Was this threshold crossed when students disrupted your lectures with noise and sexual theatrics?

Adorno: To think that they did this to me, of all people, someone who has always opposed any kind of erotic repression and sexual taboo! To mock me and to loose three girls dressed up as hippies on me! I found that repulsive. The comic effect achieved by this was nothing more than the reaction of a philistine [*Spießbürger*] who giggles "he-he!" [*der Hihi! kichert*] at the sight of a girl with naked breasts. This nonsense was naturally planned in advance.

Spiegel: Was this unusual act perhaps intended to ruffle your theory?

Adorno: It seems to me that these actions against me have little to do with the content of my lectures; what is more important to the extreme wing is the publicity. They suffer from the fear of being forgotten. In this way they become slaves of their own publicity. A lecture such as mine, which is attended by about 1,000 people, is obviously a magnificent forum for activist propaganda.

Spiegel: Can this deed not also be interpreted as an act of despair? Perhaps the students felt left in the lurch by a theory that they had considered at least capable of being translated into societal praxis?

Adorno: The students did not even attempt to have a discussion with me. What makes my dealings with students so much more difficult today is the prioritization of tactics. My friends and I have the feeling that we have been reduced to mere objects in precisely calculated plans. The idea of minority rights, which after all is constitutive of freedom, no longer plays any role whatsoever. One blinds oneself to the objectivity of the matter [*Objektivität der Sache*].

Spiegel: And in the face of such abuses you make do without a defensive strategy?

Adorno: My interests are turning increasingly toward philosophical theory. If I were to give practical advice, as Herbert Marcuse has done to a certain degree, it would detract from my productivity.[28] Much can be said against the division of labor; but even Marx, who in his youth attacked it vehemently, later on conceded that we cannot do without the division of labor after all.[29]

Spiegel: You have chosen for yourself the theoretical part, then, leaving the practical part to others; indeed, they are already working on it. Would it not be preferable if theory simultaneously reflected praxis? And, by extension, also the present actions?

Adorno: There are situations in which I would do this. At the moment, however, it seems much more important to me to think through the anatomy of actionism.

Spiegel: So, mere theory again?

Adorno: I value theory more highly at this point. I dealt with these issues—especially in my *Negative Dialectics*—long before the current conflict erupted.

Spiegel: In *Negative Dialectics*, we find the following resigned observation: "Philosophy, which once seemed passé, remains alive because the moment of its realization was missed."[30] All conflicts aside, does such a philosophy not become "foolishness"? A question that you have asked yourself.

Adorno: I still believe that one should hold on to theory, precisely under the general coercion toward praxis in a functional and pragmatized world. And I will not permit even the most recent events to dissuade me from what I have written.

Spiegel: So far, as your friend Habermas once put it, your dialectic has, at its "blackest spots" of resignation, surrendered to "the destructive pull of the death drive."[31]

Adorno: I would rather say that the compulsive clinging to what is positive stems from the death drive.

Spiegel: Then, would it be the virtue of philosophy to look the negative in the eye but not to change it?[32]

Adorno: Philosophy cannot in and of itself recommend immediate measures or changes. It effects change precisely by remaining theory. I think that for once the question should be asked whether it is not also a form of resistance when a human being thinks and writes things the way I write them. Is theory not also a genuine form of praxis?

Spiegel: Are there not situations, for example in Greece, in which you endorse action that goes beyond critical reflection?[33]

Adorno: It goes without saying that in Greece I would approve of any kind of action. The situation that prevails there is totally different. But for someone who is ensconced in safety to advise others to start a revolution is so ridiculous that one ought to be ashamed of oneself.

Spiegel: So, you continue to view the advancement of an analysis of societal conditions as the most meaningful and necessary aspect of your activities in the Federal Republic?

Adorno: Yes, and to immerse myself in very specific individual phenomena. I am not in the least ashamed to say very publicly that I am working on a major book on aesthetics.[34]

Spiegel: Professor Adorno, we thank you for this conversation.

NOTES

INTRODUCTION
Gerhard Richter

1. Besides the major new intellectual biographies occasioned by the recent centenary of Adorno's birth—Detlev Claussen, *Theodor W. Adorno: Ein letztes Genie* (Frankfurt am Main: Fischer, 2002); Lorenz Jäger, *Adorno: Eine politische Biographie* (Munich: Deutsche Verlagsanstalt, 2003); and Stefan Müller-Doohm, *Adorno: Eine Biographie* (Frankfurt am Main: Suhrkamp, 2003)—examples of the most significant recent work engaging Adorno's orbit of thought include the account of modernism based on Adorno's aesthetic theory offered by J. M. Bernstein, *Against Voluptuous Bodies: Late Modernism and the Meaning of Painting* (Stanford, Calif.: Stanford University Press, 2006), as well as the discussions of Adorno's unorthodox ethical thought in Judith Butler, *Kritik der ethischen Gewalt* (Frankfurt am Main: Suhrkamp, 2003); Jochen Hörisch, *Es gibt (k)ein richtiges Leben im Falschen* (Frankfurt am Main: Suhrkamp, 2003); and Alexander García Düttmann, *So ist es: Ein philosophischer Kommentar zu Adornos "Minima Moralia"* (Frankfurt am Main: Suhrkamp, 2004). These works are joined, most recently, by an attempt at a sustained comparison between Adorno and the fundamental ontology of Martin Heidegger: *Adorno and Heidegger: Philosophical Questions*, ed. Iain Mcdonald and Krzysztof Ziarek (Stanford, Calif.: Stanford University Press, 2008).

2. *Traumprotokolle*, eds. Christoph Gödde and Henri Lonitz, with an afterword by Jan Phillip Reemtsma (Frankfurt am Main: Suhrkamp, 2005).

3. Theodor W. Adorno, "A Portrait of Walter Benjamin," *Prisms*, trans. Samuel Weber and Shierry Weber (Cambridge, Mass.: MIT Press, 1992), 227–41, here 241.

4. Adorno, *Negative Dialektik*, in *Gesammelte Schriften*, ed. Rolf Tiedemann (Frankfurt am Main: Suhrkamp, 1997), 6:15.

5. Adorno, "Spätstil Beethovens," *Musikalische Schriften IV: Moments musicaux, Impromptus*, in *Gesammelte Schriften*, 17:13–17. For a general meditation on late style in the arts, see the posthumously published notes by Edward Said, *On Late Style: Music and Language Against the Grain* (New York: Pantheon, 2006).

6. Adorno, "Aus einem Schulheft ohne Deckel. Bar Harbor, Sommer 1939," in *Frankfurter Adorno Blätter* 4 (1995): 7.

7. Adorno, "Wörter aus der Fremde," *Noten zur Literatur*, in *Gesammelte Schriften*, 11:216–32, here 224.

8. Ibid., 218.

9. Ibid.

10. Ibid., 224.

11. For an extended analysis of this mode of writing in the orbit of Adorno's aesthetics, see Gerhard Richter, *Thought-Images: Frankfurt School Writers' Reflections from Damaged Life* (Stanford, Calif.: Stanford University Press, 2007).

12. Adorno, "Commitment," *Notes to Literature*, trans. Shierry Weber Nicholsen (New York: Columbia University Press, 1992), 2:76–94, here 93f; and "Engagement," *Noten zur Literatur*, in *Gesammelte Schriften*, ed. Rolf Tiedemann (Frankfurt am Main: Suhrkamp, 1997), 11:409–30, here 430.

13. Franz Kafka, "Letter to Oskar Pollak, January 27, 1904," *Kafka's Selected Stories*, ed. and trans. Stanley Corngold (New York: Norton, 2007), 193.

14. Adorno, "Notes on Kafka," *Prisms*, 243–71, here 246.

15. For a useful overview of this project, see *Stolpersteine: Gunter Demnig und sein Projekt*, ed. NS-Dokumentationszentrum (Cologne: Emons, 2007).

16. Adorno, "Sexual Taboos and Law Today," *Critical Models: Catchwords and Interventions*, trans. Henry W. Pickford, introduction by Lydia Goehr (New York: Columbia University Press, 2005), 71–88, here 71.

17. Adorno, *Negative Dialektik*, 358.

1. WITHOUT SOIL: A FIGURE IN ADORNO'S THOUGHT
Alexander García Düttmann

1. Theodor W. Adorno, *Negative Dialectics*, trans. E. B. Ashton (New York: Seabury Press, 1973), 391–92.

2. Ibid., 392.

3. Joseph Margolis, *Moral Philosophy After 9/11* (University Park: Pennsylvania State University Press, 2004), xvi.

4. Ibid., ix.

5. Ibid., 45.

6. Ibid., 99.

7. Raimond Gaita, *Good and Evil: An Absolute Conception* (London: Routledge, 2004), xv.

8. Ludwig Wittgenstein, "Nächtliches (Traum-)Erlebnis," in Wittgenstein, *Licht und Schatten*, ed. Ilse Somavilla (Innsbruck and Vienna: Haymon Verlag, 2004), 20–21.

9. Adorno, *Notes to Literature*, trans. Shierry Weber Nicholsen (New York: Columbia University Press, 1991), 1:192; translation amended. "Earth" and "soil" have been used throughout to translate Adorno's *Erde*.—Trans.

10. Adorno and Max Horkheimer, *Briefwechsel, Band II, 1938–1944* (Frankfurt am Main: Suhrkamp, 2004), 101.

11. In the early essay on Schubert, Adorno speaks of a "dialect without soil," that is, a dialect that has relinquished its immediate ties to the homeland, because the homeland has receded into the distance; *Gesammelte Schriften*, 17:33. The earth frequently signifies the spell of myth, unfreedom; in texts on Mahler, above all, the melancholy gaze upon the faraway or vanishing earth is one that perceives its beauty from a distance and is reconciled with it, so to speak: "But the earth, remote even to itself, is without the hope once promised by the stars. It falls away into empty galaxies. Beauty casts its glow upon it as the reflection of past hope, filling the dying eye until it freezes under the snowdrift of immeasurable space. The moment of rapture in the face of such beauty presumes to withstand captivity to disenchanted nature"; *Gesammelte Schriften*, 13:296–97.

12. See Ulrich Plass, *The Art of Transition: Language and History in Theodor W. Adorno's* Notes to Literature (New York: Routledge, 2007).

13. Adorno, *Philosophy of Modern Music*, trans. Anne G. Mitchell and Wesley V. Blomster (New York: Continuum, 2004), 128.

14. Adorno, *Prisms*, trans. Samuel Weber and Shierry Weber (Letchworth, U.K.: Neville Spearman, 1967), 208.

15. Adorno, *Philosophy of Modern Music*, 128–29.

2. TAKING ON THE STIGMA OF INAUTHENTICITY: ADORNO'S CRITIQUE OF GENUINENESS
Martin Jay

1. Paul de Man, *Blindness and Insight: Essays in the Rhetoric of Contemporary Criticism*. Second rev. ed. (Minneapolis: University of Minnesota Press, 1983), 214.

2. Marshall Berman, *The Politics of Authenticity: Radical Individualism and the Emergence of Modern Society* (New York: Atheneum, 1972), xix.

3. Lionel Trilling, *Sincerity and Authenticity* (Cambridge, Mass.: Harvard University Press, 1972), 156. A few years earlier, albeit with somewhat more skepticism, Philip Rieff had noted in his influential *Freud: The Mind of the Moralist* (Garden City, N.Y.: Doubleday, 1961) that "Freud's ethic resembles Sartre's existentialism, which offers a related criterion, authenticity, as a way of judging what is good in human action" (352). For a later discussion, see Charles Taylor, *The Ethics of Authenticity* (Cambridge, Mass.: Harvard University Press, 1991).

4. Trilling, *Sincerity and Authenticity*, 158.

5. See Ann Fulton, *Apostles of Sartre: Existentialism in America, 1945–1963* (Evanston, Ill.: Northwestern University Press, 1999), 74–76.

6. Alexander Nehamas, *Virtues of Authenticity: Essays on Plato and Socrates* (Princeton, N.J.: Princeton University Press, 1999); Geoffrey Hartman, *Scars of the Spirit: The Struggle Against Inauthenticity* (New York: Palgrave/Macmillan, 2002). Nehamas, it should be noted, does not endorse the Platonic notion of authentic forms, but he nonetheless concludes that "Plato remains, if I may use these terms here, the perfect model of a genuine philosopher, the authentic standard by which philosophy, including especially the philosophy of today, must measure itself" (xxxv). For an even more recent discussion of the issue, which links it to contemporary popular culture, see Charles Guignon, *On Being Authentic* (London: Routledge, 2004).

7. Theodor W. Adorno, *The Jargon of Authenticity*, trans. Knut Tarnowski and Frederic Will (Evanston, Ill.: Northwestern University Press, 1973). The original *Jargon der Eigentlichkeit: Zur deutschen Ideologie* was published in Frankfurt in 1964, but had no impact on the American discussion.

8. Adorno, *Minima Moralia: Reflections from Damaged Life*, trans. E. F. N. Jephcott (London: NLB, 1974), 152–55.

9. Walter Benjamin, "The Work of Art in the Age of Mechanical Reproduction," *Illuminations: Essays and Reflections*, ed. Hannah Arendt, trans. Harry Zohn (New York: Schocken, 1969).

10. Adorno, *Kierkegaard: Construction of the Aesthetic*, trans. and ed. Robert Hullot-Kentor (Minneapolis: University of Minnesota Press, 1989). The debts of this work to Benjamin are themselves strong, one commentator going so far as to call it little more than the application of *The Origin of German Tragic Drama* to Kierkegaard; see Peter Fenves, "Image and Chatter: Adorno's Construction of Kierkegaard," *Diacritics* 22 (1992): 110. For an analysis of Benjamin's distance from Heidegger's notion of authentic time in this work and in an earlier fragment of 1916 called "Tragedy and *Trauerspiel*," see Howard Caygill, "Benjamin, Heidegger and the Destruction of Tradition," in *Walter Benjamin's Philosophy: Destruction and Experience*, eds. Andrew Benjamin and Peter Osborne (London: Routledge, 1994). Caygill argues that for Benjamin "Tragic time is authentic, and marks a present which is redeemed and completed by gathering the past to itself, while time for the *Trauerspiel* is inauthentic: the past ruining the present and making it entirely in vain. . . . The fragmentary and elliptical form of the essay resists the temptation present in Heidegger's treatise to restore authenticity by any move towards dialectical resolution" (9).

11. Martin Heidegger, *Being and Time*, trans. J. MacQuarrie and E. Robinson (Oxford: Blackwell, 1962), 146. For an analysis of his use of the term,

see the entry "authenticity and inauthenticity" in Michael Inwood, *A Heidegger Dictionary* (Oxford: Blackwell, 1999).

12. See, in particular, his lengthy letter of 16 March 1936 to Benjamin, which details his qualms; in Adorno and Walter Benjamin, *The Complete Correspondence, 1928–1940*, ed. Henri Lonitz, trans. Nicholas Walker (Cambridge, Mass.: Harvard University Press, 1999), 127–32.

13. Adorno, *Aesthetic Theory*, trans. Robert Hullot-Kentor (Minneapolis: University of Minnesota Press, 1997), 311.

14. Benjamin, "The Work of Art in the Age of Mechanical Reproduction," 226. A decade earlier in *The Origin of German Tragic Drama*, trans. John Osborne (London: Verso, 1977), Benjamin had raised the question of origin and authenticity in ways that suggest he had not yet arrived at the position defended in this essay. See, for example, such statements in the "epistemo-critical prologue" as the following: "Origin [*Ursprung*], although an entirely historical category, has, nevertheless, nothing to do with genesis [*Entstehung*]. The term origin is not intended to describe the process by which the existent came into being, but rather that which emerges from the process of becoming and disappearance. Origin is an eddy in the stream of becoming, and in its current it swallows the material involved in the process of genesis. . . . The authentic—the hallmark of origin in phenomena—is the object of discovery, a discovery which is connected in a unique way with the process of recognition" (45–46). For a subtle account of the neo-Platonic, neo-Leibnizian use of "origin" in this work, see John Pizer, *Toward a Theory of Radical Origin: Essays on Modern German Thought* (Lincoln: University of Nebraska Press, 1995), chap. 2.

15. Benjamin, "The Work of Art in the Age of Mechanical Reproduction," 226.

16. Ibid., 246.

17. Ibid., 223.

18. Ibid., 226.

19. Ibid., 245.

20. Eva Geulen, "Walter Benjamin's 'The Work of Art in the Age of Mechanical Reproduction,'" in *Benjamin's Ghosts: Interventions in Contemporary Literary and Cultural Theory*, ed. Gerhard Richter (Stanford, Calif.: Stanford University Press, 2002), 135.

21. There are still earlier expressions of Adorno's debts to Benjamin on this question. For example, in his 1932 essay "The Idea of Natural History," he acknowledged the importance of the theory of allegory in *The Origin of German Tragic Drama* as an antidote to the myth of *Urgeschichte*; see Adorno, "Die Idee der Naturgeschichte," *Philosophische Frühschriften*, in *Gesammelte Schriften*, ed. Rolf Tiedemann (Frankfurt am Main: Suhrkamp, 1973),

1:357–60. In the same year, he wrote a short piece entitled "The Primal" ("*Der Ur*"), which anticipated the critique of the Nazi use of the argument from origins in the aphorism in *Minima Moralia* discussed in this essay; see Adorno, "Der Ur," *Minima Moralia*, in *Gesammelte Schriften*, ed. Rolf Tiedemann (Frankfurt am Main: Suhrkamp, 1986), 20:562–64.

22. It should be noted that the international gold standard for currencies was itself terminated only during the Depression, with the United States' decision to abandon it in 1933 serving as the last straw. For a classic discussion of the implications of its abandonment as a symptom of the crisis of liberal capitalism, see Karl Polanyi, *The Great Transformation: The Political and Economic Origins of our Time* (Boston: Beacon, 1965). It is worth mentioning that this book was written in 1944, also by a Leftist exile from fascism.

23. Adorno, *Minima Moralia*, 152. Benjamin's strategies for resisting the idea of an integral, unified, substantial self are sensitively explored in Gerhard Richter, *Walter Benjamin and the Corpus of Autobiography* (Detroit, Mich.: Wayne State University Press, 2000).

24. Adorno, *Minima Moralia*, 153.

25. Benjamin's most important discussions come in his 1933 essays "Doctrine of the Similar" and "On the Mimetic Faculty," in *Selected Writings*, vol. 2, eds. Michael W. Jennings, Howard Eiland, and Gary Smith, trans. Rodney Livingstone et al. (Cambridge, Mass.: Harvard University Press, 1999). There is an extensive literature on Adorno's use of mimesis; for relevant texts and my own interpretation, see Martin Jay, "Mimesis and Mimetology: Adorno and Lacoue-Labarthe," in *Cultural Semantics: Keywords of our Time* (Amherst: University of Massachusetts Press, 1998).

26. There were, to be sure, less beneficial variants of mimicry and repetition, for example what psychoanalysis had called "identification with the aggressor," which Adorno, along with Horkheimer, criticized in *Dialectic of Enlightenment* and elsewhere.

27. Arthur Schopenhauer, *The World as Will and Idea* (London: Routledge and Kegan Paul, 1950), 358; cited by Adorno in *Minima Moralia*, 153.

28. Adorno, *Minima Moralia*, 153–54.

29. Ibid., 154.

30. Ibid., 155.

31. Ibid.

32. Ibid. Adorno's critique of those who tried to find authenticity in Bach appeared in his "Bach Defended against His Devotees," in *Prisms*, trans. Samuel Weber and Shierry Weber (Cambridge, Mass.: MIT Press, 1967). It might be noted, as John Pizer has pointed out, that Adorno's distrust of the "false origins" of modern jazz in African music also reflects his suspicion of any prioritizing of the earliest as the most authentic; see Pizer, *Toward a Theory*

of Radical Origin, 93. This study has many shrewd things to say about Adorno's critique of the simple idea of *Ursprung*.

33. Ibid.

34. Adorno, *Philosophy of Modern Music*, trans. Ann G. Mitchell and Wesley V. Blomster (New York: Continuum, 1973), 139–40.

35. Adorno, *Against Epistemology: A Metacritique*, trans. Willis Domingo (Cambridge, Mass.: MIT Press, 1983), 34.

36. Adorno, *The Jargon of Authenticity*, 4.

37. Ibid., 3. The possibility that Kracauer was the friend is suggested by his 1925 critique of the Buber-Rosenzweig translation of the Hebrew Bible, which was motivated in part by his skepticism about their ability to revive the authenticity of the divine word in current language. For my attempt to sort out the implications of the dispute, see Martin Jay, "Politics of Translation: Siegfried Kracauer and Walter Benjamin on the Buber-Rosenzweig Bible," in *Permanent Exiles: Essays on the Intellectual Migration from Germany to American* (New York: Continuum, 1985). For a more recent treatment, which stresses important differences between Rosenzweig and Buber, see Leora Batnitsky, *Idolatry and Representation: The Philosophy of Franz Rosenzweig Reconsidered* (Princeton, N.J.: Princeton University Press, 2000), 135–41.

38. Adorno, *The Jargon of Authenticity*, 9–10.

39. Ibid., 70.

40. Ibid., 115. Another Marxist critique of the same reification can be found in C. B. McPherson, *The Political Theory of Possessive Individualism: Hobbes to Locke* (Oxford: Clarendon, 1962), which traces it back to early liberal political thought and the nascent market economy.

41. Ibid., 123.

42. Adorno, *Negative Dialectics*, trans. E. B. Ashton (New York: Seabury, 1973), 183.

43. Adorno, *Jargon of Authenticity*, 125 (emended translation).

44. Personal communication, 18 April 2003. As elsewhere, Adorno was eager to disrupt the "native" origin of words by using their "foreign" equivalents.

45. Adorno, "Bach Defended against His Devotees," 143.

46. See *Authenticity and Early Music*, ed. Nicholas Kenyon (Oxford: Oxford University Press, 1988).

47. Adorno, "Reaktion und Fortschritt," in Adorno and Ernst Krenek, *Briefwechsel*, ed. Wolfgang Rogge (Frankfurt am Main: Suhrkamp, 1974), 179; this is cited in Max Paddison, *Adorno's Aesthetics of Music* (Cambridge: Cambridge University Press, 1993), 91. See also his very helpful "Authenticity and Failure in Adorno's Aesthetics of Music," in *The Cambridge Companion to Adorno*, ed. Tom Huhn (Cambridge: Cambridge University Press, 2004).

48. Adorno, "Jene zwanziger Jahre," *Eingriffe*, in *Gesammelte Schriften*, ed. Rolf Tiedemann (Frankfurt am Main: Suhrkamp, 1977), 10:506.

49. Adorno, *Aesthetic Theory*, 23.

50. Douglas Kellner, "Adorno and the Dialectics of Mass Culture," *Adorno: A Critical Reader*, ed. Nigel Gibson and Andrew Rubin (Oxford: Blackwell, 2002), 105.

51. Adorno, *Aesthetic Theory*, 311.

52. Adorno, *Minima Moralia*, 154.

53. Paddison, "Authenticity and Failure in Adorno's Aesthetics of Music."

54. For another example in *Minima Moralia*, see aphorism 33, "Out of the Firing Line," where Adorno writes that the Second World War is "as totally divorced from experience as is the functioning of a machine from the movement of the body, which only begins to resemble it in pathological states.... Life has changed into a timeless succession of shocks, interspersed with empty, paralyzed intervals.... The total obliteration of the war by information, propaganda commentaries, with cameramen in the first tanks and war reporters dying heroic deaths, the mishmash of enlightened manipulation of public opinion and oblivious activity: all this is another expression for the withering of experience, the vacuum between men and their fate, in which their real fate lies" (54–55). This passage duplicates without any attribution exactly what Benjamin had said about the First World War in his 1936 essay "The Storyteller," *Illuminations*, 83–84.

55. Detlev Claussen, *Theodor W. Adorno: Ein letzes Genie* (Frankfurt am Main: Fischer, 2003). The issue of what constitutes a genius is, to be sure, a highly complicated one, and cannot be dealt with fully here. One place to begin would be Kant's *Critique of Judgment*, trans. J. B. Bernard (New York: Hafner, 1951), where he argues that the genius produces "an example, not to be imitated (for then that which in it is genius and constitutes the spirit of the work would be lost), but to be followed by another genius, whom it awakens to a feeling of his own originality" (162). One might well argue that Adorno, despite the imitations discussed in this paper, was inspired to his own originality by Benjamin's example.

56. Those whose ideas Adorno may have borrowed were not always as generous in their reading of his mimetic impulse. In the unpublished memorandum Siegfried Kracauer wrote in 1960 after a meeting they had to discuss the forthcoming *Negative Dialectics*, Kracauer described a moment in their interaction in the following terms: "At this point, I believe, Teddie was at the end of his rope. I am sure, however, he will not admit this to himself but immediately manage to believe that all my thoughts are really his own, annex these thoughts, which he already considers his property, to his 'system' and pass them off as the natural outgrowth of the latter. As Benjamin said: he grabs

everything he is told, digests it and its consequences and then takes over"; cited and discussed in Jay, "Adorno and Kracauer: Notes on a Troubled Friendship," in *Permanent Exiles*, 229. Whether or not either Benjamin or Kracauer can be seen as an utterly "original" thinker is another issue, which cannot be addressed here.

3. SUFFERING INJUSTICE: MISRECOGNITION AS MORAL INJURY IN CRITICAL THEORY
J. M. Bernstein

1. Jürgen Habermas, "Rightness versus Truth: On the Sense of Normative Validity in Moral Judgments and Norms," in his *Truth and Justification*, trans. Barbara Fuller (Cambridge, Mass.: MIT Press, 2003), 248.

2. Theodor W. Adorno, "Why Still Philosophy," in his *Critical Models: Interventions and Catchwords*, trans. Henry W. Pickford (New York: Columbia University Press, 1998), 14.

3. Four recent articles work up this thought from different angles: Espen Hammer, "Adorno and Extreme Evil," *Philosophy and Social Criticism* 26, no. 4 (2000): 75–93; Deborah Cook, "Ein Reaktionäres Schwein? Political Activism and Prospects for Change in Adorno," *Revue Internationale de Philosophie*, 63, no. 227 (January 2004): 47–67; Simon Jarvis, "What is Speculative Thinking?" in ibid., 69–83; and Lambert Zuidervaart, "Metaphysics after Auschwitz: Suffering and Hope in Adorno's *Negative Dialectics*," *Adorno and the Need in Thinking: New Critical Essays*, ed. Donald A. Burke, Colin J. Campbell, Kathy Kiloh, Michael K. Palamarek, and Jonathan Short (Toronto: University of Toronto Press, 2007). The existence of this splendid set of essays means that in this essay I shall be able to concentrate on philosophical matters, since so much of the hard work of textual analysis and interpretation has already been done.

4. For a potent critique of liberal justice along these lines, see Norman Geras, *The Contract of Mutual Indifference: Political Philosophy after the Holocaust* (London: Verso, 1998). For an elaboration of the thesis that liberal justice, Kantian liberal universalism, has already internalized Hobbesian instrumentalism as its premise, see J. M. Bernstein, *Adorno: Disenchantment and Ethics* (New York: Cambridge University Press, 2001), chap. 3.

5. Adorno, *Negative Dialectics*, translated by E.B. Ashton (London: Routledge, 1973), 400; emphasis mine.

6. See, for example, Deborah Cook, *Adorno, Habermas, and the Search for a Rational Society* (London: Routledge, 2004); Yvonne Sherratt, *Adorno's Positive Dialectic* (Cambridge: Cambridge University Press, 2002); Gerhard Schweppenhäuser, *Ethik nach Auschwitz: Adornos negative Moralphilosophie* (Hamburg: Argument Verlag, 1993); and Schweppenhäuser, "Adorno's Negative Moral

Philosophy," in *The Cambridge Companion to Adorno*, ed. Tom Huhn (Cambridge: Cambridge University Press, 2004), chap. 13; and in the same volume, Christoph Menke, "Genealogy and Critique: Two Forms of Ethical Questioning of Morality," chap. 12.

7. Axel Honneth, *The Struggle for Recognition: The Moral Grammar of Social Conflicts*, trans. Joel Anderson (Cambridge: Polity Press, 1995).

8. Quoted by Rolf Tiedemann in his introduction to Adorno, *Can One Life after Auschwitz: A Philosophical Reader* (Stanford, Calif.: Stanford University Press, 2003), xviii–xix.

9. Hannah Arendt, *The Origins of Totalitarianism* (New York: Meridian Books, 1958), pt. 2.

10. Honneth, "The Social Dynamics of Disrespect: Situating Critical Theory Today," in *Habermas: A Critical Reader*, ed. Peter Dews (Oxford: Blackwell Publishers, 1999), 326.

11. Ibid., 324.

12. It should be acknowledged that the collapse in the authority of liberal ideals in democratic societies over the past twenty-five years has made the business of once again elaborating them have more point than I would have imagined possible in 1968, say. But that reasonable task still should not be confused with the generation of a Critical Theory of society.

13. Honneth, "The Social Dynamics of Disrespect," 328. Notice that the price Honneth must immediately pay for his theory of misrecognition is its divorce from the fundamental mechanisms of societal rationalization. The right thing to say here is that, post–Marx and Weber, there is a systematic dislocation between social suffering and macrosocietal rationalization, and hence the hope of building a social theory in which the movement of the former becomes the route for the resolution of the latter—the classical model of revolutionary praxis—is now unavailable.

14. Ibid., 329.

15. Ibid.

16. Honneth, *The Struggle for Recognition*, 135.

17. Nancy Fraser and Honneth, *Redistribution or Recognition? A Political-Philosophical Exchange*, trans. Joel Golb, James Ingram, and Christiane Wilke (London: Verso, 2003), 203.

18. Ibid., 204.

19. Ibid., 36.

20. For a pointed set of criticisms of Honneth's program, see Nikolas Kompridis, "From Reason to Self-Realization: On the 'Ethical Turn' in Critical Theory," *Critical Horizons*, Vol. 5.1, Summer 2004.

21. Frazer and Honneth, *Redistribution or Recognition*, 229; emphasis mine.

22. Habermas, "The Debate on the Ethical Self-Understanding of the Species," in *The Future of Human Nature*, trans. Hella Beister and Max Pensky (Cambridge: Polity Press, 2003), 33–34.

23. Ibid., 50. The idea of being a body and at the same time having a body—*Leibsein und Körperhaben*—is an idea Habermas borrows from Helmuth Plessner.

24. Ibid., 34.

25. Judith Butler, *Precarious Life: The Powers of Mourning and Violence* (London: Verso, 2004), 26. In the introduction and chapter 4 of her *Excitable Speech: A Politics of Performance* (New York: Routledge, 1997), Butler gives a first sketch of how "words wound," that is, how our socially constituted independence and vulnerability are reiterated at the linguistic level.

26. Adorno, *Negative Dialectics*, 203.

27. Honneth, "The Social Dynamics of Self-Respect," 332. In "A Social Pathology of Reason: On the Intellectual Legacy of Critical Theory," trans. James Hebbeler, in *The Cambridge Companion to Critical Theory*, ed. Fred Rush (Cambridge: Cambridge University Press, 2004), 338–45, Honneth states that the ethical core contained in the idea of Critical Theory is of a social deficient rationality; in this instance, I cannot tell if Honneth is associating himself with that idea, or just recording it as a historical matter of fact.

28. Adorno, "Progress," in *Critical Models*, 152.

29. Schweppenhäuser, "Adorno's Negative Moral Philosophy," 330.

30. Of course, I am not denying that *in part* "the social pathologies of the present can be understood as the result of the inability of society to properly express the rational potential already inherent in its institutions, practices, and everyday routines" (Honneth, "A Social Pathology of Reason," 340), only that, as will be evident directly, in purveying a formal theory of the good, Honneth cleanses present ideals of their implication in social pathology. Part of the reason I find Marx's "On the Jewish Question" so exemplary is that he there manages both to continue the argument of the *Philosophy of Right* whilst simultaneously providing an immanent critique. This might just be a debate about how to identify "societies' inabilities."

31. Simon Jarvis, "Adorno, Marx, Materialism," in *The Cambridge Companion to Adorno*, 88–89.

32. Adorno, "Progress," 149.

33. When Marx urges that all rights are rights to inequality he should not be interpreted as urging that no one should (need to) have rights (because in an ideal state of affairs they would not be necessary); his point is rather the dialectical one: that rights as they now are preserve the very lacks their possession promises—the right to vote as a continuation of disenfranchisement, the right to welfare as a way of keeping people impoverished.

34. Jacques Rancière, *The Politics of Aesthetics: The Distribution of the Sensible*, trans. Gabriel Rockhill (New York: Continuum, 2004), 27.

35. Adorno, *Negative Dialectics*, 17–18.

36. Ibid., 356.

37. I have detailed this claim in my *Adorno: Disenchantment and Ethics* (Cambridge: Cambridge University Press, 2001), chap. 8.

38. Jeffrey Alexander, "On the Social Construction of Moral Universals: The 'Holocaust' from War Crime to Trauma Drama," *European Journal of Social Theory* 5, no. 1 (2002): 5–85.

39. Ibid., 31.

40. Ibid., 51.

41. Ibid.

42. Arendt, *The Origins of Totalitarianism*, chap. 9.

43. Helmut Dubiel, "The Remembrance of the Holocaust as a Catalyst for a Transnational Ethic?" *New German Critique* 90 (Fall 2003): 70; Dubiel's fine essay draws from Alexander the same normative conclusion as I am promoting here.

4. IDIOSYNCRASIES: OF ANTI-SEMITISM
Jan Plug

1. For a consideration of Adorno's theory of the subject in relation to poststructuralism, see Peter Dews, "Adorno, Poststructuralism and the Critique of Identity," in *The Problems of Modernity: Adorno and Benjamin*, ed. Andrew Benjamin (London and New York: Routledge, 1989), 1–22.

2. Max Horkheimer and Theodor W. Adorno, *Dialectic of Enlightenment*, trans. John Cumming (New York: Continuum, 1989), 204; references to the German are from *Dialektik der Aufklärung: Philosophische Fragmente* (Frankfurt am Main: Fischer Verlag, 1988).

3. Ibid., 205.

4. Ibid., 204.

5. The masculine pronoun is used deliberately here to signal Horkheimer and Adorno's own sense of individualization as a process reserved, in contemporary society, for men.

6. An argument very similar to this is made by Andrew Hewitt in the context of the representation of "woman" in *Dialectic of Enlightenment*. In fact, a number of points in my argument resemble points made by Hewitt. This coincidence is not a sign that there is no difference between the Jews and "woman," nor does it either feminize the Jews or make Jews of all women. Rather, it signals a certain approximation (at a distance) in the treatment of both as particular moments or figures of singularity; see Hewitt, "A Feminine Dialectic of Enlightenment? Horkheimer and Adorno Revisited," *New German Critique* 56 (1992): 143–70; see also Simon Jarvis, *Adorno: A Critical Introduction* (Cambridge: Polity Press, 1998).

7. Adorno, *Minima Moralia: Reflections from Damaged Life*, trans. E. F. N. Jephcott (London: Verso, 1974), 45.

8. Ibid.

9. Ibid.

10. Fredric Jameson, *Late Marxism: Adorno, or the Persistence of the Dialectic* (New York: Verso, 1990), 73. A fuller consideration of conceptuality in Adorno would have to take up Jameson's reading more extensively than I can do here.

11. For a superb account of this thinking of the limit in the context of Kant's work, see Cathy Caruth, *Empirical Truths and Critical Fictions* (Baltimore, Md.: Johns Hopkins University Press, 1991).

12. I refer, of course, to Hannah Arendt's seminal "Antisemitism," in *The Origins of Totalitarianism* (New York: Harcourt, Brace, 1978).

13. Jameson, *Late Marxism*, 153–54. A succinct but forceful account of Horkheimer and Adorno's understanding of anti-Semitism is also offered by Peter Hohendahl in *Prismatic Thought: Theodor W. Adorno* (Lincoln: Nebraska University Press, 1995), 114–15. For quite a different approach that also focuses somewhat on the question of the subject and idiosyncrasy, see Thomas Mirbach, *Kritik der Herrschaft: Zum Verhältnis von Geschichtsphilosophie, Ideologiekritik und Methodenreflexion in der Gesellschaftstheorie Adornos* (Frankfurt: Campus, 1979), 98–113. Also on the subject (though not necessarily directly in relation to *Dialectic of Enlightenment*), see Joseph F. Schmucker, *Adorno—Logic des Zerfalls* (Stuttgart: Friedrich Frommann, 1977) and Anke Thyen, *Negative Dialektik und Erfahrung: Zur Rationalität des Nichtidentischen bei Adorno* (Frankfurt am Main: Suhrkamp, 1989).

14. Horkheimer and Adorno, *Dialectic of Enlightenment*, 179–80.

15. In fact, according to their own argument, this must be true of other "groups" as well: "And since the victims are interchangable according to circumstances—gypsies, Jews, Protestants, and so on—any one of them may take the place of the murderers, with the same blind lust for blood, should they be invested with the title of the norm" (Ibid., 171). The result is that "[t]here is no genuine anti-Semitism" (Ibid.), which is also to say that the Jews, like any other group, can be incorporated into the social order that represses them. The point is not to deny Jews—or anyone else—their singularity, but rather to disclose the logic of exchange that characterizes fascism. The Jews here stand as the figure for particularity. Something similar could be argued of Lyotard's argument in *Heidegger and "the jews"* (Minneapolis: Minnesota University Press, 1986): "I write 'the jews' this way neither out of prudence nor lack of something better. I use lower case to indicate that I am not thinking of a nation. I make it plural to signify that it is neither a figure nor a political (Zionism), religious (Judaism), or philosophical (Jewish philosophy) subject that I put forward under this name. I use quotation marks to avoid confusing these 'jews' with real Jews. What is most real about Jews is that Europe, in any

case, does not know what to do with them; Christians demand their conversion; monarchs expel them; Nazis exterminate them. 'The jews' are the object of a dismissal with which Jews, in particular, are afflicted in reality" (4).

16. Werner Hamacher's brilliant deconstruction of individuality in Nietzsche is relevant not only here but for any consideration of the subject; see "'Disgregation of the Will': Nietzsche on the Individual and Individuality," in *Premises: Essays on Philosophy and Literature from Kant to Celan* (Stanford, Calif.: Stanford University Press, 1996), 143–80.

17. Rodolphe Gasché gives an excellent account of what is at stake in the notion: "while the term *idiosyncratic* commonly denotes mere eccentricity, it names first and foremost the characteristic habit (or structure) peculiar to one person only, peculiar to the point of being private and thus at the limit, unintelligible. Etymologically speaking, *idiosyncratic* signifies a personal and distinct way of blending or mixing together. It derives, indeed, from *idio*, meaning 'one's own,' and *sugkrasis*, 'commixture, blending, tempering.' But, as Émile Benveniste has demonstrated in his investigations of the Indo-European terms that define the free human being (as distinct from the slave) and, in particular, the individual in his or her personal quality (*idiotes*), that is, nonpublic status, the adjective *idios*, while referring to the notion of the private, to that which is particular to one person only, does not denote an absolute particularity, for the particularity of a given individual is the particularity of a social being confined to him or herself. In other words, the possibility of being oneself in all one's particularity is a function of one's belonging to a social unit. Only within this unity is it possible to be *idios*, and an *idiotes*"; Gasché, *The Wild Card of Reading: On Paul de Man* (Cambridge, Mass.: Harvard University Press, 1998), 4–5.

18. See Jean-Luc Nancy, *La communauté désoeuvrée* (Paris: Christian Bourgois, 1990).

19. Adorno, *Negative Dialectics*, trans. E. B. Ashton (New York: Continuum, 1973), 9–10.

20. Ibid., 15.

21. Immanuel Kant, *Critique of Judgement*, trans. J. H. Bernard (New York: Hafner, 1951), 15–16.

22. Hewitt is particularly astute in his analysis of how philosophical discourse constitutes itself even on the basis of this problematic; see Hewitt, "A Feminine Dialectic of Enlightenment?"

23. I have explored more fully the historical claims made for a criticism that places itself in a dialectical relation with its object in a very different context; see *Borders of a Lip: Romanticism, Language, History, Politics* (Albany: SUNY Press, 2003).

24. One need not think of conceptuality as removed from socioeconomic conditions or phenomena, nor from historical individuals in the most immediate sense. Susan Buck-Morss, for instance, has shown that *The Authoritarian*

Personality equates political tendencies to personality types, with the "fixity" of the fascist personality being "due to its unmediated reflection of the fixed, social structure, whereas the antifascist type, as critical, nonconforming individual, had, predictably, more diverse characteristics," in Buck-Morss, *The Origin of Negative Dialectics: Theodor W. Adorno, Walter Benjamin, and the Frankfurt Institute* (New York: Free Press, 1977), 181.

25. Horkheimer and Adorno, *Dialectic of Enlightenment*, 16.
26. Ibid., 15.
27. See Alexander García Düttmann, *The Gift of Language: Memory and Promise in Adorno, Benjamin, Heidegger, and Rosenzweig*, trans. Arline Lyons (Syracuse, N.Y.: Syracuse University Press, 2000).
28. Horkheimer and Adorno, *Dialectic of Enlightenment*, 15.
29. Ibid., 15 n. 20.
30. No doubt the most influential account of this structure, and still perhaps the best, is Paul de Man's in "The Rhetoric of Temporality," in *Blindness and Insight*, 2nd ed. (Minneapolis: University of Minnesota Press, 1983); see also Jochen Schulte-Sasse's excellent introduction to *Theory as Practice: A Critical Anthology of Early German Romantic Writing*, ed. Jochen Schulte-Sasse, et al. (Minneapolis: University of Minnesota Press, 1997).
31. For a reading of Adorno's theory of language that undertakes a fuller account of his other writings, see Hohendahl, "The Discourse of Philosophy and the Problem of Language," in *Prismatic Thought*.
32. Horkheimer and Adorno, *Dialectic of Enlightenment*, 16.
33. This, of course, is how Adorno characterizes a negative dialectics: "Dialectics unfolds the difference between the particular and the universal dictated by the universal" (*Negative Dialectics*, 6); "The fundament and result of Hegel's substantive philosophizing was the primacy of the subject, or—in the famous phrase from the Introduction to his *Logic*—the 'identity of identity and non-identity.' He held the definite particular to be definable by the mind because its immanent definition was to be nothing but the mind. . . . The matters of true philosophical interest at this point in history are those in which Hegel, agreeing with tradition, expressed his disinterest. They are nonconceptuality, individuality, and particularity—things which ever since Plato used to be dismissed as transitory and insignificant" (Ibid., 7–8).
34. In fact, one could show that the phrase enacts the notion of mimesis as narrative that Jameson has argued for: the phrase lays out a historical development, one that the note relates back to the concept of mimesis. Yet, the development and the narrative are also cut short in a sense by the tautology of the narrative. For an outstanding reading of narrative in *Dialectic of Enlightenment*, see Hohendahl, *Prismatic Thought*, 250.
35. Horkheimer and Adorno, *Dialectic of Enlightenment*, xii.

36. See Immanuel Kant, *The Metaphysics of Morals*, trans. Mary Gregor (Cambridge: Cambridge University Press, 1996), 3–4; and Jacques Derrida, *Who's Afraid of Philosophy? Right to Philosophy*, vol. 1, trans. Jan Plug and others (Stanford, Calif.: Stanford University Press, 2002).

37. Horkheimer and Adorno, *Dialectic of Enlightenment*, xiv.

38. Ibid.

39. This is not to suggest that there was a time "before" domination, which, as Jarvis points out, is a fiction; Jarvis, *Adorno: A Critical Introduction*, 30. Rather, it is to argue for a mode that would precede domination in its (onto-)logic.

40. Adorno, *Minima Moralia*, 110.

41. See "Words from Abroad," in Adorno, *Notes to Literature*, trans. Shierry Weber Nicholsen (New York: Columbia University Press, 1991), 1:185–99.

42. Perhaps this is simply to emphasize Silvia Bovenschen's reading of idiosyncrasy, and in particular Adorno's professed "idiosyncrasy against the word 'synthesis'" in *Negative Dialectics*. Bovenschen reads this statement, and the treatment of idiosyncrasy in *Dialectic of Enlightenment*, to find that idiosyncrasy is always necessarily an idiosyncrasy against hasty syntheses. The implications of this statement for a thinking of dialectics would have to be worked out more fully than I can here; see *"Über-Empfindlichkeit: Versuch über den Begriff Idiosynkrasie," Neue Rundschau* 105, no. 2 (1994): 126–52. For another excellent account of idiosyncrasy, see Alexander García Düttmann, *Das Gedächtnis des Denkens: Versuch über Heidegger und Adorno* (Frankfurt am Main: Suhrkamp, 1991), 117–20.

43. Horkheimer and Adorno, *Dialectic of Enlightenment*, 180.

44. Hardly anything in Adorno has received more critical attention than his notion of mimesis. For a sampling of this criticism, see Karla L. Schultz, *Mimesis on the Move: Theodor W. Adorno's Concept of Imitation* (New York: Lang, 1990); Josef Früchtl, *Mimesis: Konstellation eines Zentralbegriffs bei Adorno* (Würzburg: Königshausen und Neumann, 1986); Michael Cahn, "Subversive Mimesis: T. W. Adorno and the Modern Impasse of Critique," in *Mimesis and Contemporary Theory*, ed. Mihai Spariosu (Philadelphia: John Benjamins, 1984), 27–64; Miriam Hansen, "Mass Culture as Hieroglyphic Writing: Adorno, Derrida, Kracauer," in *New German Critique* 56 (1992): 43–73; Marc Jimenez, *Vers une esthétique négative: Adorno et la modernité* (Paris: Sycomore, 1983); Jameson, *Late Marxism*; and Jarvis, *Adorno: A Critical Introduction*, 31. For a thoughtful account of mimesis in the anti-Semitism chapter in particular, see Anson Rabinbach, "Why Were the Jews Sacrificed? The Place of Anti-Semitism in *Dialectic of Enlightenment*," *New German Critique* 81 (Autumn 2000), 49–64.

45. Horkheimer and Adorno, *Dialectic of Enlightenment*, 180.
46. Ibid.
47. Ibid., 111.
48. Ibid., 181.
49. This is just part of the brilliant reading developed by Andrew Hewitt in "A Feminine Dialectic of Enlightenment?"
50. Philippe Lacoue-Labarthe, *L'imitation des modernes: Typographies* (Paris: Galilée, 1986), 2:27. For a different reading of the relation between Adorno and Lacoue-Labarthe's understanding of mimesis, see Martin Jay, "Mimesis and Mimetology: Adorno and Lacoue-Labarthe," in *The Semblance of Subjectivity: Essays in Adorno's Aesthetic Theory*, ed. Tom Huhn and Lambert Zuidervaart (Cambridge, Mass.: MIT Press, 1997), 29–53.
51. Horkheimer and Adorno, *Dialectic of Enlightenment*, 183.
52. See Jean-Luc Nancy, *L'expérience de la liberté* (Paris: Galilée, 1988).
53. Horkheimer and Adorno, *Dialectic of Enlightenment*, 84.
54. Ibid., 184.
55. Ibid., 185.
56. Paul de Man, "Aesthetic Formalization: Kleist's *Über das Marionettentheater*," in *The Rhetoric of Romanticism* (New York: Columbia, 1984), 263–90. One cannot, no doubt, mention de Man in the context of a discussion of anti-Semitism without some justification. Clearly, there is not enough space here to enter into the subject adequately. What this reference to de Man's later work might suggest, though, is a reading not only of anti-Semitism, but of de Man himself, of how his late work might offer a reading of his wartime journalism. On the relation between de Man's journalism and his mature criticism, see Gasché, *The Wild Card of Reading*.
57. "The mathematical formula is regression handled consciously, just as the magic ritual used to be; it is the most sublimated manifestation of mimicry."
58. Horkheimer and Adorno, *Dialectic of Enlightenment*, 185.
59. Ibid., 171.
60. On reflection and the constitution of the subject, see Gasché's seminal *The Tain of the Mirror: Derrida and the Philosophy of Reflection* (Cambridge, Mass.: Harvard University Press, 1986).
61. Horkheimer and Adorno, *Dialectic of Enlightenment*, 189.
62. "Perception is directness at one remove, reflection in the seductive power of sensuality. By it, the subjective is blindly transferred . . . into the apparent obviousness of the object. . . . When thought in the process of cognition identifies as conceptual the conceptual elements which are directly posited in perception and hence so compelling, it progressively draws them back into the subject and rids them of perceptive power" (Ibid., 194).

63. Ibid., 188.
64. Ibid., 189.
65. Ibid.
66. Ibid., 188.
67. Ibid., 189.
68. Ibid., 187.
69. Ibid., 189.
70. Ibid.
71. Ibid., 189–90.
72. Ibid., 189.
73. Ibid., 199–200.

5. ADORNO'S LESSON PLANS? THE ETHICS OF (RE)EDUCATION IN "THE MEANING OF 'WORKING THROUGH THE PAST'"
Jaimey Fisher

1. Theodor W. Adorno, "Who's Afraid of the Ivory Tower?": A Conversation with Theodor W. Adorno," translated, edited, and with an introduction by Gerhard Richter, in this volume. In this interview, Adorno weighs, among other topics, the duality of theory versus practice in his own life and work. In defending himself against the students of the 1960s student movement—who criticized him for not taking a more radical stand against the politics and society of West Germany—he walks a thin theoretical line between theory and practice throughout the interview, suggesting that, for him, theorizing is a kind of praxis and is certainly required for any effective practice. Whatever one thinks of this defense, I would argue that he actually did advocate certain types of practices in this series of educational essays.

2. The essay has been especially influential on German history in its treatment of one of its key postwar themes, that of *"Vergangenheitsbewältigung"* (mastering the past). Adorno's essay is quoted, for instance, in Jeffrey Herf, *Divided Memory: The Nazi Past in the Two Germanys* (Cambridge, Mass.: Harvard University Press, 1997); Robert Moeller, *War Stories: The Search for a Usable Past in the Federal Republic of Germany* (Berkeley: University of California Press, 2001); Alon Confino, "Traveling as a Cultural Remembrance: Traces of National Socialism in West Germany, 1945–1960," *History and Memory* 12 (2000): 98; Alf Lüdtke, "'Coming to Terms with the Past': Illusions of Remembering, Way of Forgetting Nazism in West Germany," *Journal of Modern History* 65 (Sept. 1993): 542–72.

3. Peter Uwe Hohendahl, *Prismatic Thought: Theodor W. Adorno* (Lincoln: University of Nebraska Press, 1995), esp. chap. 3, "Education after the Holocaust."

4. For example, one U.S. educational mission that returned home after the summer of 1946 reported: "the re-education of the German people is an

undertaking of the greatest magnitude ... at once the hardest and most important task facing the Military Government in Germany today"; William E. Hocking, *Experiment in Education: What We Can Learn from Teaching Germany* (Chicago: H. Regency, 1954), 221. This U.S. educational mission was also covered in the German press: "*Die Hoffnung: Neue Wege für die Jugend*," *Süddeutsche Zeitung* (18 October 1946), 2.

5. "Reeducation" covered not only primary and secondary schools and higher education, but also all areas of cultural policy, including literature, the press, and film.

6. Recent publications in English have begun to indicate this public-sphere engagement of Adorno, but much analysis remains to be done. For primary texts on his public-sphere activities in English, see, for instance, Gerhard Richter's translation of "Who's Afraid of the Ivory Tower?" cited in note 1 above, as well as the translations in Adorno, "The Meaning of 'Working Through the Past,'" in *Critical Models*, ed. and trans. by Henry W. Pickford (New York: Columbia University Press, 1998).

7. J. M. Bernstein, *Adorno: Disenchantment and Ethics* (Cambridge: Cambridge University Press, 2001); Judith Butler, *Kritik der ethischen Gewalt: Adorno-Vorlesungen 2002* (Frankfurt am Main: Suhrkamp, 2003).

8. For example, "Education after Auschwitz" leads Adorno to confront questions about authority and normativity: it is not an accident that one of his strongest normative statements about ethics arises from this educational line of thought or that Adorno started to unfold these thoughts in the reeducation-inflected 1950s. In a fashion that confirms this trend in Anglophone scholarship, Bernstein quotes "Education after Auschwitz" at length and analyzes the essay's various ethical consequences without developing its educational context. Bernstein quotes a very long passage from "*Erziehung nach Auschwitz*," one of the longest single passages from Adorno he offers, to explicate the perils of bourgeois coldness, but does not unfold how the passage is woven into an essay about education; Bernstein, *Adorno: Disenchantment and Ethics*, 398–400.

9. Stefan Müller-Doohm, *Adorno: A Biography*, trans. Rodney Livingstone (2003; Cambridge: Polity, 2005), 375.

10. In Jaimey Fisher, *Disciplining Germany: Youth, Reeducation, and Reconstruction after the Second World War* (Detroit, Mich.: Wayne State University Press, 2007), I argue that this kind of contrastive exculpation vis-à-vis the young was an important aspect of postwar Germany's coming to terms with the past.

11. Adorno, "The Democratization of German Universities," in *Gesammelte Schriften* (Frankfurt am Main: Suhrkamp, 1970), 20:332.

12. Norman Naimark, *The Russians in Germany: A History of the Soviet Zone of Occupation, 1945–49* (Cambridge, Mass.: Harvard University Press, 1995), 445.

13. Ibid., 444.

14. Ibid., 440–59, esp. 444; although the Soviets trumpeted their efforts to increase the number of students from working-class and farmer backgrounds, the execution of this policy proved much more difficult than anticipated.

15. See, for example, Wilhelm Karl Gerst, "Wer darf studieren?" *Frankfurter Rundschau* (29 January 1946); or Walter Dirks, "Wer soll studieren dürfen?" *Frankfurter Hefte* 2, no. 5 (1947): 435–37.

16. Though he admitted that there were social groups that had long been underrepresented among students, Jaspers characteristically insisted on intellectual "excellence" for students, which, he admitted, would favor those families equipped to foster such excellence.

17. Adorno, "The Democratization of German Universities," in *Gesammelte Schriften*, 20:332.

18. Ibid., 333.

19. Ibid.

20. Also revealing for his other writings on education, against some of the scholarship on the topic, is the way in which Adorno cites but also unflinchingly problematizes traditional *Bildung*, be it in the pejorative use of "*Bildungsmonopol*" to describe those with conventional access to *Bildung* or the false consciousness of the petty bourgeoisie and their working-class discontents to which he points at the end. For Adorno and his emphasis on complex rather than simple concepts, *Bildung* is very much a historical concept, one that harbors contradictory and antidemocratic trends.

21. Adorno, "The Democratization of German Universities," in *Gesammelte Schriften*, 20:334.

22. James Tent, *Mission on the Rhine: Reeducation and Denazification in American-Occupied Germany* (Chicago: University of Chicago Press, 1982), 79.

23. In the first wave of American denazification, for instance, roughly four out of ten professors were removed. At some universities, like Heidelberg, the percentages were even higher: around sixty percent for medicine, natural science, and political science were not permitted to resume their posts.

24. See Eike Wolgast, "Karl-Heinz Bauer—der erste Heidelberger Nachkriegsrektor: Weltbild und Handeln, 1945–46," in *Heidelberg 1945*, ed. Jürgen Heß (Stuttgart: Steiner, 1996), 107–29; also discussed in Anson Rabinbach, *In the Shadow of Catastrophe: German Intellectuals between Apocalypse and Enlightenment* (Berkeley: University of California Press, 1997), 134–35.

25. As Stefan Müller-Doohm recounts, Horkheimer wrote his wife from Germany in 1948 about his return to the university: "I was respectfully welcomed by the rector and the two deans and others. They were all as sweet as pie, smooth as eels and hypocritical. . . . All these people sit there as they did before the Third Reich . . . just as if nothing had happened"; quoted in Müller-Doohm, *Adorno: A Biography*, n. 5, 565.

26. Adorno, letter to Thomas Mann, 28 December 1949, in *Theodor W. Adorno/Thomas Mann: Briefwechsel, 1943–1955*, eds. Christoph Gödde and Thomas Sprecher, in *Theodor Adorno: Brief und Briefwechsel* (Frankfurt am Main: Suhrkamp, 2002), 3:48.

27. See, for instance, "Sieht so die neue akademische Jugend aus? Störungen eines Vortrages von Pastor Niemöller," *Mittelbayerische Zeitung* (25 June 1946), 2; Kn., "Militaristische Studentenschaft: Die Hochschule ist kein Unterschlupf für arbeitslose Offiziere," *Frankenpost* (13 February 1946), 3.

28. Adorno, "Zur Demokratisierung der deutschen Universitäten," in *Gesammelte Schriften*, 20:334–35.

29. Ibid., 335d.

30. Ibid., 335.

31. Ibid., 336.

32. For instance: "The rejection of the parties by the young generation in Germany is not only to be explained with youthful immaturity, lacking experience and insight. . . . Apparently, the young do not find, in the confined space of the present, any suitable opportunity to become involved in politics that they see daily around them . . ."; Karl Wilhelm Böttcher, "Die junge Generation und die Parteien: Bericht über ein Gesprach," *Frankfurter Hefte* 3, no. 8 (August 1948): 761.

33. In his voluminous correspondence with Hannah Arendt, Jaspers praised his small-seminar students, who manifested "evidence of irrepressible German youth however small their numbers," but a few months later observed how he sees, in the following semester's philosophy seminar, a "few excellent people," who "have no interest in politics, only scorn and mistrust, but despite that they are extremely well informed . . ."; Jaspers' letter to Arendt, number 44, 18 September 1946, in Karl Jaspers and Hannah Arendt, *Hannah Arendt-Karl Jaspers: Correspondence 1926–1969*, ed. Lotte Kohler and Hans Saner, trans. Robert Kimber and Rita Kimber (New York: Harcourt Brace Jovanovich, 1992). In his own self-declared "report" to a German in exile about his experiences on the ground in postwar Germany, Adorno wrote Thomas Mann that he was very impressed with the students he encountered; that, as far as he could tell, there had been no decline in the quality of the students, but that it is remarkable how they seem completely focused on their studies, perhaps precisely because there was no politics in which to be interested: "Nevertheless, I think that there can be no talk of a 'loss in the level' of the academic youth . . . we discuss highly opaque questions at the limits of logic and metaphysics as if they were politics—maybe because, in truth, there are no more politics"; Adorno, letter to Thomas Mann, 28 December 1949, *Theodor W. Adorno/Thomas Mann: Briefwechsel, 1943–1955*, 46.

34. See chap. 4, "The German as Pariah: Karl Jaspers' 'The Question of German Guilt,'" in Rabinbach, *In the Shadow of Catastrophe*, esp. 138–40;

Hannah Arendt, "Jaspers as a Citizen of the World," in *The Philosophy of Karl Jaspers*, ed. by Paul Arthur Schlipp (La Salle, Ill.: Open Court Publishers, 1981), 543, quoted in Rabinbach, *In the Shadow of Catastrophe*, 139.

35. In a revealing passage from his "Volk und Universität," Jaspers writes: "The meaning of higher education excludes active politics from higher education itself. Each student can, when he would like to, belong to a party and be active in it. He can, as a youth, link himself politically to all the other youths of the nation. But as a student with other students, he is not to form party groups within the university. Here he researches the party in a politically windless space . . . no political action will be taken"; Karl Jaspers, "Volk und Universität," in *Erneuerung der Universität: Reden und Schriften, 1945/46*, ed. Renato de Rosa (Heidelberg: Lambert Schneider, 1986), 275–88. In order to depoliticize the university in an increasingly politicized climate, Jaspers depoliticizes the student as opposed to the "*Jugend*": he endorses the lack of interest and enthusiasm that the Nazis and war yielded but that quotidian politics demands.

36. Adorno, "The Democratization of German Universities,"in *Gesammelte Schriften*, 20:337.

37. Ibid., 337–38.

38. The questions and answers after the first lecture were published with the original appearance of the lecture in print. Reprinted and translated in *Critical Models*, here 303.

39. For its importance in *Vergangenheitsbewältigung* studies, see Moeller, *War Stories;* the important essay by Y. Michal Bodemann, "Eclipse of Memory: German Representations of Auschwitz in the Early Postwar Period," *New German Critique* 75 (Fall 1998); as well as Confino, "Traveling as a Cultural Remembrance." For readings that focus on its consequences for studies of the Holocaust and anti-Semitism, see Hohendahl, "Education after the Holocaust," in *Prismatic Thought*; and Michael Rothberg, *Traumatic Realism: The Demands of Holocaust Representation* (Minneapolis: University of Minnesota Press, 2000).

40. Adorno, "The Meaning of 'Working Through the Past,'" in *Critical Models*, 91–92.

41. Ibid., 92.

42. Ibid., 89.

43. Hohendahl, for instance, regards Adorno as emphasizing the psychoanalytic aspect of these essays on education; Hohendahl, "Education after the Holocaust," *Prismatic Thought*, 69–72.

44. Adorno, "The Meaning of 'Working through the Past,'" 99; translation modified—J. Fisher; the original reads "*verweist unmittelbar*"; in *Gesammelte Schriften*, 10:568.

45. Adorno, letter to Thomas Mann, 28 December 1949, *Theodor W. Adorno/Thomas Mann: Briefwechsel, 1943–1955*, 47.

46. Bernstein characterizes the decline of ethics in late modernity as the shift from an ethics based on thick concepts to one based on "centralism" that tries to prop up increasingly outdated norms by mandating them as ethics on high; see Bernstein, *Adorno: Disenchantment and Ethics*, 61–63.

47. Adorno, "Was bedeutet: Aufarbeitung der Vergangenheit,'" in *Gesammelte Schriften*, 10:100; translation modified.

48. The report was, by all accounts, the watershed in the shift from a negative reeducation program (primarily denazification) to a positive program in which the U.S. (and then other Allies, who also adopted its directives) would try to positively retool the German educational system; see *Report of the United States Education Mission to Germany* ("Zook" report), Department of State, Publication 2664, European Series 16, 1946.

49. Reprinted in Adorno, *Gesammelte Schriften*, 10:816–17; also translated in Adorno, *Critical Models*, 307–08.

50. For evidence that Adorno understood his lecture "Arbeitung der Vergangenheit" as engaged with ethics and norms—even if they were intended to render more complex their current understanding—see Adorno's answers to the "seventh question" in his *Critical Models*, 303–04.

51. In his chapter on *Minima Moralia*, "Wrong Life Cannot be Lived Rightly," Bernstein argues that Adorno's project was focused primarily on private existence: "To the degree to which it remains, the ethical has retreated into forms of practice that are most remote from and least necessary for capital reproduction—private existence"; Bernstein, *Adorno: Disenchantment and Ethics*, 41. In her 2002 Adorno lectures, Judith Butler makes similar points based on *Minima Moralia*: she suggests Adorno's was primarily a private ethos that we have to read politically; Butler, *Kritik der ethischen Gewalt*, 101.

52. Adorno, "Erziehung nach Auschwitz," is translated in *Critical Models: Interventions and Catch Words*, trans. and preface by Henry W. Pickford (New York: Columbia University Press, 1998), 191–204, here 191.

53. Peter Hohendahl leaves the impression that Adorno makes no specific curricular suggestions in "Education after Auschwitz" (Hohendahl, *Prismatic Thought*, 58), but I think it is remarkable, given the character of much of his work, that Adorno makes suggestions as specific as he does, for instance about the mobile education units that go unremarked upon in Hohendahl's text.

54. Such is Bernstein's argument throughout his rich chapter on Auschwitz, "Chapter 8: After Auschwitz," in Bernstein, *Adorno: Disenchantment and Ethics*, 371–414.

55. For just a sample of how important the July 1944 conspiracy was for the German public sphere, see "Gab es ein anderes Deutschland: zum 20. Juli

1944," *Süddeutsche Zeitung* (19 July 1946), 3; "Das Attentat vom 20. Juli 1944: Die Rolle des Obersten von Stauffenberg—Der Verräter Remer war kein Nazi," *Frankenpost* (20 July 1946), 8; Gerhard Ritter, "Die aussenpolitischen Hoffnungen der Verschwörer des 20. Juli 1944," *Merkur* 3, no. 11 (Nov 1949): 1121–38.

56. Adorno, "Erziehung nach Auschwitz," in *Gesammelte Schriften*, 10:680.

57. "Erziehung zur Mündigkeit" has been translated as "Education for Maturity and Responsibility"; Adorno, "Erziehung zur Mündigkeit," trans. Robert French, Jem Thomas, and Dorothee Wymann, *History of the Human Sciences* 12, no. 3 (1999): 21–34, here 21; translation modified.

58. Immanuel Kant, "Answer to the Question: What is Enlightenment? [1784]" in *Kant: Basic Writings*, ed. Allen Wood (New York: Random House, 2001), 135; on page 137, Kant openly contrasts the clergy's role as educators with the more enlightened activities as "scholars" in a public sphere.

59. "[Adorno] siedelt die Moral auf der Seite der Zurückhaltung an, beim 'nicht Mitmachen'. . ."; Butler, *Kritik der ethischen Gewalt*, 106c.

60. Adorno, "Erziehung zur Mündigkeit," 24.

6. ADORNO—NATURE—HEGEL
Theresa M. Kelley

1. For a glimpse of Hegel's claim that abstraction is unphilosophical, see his 1807 essay "Who Thinks Abstractly," in *Miscellaneous Writings of G. W. F. Hegel*, trans. Walter Kaufmann, ed. Jon Stewart (Evanston, Ill.: Northwestern University Press, 2002), 284–88; German, "Wer denkt abstrakt," in Hegel, *Werke*, ed. Eva Moldenhauer and Karl Markus Michel (Frankfurt am Main: Suhrkamp, 1970), 2:575–81. For a reading of the Hegel that Adorno seeks to recuperate for modern philosophy, see Jean-Luc Nancy, *Hegel: The Restlessness of the Negative*, trans. Jason Smith and Steven Miller (Minneapolis: University of Minnesota Press, 2002).

2. Martin Jay and Alexander Düttmann made these remarks in papers each delivered as participants in the year-long Mellon Workshop on Adorno and Late Philosophical Modernity held at the University of Wisconsin in 2004–2005; the published versions of the papers appear in this volume.

3. J. M. Bernstein emphasizes the role of nonidentity in Adorno's negative dialectics in *Adorno: Disenchantment and Ethics* (Cambridge: Cambridge University Press, 2001), 243.

4. See Ian Hacking, *The Emergence of Probability* (Cambridge: Cambridge University Press, 1975); Hacking, *The Taming of Chance* (Cambridge: Cambridge University Press, 1990); and Lorraine Daston, *Classical Probability in the Enlightenment* (Princeton, N.J.: Princeton University Press, 1988).

5. G. W. F. Hegel, *Philosophy of History*, trans. J. Sibree (Amherst, N.Y.: Prometheus Books, 1991), 32–33; German, *Werke*, ed. Eva Moldenhauer and

Karl Markus Michel (Frankfurt am Main: Suhrkamp Verlag, 1970), 12:49. The textual and philosophical history of Hegel's philosophy of nature is recorded in unpublished manuscript and student notes for lectures he gave in Jena after 1801, when Schelling's own philosophy of nature apparently prompted Hegel's attention to the topic, and in successive versions and expansions, first in 1804–1805, then in part 2 of his 1817 *Encyclopaedia of the Philosophical Sciences*, and finally in the 1830 edition of this work. Much of this development registers Hegel's gradual extrication of his views on nature from those of Schelling, such that Hegel could in the end offer spirit's decisive triumph over nature. For attentive summaries of the history of Hegel's views on the philosophy of nature, see David Farrell Krell, "Contagion: Sexuality, Disease, and Death," in *German Idealism and Romanticism* (Bloomington and Indianapolis: Indiana University Press, 1998), 118–20, and Elaine P. Miller, *The Vegetative Soul: From Philosophy of Nature to Subjectivity in the Feminine* (Albany: State University of New York Press, 2002), 209–10 n. 2. The Jena-period manuscripts on the philosophy of nature appear in Hegel, *Jenaer Systementwürfe*, vol. 3, ed. Johann Heinrich Trede and Rolf-Peter Horstmann; and in Hegel, *Gesammelte Werke*, vol. 8 (Hamburg: Felix Meiner Verlag, 1976). The version that appears in the 1830 *Encyclopaedia* is presented in Hegel's *Werke in zwansig banden: Theorie Werkausgabe* as *Enzyklopädie der Philosophischen Wissenschaften im Grundrisse (1830), Die Naturphilosophie mit den mündlichen Zusätzen*, vol. 9, ed. Eva Moldenhauer and Mark Markus Michel (Frankfurt am Main: Suhrkamp Verlag, 1970). Two English translations present different versions: Michael John Petry's translation (Hegel, *Philosophy of Nature*, 3 vols., London: Allen and Unwin; and New York: Humanities Press, 1970) distinguishes different periods of its composition by using different typefaces; A. V. Miller's translation presents Hegel's final version (*Hegel's Philosophy of Nature*, part 2, *Encyclopaedia of the Philosophical Sciences* (1830), trans. A. V. Miller [Oxford: Clarendon Press, 1970]). For important analyses of Hegel's philosophy of nature, see: Gerd Buchdahl, "Hegel's Philosophy of Nature," *British Journal for the Philosophy of Science* 23, no. 3 (August 1972): 257–66; Martin Drees, "The Logic of Hegel's Philosophy of Nature," in *Hegel and Newtonianism*, ed. Michael John Petry (Dordrecht: Kluwer, 1993), 91–101; Jean-Louis Vieillard-Baron, "L'Interpretation Hégélienne du *Timée*, ou La Philosophie de la Nature," *Revue de Métaphysique et de Morale* 81, no. 3 (July–September 1976): 376–95; Johannes Hoffmeister, *Goethe und der Deutsche Idealismus: Eine Einführung zu Hegel's Realphilosophie* (Leipzig: Felix Meiner Verlag, 1932); George R. Lucas, Jr., "A Re-Interpretation of Hegel's Philosophy of Nature," *Journal of the History of Philosophy* 22, no. 1 (January 1984): 104–13; Hans-Christian Lucas, "The 'Sovereign Ingratitude' of Spirit toward Nature: Logical Qualities, Corporeity, Animal Magnetism, and Madness in Hegel's 'Anthropology,'" *Owl of Minerva* 23, no. 2 (Spring 1992): 131–50.

6. Theresa M. Kelley, "Romanticism Bites Back: Adorno and Romantic Natural History," *European Romantic Review* 15 (June 2004): 193–204.

7. Adorno, "Parataxis: On Hölderlin's Late Poetry," *Notes to Literature*, trans. Shierry Weber Nicholsen, ed. Rolf Tiedemann (New York: Columbia University Press, 1992), 2:109–152; German, Adorno, *Noten zur Literatur*, in *Gesammelte Schriften*, ed. Rolf Tiedemann (Frankfurt am Main: Suhrkamp, 1974), 446–91; Hegel: Three Studies, trans. Shierry Weber Nicholsen (Cambridge, Mass., and London: MIT Press, 1999; German, *Zur Metakritik der Erkenntnistheorie: Drei Studien zu Hegel*, in Hegel, *Gesammelte Schriften*, vol. 5, ed. Rolf Tiedemann, Gretel Adorno, Susan Buck-Morss, and Klaus Schultz (Frankfurt am Main: Suhrkamp Verlag, 1970).

8. Adorno, "Parataxis," in *Notes to Literature*, 2:131; German, "Parataxis," in Adorno, *Gesammelte Schriften*, 11:471.

9. Hegel, "Skoteinos," in *Hegel: Three Studies*, 105–06; German, *Zur Metakritik der Erkenntnistheorie: Drei Studien zu Hegel*, in Hegel, *Gesammelte Schriften*, 5:339–40.

10. Adorno, *Negative Dialectics*, trans. E. B. Ashton (New York: Continuum, 1995), 150; German, *Negative Dialektik* (Frankfurt am Main: Suhrkamp, 1966), 153.

11. Adorno's critique of Hegel on nature turns up more incidentally, with and without Hegel's name attached, in ways that signal how deeply that critique works in Adorno's philosophical thought, even within the current of his admiration for Hegelian dialectics. It is as though the thread of that critique signaled a hidden skein that, once pulled taut and made apparent, would reveal Hegel's difficult presence throughout; see, for example, Adorno and Horkheimer, *Dialectic of Enlightenment*, trans. John Cumming (1972 rpt.; New York: Continuum, 1988), 57: "The subjective spirit which cancels the animation of nature can master a despiritualized nature only by imitating its rigidity and despiritualizing itself in turn"; German, Adorno and Horkheimer, *Dialektik der Aufklärung* (Frankfurt am Main: Fischer, 2000), 64; and Adorno's essay on cultural criticism in *Prisms*, trans. Samuel Weber and Shierry Weber (Cambridge, Mass.: MIT Press, 1967), 19–34, where the faults of the cultural critic are, Adorno suggests at the outset, those of Hegel as cultural critic.

12. Adorno, *Aesthetics: Lectures on Fine Art*, trans. T. M. Knox, 1:291 (Oxford: Clarendon Press, 1975); German, *Vorlesungen über die Aesthetik*, in *Sämtliche Werke*, ed. Hermann Glockner (Stuttgart: Frommans Verlag, 1964), 12:390; quoted by Adorno, "Parataxis," in *Notes to Literature*, 2:110; German, "Parataxis," in *Noten zur Literatur, Gesammelte Schriften*, 11:449.

13. Adorno, "Parataxis," in *Notes to Literature*, 2:112–13; in the German, the verbs are "*durchbricht*," "to break through" and *hinausschließen*, "to shoot

out, to overshoot": see "Parataxis," in *Noten zur Literatur, Gesammelte Schriften*, 11:350–51.

14. Hölderlin, "Der Einzige" ["The Only One," second version], *Poems and Fragments*, trans. Michael Hamburger (Cambridge: Cambridge University Press, 1980), 458–59; quoted by Adorno, "Parataxis," in *Notes to Literature*, 2:131 (with a different English translation); German, "Parataxis," *Noten zur Literatur, Gesammelte Schriften*, 11:471–72.

15. Adorno, "Parataxis," in *Notes to Literature*, 2:131; German, "Parataxis," *Noten zur Literatur, Gesammelte Schriften*, 11:471–72.

16. Ibid., 132; German, 472–73.

17. Ibid., 131; German, 472.

18. I am indebted to Gerhard Richter for this account of the logic of Adorno's neologism.

19. Adorno, *Negative Dialectics*, 145; German, *Negative Dialektik*, 148.

20. Ibid., 149; German, 151.

21. Hegel, introduction, *Philosophy of History*, ed. John Sibree (Amherst, N.Y.: Prometheus Books, 1991), 33; German, *Werke*, 12: 49.

22. Krell, *Contagion*, 119, citing Hegel, *Werke*, 9:19; see also 17 and 42.

23. Johann Wolfgang von Goethe, *Versuch die Metamorphose der Pflanzen* [*The Metamorphosis of Plants*] (Gotha: Carl Wilhelm Ettinger, 1790); see for example his discussion of how the plant forms its flowers, together with notice of "Nature's power" in this process (para. 36, 24–25); English edition: *Goethe: Scientific Studies*, trans. Douglas Miller, *Goethe's Collected Works* (New York: Suhrkamp, 1988), 12:81. Elaine Miller describes Hegel's decisive turn from *Naturphilosophie* thinking about nature in *The Vegetative Soul* (Albany: State University of New York Press, 2002), 124. Timothy Lenoir summarizes the differences between the *Naturphilosophen* and the vital mechanists in *The Strategy of Life* (Chicago: University of Chicago Press, 1982), 76.

24. Miller, *Vegetative Soul*, 141.

25. Quoted by Miller, *Vegetative Soul*, 124, citing Hegel, *Jenaer Systementwürfe III*, in Hegel, *Gesammelte Werke*, 8:131–32; see as well Hegel, *Werke*, 9:396; and Petry's translation, *Philosophy of Nature*, 3:68.

26. Miller, *Vegetative Soul*, 135, citing Bataille, "Hegel, Death and Sacrifice," trans. Jonathan Strauss, *Yale French Studies* 78 (1990): 9–28.

27. Nicholsen and Shapiro note the affinities among the three Hegel essays (*Hegel: Three Studies*) given as a talk in 1956, published in 1957; "Experiential Content," written in 1958 and published in 1959; and "Skoteinos," written in 1962–1963 and first published as the last of the three essays in 1963. Adorno's composition of these essays is roughly contemporaneous with his work on the essays he published together as *Notes to Literature*, especially

"Essay as Form." The period of their composition also precedes and overlaps the years in which Adorno wrote *Negative Dialectics* and *Aesthetic Theory*.

28. Editors' introduction, Adorno, *Hegel: Three Studies*, xxxvi; German, *Zur Metakritik der Erkenntnistheory: Drei Studien zu Hegel*, in Hegel, *Gesammelte Schriften*, ed. Rolf Tiedemann, Gretel Adorno, Susan Buck-Morss, and Klaus Schultz (Frankfurt am Main: Suhrkamp Verlag, 1970), 5:250.

29. Adorno, "Aspects of Hegel's Philosophy," in *Hegel: Three Studies*, 13; German, *Zur Metakritik der Erkenntnistheory*, in Hegel, *Gesammelte Schriften*, 5:261.

30. Adorno, "The Experiential Content of Hegel's Philosophy," in *Hegel: Three Studies*, 80; German, *Zur Metakritik der Erkenntnistheory*, in Hegel, *Gesammelte Schriften*, 5:318.

31. Ibid., 83; German, 320.

32. Ibid., 80; German, 319.

33. Ibid., 82; German, 320.

34. Ibid., 87; German, 324.

35. Nicholsen and Shapiro, introduction, Adorno, *Hegel: Three Studies*, xxix.

36. H. G. Hotho, quoted by Adorno, "Skoteinos," in *Hegel: Three Studies*, 120; German, *Zur Metakritik der Erkenntnistheory*, in Hegel, *Gesammelte Schriften*, 5: 351–52.

37. Adorno, "Skoteinos," in *Hegel: Three Studies*, 91; German, *Zur Metakritik der Erkenntnistheory*, in Hegel, *Gesammelte Schriften*, 5:328.

38. Ibid., 119; German, 351.

39. Ibid., 121; German, 353.

40. Ibid.

41. Ibid., 122; German, 353–54.

42. Hegel, *Wissenschaft der Logik*, 1. Teil, p. 665; *Logic: Encyclopaedia 1: Part One of the Encyclopaedia of the Philosophical Sciences*, trans. William Wallace (Oxford: Oxford University Press, 1975), p. 531; quoted by Adorno, "Skoteinos," in *Hegel: Three Studies*, 122; German, 353–54.

43. Adorno, "Skoteinos," in *Hegel: Three Studies*, 133; German, *Zur Metakritik der Erkenntnistheory*, in Hegel, *Gesammelte Schriften*, 5:364.

44. Ibid., 136; German 366.

45. Reinhard Koselleck, *Futures Past: On the Semantics of Historical Time*, trans. Keith Tribe (New York: Columbia University Press, 1979), 126.

46. Hegel, *Philosophy of History*, 33; German, Hegel, *Werke*, 12:49.

47. Adorno, "Aspects," in *Hegel: Three Studies*, 42; German, *Zur Metakritik der Erkenntnistheory*, in Hegel, *Gesammelte Schriften*, 5:286.

48. Ibid., 42; German, 286–87.

49. Hegel, *Phenomenology of Spirit*, trans. A. V. Miller (Oxford: Oxford University Press, 1977), 104–19; German, *Phänomenologie des Geistes*, ed.

Hans-Friedrich Wessels and Heinrich Clairmont (Hamburg: Felix Meiner Verlag, 1988), 120–36.

50. Adorno, "Skoteinos," in *Hegel: Three Studies*, 112; German, *Zur Metakritik der Erkenntnistheory*, in Hegel, *Gesammelte Schriften*, 5:345.

51. Adorno, *Minima Moralia: Reflections from Damaged Life*, trans. E. F. N. Jephcott (London: Verso, 1978), 200; German, *Minima Moralia: Reflexionen aus dem beschädigten Leben*, in Adorno, *Gesammelte Schriften*, 4:227–28.

52. Adorno, "The Meaning of Working through the Past," in *Can One Live after Auschwitz: A Philosophical Reader*, trans. Henry W. Pickford (Stanford, Calif.: Stanford University Press, 2003), esp. 4–7.

53. Thomas Wheatland, reprising his 1997 interview with Bell, "Critical Theory on Morningside Heights," *German Politics and Society* 22, no. 4 (Winter 2004): 66–68.

7. THE IDIOM OF CRISIS: ON THE HISTORICAL IMMANENCE OF LANGUAGE IN ADORNO
Neil Larsen

1. My translation; the German original reads: "*Das Ganze ist das Unwahre*" (Frankurt am Main: Suhrkamp, 1969), 57. In a footnote to his translation of Theodor W. Adorno, *Minima Moralia* (London: NLB, 1974), 50, E. F. N. Jephcott notes Adorno's inversion of Hegel's dictum from *The Phenomenology of Mind*, "*Das Wahre ist das Ganze*," but, curiously, opts for the word "false" rather than "untrue."

2. Adorno, *Minima Moralia*, 71; these are the opening lines of fragment 45 ("'How sickly seem all growing things'"), which, together with 44 ("For Post-Socratics") and 46 ("On the morality of thinking") are this work's most sustained reflection on dialectics. Similar language can be found throughout Adorno's works, but the following passage from "Why Still Philosophy" (1962)—no less paralogical in its way than the earlier aphorism it qualifies— seems especially pertinent in this regard: "Traditional philosophy's claim to totality, culminating in the thesis that the real is rational, is indistinguishable from apologetics. But this thesis has become absurd. A philosophy that would still set itself up as total, as a system, would become a delusional system. Yet if philosophy renounces the claim to totality and no longer claims to develop out of itself *the whole that should be the truth*, then it comes into conflict with its entire tradition"—my emphasis; Adorno, *Critical Models: Interventions and Catchwords*, trans. Henry W. Pickford (New York: Columbia University Press, 1998), 7.

3. Max Horkheimer and Adorno, *Dialectic of Enlightenment: Philosophical Fragments*, trans. E. F. N. Jephcott (Stanford, Calif.: Stanford University Press, 2002), 94.

4. Adorno and Horkheimer, *Dialectic of Enlightenment*, 112.
5. Ibid., 119.
6. Ibid., 128.
7. See, for example, the concluding paragraph of the dedication in *Minima Moralia*, 18.
8. Adorno, *Notes to Literature*, trans. Shierry Weber Nicholsen (New York: Columbia University Press, 1991), 1:3–23.
9. Adorno, "The Essay as Form," 9.
10. Ibid., 13.
11. Karl Marx, *Capital*, trans. Ben Fowkes (London: Penguin Books, 1990), 1:167.
12. Adorno, "The Essay as Form," 18.
13. Marx, "The Method of Political Economy," in *Grundrisse: Foundations of the Critique of Political Economy*, trans. Martin Nicolaus (London: Penguin Books, 1993), 100–08.
14. Ibid., 100.
15. Ibid., 101.
16. Ibid., 105.
17. Marx, *Capital*, 1:102.
18. Moishe Postone, *Time, Labor, and Social Domination: a Reinterpretation of Marx's Critical Theory* (Cambridge: Cambridge University Press, 1996).
19. Ibid., 84–85.
20. Ibid., 86.
21. "The world constituted by such [abstract] labor is not only the material environment, formed by concrete social labor, but the social world as well." (Postone, 231)
22. Ibid., 113–14.
23. See Norbert Trenkle, "Gebrochene Negativität: Anmerkungen zu Adornos und Horkheimers Aufklärungskritik," *Krisis: Beitrage zur Kritik der Warengesellschaft* 25 (2002): 39–65.
24. Ibid., 39; my translations throughout, in consultation with the author. The German original states: "*das Dokument einer Kritik, die sich immer wieder partiell zurücknimmt, weil sie vor sich selbst erschrickt. Ihre argumentative Bewegung ist wenigstens teilweise eine, die nicht in der Dialektik der Sache liegt, sondern sich dieser entgegenstemmt.*"
25. Ibid., 47; my translation. The German original states: "*ganz bestimmte, von Ware und Werte konstituierte gesellschaftliche Verhältnisse.*"
26. Ibid., 47.
27. Ibid., 46.
28. Ibid; my translation. The German original states: "*Nicht mehr der glorreiche Siegesmarsch des Fortschritts wird beschrieben, sondern der düstere Gang des*

Verhängnisses. Befreiung von Herrschaft ist allenfalls noch eine aufblitzende Möglichkeit, die nicht mehr begründet werden kann, auf jeden Fall aber nicht mehr notwendiger Endpunkt der Geschichte. So richtig und wichtig die Kritik des Fortschrittsdenkens auch ist, sie bleibt doch in ihm befangen. Indem sie bloss seinen Optimismus (die angebliche Notwendigkeit der Befreiung) verwirft, reproduziert sie negative das ihm Zugrunde liegende geschichtsphilosophische Konstrukt. . . ."

29. See Trenkle, "Gebrochene Negativität," 51–65.

30. Although, to be precise here, it should be noted that Postone does not extrapolate from his critique of "traditional Marxism" in *Time, Labor, and Social Domination* any explicit theory of crisis as such.

8. AESTHETIC THEORY AND NONPROPOSITIONAL TRUTH CONTENT IN ADORNO
Gerhard Richter

1. Theodor W. Adorno, *Ästhetische Theorie*, in *Gesammelte Schriften* (Frankfurt am Main: Suhrkamp, 1997), 7:140. Unless indicated otherwise, translations are my own.

2. Martin Heidegger, *Hölderlins Hymne "Andenken,"* in *Gesamtausgabe*, vol. 52 (Frankfurt am Main: Vittorio Klostermann, 1992).

3. I borrow this delightful image from Stanley Corngold.

4. Adorno, *Beethoven: Philosophie der Musik*, in *Nachgelassene Schriften*, sect. I (Frankfurt am Main: Suhrkamp, 1993), 1:39.

5. See Christine Eichel, *Vom Ermatten der Avantgarde zur Vernetzung der Künste: Perspektiven einer interdisziplinären Ästhetik im Spätwerk Theodor W. Adornos* (Frankfurt am Main: Suhrkamp, 1993), and Hauke Brunkhorst, "Kritik statt Theorie: Adornos experimentelles Freiheitsverständnis," in *Impuls und Negativität: Ethik und Ästhetik bei Adorno*, eds. Gerhard Schweppenhäuser and Mirko Wischke (Berlin: Argument-Verlag, 1995), 117–35. Adorno mentions his notion of "Verfransung," for instance, in his late essay, "Die Kunst und die Künste," *Ohne Leitbild: Parva Aesthetica, Kulturkritik und Gesellschaft*, in *Gesammelte Schriften* (Frankfurt am Main: Suhrkamp, 1997), 10:432–53.

6. Rüdiger Bubner, "Kann Theorie ästhetisch werden? Zum Hauptmotiv der Philosophie Adornos," in *Materialien zur Ästhetischen Theorie Theodor W. Adornos: Konstruktionen der Moderne*, eds. Burkhardt Lindner and W. Martin Lüdke (Frankfurt am Main: Suhrkamp, 1980), 108–37, here 133.

7. Adorno, *Ästhetische Theorie*, 113.

8. Adorno, *Vorlesung über Negative Dialektik: Nachgelassene Schriften*, sect. IV: *Vorlesungen* (Frankfurt am Main: Suhrkamp, 2003), 16:115.

9. J. Hillis Miller, "'Reading' Part of a Paragraph in *Allegories of Reading*," in *Theory Now and Then* (Durham, N.C.: Duke University Press, 1991), 341–58, here 348.

10. It would also be necessary in this context to examine in some detail Adorno's relationship to Walter Benjamin's philosophical transformation of allegory as ruin and otherness in *Ursprung des deutschen Trauerspiels*. That the early Adorno already was deeply familiar with Benjamin's 1928 study, originally designed as a *Habilitation* thesis, is well known. He even offered a seminar on Benjamin's text at the University of Frankfurt in 1931–1932, the first university course on Benjamin ever. Compare further the surviving class minutes prepared by various participants in Adorno's seminar: "Adornos Seminar vom Sommersemester 1932 über Benjamins Ursprung des deutschen Trauerspiels: Protokolle," *Frankfurter Adorno Blätter* 4 (1995), 52–77. For a general discussion of Adorno's seminar on Benjamin, see Stefan Müller-Doohm, *Adorno: Eine Biographie* (Frankfurt am Main: Suhrkamp, 2003), 220–28.

11. These problems deserve to be inflected by Adorno's warning against "the illusion that what is said is immediately what is meant [*die Illusion, es wäre, was geredet wird, unmittelbar das Gemeinte*]." Instead the character of language as an elusive token [*Spielmarke*] reveals "the way that all words behave: that language imprisons its speakers one more time; that language, as the proper medium of its speakers, is a failure"; "Wörter aus der Fremde," *Noten zur Literatur*, in *Gesammelte Schriften* (Frankfurt am Main: Suhrkamp, 1997), 11:216–32, here 221.

12. Adorno, "Parataxis: Zur späten Lyrik Hölderlins," *Noten zur Literatur*, in *Gesammelte Schriften* (Frankfurt am Main: Suhrkamp, 1997), 11:447–91, here 452.

13. In the original, Hölderlin's rich passage reads: "*Ich verspräche gerne diesem Buche die Liebe der Deutschen. Aber ich fürchte, die einen werden es lesen, wie ein Compendium, und um das fabula docet sich zu sehr bekümmern, indem die andern gar zu leicht es nehmen, und beede Theile verstehen es nicht. Wer blos an meiner Pflanze riecht, der kennt sie nicht, und wer sie pflückt, blos, um daran zu lernen, kennt sie auch nicht. Die Auflösung der Dissonanzen in einem gewissen Charakter ist weder für das bloße Nachdenken, noch für die leere Lust*"; Friedrich Hölderlin, *Hyperion oder der Eremit in Griechenland*, in *Sämtliche Werke und Briefe*, ed. Michael Knaupp (Munich: Hanser, 1992), 1:609–760, here 611.

14. Adorno, *Ästhetische Theorie*, 27.

15. Ibid., 199.

16. Christoph Menke, *Die Souveränität der Kunst: Ästhetische Erfahrung nach Adorno und Derrida* (Frankfurt am Main: Suhrkamp, 1991).

17. Simon Jarvis, "Art, Truth, and Ideology," in *Adorno: A Critical Introduction* (New York: Routledge, 1998), 90–123, here 90. As Jarvis suggests, the idea of a nonpropositional truth content is tied to the intuition that the cognitive significance of an artwork or a philosophical text "is not exhausted by the sum of the correct propositions contained in it, because it depends also on the

relations between these propositions and the way in which they are organized." Adorno terms this differential or relational structure the work's *Sprachähnlichkeit* [similarity to language or language-likeness], its *Sprachcharakter* [linguistic character], in short, its status as *Schrift* [writing or script]; Jarvis, 103.

18. Andreas Bernard and Ulrich Raulff, *Theodor W. Adorno:* Minima Moralia *neu gelesen* (Frankfurt am Main: Suhrkamp, 2003).

19. Adorno, "Zum Ende," *Minima Moralia: Reflexionen aus dem beschädigten Leben*, in *Gesammelte Schriften* (Frankfurt am Main: Suhrkamp, 1997), 4:283.

20. I am grateful to Elke Siegel for reminding me of the third meaning of the preposition. I also thank Liliane Weissberg for suggesting to me that the translator may have attempted to "out-Adorno" Adorno by choosing a technical term drawn from music. And, indeed, the Italian term "finale" can signify the concluding movement or part of a musical piece or performance, such as an opera, a symphony, a sonata, or a concert more generally. Given the high esteem in which Adorno holds composers such as Mozart and Beethoven, for whom the "finale" is especially significant, this is an intriguing possibility. If this musical inflection had been the marching plan of Adorno's text, however, he doubtless would have employed the term "finale" in his original text, as he does throughout his musicological writings.

21. Adorno, *Negative Dialektik*, in *Gesammelte Schriften* (Frankfurt am Main: Suhrkamp, 1997), 6:148.

22. Adorno, "Kulturkritik und Gesellschaft," *Kulturkritik und Gesellschaft* 1, in *Gesammelte Schriften* (Frankfurt am Main: Suhrkamp, 1997), 10:11–30, here 27.

23. Adorno, "Aus einem Schulheft ohne Deckel. Bar Harbor, Sommer 1939," in *Frankfurter Adorno Blätter* 4 (1995): 7.

24. Adorno, "Thesen über die Sprache des Philosophen," *Philosophische Frühschriften*, in *Gesammelte Schriften* (Frankfurt am Main: Suhrkamp, 1997), 1:366–71, here 368.

25. Ibid.

26. J. M. Bernstein, "Fragment, Fascination, Damaged Life: 'The Truth about Hedda Gabler,'" in *The Actuality of Adorno: Critical Essays on Adorno and the Postmodern*, ed. Max Pensky (Albany: State University of New York Press, 1997), 154–82, here 155.

27. For a reading of this Adornean extension of a Marxian transformation of Kantian aesthetics in the context of his essay "On Lyric Poetry and Society," see Robert Kaufman, "Adorno's Social Lyric, and Literary Criticism Today: Poetics, Aesthetics, Modernity," in *The Cambridge Companion to Adorno*, ed. Thomas Huhn (Cambridge: Cambridge University Press, 2004), 354–75.

28. Adorno, *Negative Dialektik*, 21.

29. Ibid., 27.

30. Martin Heidegger, *Über den Humanismus* (Frankfurt am Main: Vittorio Klostermann, 2000), 49.

9. THE HOMELAND OF LANGUAGE: A NOTE ON TRUTH AND KNOWLEDGE IN ADORNO
Mirko Wischke

1. Theodor W. Adorno, *Minima Moralia*, trans. E. F. N. Jephcott (New York: Verso, 1978), 99; this essay is based on a paper delivered at the 2004 German Studies Association Conference in Washington, D.C. For a related discussion, see Mirko Wischke, "Keine Erkenntnis von Dingen," *Zeitschrift für kritische Theorie* 9, no. 7 (2003), 73–88.

2. Adorno, *Minima Moralia*, 219.

3. Ibid., 101.

4. Adorno, "Thesen über die Sprache der Philosophen," *Philosophische Frühschriften*, in *Gesammelte Schriften* (Frankfurt am Main: Suhrkamp, 1997), 1:367.

5. Adorno, *Negative Dialectics*, trans. E. B. Ashton (New York: Seabury Press, 1973), 56, 10.

6. Josef Kopperschmidt, "Nietzsches Entdeckung der Rhetorik: Rhetorik im Dienste der unreinen Vernunft," in *Nietzsche oder "Die Sprache ist Rhetorik,"* ed. Josef Kopperschmidt, et al. (Munich: Fink, 1994), 48.

7. Adorno, *Negative Dialectics*, 154.

8. Hans-Georg Gadamer, "Die Philosophie und ihre Geschichte," in *Hermeneutische Entwürfe: Vorträge und Aufsätze* (Tübingen: Mohr, 2000), 205.

9. Friedrich Nietzsche, *Nachlass 1885–1887*, in *Kritische Studienausgabe*, ed. G. Colli and M. Montinari (München: DTV, 1988), 12:103.

10. Nietzsche, "Über Wahrheit und Lüge im außermoralischen Sinne," in *Kritische Studienausgabe*, 1:879.

11. For more on this problem, see the excellent study by Wolfgang Müller-Lauter, *Über Werden und Wille zur Macht: Nietzsche Interpretationen* 1 (Berlin: de Gruyter, 1999).

12. Adorno, *Negative Dialectics*, 64.

13. Ibid., 12.

14. Ibid.

15. Immanuel Kant, *Kritik der reinen Vernunft*, in *Werkausgabe*, ed. Wilhelm Weischedel (Frankfurt am Main: Suhrkamp, 1990), 3:109.

16. Adorno, *Negative Dialectics*, 162.

17. Adorno, "Thesen über die Sprache der Philosophen," 369.

18. Walter Benjamin, *The Origin of German Tragic Drama*, trans. John Osborne (London: Verso, 1998), 29–30.

19. Adorno, *Negative Dialectics*, 164.
20. Adorno, *Ästhetische Theorie* (Frankfurt am Main: Suhrkamp, 1973), 96.
21. Adorno, "Valérys Abweichungen" in *Noten zur Literatur* (Frankfurt am Main: Suhrkamp, 1974), 199.
22. Benjamin, "On Language as Such and on the Language of Man," in *Walter Benjamin: Selected Writings, 1913–1926*, ed. Marcus Bullock and Michael W. Jennings, trans. E. F. N. Jephcott (Cambridge, Mass.: Belknap, 1996), 1:67.
23. Ibid., 67.
24. Ibid., 65.
25. Adorno, *Aesthetic Theory*, trans. Robert Hullot-Kentor (Minneapolis: University of Minnesota Press, 1997), 112.
26. Adorno, "Presuppositions," in *Notes to Literature*, trans. Shierry Weber Nicholsen (New York: Columbia University Press, 1992), 2:99.
27. Adorno, *Philosophie der neuen Musik* (Frankfurt am Main: Suhrkamp, 1976), 121.
28. That this is a highly complex process that can only be hinted at here emerges from the way in which Adorno determines the dialectic of form and content: "The demands . . . made by the material are a result of the fact that 'material' itself is sedimented spirit, something social, thoroughly preformed by human consciousness. This objective spirit of the material, as a former subjectivity that has forgotten itself, possesses its own laws of movement. Stemming from the same origin as the social process and always shot through with its traces, that which appears to be mere self-movement of the material runs along the same lines and in the same sense as empirical society"; Adorno, *Philosophie der neuen Musik*, 39f.
29. Adorno, "Der Essay als Form," in *Noten zur Literatur*, 31. It is evident that Adorno is familiar with the following objections when he writes that "association, polyvalence of words, and the loosening of logical synthesis all made it easier for the listener and subjected the one thus weakened to the will of the speaker."
30. Adorno, *Minima Moralia*, 81; according to Adorno, "this inadequacy resembles that of life, which describes a wavering, deviating line, disappointing by comparison with its premises, and yet which only in this actual course, always less than it should be, is able, under given conditions of existence, to represent an unregimented one."
31. Adorno, "Parataxis," in *Notes to Literature*, 136.
32. Adorno, "Der Essay als Form," 21.
33. Adorno, *Aesthetic Theory*, 117; this limitation of rhetorical means will allow us to postulate neither an "act of recreation" through language nor an attempt at an "aesthetic rediscovery of existing reality," as Scholze claims.

Britta Scholze, *Kunst als Kritik: Adornos Weg aus der Dialektik* (Würzburg: Königshausen & Neumann, 2000), 194.

34. Adorno, "Parataxis," 130.

10. OF STONES AND GLASS HOUSES: *MINIMA MORALIA* AS CRITIQUE OF TRANSPARENCY
Eric Jarosinski

1. Claudia Michels, "Vom Wunschziel zur Zielscheibe," *Frankfurter Rundschau* (6 January 2004), 37.

2. Ibid.

3. "Adorno spaltet noch immer: Denkmal und Platz zum 100. Geburtstag stoßen Debatten an," *Frankfurter Rundschau* (11 September 2003), 26.

4. Adorno, *Dream Notes*, trans. Rodney Livingstone (Cambridge, UK: Polity, 2007), 10.

5. Axel Bernatzki, "Theodor W. Adorno: Ein Schreibtisch hinter Panzerglas als Denkmal," *Frankfurter Rundschau* (13 May 2003), 24.

6. Michels, "Vom Wunschziel zur Zielscheibe," 26.

7. Heiko Rehmann, "Gewalt gegen Adorno: Diskussion über Denkmal," *Frankfurter Allgemeine Zeitung* (15 November 2004), 42.

8. Claus-Jürgen Göpfert, "Wie ein Hinrichtungsplatz!" *Frankfurter Rundschau* (15 November 2004), 35.

9. Heiko Rehmann, "BFF: Adorno Denkmal Besser Sichern," *Frankfurter Allgemeine Zeitung* (17 November 2004), 44.

10. Claus-Jürgen Göpfert, "Adornos Denkmal bekommt Video-Schutz," *Frankfurter Rundschau* (20 November 2004), 37.

11. Michael Hirsch and Vanessa Joan Müller, preface, in *Adorno: Die Möglichkeit des Unmöglichen*, ed. Nicolaus Schafhausen, et al. (Frankfurt am Main: Lukas and Sternberg, 2003), 7.

12. Theodor W. Adorno, *Critical Models*, trans. Henry W. Pickford (New York: Columbia University Press, 1998), 43.

13. Ibid., 42–43.

14. Ibid., 78.

15. Adorno, *Minima Moralia*, trans. E. F. N. Jephcott (New York: Verso, 1978), 182.

16. Adorno, *Prisms*, trans. Samuel and Sherry Weber (Cambridge, Mass.: MIT Press, 1995), 105.

17. Adorno, *Minima Moralia*, 150.

18. Max Horkheimer and Adorno, *Dialectic of Enlightenment*, ed. Gunzelin Schmid Noerr, trans. E. F. N. Jephcott (Stanford, Calif.: Stanford University Press, 2002), 183.

19. Adorno, *Critical Models*, 136.

20. Adorno, *Prisms*, 19.
21. Ibid., 20.
22. Adorno, *Minima Moralia*, 197.
23. Ibid., 15.
24. Ibid., 247.
25. Samuel Weber, "Translating the Untranslatable," in *Prisms*, 12.
26. Alexander García Düttmann offers an insightful analysis of Adorno's style through a meditation on *Darstellung*: "*Darstellung* is language as constellation or configuration. It is in no way the representation of a sublating movement which reaches a result. Language designates here the non-negative other of speculation. By definition, a constellation entails the chance of an apparition. Something allows itself to be thought through a constellation, something provokes thought in a constellation." *The Gift of Language: Memory and Promise in Adorno, Benjamin, Heidegger, and Rosenzweig*, trans. Arline Lyons (Syracuse, N.Y.: Syracuse University Press, 2000), 1.
27. Adorno, *Minima Moralia*, 80.
28. Ibid., 192.
29. Ibid., 111.
30. Ibid., 73.
31. Ibid.
32. Ibid., 121.
33. Ibid.
34. Ibid.
35. Ibid., 87.
36. Ibid.
37. Adorno, *Critical Models*, 7.
38. Ibid., 140.
39. Ibid., 41.
40. Adorno, "Functionalism Today," in *Rethinking Architecture*, ed. Neil Leach, trans. Jane Newman and John Smith (New York: Routledge, 1997), 12.
41. Ibid., 7.
42. Ibid., 8–9.
43. Ibid., 10.
44. Ibid.
45. Ibid., 14.
46. Ibid.
47. Ibid., 16–17.
48. Ibid., 18.
49. Ibid., 12.
50. Ibid., 16.
51. Adorno, *The Culture Industry*, ed. J. M. Bernstein (New York: Routledge, 1991), 121.

52. Ibid.
53. Adorno, *Minima Moralia*, 123.
54. Ibid.
55. Ibid., 67.
56. Ibid.

II. THE POLEMIC OF THE LATE WORK: ADORNO'S HÖLDERLIN
Robert Savage

1. This chapter is a revised version of material that has previously appeared in my book *Hölderlin after the Catastrophe: Heidegger—Adorno—Brecht* (Rochester, N.Y.: Camden House, 2008).
2. See Rolf Tiedemann, "Concept, Image, Name: On Adorno's Utopia of Knowledge," in *The Semblance of Subjectivity: Essays in Adorno's Aesthetic Theory*, ed. Tom Huhn and Lambert Zuidevaart (Cambridge, Mass.: MIT Press, 1997), 123–45.
3. Theodor W. Adorno, *Philosophy of Modern Music*, trans. Anne G. Mitchell and Wesley V. Blomster (New York: Continuum, 2004), 49.
4. Adorno, *Notes to Literature*, trans. Shierry Weber Nicholsen (New York: Columbia University Press, 1991), 2:128.
5. Adorno, *Aesthetic Theory*, trans. Robert Hullot-Kentor (London: Athlone Press, 1997), 107; translation amended.
6. Ibid., 131; see also J. M. Bernstein, *The Fate of Art: Aesthetic Alienation from Kant to Derrida and Adorno* (Cambridge: Polity Press, 1992), 252.
7. Martin Seel has developed this aspect of Adorno's aesthetics in his *Aesthetics of Appearing*, trans. John Farrell (Stanford, Calif.: Stanford University Press, 2005).
8. Bernstein, *The Fate of Art*, 269; see also Bernstein, "Why Rescue Semblance? Metaphysical Experience and the Possibility of Ethics," in *The Semblance of Subjectivity*, ed. Tom Huhn and Lambert Zuidevaart, 177–212.
9. Albrecht Wellmer writes of the "polemical relationship of art to reality" in Adorno's thought; Wellmer, "Wahrheit, Schein, Versöhnung: Adornos ästhetische Rettung der Modernität," in *Adorno-Konferenz 1983*, ed. Ludwig von Friedburg and Jürgen Habermas (Frankfurt am Main: Suhrkamp, 1983), 143. Moreover, Adorno holds that each individual artwork polemicizes against the institution of art. Asked to name the ten greatest novels of German literature, Adorno replies: "one artwork is the mortal enemy of the other and can tolerate no other beside it" (Adorno, *Gesammelte Schriften*, ed. Rolf Tiedemann et al. [Frankfurt am Main: Suhrkamp, 1970–1986], 20:736); see also Adorno, *Minima Moralia: Reflections from Damaged Life*, trans. E. F. N. Jephcott (London: New Left Books, 1974), 75–76: "Aesthetic tolerance that simply acknowledges works of art in their limitation, without breaking it, leads them

only to a false downfall, that of a juxtaposition which denies their claims to indivisible truth."

10. Adorno, *Notes to Literature*, 2:137.
11. Ibid., 114.
12. Ibid., 121.
13. Ibid.; translation amended.
14. Ibid., 109; "Great works wait," Adorno writes in *Aesthetic Theory*, 40.
15. Adorno, *Notes to Literature*, 2:110.
16. Adorno, *Einführung in die Musiksoziologie* (Frankfurt am Main: Suhrkamp, 1975), 179. The metaphor applies quite literally in the case of Hölderlin. A comparative study of editions of his late work, from Hellingrath to Burdorf, could demonstrate how differing conceptions of the poetized rebound upon the material constitution of the poem. In Beißner the textual layers discarded by Hellingrath as inessential find their way into the critical apparatus; in Sattler they are superimposed upon the "final version." In each case an underlying interpretation produces the poem that inspired it.
17. Adorno, *Notes to Literature*, 2:96.
18. See Fred Dallmayr, *The Other Heidegger* (Ithaca, N.Y.: Cornell University Press, 1993), 176; Christopher Fynsk, *Heidegger, Thought and Historicity* (Ithaca, N.Y.: Cornell University Press, 1986), 204; Marc Froment-Meurice, *That Is to Say: Heidegger's Poetics*, trans. Jan Plug (Stanford, Calif.: Stanford University Press, 1998), chap. 5.
19. Adorno, *Gesammelte Schriften*, 2:239.
20. Ibid., 244.
21. Adorno, *Notes to Literature*, 2:109.
22. Max Horkheimer and Adorno, *Dialectic of Enlightenment*, trans. John Cumming (London: Allen Lane, 1973), 210. Similarly, Benjamin argues that "one reason why Fascism has a chance is that in the name of progress its opponents treat it as a historical norm"; Walter Benjamin, *Illuminations*, trans. Harry Zohn (London: Fontana, 1968), 257.
23. Peter Sloterdijk, *Kritik der zynischen Vernunft* (Frankfurt am Main: Suhrkamp, 1983), 1:53.
24. Adorno, *Gesammelte Schriften*, 19:638; for a detailed discussion of this reproach, see Philippe Lacoue-Labarthe, *Heidegger, Art and Politics*, trans. Chris Turner (Oxford: Blackwell, 1990).
25. On other occasions, Adorno compares his role in relation to Heidegger with that of the little boy in Andersen's tale of the Emperor's new clothes, e.g. Adorno, *Ontologie und Dialektik*, ed. Rolf Tiedemann (Frankfurt am Main: Suhrkamp, 2002), 232; the analogy is wishful but exact: in both cases, an outsider breaks the spell cast by a figure who, until then, had unquestioningly been *granted an audience*, by bringing that audience to *see reason*. The allusion

to the court ceremony of Todtnauberg, to the nimbus of regal dignity cultivated by Heidegger and his followers, is also not to be overheard.

26. Adorno, *Notes to Literature*, 2:119.

27. Adorno, *Aesthetic Theory*, 364.

28. I disregard Adorno's early musical setting of Hölderlin's poem "An Zimmern."

29. Adorno, *Notes to Literature*, 2:132–33.

30. See, in particular, Adorno's reading of the ode "Natur und Kunst," in *Notes to Literature*, 2:140–41.

31. Hellingrath's term is apposite here. Adorno cites it approvingly in a footnote: "According to Peter Szondi, Hellingrath, in his dissertation 'Pindarübertragungen Hölderlins' (1910), was the first to describe the language of the late Hölderlin with the term from classical rhetoric, '*harte Fügung*' [literally, harsh arrangement or jointure]. The hiatus was another of his linguistic techniques"; Adorno, *Notes to Literature*, 2:340n.

32. Friedrich Hölderlin, *Selected Poems and Fragments*, trans. Michael Hamburger (Harmondsworth: Penguin, 1998), 170; translation amended.

33. Adorno, *Notes to Literature*, 2:142.

34. Hölderlin, *Selected Poems and Fragments*, 170; translation amended.

35. Adorno, *Notes to Literature*, 2:113.

36. Ibid., 126.

37. See Walter Benjamin, *Gesammelte Briefe*, ed. Christoph Gödde and Henri Lonitz (Frankfurt am Main: Suhrkamp, 1996), 3:522.

38. The opening salvo was launched in 1960–61 with a lecture course on "Ontology and Dialectics"; the barrage culminated in 1966 with the appearance of Adorno's philosophical magnum opus, *Negative Dialectics*, petering out to the occasional potshot in the works that followed. The corpus of anti-Heideggeriana that emerged from Frankfurt during this period also included a series of talks held in Paris and Rome in early 1961 that set out "to prosecute the case against Heidegger with the greatest thoroughness" ("Merleau-Ponty shocked," Adorno noted in his diary afterward), and the influential *Jargon of Authenticity*, published in 1964 and conceived as a pamphlet against the rhetoric of the German existentialists and their epigones. While the broad acceptance that met his efforts doubtless testified to Adorno's polemical talent, the apparent ease of his victory showed that the assault may have come too late. The wave of popularity enjoyed by Heidegger during the 1950s was already beginning to ebb by the time Adorno embarked upon his crusade, while the productive reception taking place across the Rhine remained blithe to his warnings, notwithstanding his personal appearance in Paris. Certainly, to maintain, as he did in "Parataxis," that contemporary Hölderlin interpretation clung heteronomously "in large measure . . . upon the unquestioned authority

of a thought that sought out Hölderlin's of its own accord" (*Notes to Literature*, 2:114) was to indulge in a wild and potentially insulting exaggeration of Heidegger's hold upon his audience. Even those few scholars who stood close to Heidegger, such as Wolfgang Binder and Emil Staiger, were by no means willing to believe his every pronouncement. That Adorno should be so quick to grant Heidegger unquestioned authority over his more tolerant readers, excluding the possibility of a form of reception that avoided the twin extremes of gullible acceptance and emphatic repudiation, cannot simply be ascribed to his ignorance of the state of Hölderlin research or his fondness for hyperbole. Adorno could find no other explanation for the success of a philosophy that seemed to him an obvious swindle than that it exploited an "ontological need" prepared at all costs to lend it credence. For Adorno, *Daseinsphilosophie* appealed to a deep-seated affect, the need to believe one's life has meaning and substance, rather than to reason, which tells us that a transcendental rooftop is not to be had so cheaply. "The ontological need can no more guarantee its object than the agony of the starving assures them of food," he writes in *Negative Dialectics* (New York: Seabury Press, 1973), 65. Heidegger quite correctly recognized that the binding ties once provided by religion—T. S. Eliot's "roots that clutch"—had unraveled over the course of enlightenment, leaving the modern subject face-to-face with its own nullity. But instead of reflecting upon the cause of this nullity, the subject's integration into a system of total domination and exchange, Heidegger turned his back on the contaminated realm of the existent to find solace in a numinous Being. He thereby not only committed a philosophical error, rescinding the Copernican turn by endowing the *An sich* with a positivity strictly denied it by Kant; he also played into the hands of those interested in maintaining the bad status quo. For Adorno, the pseudo-satisfactions offered by fundamental ontology stood in the way of the real satisfactions we might all experience in a reconciled world.

39. Adorno, *Notes to Literature*, 2:128.

40. See Benjamin's important wartime essay "Two Poems of Friedrich Hölderlin." The poetized is defined there as the "synthetic unity of the intellectual and perceptual orders" of the poem, which, as *synthetic* unity, forms as much the "product" as the "subject of the investigation"; Walter Benjamin, *Selected Writings*, ed. Marcus Bullock and Michael W. Jennings (Cambridge, Mass.: Belknap Press, 1996), 1:18–19. On this essay and its influence on "Parataxis," see Alexander Honold, *Der Leser Walter Benjamin: Bruchstücke einer deutschen Literaturgeschichte* (Berlin: Verlag Vorwerk 8, 2000), chap. 2; Peter-André Alt, "Das Problem der inneren Form: Zur Hölderlin-Rezeption Benjamins und Adornos," *Deutsche Vierteljahresschrift* 61, no. 3 (1987): 531–63.

41. Adorno, *Notes to Literature*, 2:128.

42. Benjamin, *The Origin of German Tragic Drama*, trans. John Osborne (London: New Left Books, 1977), 28.

43. See Carl Dahlhaus, *Richard Wagners Musikdramen* (Stuttgart: Philip Reclam, 1996), 7.

44. Adorno and Benjamin, *The Complete Correspondence, 1928–1940*, ed. Henri Lonitz, trans. Nicholas Walker (Cambridge, Mass.: Harvard University Press), 228–29. In the commentary he devotes to this passage, Richard Leppert claims that Benjamin is "essentially" accusing Adorno of a "lack of mediation": "The progressive aspects of Wagner, though acknowledged by Adorno, are insufficiently set in tension with the regressive tendencies that principally define the study." Nothing could be further from the truth. For Benjamin, the inadequacy of Adorno's polemic against Wagner does not lie in any one-sided, Beckmesser-like preoccupation with his blatantly regressive tendencies, nor, correspondingly, in its insufficient illumination of the progressive aspect of Wagner's achievement, but in its continuing indebtedness to a conception of history that operates with precisely these categories. Benjamin's letter makes clear that the *Rettung* he has in mind is to be identified with neither progress nor regress, *both* of which it assigns to the purview of the polemic. As we will see, it is *Adorno* who is "essentially" (if indirectly) accusing *Benjamin* of a "lack of mediation"—much as he would five months later, this time with all desirable explicitness, in his critique of Benjamin's essay on Baudelaire; Richard Leppert, "Commentary," in Adorno, *Essays on Music*, ed. Richard Leppert, trans. Susan H. Gillespie, et al. (Berkeley: University of California Press, 2002), 528–31.

45. An allusion to Adorno's libretto *The Treasure of Indian Joe*, but also, no doubt, to his already virulent philopolemology.

46. Benjamin, *Illuminations*, 264.

47. Ibid., 261.

48. "Our consideration . . . seeks to convey an idea of the high price our accustomed thinking will have to pay for a conception of history that avoids *any complicity* with the thinking to which these politicians [the social-democratic and liberal politicians who proved powerless to prevent the rise of fascism] continue to adhere"; ibid., 258; my italics.

49. "As far as your critical remarks are concerned, I am uncommonly delighted by your positive response. As far as the more negative side is concerned, I am forced to respond rather laconically, if only because I cannot help agreeing with you"; Adorno and Benjamin, *Complete Correspondence*, 265.

50. Ibid., 265; see also Adorno's letter to Horkheimer from 29 November 1937, in Adorno and Horkheimer, *Briefwechsel 1927–1969: Band 1: 1927–1937*, eds. Christoph Gödde and Henri Lonitz (Frankfurt am Main: Suhrkamp, 2003), 492.

51. Adorno and Benjamin, *Complete Correspondence*, 265.

52. Hölderlin, *Essays and Letters on Theory*, trans. Thomas Pfau (Albany: State University of New York Press, 1988), 101, 107.

53. Ibid., 102.
54. Ibid., 101: "For indeed, the tragic *transport* is actually empty and the least restrained."
55. Hölderlin in fact locates the caesura, in both of the Sophoclean plays he translated, in the speeches of the prophet Tiresias.
56. Lacoue-Labarthe, *Musica Ficta (Figures of Wagner)*, trans. Felicia McCarren (Stanford, Calif.: Stanford University Press, 1994), 141; see also Lacoue-Labarthe, "The Caesura of the Speculative," trans. Christopher Fynsk, in *Typography* (Stanford, Calif.: Stanford University Press, 1998), 208–35.
57. See Adorno, *Beethoven: Philosophie der Musik*, ed. Rolf Tiedemann (Frankfurt am Main: Suhrkamp, 1993), 102.
58. Benjamin, *Selected Writings*, 1:340.
59. Ibid., 341.
60. Winfried Menninghaus, *Ekel: Theorie und Geschichte einer starken Empfindung* (Frankfurt am Main: Suhrkamp, 2002), 436.
61. The other, passing reference is in Adorno, *Notes to Literature*, 2:132.
62. Ibid., 113.
63. Adorno writes at the end of his introduction to *Stichworte [Catchwords]*: "The association with polemics that the title conveys is a welcome one to the author"; Adorno, *Critical Models: Interventions and Catchwords*, trans. Henry W. Pickford (New York: Columbia University Press, 1998), 126.
64. Adorno, *Notes to Literature*, 2:113.
65. Adorno, "Wagner's Relevance for Today," trans. Susan H. Gillespie, in Adorno, *Essays on Music*, 599.
66. Adorno, *Notes to Literature*, 2:134–35.
67. Ibid., 149.
68. Adorno, *Gesammelte Schriften*, 13:139.
69. See Adorno, "Wagner's Relevance for Today," 598: "Wagner conceives no music of world destruction adequate to the one he prophesies. It falls off, fails to fulfill the expectation of the maximal catastrophe that it has aroused."
70. For Benjamin, the caesura is the force that "completes the work, by shattering it into a thing of shards"; Benjamin, *Selected Writings*, 1:340.
71. Adorno, *Notes to Literature*, 2:116; see also Adorno, *Aesthetic Theory*, 85: "art today is scarcely conceivable except as a form of reaction that anticipates the apocalypse."
72. In Adorno, "Parataxis," in *Notes to Literature*, 2:117, 133, 137, 340n; elsewhere: Adorno, *Beethoven*, 102, 268.
73. See Benjamin's distinction between symbol and allegory in his book *The Origin of German Tragic Drama*. On Adorno's concept of allegory, see Britta Scholze, *Kunst als Kritik: Adornos Weg aus der Dialektik* (Würzburg: Königshausen and Neumann, 2000), 209–86.

74. See Adorno, *Aesthetic Theory*, 110.
75. Adorno, "Late Style in Beethoven," trans. Susan H. Gillespie, in Adorno, *Essays on Music*, 564; on "Late Style in Beethoven," see also Edward Said, "Adorno as Lateness Itself," in *Adorno: A Critical Reader*, ed. Nigel Gibson and Andrew Rubin (Oxford: Blackwell, 2002), 193–208.
76. Adorno, *Beethoven*, 232–33.
77. Adorno, "Late Style in Beethoven," 566.
78. Adorno, *Beethoven*, 26.
79. Adorno, *Notes to Literature*, 2:139. Adorno held fireworks to be the prototype of aesthetic semblance; see *Aesthetic Theory*, 81.
80. On the problem of latency and contingency, see David Roberts, *Art and Enlightenment: Aesthetic Theory after Adorno* (Lincoln: University of Nebraska Press, 1991).
81. Adorno, "Late Style in Beethoven," 567; translation amended.
82. Ibid., 567.
83. Husserl's example of a nonsensical sentence (*Unsinn*) is "King but or similar and," which, although intelligible in its component parts, "is not to be understood as a unity." His example of a contrasensical sentence [*Widersinn*], "A square is round," makes perfect sense as a grammatical construct but suffers from the a priori impossibility of its implied object; Edmund Husserl, *Logische Untersuchungen*, ed. Ursula Panzer (The Hague: Martinus Nijhoff, 1984), 2:342–43.
84. For an excellent account of Adorno's theory of the (perpetually frustrated) constitution of meaning in aesthetic texts, an account that nonetheless skirts the problem of *Widersinn* (and thus the problem of the polemic), see Christoph Menke, *The Sovereignty of Art: Aesthetic Negativity in Adorno and Derrida*, trans. Neil Solomon (Cambridge, Mass.: MIT Press, 1998).
85. Adorno, *Notes to Literature*, 2:111.
86. Ibid., 111.
87. Wolfgang Binder, *Hölderlin-Aufsätze* (Frankfurt am Main: Insel, 1970), 353.
88. Adorno, *Kierkegaard: Construction of the Aesthetic*, trans. Robert Hullot-Kentor (Minnesota: University of Minneapolis Press, 1989), 133; translation amended. A few pages earlier: "it [the realm of images] is not imageless truth, but promises paradoxically [*widersinnig*] unreachable truth in opposition to its semblance"; ibid., 127.

12. TWELVE ANACOLUTHIC THESES ON ADORNO'S "PARATAXIS: ON HÖLDERLIN'S LATE POETRY"
David Farrell Krell

1. "Parataxis: Zur späten Lyrik Hölderlins" was first a lecture given at the annual meeting of the Hölderlin-Gesellschaft in Berlin on 7 June 1963. An

expanded version was then published in *Neue Rundschau* 75:1 (1964). The piece appears now in Theodor W. Adorno, *Noten zur Literatur*, ed. Rolf Tiedemann (Frankfurt am Main: Suhrkamp, 1981), 447–91; I will refer to the Suhrkamp volume throughout, citing it by page number in the body of my text. For an English translation, see Adorno, *Notes to Literature*, trans. Shierry Weber Nicholsen (New York: Columbia University Press, 1992), 2:109–49; notes on 338–41.

2. The seminar took place in February 2005 at the University of Wisconsin upon the kind invitation of Gerhard Richter and Theresa Kelley. My thanks to them and to Sabine Mödersheim for their hospitality.

3. See Martin Heidegger, *Ursprung des Kunstwerkes*, ed. Hans-Georg Gadamer (Stuttgart: P. Reclam, 1960); see also Jacques Derrida, "Les fins de l'homme," in *Marges de la philosophie* (Paris: Minuit, 1972), 129–64; translated by Alan Bass as *Margins—Of Philosophy* (Chicago: University of Chicago Press, 1982), 109–36; Derrida, *La Carte postale de Socrate à Freud et au-delà* (Paris: Aubier-Flammarion, 1980); translated by Alan Bass as *The Post Card from Socrates to Freud and Beyond* (Chicago: University of Chicago Press, 1987); Derrida, *De l'esprit: Heidegger et la question* (Paris: Galilée, 1987); translated by Geoff Bennington and Rachel Bowlby as *Of Spirit: Heidegger and the Question* (Chicago: University of Chicago Press, 1989).

4. For the literature, which is vast, let the following references for the moment suffice: Martin Heidegger, "Germanien" and "Der Rhein," in *Gesamtausgabe*, vol. 39 (Frankfurt am Main: V. Klostermann, 1980); *Hölderlins Hymne "Andenken,"* in *Gesamtausgabe*, vol. 52 (1982); *Hölderlins Hymne "Der Ister,"* in *Gesamtausgabe*, vol. 53 (1984); see also, and above all, "Die Zu-Künftigen" and "Der letzte Gott," *Beiträge zur Philosophie (Vom Ereignis)*, in *Gesamtausgabe* (1989), 65:395–417. For an English translation of Heidegger's "Essence of Technology," first published in *Vorträge und Aufsätze* (Pfullingen: G. Neske Verlag, 1954), 13–44, see Reading VII in *Basic Writings*, ed. D. F. Krell (San Francisco: HarperCollins, 1993), 307–41.

5. See David Farrell Krell, *Lunar Voices: Of Tragedy, Poetry, Fiction, and Thought* (Chicago: University of Chicago Press, 1995), chap. 4, which discusses Derrida's *Geschlecht* series in this respect. Much work remains to be done here, especially by bringing Derrida's and Adorno's readings into closer association with Luce Irigaray, *L'Oubli de l'air chez Martin Heidegger* (Paris: Minuit, 1983); translated by Mary Beth Mader as *The Forgetting of Air in Martin Heidegger* (Austin: University of Texas Press, 1999). I am thinking in particular of Adorno's statement that "since Parmenides the One and Being have been coupled" (459), which is Irigaray's plaint throughout her book.

6. Perhaps I ought to add here a note written long after the seminar—on 10 June 2005, in Germany, as I was preparing these notes for publication—

concerning Adorno's Heidegger critique. The note: Adorno's "Parataxis" improves on second reading. This time I read it in translation [see note 1, above]. Is my German that bad? No, it was the haste with which I read it in January, under the pressure of the need to prepare a seminar on it. Whereas on first reading [not really the first, inasmuch as I had read "Parataxis" two decades ago in the French translation appended to a text edited by Philippe Lacoue-Labarthe] I took glee in noting the places where Adorno had to cede to Heidegger, on second reading the critique of Heidegger seemed quite right: Heidegger does foist his history of being onto Hölderlin's poems. Heidegger's *Leitworte*, seemingly derived from Hölderlin, import into the poetry a preoccupation that is not Hölderlin's. Lacoue-Labarthe was therefore right to hold "Parataxis" in such high esteem. Above all, Adorno's nuanced treatment of Hölderlin's use of *myth* and of Hölderlin's invocation of the *names* of persons and places—myth without magic and names without meaning—seems to me now to merit a more careful reading. If in the end Adorno has recourse to Heidegger's favorite lines—on the mortals who are closer to the abyss than gods can be—he retains the difference of utopia, that is, of a peace and a celebration of peace that enact a reconciliation beyond anything Hegel or Heidegger ever dreamt of; likewise, Adorno retains far better than Heidegger ever could the difference of what is profoundly different, namely, the foreign, the brown women of southern France, who, to repeat, for Heidegger could only represent the threat of a foreign invasion.

7. Maurice Blanchot, "Itinéraire de Hölderlin," in *L'Espace littéraire* (Paris: Gallimard, 1955), 367–79.

8. Adorno cites Walter Benjamin, *Schriften*, ed. Theodor W. Adorno and Gretel Adorno, with the assistance of Friedrich Podszus (Frankfurt am Main: Suhrkamp, 1955), 2:385.

9. I have here quoted the English translation cited above in note 1 (see 130–32 of the translation) with only a few alternative suggestions, especially in the translation of Hölderlin's lines.

10. Friedrich Hölderlin, *Friedrich Hölderlin Sämtliche Werke und Briefe*, ed. Jochen Schmidt (Frankfurt am Main: Deutscher Klassiker Verlag, 1992), 1:320.

11. Ibid.

12. Ibid., 1:354; 2:149–51.

13. See Novalis, *Werke, Tagebücher und Briefe Friedrich von Hardenbergs*, ed. Hans-Joachim Mähl (Munich: C. Hanser Verlag, 1978), 2:438–39.

14. Hölderlin, *Sämtliche Werke und Briefe*, 2:917. For "fragmentary writing," see Maurice Blanchot, *Entretien infini* (Paris: Gallimard, 1969), 227–55; on theophany, see Lacoue-Labarthe, *Métaphrasis* (Paris: Presses Universitaires de France, 1998), 34, 40–41.

15. Hölderlin, *Sämtliche Werke und Briefe*, 1:364.

16. In a discussion that followed the Wisconsin seminar, Venkat Mani suggested that this would be the place to take up the question of *Geschick* in Hölderlin, Heidegger, and Adorno. *Geschick* is both destiny and address, the fateful skill that is attuned to myths of beginnings and ends. A discussion of *Geschick*, which Adorno invokes some five or six pages into his piece, would no doubt give us the opportunity to place Adorno and Heidegger in the closest possible proximity—at which point their differences would also emerge with the greatest possible clarity. Another time, perhaps. I thank Venkat Mani for his question and Sabine Mödersheim for the many discussions from which, over the years, I have profited so greatly.

17. Hölderlin, *Sämtliche Werke und Briefe*, 1:1033, cf. 1:331.

13. THE EPHEMERAL AND THE ABSOLUTE: PROVISIONAL NOTES TO ADORNO'S *AESTHETIC THEORY*
Peter Uwe Hohendahl

1. A strong restatement of this position we find in Fabio Akcelried Durão, "Adorno Thrice Engaged," *Cultural Critique* 60 (Spring 2005), 261–76.

2. See, for instance, Albrecht Wellmer, *The Persistence of Modernity* (Cambridge, Mass.: MIT Press, 1993); David Roberts, *Art and Enlightenment: Aesthetic Theory after Adorno* (Lincoln and London: University of Nebraska Press, 1991).

3. See, for example, Christoph Menke, *The Sovereignty of Art: Aesthetic Negativity in Adorno and Derrida* (Cambridge, Mass.: MIT Press, 1998); Eva Geulen, "Reconstructing Adorno's 'End of Art,'" *New German Critique* 81 (Autumn 2000), 153–68; and Carsten Strathausen, "Adorno: or, the End of Aesthetics," in *Globalizing Critical Theory*, ed. Max Pensky (Lanham: Rowman and Littlefield, 2005), 221–40.

4. For a discussion of Adorno's position on religion, see John Hughes, "Unspeakable Utopia: Art and the Return to the Theological in the Marxism of Adorno and Horkheimer," *Cross Currents* 53 (Winter 2004), 475–92.

5. J. M. Bernstein, "'The dead speaking of stones and stars': Adorno's *Aesthetic Theory*," in *The Cambridge Companion to Critical Theory*, ed. Fred Rush (New York: Cambridge University Press, 2004), 139–64, here 141.

6. Ibid., 145.

7. Ibid., 146.

8. Ibid., 147.

9. Theodor W. Adorno, *Aesthetic Theory*, trans. Robert Hullot-Kentor (Minneapolis: University of Minnesota Press, 1997), 29; subsequently all quotations from this edition will be cited in parentheses in the text as *AT*.

10. Bernstein, "'The dead speaking of stones and stars': Adorno's *Aesthetic Theory*," 157.

11. See Hohendahl, "Aesthetic Violence: The Concept of the Ugly in Adorno's *Aesthetic Theory,*" *Cultural Critique* 60 (Spring 2005): 170–96.

12. In *Negative Dialectics* Adorno explicates the philosophical problematic of the concept of the absolute. As part of metaphysics the concept has to be thought as part of a system. "Although dialectics allows us to think the absolute, the absolute as transmitted by dialectics remains in bondage to conditioned thinking. If Hegel's absolute was a secularization of the deity, it was still the deity's secularization; even as the totality of mind and spirit, that absolute remained chained to its finite human model"; Adorno, *Negative Dialectics* trans. E. B. Ashton (New York: Continuum, 1973), 405. While the project of metaphysics, as Adorno insists, has failed, the concept of the absolute as a point of reference remains legitimate for the examination of the crisis of modernity and specifically for the reflection on given metaphysical needs.

13. Hidden in an exemplary manner; see Rose Rosengard Subotnik, "Adorno's Diagnosis of Beethoven's Late Style: Early Symptoms of a Fatal Condition," *Journal of the American Musicological Society* 29, no. 2 (Summer 1976): 242–75.

14. Adorno, *Philosophy of Modern Music*, trans. Anne G. Mitchell and Wesley V. Blomster (New York: Seabury Press, 1973), 133.

15. Michael Pauen, *Dithyrambiker des Untergangs: Gnostizismus in Ästhetik und Philosophie der Moderne* (Berlin: Akademie Verlag, 1994), 381.

16. Ibid., 383.

17. From a different perspective Eva Geulen has drawn our attention to the apocalyptic tone in *Dialectic of Enlightenment*. In her discussion of the topic of the end of art she points to the strong similarities between genuine art and the culture industry in the author's description. The supposed opposition collapses in light of the presumed end of history. "The epistemological pattern of this all-encompassing knowledge . . . is grounded in the spectacle of the apocalypse"; Geulen, "Reconstructing Adorno's 'End of Art,'" *New German Critique* 81:160. What is not stressed in Geulen's assessment is the affinity to Gnosis. For this reason she interprets as process what can be read as a fundamental pattern that determines the understanding of empirical reality and the process of history in general. In Gnostic thought the end of history (and by extension art) is already found in its origin. The depravity of the material world can be shown but does not have to be proved in empirical terms.

18. See Pauen, *Dithyrambiker des Untergangs*, 383.

19. Frederic Jameson, *Late Marxism Adorno: or, the Persistence of the Dialectic* (London and New York: Verso, 1990), 1–12.

20. It seems that Geulen, in her attempt to understand the logic of endings in Adorno, merges the aesthetic and the ethical dimension and thereby conflates Adorno's ethical challenge, which was immediately misunderstood by

contemporary critics as a historical indictment, with the intrinsic aesthetic problematic. Adorno's extreme formulations encourage such conflation, since they do not carefully mark the range of their meaningful application; Geulen, "Reconstructing Adorno's 'End of Art,'" *New German Critique* 81:155–56.

21. John Hughes tends to be a rather sympathetic reader of Adorno and Horkheimer's critique of Christianity; he provides a good interpretation of their position, which he defines as Jewish Enlightenment focused on a negative dimension of messianic expectation. Ultimately, however, Hughes means to rescue Christian theology from Adorno's overly negative critique; Hughes, "Unspeakable Utopia: Art and the Return to the Theological," *Cross Currents* 53:430–52).

22. Adorno, *Minima Moralia: Reflections from Damaged Life*, trans. E. F. N. Jephcott (London and New York, Verso 1978), 247.

23. I follow the more accurate translation of the text of *Minima Moralia* by Gerhard Richter in his essay "Aesthetic Theory and Nonpropositional Truth Content in Adorno," in this volume, 137.

24. Ibid.

25. Ibid.

26. Ibid., 141.

APPENDIX. WHO'S AFRAID OF THE IVORY TOWER?
A CONVERSATION WITH THEODOR W. ADORNO
Gerhard Richter

1. Theodor W. Adorno, *Negative Dialektik* (Frankfurt am Main: Suhrkamp, 1975), 15; all translations are my own.

2. Samuel Weber, "Translating the Untranslatable," introduction to Adorno, *Prisms*, trans. Samuel Weber and Shierry Weber (Cambridge, Mass.: MIT Press, 1981), 9–15, here 11f.

3. Robert Hullot-Kentor, "Translator's Introduction," in Adorno, *Aesthetic Theory*, trans. Robert Hullot-Kentor (Minneapolis: University of Minnesota Press, 1997), xi–xxi, here xv.

4. In addition to his "Translator's Introduction" to *Aesthetic Theory*, see also, for instance, his commentary on his retranslation of the Odysseus essay of Horkheimer and Adorno's *Dialectic of Enlightenment*: Hullot-Kentor, "Notes on Dialectic of Enlightenment: Translating the Odysseus Essay," *New German Critique* 56 (Spring–Summer 1992): 101–08.

5. *Der Spiegel*, 5 May 1969, 204–09.

6. It appeared under the title "Of Barricades and Ivory Towers: An Interview with T. W. Adorno," in *Encounter* 33, no. 3 (1969): 63–69.

7. Adorno, *Vermischte Schriften* 1, in *Gesammelte Schriften* (Frankfurt am Main: Suhrkamp, 1986), 20: 402–09.

8. Habermas first used this term in a discussion at the 1967 conference on "Bedingungen und Organisation des Widerstands" ["Conditions and Organization of Resistance"] in Hannover. Specifically, he accused student leader Rudi Dutschke of an ideology that "under today's condition—at least I believe to have reason to suggest this terminology—one must call 'left-wing fascism'" ["'linken Faschismus' nennen muß"]. Today, Habermas's remarks, along with others he made in the context of the Protest Movement, can be found in Jürgen Habermas, *Kleine Politische Schriften*, vols. 1–4 (Frankfurt am Main: Suhrkamp, 1981), 199–307, here 214.

9. Daniel Cohn-Bendit, today a Green Party member of the European Parliament, was one of the most influential and charismatic figures in the Protest Movement in both Germany and France. For book-length articulations of Cohn-Bendit's views on political activism in the context of the Protest Movement, see Daniel Cohn-Bendit and Gabriel Cohn-Bendit, *Linksradikalismus: Gewaltkur gegen die Alterskrankheit des Kommunismus* (Reinbek: Rowohlt, 1968), and, more recently, Daniel Cohn-Bendit, *Wir haben sie so geliebt: Die Revolution* (Bodenheim: Philo.-Verlag, 1998).

Adorno's letter has been made available in the comprehensive three-volume collection of documents *Frankfurter Schule und Studentenbewegung: Von der Flaschenpost zum Molotowcoctail 1946–1995*, ed. Wolfgang Kraushaar (Frankfurt am Main: Roger und Bernhard bei Zweitausendeins, 1998), 2:624–25, here 624. This collection also contains a series of interesting essays by a variety of scholars on the relationship between the Student Movement and the Frankfurt School. For more general assessments of the German Student Movement, see, among others, Gerhard Bauß, *Die Studentenbewegung der sechziger Jahre in der Bundesrebublik und Westberlin: Ein Handbuch* (Cologne: Pahl-Rugenstein, 1977) and *Provokation: Die Studenten- und Jugendrevolte in ihren Flugblättern 1965–1971*, ed. Jürgen Miermeister and Jochen Staadt (Darmstadt: Luchterhand, 1980).

10. "Gegen die Notstandsgesetze," *Vermischte Schriften* 1, in *Gesammelte Schriften*, 20:396–97.

11. Adorno's letter is reproduced in *Frankfurter Schule und Studentenbewegung*, 472–74, here 474.

12. The essays can be found in his *Kulturkritik und Gesellschaft* 2, in *Gesammelte Schriften*, 10:794–99, 759–82, respectively. The interview with *Süddeutsche Zeitung* can be found in *Vermischte Schriften* 1, in *Gesammelte Schriften* 20:398–401.

13. Adorno, *Aufarbeitung der Vergangenheit: Reden und Gespräche*, selected and with an accompanying text by Rolf Tiedemann, 5 Compact Disks (Munich: Der HörVerlag, 1999).

14. "SDS" is an abbreviation of *Sozialistischer Deutscher Studentenbund* [Socialist German Students' Union], founded in 1946 with the support of West Germany's Social Democratic Party (SPD) and dissolved in 1970.

15. The critic in question is Ralf Dahrendorf, the German-born British sociologist and former FDP (Free Democratic Party) politician. The controversy between Adorno and Dahrendorf regarding the relationship between theory and praxis took place in Frankfurt in April 1968 at the *Deutscher Soziologentag*, the conference of German sociologists, where Adorno had held the opening keynote address on "Late Capitalism or Industrial Society?" The following day, Dahrendorf responded critically to Adorno's lecture with his own presentation, initiating an intense debate. Dahrendorf's and Adorno's papers, along with their discussions, are documented in the conference's published proceedings, *Spätkapitalismus oder Industriegesellschaft? Verhandlungen des 16. Soziologentages*, in *Auftrag der Deutschen Gesellschaft für Soziologie herausgeben von Theodor W. Adorno* (Stuttgart: Elms, 1969).

16. Adorno here alludes to his conviction, expressed most memorably in *Minima Moralia*: "There is no right life within the wrong one [*Es gibt kein richtiges Leben im falschen*]; Adorno, *Minima Moralia* (Frankfurt am Main: Suhrkamp, 1969), 42.

17. Among other things, Adorno here alludes to Baudelaire's initial support of the 1848 revolution that initiated France's Second Republic and his later retreat from political life following his disenchantment with that revolution's results.

18. The implicit reference here is to Lenin's famous 1902 meditation on "What Is to Be Done?"; see Vladimir I. Lenin, *What Is to Be Done?* trans. S. V. Utechin and Patricia Utechin, ed. S. V. Utechin (Oxford: Claredon, 1963).

19. Adorno here refers to the so-called *Positivismusstreit* [Positivism debate] in which he was engaged, arguing against what he perceived as uncritical, positivistic sociological paradigms like those propagated by Karl Popper and Alphons Silbermann; see especially Adorno et.al., *Der Positivismusstreit in der deutschen Soziologie* (Neuwied: Luchterhand, 1969).

20. I have rendered Adorno's German term *"Aktionismus"* as the somewhat strange-sounding English term "actionism" in order to preserve in the neologism his critical emphasis on the ideological dimension of a belief that favors action and intervention at all cost and with dogmatic fervor.

21. Adorno here evokes the May 1968 events in France, during which Paris was subjected to violent police oppression following a series of strikes and an attempted general revolt, in which many French intellectuals, among them Jean-Paul Sartre, Michel Foucault, and Jacques Derrida, had taken part. In the wake of bloody street battles and civil war–like unrest, Charles de Gaulle dissolved the French National Assembly and instigated new parliamentary elections.

22. The original sentence quoted by Adorno reads *"Denn nichts als nur Verzweiflung kann uns retten."* Such formulations were often used, in different

variations, by the early nineteenth-century dramatist Christian Dietrich Grabbe in such plays as *Herzog Theodor von Gothland, Die Hermannsschlacht,* and *Marius und Sulla*. They are often considered "nihilistic."

23. Implicitly, Adorno here also alludes to others on the Left, such as Georg Lukács, who had risked his life in the 1956 Hungarian uprising and who had faulted Adorno for valorizing despair as a politically productive category. In July 1962, Lukács had in the new introduction to his *Theory of the Novel* explicitly singled out Adorno for criticism: "A good part of the leading German intelligentsia, among them Adorno, has moved into the 'Grand Hotel Abyss,' a 'beautiful hotel,' as I wrote on the occasion of my critique of Schopenhauer, 'equipped with all amenities at the edge of the abyss, nothingness, and meaninglessness. And the daily sight of this abyss, in between cozily enjoyed meals or artistic products, can only enhance the pleasure of this refined comfort"; Lukács, *Die Theorie des Romans* (Darmstadt: Luchterhand, 1984), 16.

24. The essay in question is Habermas's 1969 "Protestbewegung und Hochschulreform" [Protest Movement and university reform], now collected in his *Kleine Politische Schriften*, vols. 1–4 (Frankfurt am Main: Suhrkamp, 1981), 265–303. Habermas speaks of the students' *"phantasiereichen Provokationismus"* on page 284.

25. At stake in this university reform was a far-reaching democratization of the academic system in the Federal Republic. One of the most pervasive slogans associated with the reform movement was the students' assessment of their professors: *"Unter den Talaren—der Muff von 1,000 Jahren"* ["Under their robes—the smell of 1,000 years"]. One of the earliest and most influential publications that helped to set the reform movement into motion was Georg Picht, *Die deutsche Bildungskatastrophe* (Olten: Walter Verlag, 1964).

26. The student Benno Ohnesorg was shot and killed on 2 June 1967 in Berlin during a demonstration against the visit by Shah Risa Pehlewi of Persia, who had crushed democratic uprisings and who had come to stand as a symbol for political oppression.

27. Germany's Springer Publishing House is considered by many to have a conservative or even right-wing agenda. It is the publisher of Germany's most widely read daily, the tabloid *Bild-Zeitung*, and of newspapers such as *Die Welt* and *Die Welt am Sonntag*. In fact, there was an extensive grassroots anti-Springer campaign, and members of the APO, along with writers such as Hans Magnus Enzensberger and Peter Schneider, conducted the so-called Springer-Hearings in West Berlin from September 1967 through April 1968. During these Springer tribunals led by students and intellectuals, one of the most memorable slogans was *"Bild schießt mit"* ["*Bild* shoots along," or "*Bild* shoots as well"].

28. It should be noted that Marcuse, who played an active role both in the U.S. and in West Germany during the revolts, later took exception to Adorno's characterization of his stance. As Marcuse writes to Adorno on 4 June 1969, about a month after the *Spiegel* interview appeared: "You know that you and I both reject any unmediated politicization of theory. But our (old) theory has an inner political content, an inner political dynamic, which today more than ever pushes toward a concrete political position. This does not mean giving 'practical advice,' as you claim of me in your *Spiegel* interview. I have never done that. Like you, I find it irresponsible to encourage, from one's desk, action in those who, in full awareness, are prepared to have their heads smashed in the service of the cause. But this means, in my view, that in order for us to remain our 'old' Institute, we must write and act differently than we did thirty years ago. Even undamaged theory is not immune to reality. While it is wrong to negate the difference between the two (as you justly accuse the students), it is just as wrong to hold on abstractly to this difference in its previous form, if it changes in a reality that comprises (or opens up) both theory and praxis"; *Frankfurter Schule und Studentenbewegung*, 649–50.

29. In his discussion of the division of labor, Adorno is presumably referring, on the one hand, to the early Marx's *Pariser Manuskript*, which criticizes the division of labor, and, on the other hand, to the later Marx of the third volume of *Das Kapital*, in which he juxtaposes, more pragmatically, what he names "the realm of freedom" and "the realm of necessity"; Karl Marx, *Das Kapital* (Berlin: Dietz, 1987), 3:828.

30. See note 1.

31. *Spiegel* is quoting from Habermas's 1963 essay on Adorno, "Ein philosophierender Intellektueller." There, Habermas worries that the "dialectic of enlightenment," "at its blackest spots" ["*an ihren schwärzesten Stellen*"] "despairs in light of its final turnover." In that case, Habermas writes, the "dialectic of enlightenment" resigns itself to the thesis of the "counter-enlightenment," which argues that horror cannot be abolished without also the obliteration of civilization itself. In this scenario, the dialectic of which Habermas speaks would "surrender to the destructive pull of the death drive" ["*überläßt sie sich dem destruktiven Sog des Todestriebs*"]. But because Habermas does not italicize or put into quotation marks the phrase "dialectic of enlightenment," it cannot be decided for certain whether he means Adorno and Horkheimer's specific work by that name or the actual dialectic that is at play in the enlightenment. This is an important difference that the *Spiegel* ignores. By foreclosing the double reading that Habermas's passage enables, the question misses the opportunity to conceive of this undecidability as the very *enactment* of the dialectical structure that it addresses; Habermas, "*Ein philosophierender Intellektueller*," in his *Philosophisch-Politische Profile*, enlarged edition (Frankfurt

am Main: Suhrkamp, 1987), 160–66, here 165. Be that as it may, we might note that Habermas's reference to the death drive [*"Todestrieb"*] is overdetermined in that it also evokes the Freudian elements in Adorno's philosophy. Compare further, for instance, Freud's elaborations on the death drive in Sigmund Freud, *Das Ich und das Es* (1923), in his *Studienausgabe* (Frankfurt am Main: Fischer, 2000), 3:273–330. Adorno shared with the rest of the Frankfurt School an interest in the development of a new Critical Theory founded on an innovative constellation of the theories of Hegel, Marx, and Freud.

32. The reference here is to the eleventh of Marx's "Thesen über Feuerbach": "The philosophers have only *interpreted* the world in different ways; the point is to *change* it [*Die Philosophen haben die Welt nur verschieden* interpretiert; *es kömmt darauf an, sie zu* verändern]"; Karl Marx and Friedrich Engels, *Werke* (Berlin: Dietz, 1987), 3:7. The *Spiegel* interviewer seems to miss the point—already implied in Marx's own perspective—that for a change of the world to occur, this change must be based on a prior interpretation or reinterpretation of the world and the ideologies that traverse it. This interpretation is the task of philosophical inquiry.

For Adorno's own reflections on the relation between theory and praxis in the context of a negative dialectics that perpetuates and transforms the projects of Kant, Hegel, and Marx, see the "Einleitung" to Adorno, *Negative Dialektik*, 13–66.

33. Following a coup d'état by the Greek army on 21 June 1967 under the leadership of General Gregorius Spandidakis, a military regime was installed and democratic politicians were arrested. Constantine Kollias became Greece's new prime minister. In December, Colonel Georgias Papadopoulos became Greece's new prime minister and, beginning one year later, its de facto dictator. Greece began to return to democratic conditions in late 1973.

34. This work, which remained unfinished at the time of Adorno's death in August 1969, was published posthumously one year later as *Ästhetische Theorie* under the editorship of Adorno's widow, Gretel Adorno, and his student Rolf Tiedemann; Adorno, *Ästhetische Theorie* (Frankfurt am Main: Suhrkamp, 1970).

CONTRIBUTORS

J. M. BERNSTEIN is University Distinguished Professor of Philosophy at The New School for Social Research. Among his recent books are *Against Voluptuous Bodies: Adorno's Late Modernism and the Meaning of Painting* (2007); *Classical and Romantic German Aesthetics* (editor, 2002); *Adorno: Disenchantment and Ethics* (2002); *Beyond Representation* (1996); *Recovering Ethical Life: Jürgen Habermas and the Future of Critical Theory* (1995); and *The Fate of Art: Aesthetic Alienation from Kant to Derrida and Adorno* (1992).

ALEXANDER GARCÍA DÜTTMANN teaches philosophy at Goldsmiths Collge, University of London. His recent publications include: *Philosophy Of Exaggeration* (Frankfurt: Suhrkamp, 2004; London and New York: Continuum, 2007), *That's It: A Philosophical Commentary On Adorno's "Minima Moralia"* (Frankfurt: Suhrkamp, 2004), *Erase The Traces* (Berlin and Zurich: Diaphanes, 2004), *Visconti: Insights Into Flesh And Blood* (Berlin: Kadmos 2006; Stanford: Stanford University Press, 2008) and *Derrida And I: The Problem Of Deconstruction* (Bielefeld: Transcript, 2008).

JAIMEY FISHER is Associate Professor of German at the University of California, Davis. He is the author of *Disciplining German: Youth, Reeducation, and Reconstruction after the Second World War* (Wayne State University, 2007) and co-editor of *Critical Theory: Current State and Future Prospects* (Berghahn, 2001). He is currently co-editing *Collapse of the Conventional: German Cinema and its Politics at the Turn of the New Century* as well as *Spatial Turns: Space, Place, and Mobilty in German Literary and Visual Culture*.

PETER UWE HOHENDAHL is Jacob Gould Schurman Professor of German and Comparative Literature at Cornell University. Among his books are *Literaturkritik und Öffentlichkeit* (1974); *The Institution of Criticism* (1982); *A History of German Literary Criticism* (ed., 1988); *Building a National Literature: The Case of Germany 1830–1870* (1989); *Reappraisals: Shifting Alliances in Postwar Critical Theory* (1991); *Geschichte, Opposition, Subversion: Studien zur Literatur des 19. Jahrhunderts* (1993); *Prismatic Thought:*

Theodor W. Adorno (1995); *German Studies in the United States: A Historical Handbook* (2003); and *Heinrich Heine: Europäischer Schriftsteller und Intellektueller* (2008).

ERIC JAROSINSKI is Assistant Professor of German at the University of Pennsylvania. He has published on figures such as Theodor W. Adorno, Walter Benjamin, Siegfried Kracauer, and Vladimr Nabokov. He is finishing a book on the rhetoric of "transparency" as well as co-editing a collection on reading and touch, *The Hand of the Interpreter*.

MARTIN JAY is Sidney Hellman Ehrman Professor of History at the University of California, Berkeley. Among his works are *The Dialectical Imagination* (1973 and 1996); *Marxism and Totality* (1984); *Adorno* (1984); *Permanent Exiles* (1985); *Fin-de-Siècle Socialism* (1989); *Force Fields* (1993); *Downcast Eyes* (1993); *Cultural Semantics* (l998); *Refractions of Violence* (2003) and *Songs of Experience* (2004). *The Virtues of Mendacity: On Lying In Politics* will be published in 2010.

THERESA M. KELLEY is Marjorie and Lorin Tiefenthaler Professor of English at University of Wisconsin, Madison. She is the author of *Wordsworth's Revisionary Aesthetics* (Cambridge, 1988), co-editor with Paula Feldman of *Voices and Countervoices: Romantic Women Writers* (New England, 1995), and *Reinventing Allegory* (Cambridge, 1997), awarded the South Central Modern Language Association award for best scholarly book, and many essays on Romantic poetics, aesthetics, visual culture and philosophy, including work on John Keats, Mary Shelley, Charlotte Smith, Percy Shelley, Blake, Hegel, Goethe and Theodor W. Adorno. Her current book project is *Clandestine Marriage: Botany and Romantic Culture*, for which she is the recipient of fellowships from The Henry E. Huntington Library and Art Gallery, the Yale Center for British Art, National Endowment for the Humanities and the John D. Simon Guggenheim Foundation.

DAVID FARRELL KRELL is Professor of Philosophy at DePaul University in Chicago and guest professor at the University of Freiburg, Germany. Recent books include *The Tragic Absolute: German Idealism and the Languishing of God* (Indiana University Press, 2005), *The Purest of Bastards: Works of Mourning, Art, and Affirmation in the Thought of Jacques Derrida* (Pennsylvania State University Press, 2000), and *Contagion: Sexuality, Disease, and Death in German Idealism and Romanticism* (Indiana University Press, 1998). Recently published by SUNY Press is his translation, in a critical edition, of Friedrich Hölderlin, *The Death of Empedocles: A Mourning-Play* (2008).

NEIL LARSEN is Professor of Comparative Literature at the University of California, Davis. He is the author of *Modernism and Hegemony* (University of Minnesota Press, 1990); *Reading North by South: On Latin American Literature, Culture and Politics* (University of Minnesota Press, 1995); and *Determinations: Essays on Theory, Nation and Narrative in the Americas* (Verso, 2001).

JAN PLUG is Associate Professor of English at the University of Western Ontario and also a core member of the Centre for the Study of Theory and Criticism and the program in Comparative Literature. He is the author of *Borders of a Lip: Romanticism, Language, History, Politics* (SUNY Press, 2003) and translator, among other works, of two books by Jacques Derrida, *Who's Afraid of Philosophy?: Right to Philosophy 1* (Stanford University Press, 2002) and (with others) *Eyes of the University: Right to Philosophy 2* (Stanford University Press, 2004).

GERHARD RICHTER is Professor of German and Director of the Graduate Program in Critical Theory at the University of California, Davis. He is the author of *Thought-Images: Frankfurt School Writers' Reflections from Damaged Life* (Stanford University Press, 2007); *Ästhetik des Ereignisses. Sprache—Geschichte—Medium* (Wilhelm Fink Verlag, 2005); and *Walter Benjamin and the Corpus of Autobiography* (Wayne State University Press, 2000; 2nd. ed. 2002). His edited volumes include *Sound Figures of Modernity: German Music and Philosophy*, co-edited with Jost Hermand (University of Wisconsin Press, 2006); *Literary Paternity, Literary Friendship* (University of North Carolina Press, 2002); and *Benjamin's Ghosts: Interventions in Contemporary Literary and Cultural Theory* (Stanford University Press, 2002). His *Afterness: Figures of Following in Modern Thought and Aesthetics* is forthcoming.

ROBERT SAVAGE is ARC Postdoctoral Fellow at the Centre for Comparative Literature and Cultural Studies, Monash University (Australia). He is the author of *Hölderlin after the Catastrophe* (Camden House, 2008), and has published widely in the fields of Critical Theory, literary studies, and opera studies. His translation of Hans Blumenberg's *Paradigms for a Metaphorology* is forthcoming.

MIRKO WISCHKE is Visiting Professor of Philosophy at Taras Shevchenko National University (Kiev, Ukraine). He is the author of *A Critique of the Ethics of Obedience: On the Problem of Morality in the Works of Theodor W.*

Adorno (Peter Lang, 1993); *The Birth of Ethics: Schopenhauer, Nietzsche, and Adorno* (Akademie Verlag Berlin, 1994), *The Weakness of Writing: On the Philosophical Hermeneutics of Hans-Georg Gadamer* (Böhlau Verlag, 2001). His numerous edited volumes include, among others, *Impulse and Negativity: Adorno's Ethics and Aesthetics*, co-edited with Gerhard Schweppenhäuser (Argument Verlag, 1995) and *Gadamer verstehen. Understanding Gadamer*, co-edited with Michael Hofer (Wissenschaftliche Buchgesellschaft Darmstadt, 2003. His books *Law without Justice? Hegel and the Foundation of the Law-Based State*, co-edited with Andrzej Przylebski (Königshausen & Neumann Verlag) and *Freedom without Law? Politics and Law in the Age of Globalization* (Peter Lang Verlag) are forthcoming.

INDEX

Adorno, Gretel, 179
Alexander, Jeffrey, 48–49, 250n38, 250n43
Allemann, Beda, 203
Alt, Peter-André, 279n40
Andersen, Hans Christian, 277n25
Arendt, Hannah, 49–50, 248n9, 250n42, 251n12, 259n33, 259n34

Bach, Johann Sebastian, 22, 25–26, 244n32
Bataille, Georges, 108, 265n26
Batnitsky, Leora, 245n37
Baudelaire, Charles, 4, 233, 280n44, 289n17
Bauer, Karl, 82
Bauß, Gerhard, 288–89n9
Becker, Hellmut, 96–97
Beckett, Samuel, 3, 133, 191, 203
Beethoven, Ludwig van, 3, 104, 112, 131–32, 175, 190–94, 203, 218, 271n20
Beißner, Friedrich, 180, 193, 199, 277n16
Bell, Daniel, 116, 267n53
Benjamin, Andrew, 242n10 250n1
Benjamin, Walter, 2, 4–5, 18–24, 27, 29, 109, 112, 129, 138, 152–53, 156, 182–89, 195, 199–202, 205, 220, 239, 242n9, 242n10, 243n12, 243n14, 243n15, 243n21, 244n23, 244n25, 245n37, 246n54, 246n55, 246n56, 270n10, 273n18, 273n22, 277n22, 278n37, 279n40, 280n42, 280n44, 280n46, 280n49, 281n51, 281n58, 281n70, 282n73, 284n8
Benveniste, Émile, 252n17
Berg, Alban, 4, 134
Berman, Marshall, 17–18, 281n2
Bernard, Andreas, 271n18
Bernatzki, Axel, 274n5

Bernstein, J. M., 8, 78, 85, 91, 96, 174, 208–11, 239n1, 247n4, 257n7, 257n8, 261n46, 261n51, 261n52, 261n54, 262n3, 271n26, 276n6, 276n8
Binder, Wolfgang, 193, 278n38, 282n87
Blake, William, 102, 104
Blanchot, Maurice, 199, 203, 284n7, 285n14
Bloch, Ernst, 4, 220, 228
Bodemann, Y. Michal, 260n39
Bollnow, Otto Friedrich, 24
Borchardt, Rudolf, 110
Böschenstein, Bernhard, 136
Böttcher, Karl Wilhelm, 259n32
Bourdieu, Pierre, 207
Bovenschen, Silvia, 254n42
Brandt, Willy, 229, 231
Brecht, Bertolt, 4, 27, 182
Brunkhorst, Hauke, 269n5
Buber, Martin, 18, 245n37
Bubner, Rüdiger, 133, 269n6
Buchdahl, Gerd, 262n5
Buck-Morss, Susan, 252n24
Buonarroti, Michelangelo, 190
Burdorf, Dieter, 277n16
Burke, Donald A., 247n3
Butler, Judith, 43, 78, 85, 98, 239n1, 249n25, 257n7, 261n51, 262n59

Cahn, Michael, 254n44
Campbell, Colin J., 247n3
Caruth, Cathy, 251n11
Caygill, Howard, 242n10
Claussen, Detlev, 29, 239n1, 246n55
Cohn-Bendit, Daniel, 229, 288n9
Cohn-Bendit, Gabriel, 288n9
Confino, Alon, 256n2, 260n39
Cook, Deborah, 247n3, 247n6

Dahlhaus, Carl, 280n43
Dahrendorf, Ralf, 233, 289n15

Dallmayr, Fred, 277n18
Daston, Lorraine, 262n4
De Man, Paul, 17, 241n1, 253n30, 255n56
Demnig, Gunter, 5, 240n15
Derrida, Jacques, 63, 132, 196, 254n36, 254n44, 283n3, 283n5, 290n21
Descartes, René, 69, 101
Dews, Peter, 248n10, 250n1
Dirks, Walter, 258n15
Drees, Martin, 262n5
Dubiel, Helmut, 50, 250n43
Durão, Fabio Akcelried, 285n1
Dutschke, Rudi, 288n8
Düttmann, Alexander García, 7, 99, 239n1, 253n27, 254n42, 262n2, 275n26

Eichel, Christine, 269n5
Eichmann, Adolf, 49
El Greco, 190
Eliot, T. S., 278n38
Emrich, Wilhelm, 229
Enzensberger, Hans Magnus, 291n27

Fenves, Peter, 242n10
Fisher, Jaimey, 8, 257n10
Foster, Sir Norman, 157
Foucault, Michel, 207, 290n21
Frank, Anne, 49
Fraser, Nancy, 32, 37–40, 248n17
Freud, Sigmund, 2, 17–18, 88, 90, 196, 241n3, 292n31
Friedburg, Ludwig von, 276n9
Froment-Meurice, Marc, 277n18
Früchtl, Josef, 254n44
Fulton, Ann, 242n5

Gadamer, Hans-Georg, 149–51, 272n8, 283n3
Gaita, Raimond, 13–14, 240n7
Gamboni, Dario Libero, 159
Gasché, Rodolphe, 252n17, 255n56, 255n60
de Gaulle, Charles, 290n21
George, Stefan, 4, 108, 177
Geras, Norman, 247n4
Gerst, Wilhelm Karl, 258n15
Geulen, Eva, 20, 243n20
Gibson, Nigel, 246n50, 282n75
Gillespie, Susan H., 192
Glaser, Hermann, 82

Goethe, Johann Wolfgang, 16, 107, 180, 190, 196, 230, 265n23
Göpfert, Claus-Jürgen, 274n8, 274n10
Grabbe, Christian Dietrich, 235, 290n22
Grass, Günter, 231
Grasskamp, Walter, 159
Grossman, Henryk, 116
Guignon, Charles, 242n6
Gumbrecht, Hans Ulrich, 136
Gurland, Arkady, 116

Habermas, Jürgen, 32, 34–37, 40–42, 46, 206, 223, 229, 235, 237, 247n1, 248n22, 249n23, 276n9, 288n8, 290n24, 292n31
Hacking, Ian, 262n4
Hamacher, Werner, 252n16
Hammer, Espen, 247n3
Hansen, Miriam, 254n44
Hartman, Geoffrey, 18, 242n6
Hegel, Georg Wilhelm Friedrich, 8, 21, 32–33, 39–40, 43, 46, 62, 99–116, 117, 120, 123, 126, 145, 149, 151, 156, 180, 187, 196, 198, 210, 212–13, 217, 221, 253n33, 262n1, 262n5, 264n7, 263n9, 264n11, 265n21, 265n22, 265n23, 265n25, 265n27, 266n28, 266n29, 266n30, 266n36, 266n37, 266n42, 266n43, 266n46, 266n47, 266n49, 267n50, 267n1, 284n6, 292n31, 292n32
Heidegger, Martin, 8, 18–19, 24–25, 28, 131, 145, 173–79, 181–82, 193, 195–99, 203, 205, 210, 239n1, 242n10, 242n11, 269n2, 272n30, 277n25, 278n38, 283n3, 283n4, 284n6, 285n16
Heinemann, Gustav, 231
Hellingrath, Norbert von, 203, 277n16, 278n31
Herf, Jeffrey, 256n2
Heß, Jürgen, 258n24
Hewitt, Andrew, 250n6, 252n22, 255n49
Hirsch, Emanuel, 177
Hirsch, Michael, 274n11
Hitler, Adolf, 47, 90–91, 170, 235
Hobbes, Thomas, 247n4
Hocking, William E., 256n4
Hoffmeister, Johannes, 263n5
Hohendahl, Peter Uwe, 8, 77, 95–96, 251n13, 253n31, 253n34, 256n3, 260n39, 260n43, 261n53
Hölderlin, Friedrich, 4, 8, 100–5, 112, 131, 134–35, 172–94, 195–205,

265n14, 270n13, 278n28, 278n31,
  278n32, 278n34, 278n38, 281n52,
  281n55, 284n6, 284n9, 284n10,
  285n14, 285n15, 285n17
Honneth, Axel, 32–42, 45–46, 248n7,
  248n10, 248n13, 248n16, 248n17,
  248n20, 248n21, 249n27, 249n30
Honold, Alexander, 279n40
Hörisch, Jochen, 239n1
Horkheimer, Max, 15, 33–34, 52–74, 82,
  116, 118, 124–26, 132, 136, 148, 162,
  229, 230, 234, 241n10, 244n26, 250n2,
  250n5, 250n6, 251n13, 251n14,
  253n25, 253n28, 253n32, 253n35,
  254n37, 254n43, 255n45, 255n51,
  255n53, 255n58, 255n61, 258n25,
  264n11, 267n3, 268n23, 268n26,
  275n18, 277n22, 280n50, 288n4
Hotho, H. G., 266n36
Hubert, Henri, 60
Huhn, Tom, 245n47, 248n6, 255n50,
  271n27, 276n2, 276n8
Hullot-Kentor, Robert, 25, 224, 228,
  288n3, 288n4
Husserl, Edmund, 23–24, 192, 282n83

Ibsen, Henrik, 21
Inwood, Michael, 242n11
Irigaray, Luce, 283n5

Jäger, Lorenz, 239n1
Jameson, Fredric, 55–56, 223, 251n10,
  251n13, 253n34, 254n44
Jarvis, Simon, 136, 247n3, 249n31,
  250n6, 254n39, 254n44, 270n17
Jaspers, Karl, 18, 24, 78, 80, 84–86, 89,
  258n16, 259n33, 259n34, 260n35
Jay, Martin, 8, 99, 244n25, 245n37,
  246n56, 255n50, 262n2
Jimenez, Marc, 254n44
Jung, Carl, 212
Jünger, Ernst, 96

Kafka, Franz, 5, 240n13
Kant, Immanuel, 12, 21, 35, 55–58, 63,
  97, 106, 112, 127, 145, 150–52, 196,
  208, 213, 217–18, 246n55, 247n4,
  251n11, 252n21, 254n36, 262n58,
  271n27, 272n15, 278n38, 292n32
Kaufman, Robert, 271n27
Kelley, Theresa M., 8, 264n6, 283n2
Kellner, Douglas, 27, 246n50

Kenyon, Nicholas, 245n46
Kierkegaard, Søren, 18, 21–24, 176–78,
  242n10
Kiesinger, Kurt Georg, 229
Kiloh, Kathy, 247n3
Kirchheimer, Otto, 116
Klages, Ludwig, 212
Kojève, Alexandre, 198
Kollias, Constantine, 293n33
Kompridis, Nikolas, 248n20
Kopperschmidt, Josef, 272n6
Koselleck, Reinhard, 112, 266n45
Kracauer, Siegfried, 4, 24, 245n37,
  246n56, 254n44
Kraus, Karl, 4, 184
Krell, David Farrell, 8, 107, 262n5,
  265n22, 283n5
Krenek, Ernst, 245n47
Kurz, Robert, 126

Lacoue-Labarthe, Philippe, 69, 204,
  244n25, 255n50, 277n24, 281n56,
  284n6, 285n14
Le Corbusier (Charles-Édouard Jeanne-
  ret-Gris), 168
Leach, Neil, 275n40
Lenin, Vladimir I., 289n18
Lenoir, Timothy, 265n23
Lepenies, Wolf, 136
Leppert, Richard, 280n44
Lévi-Strauss, Claude, 132
Lévinas, Emmanuel, 204
Lindner, Burkhardt, 269n6
Lohoff, Ernst, 126
Loos, Adolf, 168
Lowenthal, Leo, 116
Lucas, George R., Jr., 263n5
Lucas, Hans-Christian, 263n5
Lüdke, W. Martin, 269n6
Lüdtke, Alf, 256n2
Luhmann, Niklas, 206–7
Lukács, György 124, 219, 290n23
Lyotard, Jean-François 2, 251n15

Mani, Venkat, 285n16
Mann, Thomas, 82
Marcuse, Herbert, 116, 135, 220, 236,
  291n28
Margolis, Joseph, 13–14, 240n3
Marx, Karl, 33–34, 45–46, 108, 120–28,
  135, 145, 208, 219, 221, 236, 245n15,
  248l3, 249n30, 249n33, 268n11,

268n13, 268n17, 269n30, 271n27, 291n29, 292n31, 292n32
Mauss, Marcel, 60
Mcdonald, Iain, 239n1
McPherson, C. B., 245n40
Meinecke, Friedrich, 92
Menke, Cristoph, 135, 247n6, 270n16, 282n84
Menninghaus, Winfried, 187, 281n60
Merleau-Ponty, Maurice, 278n38
Michelangelo. *See* Buonarroti.
Michels, Claudia, 274n1, 274n6
Miermeister, Jürgen, 288n9
Miller, Elaine P., 107–8, 262n5, 265n23, 265n24, 265n25, 265n26
Miller, J. Hillis, 134, 270n9
Mirbach, Thomas, 251n13
Mitscherlich, Alexander, 88
Mödersheim, Sabine, 283n2, 285n16
Moeller, Robert, 256n2, 260n39
Müller, Vanessa Joan, 274n11
Müller-Doohm, Stefan, 79, 239n1, 257n9, 258n25, 270n10
Müller-Lauter, Wolfgang 272n11
Muschg, Walter, 195
Musil, Robert, 4

Naimark, Norman, 80, 257n12
Nancy, Jean-Luc, 252n18, 255n52, 262n1
Napoleon I (Napoleon Bonaparte), 109
Nehamas, Alexander, 18, 242n6
Neumann, Franz L., 116
Neumann, Gerhard, 136
Nicholsen, Shierry Weber, 108, 265n27, 266n35
Niemöller, Martin, 82–83, 259n27
Nietzsche, Friedrich, 4, 17–18, 21–22, 24, 36, 46, 122, 132, 138, 149–51, 252n16, 272n9, 272n10
Novalis, 132, 203, 284n13

Ohnesorg, Benno, 235, 291n26
Osborne, Peter, 242n10

Paddison, Max, 29, 245n47, 246n53
Palamarek, Michael K., 247n3
Papadopoulos, Georgias, 292n33
Pascal, Blaise, 36
Pauen, Michael, 220–23
Pehlewi, Risa, 291n26
Pensky, Max, 271n26
Petry, Michael John, 262n5

Picht, Georg, 290n25
Pizer, John, 243n14, 244n32
Plass, Ulrich, 241n12
Plato, 133, 149, 151, 242n6, 243n14, 253n33
Plessner, Helmuth, 249n23
Polanyi, Karl, 244n22
Pollock, Friedrich, 116, 124
Popper, Karl, 290n19
Postone, Moishe, 124–26, 129, 268n18, 268n21, 269n30
Proust, Marcel, 3

Rabinbach, Anson, 78, 254n44, 258n24n 259n34
Rancière, Jacques, 249n34
Raulff, Ulrich, 271n18
Rehmann, Heiko, 274n7, 274n9
Rembrandt, 190
Ricardo, David, 121–22, 126
Richter, Gerhard, 225, 240n11, 243n20, 244n23, 256n1, 257n6, 265n18, 283n2
Rieff, Philip, 241n3
Ritter, Gerhard, 261n55
Roberts, David, 282n80
Rosenzweig, Franz, 245n37
Rothberg, Michael, 260n39
Rousseau, Jean-Jacques, 17–18
Rubin, Andrew, 246n50, 282n75
Rush, Fred, 249n27

Said, Edward, 239n1, 282n75
Sartre, Jean-Paul, 4, 17–18, 241n3, 290n21
Sattler, Dietrich, 277n16
Schafhausen, Nicolaus, 274n11
Schelling, F. W. J., 107, 112, 262n5
Schiller, Friedrich, 47, 197
Schmucker, Joseph F., 251n13
Schneider, Peter, 291n27
Scholz, Roswitha, 126
Scholze, Britta, 282n73
Schönberg, Arnold, 3–4, 133, 191
Schopenhauer, Arthur, 21, 189, 244n27
Schubert, Franz, 241n11
Schulte-Sasse, Jochen, 253n30
Schultz, Karla L., 254n44
Schweppenhäuser, Gerhard, 247n6, 269n29, 269n5
Seel, Martin, 276n7
Shapiro, Jeremy J., 108, 265n27
Sherratt, Yvonne, 246n6

Short, Jonathan, 247n3
Siegel, Elke, 271n20
Silbermann, Alphons, 290n19
Sloterdijk, Peter, 178, 277n23
Smith, Adam, 121–22
Sohn-Rethel, Alfred, 127
Sonnemann, Ulrich, 24
Sophocles, 199, 204, 281n55
Spandidakis, Gregorius, 292n33
Spariosu, Mihai, 254n44
Staadt, Jochen, 288n9
Staiger, Emil, 200–1, 278n38
Stalin, Josef, 235
Stravinsky, Igor, 23
Szondi, Peter, 180, 203, 229, 278n31

Taylor, Charles, 241n3
Tent, James, 258n22
Teufel, Fritz, 230
Thyen, Anke, 251n13
Tiedemann, Rolf, 179, 248n8, 276n2
Trakl, Georg, 198–99

Trenkle, Norbert, 126–30, 268n23, 269n29
Trilling, Lionel, 17, 241n3, 242n4

Vieillard-Baron, Jean-Louis, 262n5

Wagner, Richard, 22, 183, 185, 189, 280n44, 281n69
Weber, Max, 34, 248n13
Weber, Samuel, 164, 227, 275n25, 288n2
Weissberg, Liliane, 271n20
Wellmer, Albrecht, 276n9
Wheatland, Thomas, 267n53
Wischke, Mirko, 269n5, 272n1
Wittgenstein, Ludwig, 14, 240n8
Wolgast, Eike, 258n24

Zakharov, Vadim, 157–59
Ziarek, Krzystof, 239n1
Žižek, Slavoj, 136
Zuidervaart, Lambert, 247n3, 255n50, 276n2, 276n8

www.ingramcontent.com/pod-product-compliance
Lightning Source LLC
Chambersburg PA
CBHW031235290426
44109CB00012B/297